MOBILITY AND FORCED DISPLACEMENT IN THE MIDDLE EAST

T0386734

ZAHRA BABAR (ED.)

Mobility and Forced Displacement
in the Middle East

جـامـعـة جـورجـتـاون قـطـر
GEORGETOWN UNIVERSITY QATAR

Center *for* International *and* Regional Studies

HURST & COMPANY, LONDON

First published in the United Kingdom in 2020 by
C. Hurst & Co. (Publishers) Ltd,
41 Great Russell Street, London, WC1B 3PL
© Zahra Babar and the Contributors, 2020
All rights reserved.
Printed in India

A Cataloguing-in-Publication data record for this book
is available from the British Library.

ISBN: 9781787383203

This book is printed using paper from registered sustainable
and managed sources.

www.hurstpublishers.com

CONTENTS

CONTENTS

ACKNOWLEDGMENTS

This volume emerged as the result of a grant-driven research initiative undertaken between 2016 and 2018 by the Center for International and Regional Studies (CIRS) at Georgetown University in Qatar. From the very early stages of this project a number of scholars provided their intellectual input in crafting this study of mobility and displacement in the Middle East. I would like to offer my warm thanks to Michael Ewers, Ayman Shabana, and Valbona Zenku for their support throughout the grant proposal process. Grateful acknowledgment also goes to the participants of the two working groups that were held in Doha, in particular to Amani El Jack, Sherine El Taraboulsi-McCarthy, Michael Leezenberg, Natalie Peutz, and Florian Wiedmann. This volume also benefited significantly from the efforts of my colleagues at CIRS, without whom the task of editing would have been impossible. For all their intellectual input and practical assistance, I offer my heartfelt thanks to Maram Al Qershi, Misba Bhatti, Islam Hassan, Mehran Kamrava, Suzi Mirgani, Jackie Starbird, and Elizabeth Wanucha. CURA Student Research Fellows, Aiza Khan, Irene Promodh, and Abdul Rehmaan Qayyum provided me with invaluable support in multiple ways. Finally, grateful acknowledgment goes to the Qatar Foundation for its support of such research endeavors.

ABOUT THE CONTRIBUTORS

Rogaia Mustafa Abusharaf is Professor of Anthropology, Georgetown University in Qatar. She was a recipient of postdoctoral and senior fellowships at Durham University in the UK, and at Brown University and Harvard University. She writes on culture and politics, anthropology of gender, human rights, migration, and diaspora issues in the Gulf, Sudan, Zanzibar, and the USA. She is the author of *Transforming Displaced Women in Sudan: Politics and the Body in a Squatter Settlement* (University of Chicago Press, 2009) and is the editor of *Female Circumcision: Multicultural Perspectives* (University of Pennsylvania Press, 2006) and *Wanderings: Sudanese Migrants and Exiles in North America* (Cornell University Press, 2002). She has also edited "What is Left of the Left? The View from Sudan," a special issue of *South Atlantic Quarterly* (Duke University Press), and coedited two books with Dale Eickelman—*Africa and the Gulf: Blurred Boundaries, Shifting Ties* (Gerlach Press, 2015), and *Higher Education Investment in the Arab States of the Gulf: Strategies for Excellence and Diversity* (Gerlach Press, 2016).

Pooya Alaedini is Associate Professor of Social Planning in the University of Tehran's Faculty of Social Sciences. His areas of interest are urban and regional planning, social policy, industrial and employment development, and tourism planning. His coedited volumes include *Industrial, Trade, and Employment Policies in Iran: Towards a New Agenda* (with Mohamad R. Razavi) (Springer, 2018); *Quality Services and Experiences in Hospitality and Tourism* (with Liping A. Cai) (Emerald, 2018); and *Economic Welfare and Inequality in Iran: Developments since the Revolution* (with Mohammad Reza Farzanegan) (Palgrave, 2016). His publications further include "Urban Dynamics in Iranian Port Cities: Growth, Informality, and Decay in Bandar

Abbas," in *Gateways to the World: Port Cities in the Persian Gulf*, ed. M. Kamrava (Hurst/Oxford University Press, 2016), *From Shelter to Regeneration: Slum Upgrading and Housing Policies in I.R. Iran* (coedited with Farzin Fardanesh) (UDRO, 2014), as well as a number of monographs and peer-reviewed articles. He holds a PhD in Urban Planning and Policy Development from Rutgers University.

Mustafa O. Attir is Emeritus Professor of Sociology, University of El-Fatah, Tripoli, and Director of the Center for Applied Social Research at the Libyan Academy. He has served in a number of leadership roles, including as President of the University of Benghazi and President of the Arab Sociological Association. He obtained his PhD in sociology in 1971 from the University of Minnesota. His publications include twenty-seven books, five of them in English, and more than a hundred research papers.

Emma Aubin-Boltanski is a social anthropologist and an Arabist. A senior researcher at the National Center for Scientific Research (CNRS), she is currently a member of the Centre for Social Research on Religion (CéSor). She is the author of *Pèlerinage et nationalisme en Palestine* (Ed.de l'EHESS, 2007) and *Le corps de la Passion. Expériences religieuses et politiques d'une mystique au Liban* (Ed. de l'EHESS, 2018). She is one of the principal investigators of the SHAKK research program (From Revolt to War in Syria: Conflict, Displacements, Uncertainties), funded by the Agence Nationale de la Recherche (2018–22). Since 2018, Aubin-Boltanski has developed a new body of research on the shifting roles of Syrian women in the context of revolution, war, and exile. With Nibras Chehayed, she translated (from Arabic to French) a series of testimonies gathered by the Syrian novelist Samar Yazbek: *19 femmes. Les Syriennes racontent* (Stock, 2019).

Zahra Babar is Associate Director for Research, Center for International and Regional Studies, Georgetown University in Qatar. Her research interests include rural development, migration, and citizenship in the Persian Gulf states. She has published several articles and chapters, most recently, "Im/mobile Highly Skilled Migrants in Qatar," with M. Ewers and N. Khattab, *Journal of Ethnic and Migration Studies* (2019); "Enduring 'Contested' Citizenship in the Gulf Cooperation Council," in Nils A. Butenschon and Roel Meijer (eds), *The Middle East in Transition: The Centrality of Citizenship*, (Edward Elgar, 2018); "The 'Enemy Within': Citizenship-Stripping in the

Post-Arab Spring GCC," *Middle East Journal* (2017); "The 'Humane Economy:' Migrant Labour and Islam in Qatar and the UAE," *Sociology of Islam* (2017); and "Population, Power, and Distributional Politics in Qatar," *Journal of Arabian Studies* (2015). She was editor for *Arab Migrant Communities in the GCC* (Hurst/Oxford University Press, 2017), and coedited with M. Kamrava, *Migrant Labour in the Persian Gulf* (Hurst/Columbia University Press, 2012).

Matt Buehler is Assistant Professor, University of Tennessee, and a global security Fellow at the Howard H. Baker Jr Center for Public Policy. He has held fellowships at the Middle East Initiative at Harvard University's John F. Kennedy School of Government and the Center for International and Regional Studies (CIRS) at Georgetown University in Qatar. He is the author of *Why Alliances Fail: Islamist and Leftist Coalitions in North Africa* (Syracuse University Press, 2018), which received the 2019 Southeast Regional Middle East & Islamic Studies Society Book Award (SERMEISS). His research has appeared in peer reviewed journals, including *Political Research Quarterly, the British Journal of Middle Eastern Studies*. He serves as an editor for the journal *Mediterranean Politics*.

Estella Carpi is Research Associate, Migration Research Unit, Department of Geography, University College London (UCL). Previously, she was a Research Associate at the Bartlett Development Planning Unit (UCL), and Humanitarian Affairs Advisor at Save the Children-UK. She received her PhD in Social Anthropology from the University of Sydney (Australia), with a study on the social response to crisis and crisis management in Lebanon. After studying Arabic in Milan and Damascus (2002–8), she worked as a researcher for New York University (Abu Dhabi), Lebanon Support (Beirut), Trends Research & Advisory (Abu Dhabi), UN-Habitat (Beirut), the American University of Beirut, UNDP (Cairo), and the International Development Research Center (Cairo), mostly focusing on conflict-induced displacement, identity politics and humanitarian aid provision in the Middle East. She has lectured extensively in the social sciences in Italy and Australia.

Kyung Joon Han is Associate Professor of Political Science, University of Tennessee, Knoxville. His research focuses on party politics, voting behavior, and political economy in Western Europe. His articles have appeared in the *British Journal of Political Science, International Studies Quarterly, European*

Journal of Political Research, Party Politics, West European Politics, Electoral Studies, among other outlets.

Mohamed Jouili is Professor of Sociology at the University of Tunis, and a youth outreach specialist working to assist young Tunisians with accessing job opportunities and achieving business success. He was the head (2011–17) of Tunisia's National Observatory of Youth (ONJ), and was awarded a scholarship at the Asia Pacific University. Jouili's research interests and publications have focussed on youth, identity, migration, and the prevention of violent extremism. He has conducted research on the attitudes of Tunisian youth towards civic engagement, and youth representation of Salafism. Jouili is currently conducting a research project with the Hanns Seidal foundation on the attitudes of Libyans' towards migration and migrants.

Ricardo René Larémont is Professor of Political Science and Sociology, SUNY, Binghamton, and an Atlantic Council Senior Scholar. His principal books include *Al-tasawuf al-maghrebi: qadaya muasira* (with Khalid Bekkaoui) (Moroccan Cultural Studies Centre, 2017); *Pursuing Security and Shared Development in Euro-Mediterranean Migrations* (with Emanuela Claudia del Re) (Aracne, 2017); *Revolution, Revolt, and Reform in North Africa* (Routledge, 2013); *Al-rabia al-arabi: al-intifada w'al islah w'al-thawra* (with Youssef Sawani) (Al-Maaref, 2013); *Islamic Law and Politics in Northern Nigeria* (Africa World Press, 2011); *Borders, Nationalism, and the African State* (Lynne Rienner, 2005); *The Causes of War and the Consequences of Peacekeeping in Africa* (Heinemann, 2002); and *Islam and the Politics of Resistance in Algeria, 1783–1992* (Africa World Press, 2000).

Aitemad Muhanna-Matar is Assistant Professorial Research Fellow, London School of Economics and Political Science (LSE). In 2016–19 she led a research project investigating the gender impact of Syrian displacement in Jordan and Turkey, funded by the LSE Institute of Global Affairs (IGA)–Rockefeller Foundation. In 2014–16, she conducted research on Tunisian Salafi youth and the driving factors behind their radicalization; and in 2013 managed a regional research project in five Arab countries looking at women's political participation across the Arab region, funded by Oxfam GB. Through these projects, she published several papers in peer-reviewed journals. She is the author of *Agency and Gender in Gaza: Masculinity, Femininity and Family during the Second Intifada* (Routledge, 2013). Muhanna-Matar has worked as a consultant with the World Bank, UNDP, UN Women, Oxfam GB, and Save the Children. She has also garnered substantive experience in policy analysis and development planning through her work as Policy Advisor for the Palestinian Ministry of Planning.

Natalia Ribas-Mateos is a researcher at the Universitat Autònoma, Barcelona, Spain. She has taught and conducted fieldwork in various countries, including in Mediterranean Europe (MigCities, TMR, Marie Curie, Ramón y Cajal) and other regions (with INSTRAW, ECOS Sur). Through her work in international social sciences, Ribas-Mateos links grounded empirical engagement at multiple levels, and examines new critical theoretical challenges in dialogue with gender activists. She has published extensively in different languages, including Spanish, French, and Arabic. She is the author of *The Mediterranean in the Age of Globalization* (Routledge, 2005) and *Border Shifts: New Mobilities in Europe and Beyond* (Palgrave Macmillan, 2015), editor of *Migration, Mobilities and the Arab Spring* (Edward Elgar, 2016), and coeditor of *The International Handbook on Gender, Migration and Transnationalism* (Edward Elgar, 2013).

Thomas Schmidinger is a political scientist and social and cultural anthropologist. He is Lecturer, Institute of Political Science, University of Vienna, and at Vorarlberg University of Applied Sciences. Schmidinger is Secretary-General of the Austrian Kurdish Studies Association, and is an editorial board member of the *Vienna Yearbook for Kurdish Studies*. His book, *Krieg und Revolution in Syrisch-Kurdistan: Analysen und Stimmen aus Rojava* (Wien Mandelbaum, 2017), published in Turkish and English, was awarded the Mazlum Bagok Kurdish Journalism Prize. He recently authored (with Andrej Grubacic and Michael Schiffmann) *The Battle for the Mountain of the Kurds* (PM Press, 2019) and *"Die Welt hat uns vergessen." Der Genozid des "Islamischen Staates" an den JesidInnen und die Folgen* (Wien Mandelbaum, 2019) and edited (with Bayar Mustafa Sevdeen) *Beyond ISIS: History and Future of Religious Minorities in Iraq* (Transnational Press, 2019).

Leïla Vignal is Associate Professor in Human Geography, Rennes-2 University, and a Research Fellow at the research unit ESO-Rennes (Rennes, France). She was the Principal Investigator of the research programme SYSREMO (Global Geographies: Towards a Regional System in the Middle East), funded by the Agence Nationale de la Recherche (2010–15), France.

In 2015–17 she was a Marie Curie Senior Research Fellow at the Refugee Studies Centre, University of Oxford, working on the spaces of the Syrian conflict, including the spaces of refuge. A scholar of Syria and the Middle East before the war, she has developed a new body of research on the socio-spatial transformations of the country and its society in the conflict.

LIST OF FIGURES

1

HUMAN MOBILITY IN THE MIDDLE EAST

Zahra Babar

Introduction

For centuries, the movement of people from one place to another has remained an integral aspect of human existence. On an annual basis, thousands of people all over the world leave the place they call home and travel—to a nearby city or to a distant destination in a country or continent thousands of miles away—to seek something better for themselves. People move voluntarily for a variety of reasons: perhaps for a better job, higher wages, a marriage partner, a chance to reunite with their family members, an opportunity to experience a different part of the world, to get an education, or for assorted lifestyle preferences. Others move less out of choice than necessity, as they are forced to leave circumstances that are unsafe, insecure, and generally untenable for productive human life.

Between the two poles of moving purely out of choice or moving because one has no other option but to leave, there are a variety of circumstances and nuanced motivations that lie somewhere in the middle. No matter what the personal or circumstantial drivers and reasons that propel it, migration on an

1

annual basis occurs for millions of people. The term "migration" is itself used to describe varied and complex patterns of human mobility that occur internally within a state or region, as well as those taking place across borders, internationally, and trans-continentally. Migration can be applied to the categories of people moving as a result of their own agency, voluntarily, and as an individual or familial choice. It can also be used to describe the categories of those having to move by force or under duress, and this includes the mobility experiences of forced migrants, internally displaced persons, refugees, and asylum-seekers.

Migration as an area of research, as well as an experiential phenomenon, addresses and involves multiple aspects of human life, from the most personal and individual domains to large-scale sociological and political fields. Migration influences education, income generation, employment, health, marriage choices, family and religious life, and psychological well-being, as well as broader macro domains of economic and political development, population growth, sociocultural transformation, and much else that lies in between.[1] As such, migration studies has grown to be an inherently multidisciplinary field of scholarship, as it would be impossible to understand its many elements and aspects from a single disciplinary perspective.[2]

Theoretical interpretations of international migration have traditionally considered human mobility as a response to structurally based political, economic, and social conditions.[3] Human beings are most inclined to leave their ancestral homelands or birthplace and seek alternative geographic locations for living and working if conditions at home are considered unsafe or unsatisfactory.[4] Civil war, social unrest, violent and sustained levels of crime, campaigns of ethnic cleansing, or episodes of extreme political instability may produce sudden, chaotic, and unanticipated departures of segments of populations. Lethargic economic conditions offering limited labor market opportunities, low wages, and chronic high unemployment or underemployment also create outward flows of people.[5] In addition, ongoing systems of corruption and poor governance, inadequate or unaffordable public sector services, structural hierarchies that limit upward mobility and diminish material well-being for lower- and middle-income communities, as well as persistent forms of marginalization of certain segments of a plural population, all serve to drive different forms of migration. In addition to the extensive scholarship on migration that has been carried out by economists, political scientists, and demographers, other disciplines within the social sciences have produced a vast array of work focusing on a further subset of considerations that shape and influence migratory phenomena and have drawn a great deal of attention to the influence of assorted social and cultural factors as additional drivers for people's movement.[6]

Regardless of the long history of human movement and the various dynamics, both old and new, propelling particular forms of migration, what is increasingly apparent is that migration flows in the contemporary world order of nation-states are for the most part considered to be anomalous, problematic, and potentially destabilizing. The state-centric perspective currently dominating discourses of human mobility in many parts of the world posits that migration flows in all their various forms are challenging and need to be disciplined and controlled.[7] Many states have placed migration high on their twenty-first-century policy agendas, and this is demonstrated through the public narrative that articulates the need to "manage" migration, as well as policy practices, which primarily translates into forms of state governance that rigidly curtail and restrict inward flows of people over territorial borders.[8] Even more evident is that in addition to state-led discussions and policies, in migrant-receiving states in particular, citizens are also demonstrating anxiety around migration and migrants, expressing rising anti-immigrant sentiments, and demanding political responses from their governments to address the migration problem.[9]

Fighting against the tide, a number of scholars have pushed back on the idea that migration is an abnormal and destructive condition that harms societies and nations, instead suggesting that movement and mobility have long been a natural component of human existence. Stephen Castles and a number of others have maintained, for example, that human mobility needs to be viewed from beyond the lens of the nation-state, and any analysis of migration must pay greater attention to larger, transnational economic and political processes occurring at the global level.[10] Castles argues that migration occurs in conjunction with many political, economic, and social factors on a meta-level and, rather than being viewed as a rupture to the system, needs to be understood as part of larger, naturally occurring processes of change. Moreover, Castles highlights the significant relationship between contemporary forms of globalization—which facilitate cultural interchange and integration—and current patterns of migration or human mobility. Observing migration as an isolated process, one that disrupts the seamless structures and systems of nation-based human life without acknowledging its joint causes and effects, would be highly misleading: "migrations are not isolated phenomena: movements of commodities, capital and ideas almost always give rise to movements of people."[11]

Mobility in the Middle East

The Middle East has historically served as a locus of displacement for a number of reasons, including, among other things, the legacy of imperial rule and colonial occupation, territorial rivalry and the creation of contested boundaries at the time of independence, sporadic interstate warfare and unresolved issues of geopolitical competition between nation-states, internecine conflict, and the ongoing intervention by external powers in regional affairs.[12] In addition, authoritarian rule and repressive action by the state, political and ethnic marginalization, socioeconomic exclusion, and tenuous rights to and of citizenship have also propelled internal and international displacement in the region.[13] Pervasive poverty, underdevelopment, and resource scarcity may also be contributing factors to the region's high number of internally displaced persons and its heavy volume of refugees.[14] However, while poverty and scarcity can certainly serve as catalysts for human displacement and migration, there are many parts of the world with far higher levels of poverty and inequality than the Middle East but without similar patterns of involuntary displacement.[15]

Beyond war and poverty as the obvious and most frequently cited causes for human mobility, the persistence of large numbers of displaced people in the Middle East raises fundamental questions about the political organization of power and authority in the region. In some parts of the Middle East, at the initial stages when the borders of the nation-states were being established, simultaneous forms of statelessness and the creation of future refugee populations were being generated. Palestinians have often been held up as one such example of a Middle Eastern community that suddenly found itself without access to a territorially bound nationality with the foundation of the modern state of Israel, while the Kurds experienced something similar after the First World War when the modern states of Turkey, Iraq, and Syria were created.[16] In other cases, the very processes of state formation and the consolidation of a centralized political authority have led to the permanent marginalization of certain segments of the population and established conditions for a sustained simmering of interethnic or confessional group tension that at any point can be agitated and lead to episodes of conflict and human displacement.[17] A critical component of the state-building process in the Middle East was the establishment of legal parameters for defining national citizenship. In many cases, the citizenship regimes that were rolled out were closely linked to the advancement of the interests of particular political elites and were highly exclusionary in nature. Determining who was legally given the right to belong to and participate in the state, or who was excluded, was a result of the particular political dynamics of the time.

Creating and sustaining displacement and statelessness is also a strategic tool used by political actors to satisfy particular political goals, and this is certainly not unique to the Middle East. The political science literature on the Middle East has often ignored some of these deeper questions around the politics of population displacement, and why or how rulers actively engage in it. This is perhaps due to the tendency to treat this phenomenon as either an atavistic byproduct of history, or due to lingering and unresolved interstate territorial disputes, or as a result of domestic political instability and identity politics. Nevertheless, there is growing awareness that the ongoing creation of internally displaced and refugee populations, in the Middle East and elsewhere, is more than just merely symptomatic of unresolved identity issues or a result of interstate conflicts. States and political actors actively displace people for various reasons and as a result of deliberate actions, such as asserting authority over contested territories, controlling and marginalizing specific segments of their own populations, embarking on nation-building projects steeped in exclusionary narratives of national identity and citizenship, and building on divisive political agendas to shore up their support-bases.[18] Across the Middle East, minority communities in particular have often been scapegoated by governments, both through political action and discourse, not only to consolidate power over homogeneous populations but also to garner support for political gains and to build populist agendas.

The Middle East is currently facing one of its most critical migration challenges, as the region has become the simultaneous producer of and host to the world's largest population of displaced people.[19] As a result of ongoing conflict, particularly in Syria, Libya, Iraq, and Yemen, there have been sharp increases in the numbers of the internally displaced, forced migrants, refugees, and asylum-seekers.[20] Despite the burgeoning degree of policy interest and heated public discourse on the impact of these refugees on European states, most of these dislocated populations are living within the borders of the Middle East.[21] The burden of care for this seemingly unending flow of migrants is being most critically felt by regional neighbors, not all of whom have the stable and robust economic, political, and social conditions necessary for absorbing and hosting large communities of refugees.

Patterns of refugee creation cannot be easily predicted or anticipated in the Middle East. The abrupt flight of Syrian refugees to Lebanon, Jordan, Egypt, and Turkey beginning in April and May 2011 illustrates how easily conditions can disintegrate so rapidly from strength to fragility in a national context. For many years before its descent into civil war, Syria was considered one of the strongest (albeit rigidly authoritarian) states in the Middle East, and as such an unlikely contender for sudden collapse into chaos.[22] Syria historically served as a sanctuary for many other regional refugees fleeing conditions of instability in neighboring countries, a fact that is both tragic and ironic. A country that has, in the not too distant past, frequently provided protection and refuge to those escaping persecution or declining economic and political prospects in other parts of the Middle East is now producing millions of its own refugees and contending with its own internally displaced populations.[23] While Syria's internally displaced population is currently made up almost entirely of its own citizens, as recently as 2011 the largest group of displaced people residing in Syria were Iraqis. As we can see in the cases of Lebanon and Iran, there are also circumstances in the Middle East where countries are simultaneously serving as host states for large groups of migrants and refugees as well as contributing a large diaspora of their own citizens, either to other countries within the region or elsewhere around the world.[24]

This volume is the outcome of a grants-based project to support in-depth, empirically based examinations of mobility and displacement within the Middle East and to gain a fuller understanding of the forms, causes, dimensions, patterns, and effects of migration, both voluntary and forced. As the following chapters in this volume will demonstrate, through this series of case studies we are seeking to broaden our understanding of the population movements that are seen in the Middle East and hope to emphasize that regional migration is a complex, widespread, and persistent phenomenon in the region, best studied from a multidisciplinary perspective. This volume explores the conditions, causes, and consequences of ongoing population displacements in the Middle East. In doing so, it also serves as a lens to better understand some of the profound social, economic, and political dynamics at work across the region.

The inadequacy of labeling

Along with the increasing problematization of migration is a growing trend to assign a host of labels and categories to assorted patterns of migration. These labels seek to partition human mobility into easily differentiated forms, based on the assumption that there is a common causal factor behind particular streams of migration. Assigning migrants to precise subcategories holds consequences for how they are treated, what rights they are granted at different stages of the migration process, as well as for the obligations and commitments that states are meant to adhere to when migrants enter their territory. The binding logic of systematically differentiating migrants into subgroups is that different groups of migrants need different forms of intervention and support.

It is not only states that make use of subcategories of migration as they design policies for managing inward migration but also supranational bodies that are increasingly visible and active in the global governance of human mobility. Given the cross-border and transnational nature of many forms of human mobility, over the past century a plethora of international agencies has emerged with the mandate to develop cooperative mechanisms for regulating transnational movement. Many of these organizations have their historical roots in post-Second World War Europe, when, in the aftermath of the war, many European states struggled to cope with high levels of displaced people and had to develop both normative and practical means by which to manage streams of refugees and dislocated populations. The organizations that emerged in the aftermath of the Second World War, as well as additional agencies established more recently, play a prominent role today in managing and monitoring international migration in all its various forms. While the movement of people over territorial borders remains an issue over which state sovereignty retains dominance, international organizations assert their own influence in the governance of migration, both practically and normatively, by setting the parameters and guidelines for mechanisms of cooperation between states. For both states and these international organizations, the assigning of homogenizing labels and classifications is crucial since maintaining distinctions between what rights different groups of migrants can have access to in a host state is a highly political issue. Creating categories and then assigning specific criteria to each allows for the development of a common understanding of how different migrant groupings are to be treated, what rights they are to be given, and how they are or are not accommodated by the state. Segmenting people on the move into convenient and easily understood groupings supports the development of distinct policies to apply to each of the separate categories of migrant.

However, defining who is a migrant, and then agreeing on exactly what sort of migrant a person is, remains a complicated task. Even among international organizations that work for and with communities of migrants, there is not always clear agreement or a set definition of whom they are talking about.

Earlier, the assumption used to be that migrants left their country of origin with the specific and final objective of obtaining permanent settlement in another country.[25] More recently, it is understood that migration may in fact be far more fluid: when migrants leave their home, permanent resettlement in another country may not be their primary objective. Many migrants make multiple journeys and reside in a number of locations without permanent integration into a national fold. According to the International Organization for Migration, all those who move across borders for any reason (or even those who move between different parts of a country), and for any length of time, regardless of their legal or illegal status, are to be considered migrants.[26]

The United Nations High Commissioner for Refugees (UNHCR), however, applies a different standard, and considers only those who have chosen to move to improve their lives to be migrants.[27] According to the UNHCR, this migration could be either within or across national borders, although more often the latter, and could be caused by several factors, including the desire for reunification with family members living outside the home country, for employment opportunities, or in order to seek shelter from natural disasters.[28] The UNHCR separates refugees from other categories of migrants as it views refugees as persons who have escaped dangerous conditions involuntarily and often due to a direct threat to their lives or freedoms.

A number of scholars have drawn attention to the problem of placing migrants into differentiated classes and categories.[29] While categorizing groups of migrants into separate baskets may hold appeal for policymakers and makes sense from the perspective of states and international bodies, especially those deputed to manage international migration, these classifications tend to be restrictive and analytically problematic for scholars.[30] At the broadest level, a partition has been created between refugees and asylum-seekers on the one hand and economic migrants on the other.[31] There is an evolving and complicated nature to transnational migration and movement, and people's cross-border movements go far beyond simplified categories of refugee and economic migrant. Creating a static view of refugees fleeing conflict and seeking refuge oversimplifies the causes of movement as well as the conditions of those who have been displaced. In certain circumstances, multiple labels might apply to the same individual. A person might well be a labor migrant, but at the same time they might in fact be a refugee or forced migrant, if circumstances in their country of origin have deteriorated to the extent that returning there is untenable.

Several chapters in this volume highlight the potential dangers of assigning people particular mobility categories and suggest that static yet overarching labels of refugee, economic migrant, asylum-seeker, irregular migrant, and forcibly displaced person are too simplistic and elide the highly complex forms of mobility that are being experienced at multiple locations around the Middle East.[32] The inadequacy of current designations and the lack of an appropriate conceptual language has led to analytical stasis, challenging researchers and practitioners alike as they struggle with how to define people engaged in various forms of mobility without assigning them bounded and inappropriate labels.

The current approach to categorization is based on identifying a single solid cause or reason behind an individual's migration, and then providing certain privileges and protections based on the particular vulnerabilities associated with the category itself. In Chapter 2 of this volume, Natalia Ribas-Mateos suggests that mobility filters operate in tandem with highly securitized national borders to keep out certain categories of migrants who are screened on the basis of a complex set of social, economic, and cultural inequalities. Estella Carpi's contribution focuses on international humanitarian agencies in Turkey and Lebanon that deliver support to a diverse community of Syrian refugees, demonstrating how these agencies first assign labels to diverse groups of Syrian migrants and then manage them as various "categories of need." Carpi's empirical fieldwork maps out how this process of labeling unfolds in a refugee context, and how the associated allocation of targeted services and resources is received by those designated as refugees versus citizens of the host states. As Carpi points out, through their labeling processes, humanitarian agencies operating in border regions in Turkey and Lebanon end up producing "eligible and ineligible subjects of care." Bifurcating the residents of two towns into those who can access humanitarian goods and services and those who cannot has served to trigger hostility toward refugees from the host population.

In Chapter 4, "Hosting and Being Hosted in Times of Crisis: Exploring the Multilayered Patterns of Syrian Refuge in the Dayr al-Ahmar Region, Northern Bekaa, Lebanon," Emma Aubin-Boltanski and Leïla Vignal demonstrate how, in the midst of the complexities of a refugee situation in the Middle East, categorizing who is actually a refugee and who is not is no easy or certain matter. Aubin-Boltanski and Vignal's fieldwork in Lebanon demonstrates how the legal status of "refugee" as defined in the 1951 Refugee Convention does not even apply in Lebanon as the state has not signed up to the convention. Lebanon, which is serving as host to a large Syrian refugee population, is thus not under the same obligations to accord refugees the legal recognition and rights as recognized in the convention. Instead, under a bilateral arrangement with the Lebanese government, the UNHCR is assigned to register Syrian refugees and consider their asylum requests.

As the Aubin-Boltanski and Vignal chapter suggests, this gray zone of refugee categorization means that the experience of Syrian refugees in Lebanon may vary greatly from one individual to the next, and even for members of the same family. Some Syrians might be officially "registered refugees" in Lebanon, while others might be "non-registered refugees." Some Syrians might have no legal residency status in the country, while others may have legal residency, but as they are not registered as refugees, they cannot receive the rights or benefits associated with having refugee status. Furthermore, even designating Syrians as refugees is a political and politicized issue in Lebanon, as these terms have historical resonance in a state that has had to contend with Palestinian refugees and still feels a great deal of anxiety in replicating that experience. Within Lebanon, where factions of the domestic political apparatus also have clear views, biases, and vested interests in relation to the outcome of the Syrian civil war, there is a political preference to consider Syrians as temporarily displaced people rather than actual refugees. There is no neutrality to the process of assigning labels to groups of migrants, and, in fact, these labels come heavily laden with their own political meanings and are subsequently absorbed and adopted in particular contexts that have their own political, cultural, and historical sensitivities.

Borders and mobility

Migrants, in all their forms and with all their various assigned labels, are defined by a world of nation-states and the assertion of their sovereign control over movement onto their territory and through their borders. The world as we know it today is one where the human right to free mobility is heavily undermined by the rights of state sovereignty. This is most visibly observed in the hardening of borders and the more heavily guarded territorial boundaries that have been established, mostly over the course of the past century. It can conversely also be argued that the mobility of people over borders heavily undermines state sovereignty, and that border areas have emerged as one of the most politically charged arenas for examining the tension between the rights of states versus the rights of people. Several of the chapters in this volume seek to examine how the movement of people in the Middle East is challenging core elements of state sovereignty, and how people themselves are responding to the assertion of state sovereignty at borders.

Borders do not necessarily work as hard concrete walls in the Middle East, and they can be viewed more as filters with openings that are broad or narrow, or as dams that can let in a trickle or a flood. Wars have a direct impact on borders and how states manage them, in some cases opening the borders up entirely for the flow of armaments and weapons, combatants, and other provisions and services related to a war economy. Humanitarian relief efforts and refugee-support services are also usually based at a border, and these create an entirely different form of cross-border networking and flow of people and goods.

In addition to war or political instability, forces of economic globalization have had an impact on cross-border mobility patterns across the world, as well as within the Middle East. With the increase in economic cooperation and trade, there has been a greater flow of goods and people over national borders, but this has been accompanied by a heightened level of scrutiny over what and who passes through, greater restrictions for certain forms of human mobility, and a reinforcing of border control. These processes are quite visible in the Middle East, as border cities become sites of contestation between the free market and the state.

Ribas-Mateos, in Chapter 2, "Borders and Mobilities in the Middle East: Emerging Challenges for Syrian Refugees in 'Bilad al-Sham,'" suggests that border sites in the Middle East are locations where severe social and mobility inequalities are being made profoundly visible. Ribas-Mateos sees borders emerging as a site of increasing contestation where the limitations placed on the mobility of different categories of migrant through expanded border securitization lead to vulnerable communities of people whose rights are expressly violated. By focusing on Lebanon, she maintains that borders and border cities constitute a particular space with specific dynamics within which contradictions driven by globalization appear in a very obvious manner. Borders are both a physical and a social space. On the one hand, borders and the communities that live there often share cross-border economic and social ties, common everyday practices, a shared historical memory, and other connectivities. Yet, during times of turbulence, these communities also contend with the ruptures and deterioration of their conditions due to the securitization and the reinforcement of hard borders and border closures. Human rights are also additionally precarious at the borders of a state, as this tends to be a space where state sovereignty and security needs tend to trump civilian and individual rights and liberties.

In the next chapter, Carpi examines Syrian refugees residing in the border towns of Gaziantep in southeast Turkey and Halba in northern Lebanon.

Syrian refugees who are first-time arrivals as well as those refugees who previously engaged in circular migration to Lebanon and Turkey have formed new social networks that have reconfigured these two urban settings. In addition to the impact of the refugees themselves, the large international humanitarian apparatus that has taken hold in these two border towns is having its own transformative impact on local society. The chapter investigates how everyday practices change within and between local, migrant, and refugee communities in times of emergency and in response to neoliberal humanitarian policies and emerging cultures of everyday life arrangement. Many of Carpi's discussions with her interlocutors suggest the existence of border-crossing identities and that the fluidity of the border determines many aspects of their social and economic lives. In fact, the fluid border-identities of the inhabitants of these two towns before the war superseded their ethnic and confessional identities.

Aubin-Boltanski and Vignal's chapter, "Hosting and Being Hosted in Times of Crisis: Exploring the Multilayered Patterns of Syrian Refuge in the Dayr al-Ahmar Region, Northern Bekaa, Lebanon," also focuses our attention on the importance of the border as a space for studying theories of migration and mobility, particularly when trying to understand how sudden episodes of violent displacement tie into longer histories of cross-border mobility and transnational connections between border areas. The chapter examines the predominantly Maronite Christian region of Dayr al-Ahmar in Lebanon that has historically had close economic linkages with Syria as a result of the seasonal migrant workers who come from Syria to engage in agricultural work. These preexisting patterns of circular migration have continued through the years of conflict and tension and have enabled Syrians to seek refuge in Dayr al-Ahmar in the midst of the current conflict. However, the dynamics of the Syrian civil war have certainly seen a change in intercommunity relations, and this chapter demonstrates that the presence of Syrians has led to an increase in confessional tensions in the North Bekaa.

The resilience of identity in Middle Eastern migration

Rogaia Abusharaf, in Chapter 5, "Diasporic Circularities: Omani-Zanzibaris Narrate Experiences In and Out of the Archipelago, 1964," provides an account of the resilience of identity amid the trauma of forced migration. The chapter provides a historicized analysis of the forced migration of Omani-Zanzibaris who were made to leave Zanzibar and move to Oman after the revolution in 1964. Historically, significant maritime networks have existed across the Indian Ocean and the East African littoral, and while Oman's official presence in Africa is often recognized as occurring in 1840, when the sultan of Oman, Sayyid Said, transferred the capital from Muscat to Zanzibar, many Omanis refer to migratory patterns that spanned over centuries before that. Abusharaf suggests that these historic migrations, both before and after the settlement of the Al-Busaidi dynasty in the Zanzibar archipelago, lie at the heart of the creation, and persistence, of a distinct Omani-Swahili identity and political subjectivity. Abusharaf examines the story of how the trauma of the violent forced migration of Omanis from Zanzibar back to Muscat affected their Omani-Swahili identity and how it persists today. While the Omani-Zanzibaris interviewed by Abusharaf emphasize that they and their families were welcomed in Oman, their continued identification as a diasporic "community of memory," and their affiliation to a primarily Swahili-speaking identity, provide an important account that expands our understanding of the complex sense of belonging and reintegration experienced by migrants and return migrants in a variety of contexts.

Much of the literature on gender identity and refugee communities has focused on how the material aspects of displacement result in a change in gender roles and identity. However, displacement does not only cause a change in relation to traditional gender roles within families and households: it also causes immense social change for the larger community. Examining the impact that displacement has on gender roles and gender identity must move beyond looking at changes to individuals' behavior and also study how displacement may be affecting overarching value systems in society. The displacement of value systems triggers broader transformation and social change that is manifest in the renegotiation and reconfiguration of gender roles and can have a long-term impact that even outlives the period of forced displacement. In Chapter 9, "Gendering the Triangular Relationship between Vulnerability, Resilience, and Resistance: The Experiences of Displaced Syrian Refugees in Jordan," Aitemad Muhanna-Matar explores how refugee Syrian men and women's experiences and strategies of coping with vulnerability have involved a reconfiguration of their "normative" gender roles. The chapter investigates how these reconfigured gender roles are perceived socially and culturally by both men and women, and how they accommodate or resist processes of gender reconfiguration that are seen as being driven by external humanitarian agendas and actors.

Notwithstanding the fact that Syria is currently occupying much of the world's attention when it comes to refugee flows, conflict, and displacement, the Middle East continues to contend with earlier groups of migrant and refugee communities. In Chapter 6, "Afghan Migrants in Tehran: Toward Formal Integration," Pooya Alaedini examines the impact of the prolonged conflict in Afghanistan that has led to more than forty years of Iran serving as a continuous host to large groups of Afghan refugees. As this chapter demonstrates, beyond the immediate needs of dislocated people and prolonged encampment and the immediate concerns of host states struggling with the humanitarian challenge of managing a large refugee community, many of the main debates from the *longue durée* perspective focus on issues related to the marginalization and integration of long-term refugees. Marginalization occurs when the combination of socioeconomic, cultural, legal-political, and spatial inequality, together with various additional vulnerabilities of displaced people, prevents them from successful adaptation and meaningful integration into the host state and society. Iran is one of the primary refugee-hosting countries in the Middle East; through a focused case study of Afghans in Iran, this chapter fills a key knowledge gap by providing deeper insight into the impact long-term refugee communities have on their surroundings. Alaedini argues that the unprecedented scale of Afghan migration has had a significant impact on urban development dynamics, particularly in larger Iranian cities, and that Afghan refugee communities have begun to transform local urbanism in Iranian cities. Overall, Alaedini demonstrates that despite an overarching governance system that marginalizes Afghan refugees, Afghans have become informally integrated into the Iranian cities they inhabit. Municipal authorities may not include Afghans in their development plans nor consider them as permanent residents of the city whose needs need to be met, yet viewing Afghans' housing choices, their employment behavior, their language and cultural practices, as well as their social relations, reveals clear signs that these refugees have adapted, assimilated, and found their own ways of integrating into their host state.

In Chapter 7, "Living with Uncertainty: The Story of sub-Saharan Migrants in Libya and Tunisia," Mustafa O. Attir, Mohamed Jouili, and Ricardo René Larémont focus on migration patterns in Libya and Tunisia. The authors suggest that of the three routes to Europe, the central route from Libya and Tunisia to Italy and Malta is the only one that has not been impeded but has, in fact, expanded. Despite this becoming the most viable route for migrants wishing to pass into Europe, the effects of migration on Libya and Tunisia are relatively unstudied. Attir, Jouili, and Larémont suggest that Libya and Tunisia are not only points of departure for accessing

Europe but also points of final destination and settlement for many migrants. Despite the policy perspectives that assume all African migrants are desperately trying to get to Europe, this research suggests that migrants often remain within the region for extended periods of time and that Tunisia and Libya are not just transit points but rather destinations where migrants often remain and build permanent or semi-permanent communities. Though significant work in recent years has studied the impact of trans-Mediterranean migration on Europe, little to no research has examined its effects on North Africa. This contribution provides empirical data through individual and focus group interviews and offers an analysis of foundational knowledge about the array of African and Middle Eastern migrants who have arrived in Libya and Tunisia and their motivations for migrating as well as their migratory experiences. While some of these migrants may attempt the dangerous crossing to Europe, many more choose—or are forced—to remain in these points of departure. In order to address the humanitarian tragedy and security risks that are currently unfolding in the region, this chapter helps us to understand these migrants, their experiences, and the communities of support they have formed.

Matt Buehler and Kyung Joon Han, in Chapter 8, "Integrating African Migrants? Gauging Citizen Opposition to Migrant Resettlement in Morocco's Casablanca Region," study migrants in Morocco. Their research specifically contributes to broader issues of identity inclusion, and practices of exclusion, marginalization, and "othering" that host states and host communities frequently exhibit. The extent to which migrants can be included in a state and society will be directly influenced by how different communities and groups of migrants are perceived by the host communities, where markers of difference are often based on ethnic and religious commonality. While the past few years of conflict and civil instability have increased the numbers of refugees and displaced persons within the Middle East and North Africa, there has been limited work unpicking host populations' perceptions of the various refugee communities in their countries. Buehler and Han's chapter draws on an original, nationally representative public opinion poll of 1,500 citizens in Morocco. The authors explore whether Moroccans think African or Arab refugees have better chances of social integration and acquiring citizenship. Buehler and Han claim that although Arab and Black African refugees fled similar conditions of conflict and war, ordinary Moroccans do not view them equally. Whereas Moroccans express attitudes of sympathy and compassion toward Arab refugees, they express attitudes of prejudice and racism toward African refugees. The poll explains this divergence in citizen attitudes, isolating the factors that predict why prejudice intensifies or abates if a refugee is African or Arab.

Studies have suggested that the region's many small communities of religious minorities are particularly vulnerable to experiencing repeated forms of internal displacement as well as forced migration in the Middle East, with many frequently victims of persecution and marginalization. Thomas Schmidinger, in Chapter 10, "'The World Forgot Us and Europe Doesn't Want Us': The Situation of Yazidi, Christian, and Babawat Internally Displaced Persons and Refugees from Sinjar after the Genocide of 2014," focuses on the Kurdish region of Sinjar in Iraq, and the displacement of the Yazidi and Christians by the self-proclaimed Islamic State (IS). Schmidinger demonstrates that these groups were targeted by IS as a result of their status as religious minorities, with small numbers of adherents and without a strong political presence. He highlights an important issue regarding how plural societies grapple with their history of inter-confessional tension and episodes of violent intercommunal conflict, and how this affects the building of healthy long-term social and political cohesion for nation-states in the Middle East. Religious minorities experience violent displacement, and they frequently interpret their experience through a confessionalized and historicized lens. Such an interpretation of conflict has long-term consequences and creates community discourses around victimization and distrust. Religious minorities who survived the violence of IS in Iraq consider their status as those who have been directly persecuted due to their religious or confessional identities.

In the midst of pervasive and toxic language, and equally ugly ideas that suggest migrants are invaders and human mobility is an aberration, one might be persuaded to imagine that human beings are naturally sedentary and that the desire to move from one's birthplace is an abnormality. Quite the contrary: migration and human mobility are part and parcel of the world in which we live, and the continuous flow of people and exchange of cultures is as old as the societies we have built together. Overall, the chapters in this volume emphasize the diversity of the origins, consequences, and experiences of varied patterns of human mobility in the Middle East. From multidisciplinary perspectives and by examining varied cases, these chapters together provide us with a deeper understanding of current as well as historical incidences of displacement and forced migration across the region. In addition to offering insight on multiple root causes of displacement, the chapters also address the complex challenges of host–refugee relations, migrant integration and marginalization, humanitarian agencies, and the role and responsibility of states. Cross-cutting themes also bind several of these chapters together, specifically: the challenges of categories, the dynamics of control and contestation between migrants and states at border sites, and the persistence of identity issues influencing regional patterns of migration.

2

BORDERS AND MOBILITIES IN THE MIDDLE EAST

EMERGING CHALLENGES FOR SYRIAN REFUGEES IN "BILAD AL-SHAM"

Natalia Ribas-Mateos

This chapter addresses the transformation of geopolitical lines and borders in a globalizing world. In the Middle East, this transformation has been accompanied by severe social inequalities that have been expressed in a number of different ways: increasing limitations placed on the mobility of refugees and migrants, yet decreasing limitations on the cross-border flow of goods; a proliferation of refugee encampments and settlements (formal and informal); human vulnerability and rights violations; and expanded border securitization. In the case of Lebanon, these processes play out in especially stark fashion in big cities and border sites. This chapter focuses on one such site in an area of Lebanon: the Central Bekaa.

Changing global borders

It is important to start by looking at the context of borders and mobility in the Middle East.[1] This chapter is based on original research that aims to provide

19

an examination of certain aspects of borders and mobility, including the trans-national circulation of displaced communities, cross-border networks, and how Syrian refugees in the Middle East—especially in Lebanon—navigate borders and deploy their own social capital in the process. In doing so, the chapter raises and explores a number of questions: How do refugees or migrants perceive borders? How do borders affect migrants' sense of agency? Do vulnerability and agency engender new notions of the humanitarian within global networks? And how do refugees shape the complex borders of this part of the world?

In seeking to answer these questions, this study has been guided by two main aims. The first is to develop a new approach that can be used to explore borders in the context of the unequal nature of social mobility practices.[2] The second aim, as an extension of other works, is to situate this topic in the trans-formation and proliferation of the world's borders—from the border as defined by geopolitical lines to the meaning of conflict in an era of globaliza-tion. This second aim serves as a context in which to study the problems related to "the lack of the right to have rights" in a particular border area, the Central Bekaa in Lebanon.

To achieve these aims, my fieldwork in Lebanon was based around three specific theoretical–empirical forms of inquiry: (1) the changes in borders and mobility after the Arab Spring; (2) the broader context of the "encampment of the world," which is linked to the revival of "the right to have rights"; and (3) the existing contradictions in border security/humanitarian policies and the politics of compassion,[3] with the aim of going beyond the classic para-digms of victimhood, which mostly refer to women and children.

Globalization has intensified social inequality and increased human inse-curity. Yet this broader context of mobility and globalization can also serve as a means to understand transnational connections between countries—con-nections that families find in many ways of remitting capital, objects, and information, as well as through mobility patterns. While transnationalism is not completely new, it did reach a particularly high degree of intensity at the end of the twentieth century due to the associated circular processes of glo-balization, technological changes, and decolonization.[4] If such increased cir-cularity is to be thought of as one of the elements of global migration, the feminization of international mobility is another,[5] covering equally new para-digmatic regions and new migration poles (West Africa, Southern Europe, the Gulf, China), as well as emerging countries of emigration/immigration, and new spaces of transit (sub-Saharan Africa, Maghreb, Turkey, Mexico). It is within such a framework that I examine the nature of what I have termed the "border shift."[6]

At the global level, the chapter begins by considering other types of work that emphasize the multiplication of camps containing migrant and refugee populations around the world, which also has important consequences for the construction of migration routes that contemporary migrants and refugees undertake.[7] I then take into consideration the broader existence of such areas of encampment, which are becoming a central step in refugees' journeys, as these journeys structure their mobility and drastically limit their access to human and social rights.[8]

The experiences of migrants are inevitably affected by borders, which are currently experiencing a transformation along geopolitical lines. This was apparent in the cities I examined in my previous research, which were witness to myriad contradictions between the meaning of a common shared life (memory, everyday border practices, for example between Lebanese–Syrian border neighborhood relations) and the reinforcement of borders and the deterioration of human rights conditions and the reinforcement of border closures. This chapter consequently seeks to build upon my earlier work by examining this transformation further through a case study of Syrian refugees in the Central Bekaa in Lebanon.

The chapter's point of departure from previous works set in the "transnational Mediterranean" is its analysis of a global context that repeatedly recalls metaphors of border opening and crossing—mainly opening for flows of capital, goods, and information, while closing for people. However, we rarely reflect on how the effects of mobility and border closures occur as a result of an unequal maze of practices driven by state control, which can provide crucial points for interpreting the "making and remaking" of empirical studies on globalization, where border closure is also a policy goal in the Middle East as it has been in the European Union since the late 1980s.

As such, the chapter is primarily concerned with the evolution of new forms of mobility, issues of border security, and conditions of vulnerability and agency that can be examined by the study of human (in)security in specific places encased in national territories, namely borders. The gap between the protection migrants should formally enjoy under international and national laws compared with the actual experiences of individuals reveals a severe absence of human rights as states tend to distance themselves from state-based obligations toward refugees, not only in Europe but also in the Middle East. It is also at such strategic sites as these that we encounter many of the main conflicts related to global borders: securitization, irregular migration, racism, complex gender issues, human trafficking, and globally networked surveillance.

Borders are key empirical research sites in which to study some of the insights of "the mobility turn."[9] In Lebanon, studying borders is related to what I have previously termed the "Mediterranean Caravanserai," which here implies a vision of the Mediterranean as a particular region of study characterized by highly diverse and intensified circulation. Accordingly, the Mediterranean setting is key for observing cross-border mobility as an axis of historical and contemporary interpretation. Here, borders are intertwined with mobility filters that differentiate people according to social categories in a place that is one of the most militarized and heavily patrolled areas in the world, as well as being one of the most lethal border regions in the world. In addition, this Mediterranean setting is also particularly challenging because it spills over into the interrelations between the EU, Southern Europe, North Africa, the Arab/Berber North Africa, the Middle East, Turkey, and the Balkans.

The chapter is structured around a general context defined by (1) globalization and transnationalism related to border contradictions and mobility practices; (2) the forces related to the "encampment of the world"; and (3) "the right to have rights," reviewing pity and charity toward women and children—within a conception of human vulnerability—in the humanitarian agendas. This study attempts to arrive at a clear understanding of these issues through a specific focus on the Middle East. The core argument is that the Central Bekaa is a paradigmatic case that can be used to think about the border and continuous displacement, and to think about how we understand the border vulnerability of women and children today in humanitarian programs.[10]

Focusing on the Central Bekaa in the Bilad al-Sham: the arrival
of Syrian refugees

Many of the works on borders and mobilities emphasize the *longue durée*—the historical background of mobilities in the Mediterranean. From the *longue durée* perspective, we can understand how history "has managed" to form borders that have been seen as naturally entrenched and therefore difficult to uproot.[11] In the Middle Eastern case and particularly in the Bilad al-Sham, colonial legacies in the formation of the nation-state (and the expression of nationalisms today) also need to be considered, as well as the historical context of restrictive borders and refugee mobilities in the region.[12]

Despite the natural/national assumption of borders, these spaces are much more than borders: they are strategic research sites that offer a way to look at the world today. This is especially relevant when examining a specific social relationship between two places. It is precisely in such a landscape that the nation-state can reassert itself by flying the flag of national sovereignty,[13] especially in this period of globalization, and by using its hard-security arm to territorialize and protect its own sovereignty rights, creating ripe conditions for human rights abuses in border zones.[14]

However, before proceeding further, it is necessary to first think through the historical background in a more nuanced way, because, as Judith Butler puts it, the historical context is not just a container for logic; logic cannot be extracted from every context and found to be the same.[15] The context seeps into the forms of neoliberal logic, giving them their rhythms, mechanisms, and dynamics. That, of course, can be extended to the ways in which neoliberalism provides a background for the Arab and Turkish upheavals since 2011 and to the ways in which the upheavals overlap with issues of mobility.

The current discourse on borders in the Middle East has opened a debate about how borders were delineated during the twentieth century. Much of the literature refers to the legacy of the Sykes–Picot Agreement (1916). However, since then, Middle East nation-states, their administrations, and the divisions among their peoples have created new complexities that have become embedded into contemporary mobilities. Evidently, as in any other case, a genealogy of border construction is key to understanding the contemporary complexities of these areas according to the *longue durée* perspective.

Other studies examine how exile, statelessness, and refugee crises are the result of the state-building process in the region.[16] Mohamed Doraï, for example, focuses on the complexity involved in understanding mobility, residence rights, and protection in the countries where Palestinians look for asylum. Once refugees become asylum-seekers in other conflict situations, their statelessness becomes especially evident, as they cannot even seek the protection of their country of origin. Examples include Palestinians living in Iraq in 2003 and Palestinians expelled from Libya in 1995. Community networks can be strong, yet even if a network is built on strong community ties and a sense of family, the resources of such ties inevitably grow scarce in conflict and post-conflict situations.

Since the outbreak of the Syrian conflict in 2011, over 5 million refugees have settled in neighboring countries,[17] which is why the region is now so important in refugee history.[18] In the Middle East, while Jordan and Turkey decided to open refugee camps, Lebanon did not. Although refugee camps are well documented in the literature, less attention has been paid to self-settled refugee groups,[19] despite the fact that, according to Doraï, "at a regional level less than 20% of the registered refugees reside in camps."[20]

Other mobility changes in the region since the Arab Spring include the simultaneous development of intra-regional (within the MENA region) as well as extra-regional forced mobilities (across the whole Mediterranean region as well as particular countries in Northern and Central Europe).[21] Although there are of course specific differences between the Schengen model and the Middle Eastern one, there is a growing tendency throughout this entire area to close borders to Syrian refugees.

The changes in the Mediterranean region also reveal how the post-2011 period has witnessed more pressure on external EU borders and fundamental changes in internal EU borders. In part, this has resulted from modifications to the Mediterranean migratory routes due to the Arab revolts and the wars in Libya and Syria, with new categories of people choosing to use old routes that have been partially reconfigured owing to the evolution of border surveillance and rescue policies, as well as smuggling strategies.[22]

On contrasting border sites as a research methodology

The use of contrasting border sites as a methodology can serve to demonstrate how border construction (both physically and socially) is a salient aspect of the transformation that has emerged from global changes. Research based on this methodology, which emphasizes how mobility inside and outside the space of national control is intrinsic to the study of contemporary borders, emphasizes the following elements.

Focusing on filters as part of the method

Contemporary borders sort or filter people and goods into different types, based on a complex set of social, economic, and cultural inequalities.[23] Josiah Heyman differentiates between the attitudes of certain actors who oppose open borders and more privileged ones who are more likely to be in favor of open borders, an "imagined community," as part of a prosperous globalism.[24] Heyman notes how contemporary borders in this form of differential mobility are not only open or closed but can display both characteristics simultaneously. He concludes that borders are both open and closed, and then introduces the idea of mobility filters marked by social inequality, which is also central to my chosen methodology on borders in different case studies and particularly in this one related to the Central Bekaa.

The inside–outside

Heyman's research thus highlights the relationship between the inside and the outside, the camps inside the nation-state as well as the control of people inside the nation-state (the internal border). In using the concept of the inside–outside, I aim to explore vulnerability in border areas and also in other forms of control, such as control of migrants and refugees, which is a key part of the social–structure, human–agency relationship in the construction of routes. Accordingly, the notion of the inside–outside relationship is central to the vulnerability of rights, as it affects refugees' rights to have rights in a broad sense, which in the case of Lebanon implies going through many internal checkpoints. On the one hand, the rights are provided by the nation-state, while on the other rights are provided by international legal protection and even humanitarian assistance. Humanitarianism, as Heather Hindman refers to it, is the site in which the projects of development and relief are contested and recast in light of new geopolitical landscapes and neoliberal economies that transgress the boundaries of states.[25]

The concept of rights-bearers

Giorgio Agamben has problematized the differentiation between the classic idea of refugees as victims and that of refugees as rights-bearers from a human rights approach.[26] Therefore, such ways of contrasting borders taken from these perspectives make the method itself the theoretical viewpoint of the research fieldwork, providing the strategic concepts as well as the overall social relations imposed on them.

Some notes about the fieldwork

Like many other researchers, my interest in Lebanon was initially driven, at least in part, by the media's use of humanitarian images of Syrian refugees in Lebanon. "All Lebanese borders are dangerous," my academic colleagues pointed out when I explained my research plans upon arrival in Beirut, thus signaling the difficulties I foresaw while conducting research in Beirut and in the Bekaa Valley. The methodology outlined above involved trying to listen to people's own accounts. However, getting direct access to the people with whom I wished to speak was often problematic, as we were viewed with suspicion. While I had hoped to circumvent this problem by researching legal cases, this also proved impracticable as there is no official data on the number of arrests of refugees in Lebanon, or the number of entries filed under "humanitarian cases." It was even difficult to examine maps of the region, as Lebanese maps from 1962 were labeled as secret. Reports from contextual literature were sourced from a range of international and nongovernmental organizations (NGOs).

I conducted participant observations as the basis of my fieldwork in different NGOs in the Bekaa Valley (the names of my participants have been kept anonymous). Most of the people interviewed (fifteen in total) were staff members of NGOs—social workers, project facilitators, area managers, psychologists, and United Nations High Commissioner for Refugees (UNHCR) managers and technicians—working with issues ranging from general charity to social services and social development. The expansion of NGOs after the war in Syria has brought new jobs to Lebanon, such as project facilitators and advocacy officers. Most of the NGO workers are part of a qualified Syrian and Lebanese workforce who were born in the 1980s and 1990s. Even if they work on behalf of a humanitarian agency and under the guidance of certain goals—poverty reduction, children's education, empowerment of women, and community conflict resolution—in general their jobs involve poor working conditions. Working under stress and coping with multitasking thus brings with it a need for area and project managers, employees, and donors.

In all, I visited and interviewed four associations and carried out one in-depth case analysis at the association where I was volunteering—a musical project for children.[27] I also held informal interviews with Syrian refugees of different ages, genders, ethnicities, and social classes. The outcomes generated from the ethnographic data by situational analysis and qualitative content analysis are the basis from which I examine different discourses that I will outline later in the Lebanese experience, but they also relate to the general field of refugee and forced migration studies.

The Lebanese–Syrian border as a case in point

The Lebanese–Syrian border became a source of contention between the two countries during the 1958 Lebanese civil war, when Syria—then part of the

United Arab Republic with Egypt—supplied weapons to Lebanese rebels via smuggling trails near Arsaal in the northeast Bekaa Valley. In the period since, both states have failed to properly delineate the frontier, demarcate it on the ground, and conclude a border agreement between Beirut and Damascus that can be registered with the United Nations (UN). The other problem is the lack of security and Lebanese state control along the border. It has taken the war in Syria for Lebanon to address the latter failing. The international community, especially Europe, has come to recognize the importance of securing Lebanon's border with Syria, given the refugee crisis.[28]

This part of the border—evidently very different from the extremely securitized Israeli one—was the site where Syrian troops were positioned in 2005, and a year later, where the war between Israel and Hezbollah took place. The international community pushed for a demarcation and reinforcement of a border that has long been considered porous. International interest in the Lebanon–Syria border in the wake of the 2006 war was less about the commercial smuggling of commodities, such as cigarettes and diesel fuel, and more concerned with securitization, and the ability of Hezbollah to rearm itself with new and improved weaponry brought in from Syria.[29]

The example of the Central Bekaa

The Bekaa Valley is situated as a defensive buffer zone in the Lebanese border region with Syria; however, Lebanon is so small, relatively speaking, that most of its border is with Syria. The region hosts the highest concentration of Syrian refugees in Lebanon.[30] On the one hand, the border has served as a common area of exchange ever since the Sykes–Picot Agreement and the creation of modern Lebanon and Syria,[31] and the two countries were even the same region in the time of the Ottoman Wali of Damascus. As such, a fluid community exists on both sides of the border, with all types of connections, as well as the reception of the different communities from one side to the other, as for example the Lebanese refugees in Homs during the Lebanese civil war or Syrian labor migrants with a long history of working in the agriculture and construction sectors. On the other hand, the border also implies a conflictual relationship, as I heard from one interviewee, a UNHCR technician in the organization's central office in the Bekaa:

> Here in Zahle, they have always been very reluctant towards Syrians. Yes, during the war the Syrian troops were here. Three hundred died and they can't forget it. This place was for Syrians a strategic point (you should check Fisk's book on the

Phalanx, he explains it very well). So they are very hostile to the Syrians, despite having a Syrian bishop (along with Alexandretta and Damascus).[32]

Hence the border context also explains the political tensions created by having open political connections on each side.

In the first two years of the Syrian conflict, the influx of Syrian refugees was facilitated by an agreement and an "open-door" policy where they had free crossing, as had been the case before the war. Restrictions started in 2013 with limitations established in Lebanon, followed by specific measures in 2014 that were reinforced in 2015. The closure of eighteen irregular entry points along the border between Lebanon and Syria marked the introduction of stricter policies. In May 2014, the Lebanese government agreed to cooperate with the UN in the development of the Lebanon Crisis Response Plan, which has three priorities: (1) ensuring humanitarian protection and assistance, primarily to Syrian de facto refugees and the poorest Lebanese; (2) strengthening the capacity of national and local public-delivery systems to accommodate the basic needs of the aforementioned peoples; and (3) supporting Lebanon's economic, social, institutional, and environmental stability. In October of the same year, the government proposed and approved the application of the "Policy Chapter on Syrian Refugee Displacement."[33] This document sets out the following goals regarding "displaced" Syrians in Lebanon: (1) reducing the numbers of Syrian refugees in the country by reducing access to territory and encouraging Syrian nationals to return to Syria; (2) ensuring security by, among other things, increasing regulation of the Syrian population in Lebanon, providing additional support for municipal police, and requiring municipalities to undertake regular statistical surveys; and (3) easing the burdens on the infrastructure.

The governor of the Bekaa and the Lebanese Armed Forces play a key role in managing the Syrian refugee population, reflecting a national securitized policy that imposes restrictions on Syrian residences and shelters. These relationships are managed by the municipalities, which serve as the main actors together with donors, civil society, and the *shawish*—the representative of the camp—who mainly manages the shelter.

Focusing on vulnerability in the Central Bekaa

The Central Bekaa has higher indexes of poverty and weaker infrastructures than the rest of Lebanon. In practice, this has translated into a situation of mass evictions of communities from settlement areas. Furthermore, apart from all the evictions and substandard shelters in the region, the Syrian population is considered highly vulnerable. NGOs offer psychological care according to families' basic needs and deliver winter clothes, blankets, and hygiene kits.

During the summer of 2017, conditions of vulnerability worsened for those displaced, increasing competition for already scarce resources. The conditions of vulnerability in the Central Bekaa are characterized by the context of an agricultural area stressed by border closures and water pollution, as the whole area experiences serious environmental dangers. NGO reports frequently refer to acute vulnerability and the extension of informal settlements.[34] Syrians arrive in a region where they mix with the local Lebanese, Lebanese returnees, and Palestinian refugees also arriving from Syria. More than three-quarters of the Syrian refugees are considered severely and highly vulnerable, and there are more than thirty-five highly vulnerable areas/villages in the governorate. It is often said that, in the Bekaa, refugees are three times more numerous than the Lebanese poor.

The vulnerability of children and women is often highlighted in these reports.[35] Child labor has increased significantly in Lebanon since the start of the conflict in Syria, with child labor rates even higher in the Bekaa Valley. Reports also show there is a problem with sexual trafficking and the underage marriage of young girls.[36] Such worsening conditions of vulnerability also comprise risk. The situation of Syrians is connected with political affiliations in the Future Movement, the Lebanese Forces, and so on, where refugees are often portrayed as victims, criminals, or terrorists.

A focus on women

"In Bar Elias there are 37,000 Syrian refugees ... In relation to gender, yes, we have this situation in which eighty percent are women and children. They are working in the fields. Yes, there is a very negative coping; with many burdens for them."[37] This interviewee thus confirms the vulnerability of women and children. However, by observing groups of refugees at UNHCR in the Bekaa on various occasions during the summer of 2017, surprisingly, I could tell that groups were never headed by an adult woman; there was always another male member within the group.[38] A Lebanese social worker in the Bekaa said:

> Sometimes only the mothers, often with kids, but mostly without husbands ... You are right what you say about needing a protector. The culture here is that you need a man to be protected ... Syrian women move with a protector.[39]

Various NGO workers in Bar Elias tried to explain the family context to me based on their views of the traditional Syrian family—likening them to Bedouin family structures that stood in sharp contrast to a supposedly "modernized" Lebanese family structure. Interviewees also emphasized key changes in family structures after their displacement:

> When there is no husband there is a family restructuration. Some of them are their brothers-in-law, for example. They do rearrange their families. There are many members of the family together; this is why there are also new conflicts. For example, there is no privacy for couples. They just put a simple cloth in between as a form of space division. It is not about the war. It is about what comes afterwards, the problems that generate within the family.[40]

Few resources are available for a displaced woman to escape from conditions of border vulnerability. However, after years of emergency solutions and a strong focus on relief measures, newly established NGOs are trying new strategies for transforming the role of their beneficiaries. Examples include women's workshops and embroidery ateliers, or combining relief help with micro-projects from livelihood programs, which are always implemented.[41]

According to a project manager working with women in an NGO in Bar Elias, "the women can also start their own business through the project on entrepreneurship." Most women at the embroidery atelier in Bar Elias come from Idlib, Al Qusair, Homs, Damascus, and Raqa. The program focuses on searching for sustainability, food, warmth, and security. Many of the women are employed as cheap labor, but they are nevertheless the breadwinners, as men do not work. Since 2011, the program has focused on the needs assessed: "immediate relief, food, and health. Nowadays they focus more on agency and finding long-term solutions, empowering the community, and all that can be combined with aid."[42]

These women's workshops recognize the need to invest in skills. In this sense, the ateliers are a way for women to earn an income in a safe, shared space. However, some complain about their meager earnings. One woman in the atelier told me how one piece of embroidery earns her only $7. The NGO psychologist in the Bekaa added: "This is one piece, $7 dollars. This is what they get paid for it. And for selling it. It is a luxury what they sell ... It is not cheap.... It is the stereotype of the Arabic woman, at home sewing."[43]

Rita, a Palestinian woman from the Yarmouk camp in Damascus, spoke to me about her situation for an hour:

> We have lost everything, our bombed house, the relationships I had. I look at my pictures every day, the photos of my destroyed house. The school for my girl

was better, the building was better.... And now they do not want us here, I know even by the way they look at me in the park, I feel totally discriminated aganist. Please find us a way to get out of here ... I went to INTERSOS to ask for help with legal aid. I am bored here even if I have studies, and I tried also the embroidery atelier.

Conclusion

The foregoing discussion has sought to build upon existing research providing new ways in which to approach mobilities that differ from previous narratives of movement, migration, and transportation. There are, of course, several critiques that mitigate against an overwhelming sense of newness in mobilities research, often making researchers think of a sudden revolution, which is also connected to the speed of the changes at the heart of the globalization debate.

Mobility itself is a classic concept; indeed, the Chicago school of sociology showed how inequalities in mobilities are not completely new. In the case of the Middle East, mobilities have been fully entrenched in the long history of the different communities and nation-states. The construction of blockades is also far from new, and mobility has long had a complex connection to the proliferation of borders and the reinforcement of existing borders as well as the investment in security and control measures at many levels, creating new forms of technological surveillance.

This chapter has sought to differ from the existing research is in its understanding of mobility practices, which have traditionally been viewed in a social hierarchy that differentiates people, communities, and nationalities. When seen in this traditional way, the forms of mobility regarded as movement,[44] representation, and practice can also be understood as political, where mobilities are implicated in the production of power and relations of domination. Thus, we are used to a way of thinking that addresses power through the binary concepts of domination and resistance, and structure and agency, but such a framework, while productive, has clear limitations when applied to border ethnographies.

By moving beyond those binaries, we can more effectively study fluid populations in a globalized, transnational world. Furthermore, in such relations of domination related to movement, place is also very important, underlying the "fixity" of global capitalism. Thus, we have to deal with, and make sense of, movement and restrictive places existing together. Borders are popping up everywhere, and the Middle East and the Central Bekaa are no exception.

This chapter has focused on borders and mobilities, which requires a particular framework defined by globalization and transnationalism related to border contradictions and mobility practices, an analysis of the forces related to the "encampment of the world," and, finally, "the right to have rights"—reviewing pity and charity toward women and children. Such a framework has been considered in the context of the Middle East. The Central Bekaa is a paradigmatic case to think about borders and continuous displacement, to think about how we understand the border vulnerability of women and children today, and how the Bekaa became "the desert in the Mediterranean." In this analysis, the image of the "desert," thought of as tyranny in Hannah Arendt's conception, thus becomes the center of the politics of desertification of border space.[45]

3

THE BORDERWORK OF HUMANITARIANISM DURING DISPLACEMENT FROM WAR-TORN SYRIA

LIVELIHOODS AS IDENTITY POLITICS IN NORTHERN LEBANON AND SOUTHEAST TURKEY

Estella Carpi

Introduction

Following the 2011 Syrian political crisis, large numbers of Syrians became refugees, many of whom relocated to neighboring countries.[1] Despite a historically open-border policy, the governments of the countries receiving the Syrian refugees incrementally toughened their migration policies until the ultimate closure of the Syrian–Turkish and the Syrian–Lebanese borders in 2015. Intermittent border closures affected the everyday socioeconomic capital of border populations. While normatively characterized as a symptom of crisis, human mobility, as this chapter shows, has historically sustained border residents in addition to producing their border identities—formed from a situation of residing neither here nor there. The closure of national borders and the "borderwork" of humanitarian labeling—which refers to the social effects of humanitarian action in border areas, and bases' access to assistance on pre-assigned identities—sanctioned the current identity politics of livelihoods in these regions in the wake of the Syrian crisis.[2]

Cross-border activities have always been an important source of livelihoods for border populations in the Middle Eastern region. Considering that the official declaration of the crisis—rather than the crisis itself—plays a crucial role in both the formation and dissolution of social orders and borders, local access to livelihoods has been wavering, particularly since 2011. Despite the longstanding exile of Palestinian refugees in Lebanon, and the protracted Kurdish displacement in southeast Turkey, the current presence of international humanitarian agencies in the northern Lebanese and southern Turkish regions is unprecedented. Here, humanitarianism coexists with governmental border policies that stifle everyday cross-border activities. In this sense, humanitarian borderwork is inscribed in geopolitical configurations and consequently shapes livelihoods programs intended to guarantee basic needs for refugee life (such as food, water, shelter, and clothing) along national lines. At the same time, some international humanitarian programs undercut the economic and cultural transnationalization processes of economic sustainability that normally occur within border spaces, with the presumption that border economies and identities were socially and culturally clear-cut prior to the Syrian crisis. From this perspective, forced migration flows disrupt national realms. Accordingly, the search for and access to livelihoods at the local level has gradually been defined by identity politics: regardless of the past coping strategies across borders and hybrid identities inhabiting these regions, the borderwork of humanitarian action has rendered livelihoods a discriminatory factor in line with national policies meant to reassert sovereignty over borders and control human mobility. As such, livelihoods programming is in fact able to mark out temporary guests and permanent hosts, refugees and citizens, eligible and ineligible victims of crisis.

In this chapter, I argue that it is not the crisis per se that stops the fluid livelihoods system between Syria, Lebanon, and Turkey, as these countries have historically benefited by relying on a long genealogy of smuggling and border relations. Rather, it has been the impossibility of continuing preexisting forms of border livelihoods that have further disenfranchised these regions during wartime. Border refugees, who has been facing a long series of changes in humanitarian and national governance in Lebanon and Turkey, populate these regions in large numbers. On the one hand, border refugees have been largely neglected in the specificity of their "vacillating" existential condition,[3] since they were arbitrarily believed to be the ones who would return to their homes in Syria as soon as possible.[4] Some of these refugees were unable to reach other locations within host societies. On the other hand, the initial response was a prompt form of emergency relief commitment to Syrian nationals who resided outside of camps in Lebanese and Turkish border provinces.

Border refugees often face more socioeconomic troubles, as demographic concentrations along the borders in times of crisis remain high and local infrastructures and service provision are under strain.[5] Border refugees have suffered from increasing costs in the rental and goods markets, while their per capita income has always been lower than the national average in both border regions. Similarly, state- or civil society-based welfare systems have always performed poorly in these border regions. In this framework, national borders have historically functioned as revealing factors of international and regional trade and political and diplomatic relations between neighboring countries.[6] Borders have historically been discussed as inherently contentious spaces,[7] sites of—and, at times, the reasons behind—political conflict. Scholars have therefore spoken of the "battle for the border,"[8] where only people who are recognized as victims are deemed in need of assistance.[9]

This chapter attempts to outline the new social meanings of borders in the framework of humanitarian assistance provision: not only are borders used as entry points for assisting internally displaced people in countries stricken by conflict,[10] but they can also be used by humanitarian governance to challenge or support national politics and transnational models of care. By looking at international humanitarian livelihoods programs, I show that their marginal impact on Syrian urban refugees is due to a taxonomic identity regime that has proven unable to adapt to contextual needs, being both the cause and the product of the longstanding securitization of Middle Eastern borders and states. However, historically, most Middle Eastern states, although not signatories to the 1951 Geneva Convention of Refugees, are more permeable by human mobility than the so-called Global North.

This chapter attempts to add nuance to the scholarly debate on the security politics of borders and invites its readers to consider the practices and identities of refugees, host border societies, and earlier border migrants in a way that considers their pre-crisis (im)mobility status within the hybrid human realm of the border. The vacillating status of earning a living across the border in times of peace pervades the space of local citizenship during displacement.

Against this backdrop, a clear-cut humanitarianism along borders—purporting to distinguish who is the host and who is the guest—acts as a force intended to preserve nation-state privileges. As I illustrate, this vacillating status between borders represents the local citizens' desire that the refugees return home as soon as possible; the refugees, in turn, are left to deal with the paradox of this request, as they are unable to definitively *choose* either site. It is in this vein that this chapter engages with ungraspable categories of life—and humanitarian labels—pushing border-crossing beyond a matter of life or death,[11] and draws on the taxonomies that humanitarian borderwork and national border policies engender.

Methodology

I conducted one month of fieldwork in Arabic in the small city of Halba, northern Lebanon, between February and March 2017, and another in Arabic, English, and Turkish, with the support of a local research assistant, in the city of Gaziantep, southeast Turkey, in August 2017. More specifically, I conducted semi-structured interviews with the different actors in the overall border setting in which humanitarian practices are rolled out: local residents, city authorities, urban refugees, and humanitarian aid workers in Halba, the capital of the Akkar Governorate that neighbors Syria; and in the large city of Gaziantep, located 60 miles north of Syria's Aleppo.

To explore socioeconomic practices in markets, I consider identity categories as set by the international humanitarian apparatus and nation-states; the purpose of using a practice approach rather than a normative value system resides in locating socioeconomic behavior within broader historical processes.[12] The practice approach identifies the interconnections of human practices while problematizing the construction of bounded ethnic and religious categories employed to explain social behaviors as well as facts. By focusing on the practices of these different social actors, I happened to observe Syrian nationals carrying out practices similar to those used by Lebanese and Turkish nationals with the aim of surviving or thriving economically. For instance, some Syrian businessmen who relocated to Gaziantep after 2011 identified themselves as refugees because they were unable to go back to their country of origin, and additionally, some Syrian refugees who relocated to Gaziantep while working as aid providers with the purpose of assisting their national fellows identified themselves in more than one analytical category used for the present study.

It was not possible to conduct interviews with the local authorities in Gaziantep due to recent governmental restrictions on research on refugees in border settings. In Halba, on the other hand, I conducted in-depth interviews with the city authorities: the municipality mayor (*ra'is al-baladiye*), the deputy mayor (*na'ib ar-ra'is*), the governor of the district of Akkar (*mohafez*), and the *makhatir* (central state officials). In both locations, I also had access to local archives containing Arabic and Turkish texts on urban history and the economy; and in the case of Lebanon, I collected insights from local intellectuals, namely a historian, a writer, and a poet.

I carried out in-depth interviews and participant observations in Halba with Lebanese women and men, some of whom were beneficiaries of livelihoods programs; in Gaziantep, the interviews were conducted with Turkish nationals and Syrian refugees from different social classes who did not benefit from any livelihoods program. In Halba, I conducted interviews with local residents in public spaces. This interview strategy was not feasible with Halba's urban refugees, who generally felt uncomfortable or even unsafe in outdoor spaces. In Gaziantep, it was especially inadvisable to conduct interviews in public spaces due to security concerns and political sensitivities.[13] Finally, in-depth interviews and participant observations were also conducted with six local aid workers from five international non-governmental organizations (INGOs) in Halba, and with two international and two local aid workers from four INGOs in Gaziantep, all involved in livelihoods programs. People who had been residing in Halba and Gaziantep a long time were prioritized in the sampling.

The Syrian refugee influx in Halba, northern Lebanon

Northern Lebanon is one of the country's most deprived regions, with severe poverty levels and the worst unemployment rates in the country. According to the UN Office for the Coordination of Humanitarian Affairs (OCHA), out of a total population of 1.1 million people, around 708,000 live under the poverty line: 341,000 deprived Lebanese, over 266,000 Syrian refugees, 88,000 Palestinian refugees, and almost 12,000 Lebanese returnees from overseas.[14] Akkar's families, of which the average size is 4.7 individuals—higher than the national average—constitute nearly 20.5 percent of the entire Lebanese population, maintaining a traditional sociocultural structure.[15]

As a local intellectual in Halba told me: "Halba is neither a village, nor a city" (*wa la qariye wa la medine*).[16] Too small to be called a city, some scholars would probably better define it as an urban center.[17] Halba's society continues to rest on the rural hierarchical ties and relationships that characterize the surrounding hamlets. The social architecture of power, in this sense, integrates with the rural. Urban and rural are therefore interrelated at multiple levels: not only do the local people move back and forth between these two environments and exchange products[18] but both environments are hardly distinguishable from each other. Such a hybrid physical environment is the product of an underdeveloped urban infrastructure. Indeed, local aid workers have emphasized the neglect of the Akkar region by the state and NGOs over the last century and the Beirut-centrism of the Lebanese economy.[19]

The work sectors of Akkar are subdivided into only four categories: education, military, trade, and agriculture.[20] Nonetheless, Halba became a commercial hub during the civil war, as many people living in Tripoli feared clashes and destruction and resettled outside the large northern Lebanese city to open shops and continue their lives. Despite this history, physical market spaces have gradually faded away because of the lack of urban planning, according to local intellectuals.[21] Indeed, the municipality, built in the center of the town in 1998, caused increased traffic and stunted any possibility of opening up public markets, especially from the 2000s. "There is nothing nowadays that can be called 'Halba square,'" affirmed a local resident.[22] Furthermore, Halba has suffered the indirect effects of war in Lebanon. For instance, in the July 2006 war against Israel, two Akkar bridges—used by the major Lebanese Shi'ite party, Hezbollah, to import weapons from Syria via the Dabbusiye–'Abboudiye road—were destroyed. The infrastructure destroyed during the war has yet to be rebuilt. Likewise, no political entities have invested in the reconstruction of the Nahr al-Bared refugee camp in northern Lebanon after the 2007 clashes between the Islamist group Fath al-Islam and the Lebanese army.[23] These clashes negatively affected the northern Lebanese economy, yet the United Nations Refugee Works Agency (UNRWA) did not hold the type of mandate necessary to rebuild parts of the urban area that had delineated the camp space.[24]

During the 1980s, unauthorized (*bala rokhsa*) houses proliferated in Halba, and housing emerged randomly (*bishakl fawdi*) in fields where there used to be cotton cultivation.[25] Halba's economic importance derived from its intermediary position between Homs and Tripoli, and from being the main market for the surrounding villages.[26] After Lebanese independence from France in 1946, Halba largely lost its commercial importance due to the improvement of transport between the northern city of Tripoli and the Akkar region, but it still remained one of the main junctions in northern Lebanon.[27]

Before the 1975–90 civil war, which sanctioned the *Pax Syriana* in Lebanon, unskilled and cheap Syrian labor was looked at positively due to the booming Lebanese economy. Conversely, between 1976 and 2005, Syrian workers were framed as threats to the Lebanese economy and society, reflecting local hardships caused by the Syrian military presence and the Asad regime's political interference. Syrian nationals embodied a commodity—sold and used at convenience—without claiming political and social rights or permanency.[28] After all, Syrian political power in Lebanon was neither advancing nor protecting its workers' rights, even while ensuring their access to the Lebanese labor regime. Nevertheless, there was no attempt by locals to employ a Lebanese workforce over a Syrian one, as doing so would have affected profits.[29]

With a population of 27,000 local inhabitants and 17,000 urban refugees,[30] Syrian nationals mostly reside in informal tented settlements (ITS) built on empty parcels of land on the side of public roads, occupy empty depots, or rent apartments. Since Lebanon is officially a "transit country," as a non-signatory to the 1951 Refugee Convention and the 1967 Protocol, displacement from Syria in Lebanon had not been regulated until October 2014, when the Lebanese government and the United Nations drafted a new decree for refugees—namely the 2015–16 Lebanon Crisis Response Plan (LCRP). Significantly, the plan was intended to generate livelihoods opportunities for both Lebanese and Syrian nationals,[31] thereby framing refugees as economic migrants. Before the war and the influx of Syrian refugees into Lebanon, local people were less prejudiced against temporary Syrian menial labor,[32] but their current permanent presence is unwanted due to the increasing strain on local infrastructures and labor markets. Since 2014, Syrian nationals are no longer allowed to enter Lebanon under a humanitarian framework but are eligible for business and trade if they hold $1,000 and a hotel reservation (for a tourist visa), if they own assets in Lebanon,[33] or if they are sponsored by a Lebanese employer (*kafala* system).[34] Moreover, in 2015, the United Nations High Commissioner for Refugees (UNHCR) stopped registering refugees from Syria and even de-registered a large number in order to comply with the Lebanese government's decree.

The legal constraints that Syrian refugees face in today's Lebanon are not limited to entry regulations. Indeed, the Lebanese Directorate of General Security (the central intelligence agency) issued regulations that now require a refugee to renew their residency every six months for a $200 fee, which also applies to those registered with the UNHCR.[35] This new regulation has caused large numbers of Syrian nationals to lose their legal status in Lebanon, as they are often unable to pay the fee. Their illegal status prevents them from opening bank accounts, enrolling in public schools, and owning property. Nowadays, some Syrian nationals working in Halba are engaged in the same occupation as before the crisis, providing menial labor in gardening, construction, cleaning, and agriculture.[36] Nevertheless, the belief that newcomer refugees currently play the same role within Akkar's economy as they did before the Syrian crisis is misleading.[37] In the past, Syrian migrant workers were mostly young or middle-aged men who provided seasonal labor in Lebanon before returning to Syria, where their families were living and where everyday services and resources were more affordable to them.[38] When the popular uprising and the subsequent conflict broke out in Syria in the spring of 2011, some of these migrant workers brought their families to Lebanon. The local economy of Akkar therefore became a new refuge for women, youth, and child laborers. The sociological features of the local workforce and its costs—which vary according to the age of the laborer—have changed considerably over the last six years.

The Syrian refugee influx in Gaziantep, southeast Turkey

There are close to 300,000 Syrian refugees currently sheltered in twenty-five camps in ten provinces in Turkey,[39] and, at the time of writing, nearly 2.2 million Syrian refugees dispersed across the country outside the camps. In 1990, the Gaziantep population was 738,245, rising to 1,235,815 in 2008, and growing to 1,974,244 by 2016. The 2014 city council report claimed that one person out of every three in the province was a foreign migrant. Gaziantep received the largest number of Syrians in the southeastern Anatolia region; as of February 2017, the number of Syrians in Gaziantep was around 323,283, making up 16.73 percent of the city's population, while the number of Syrian camp-dwellers in Gaziantep was around 390,696. Although Turkey is not a signatory to the 1951 Refugee Convention and the 1967 Protocol, it enacted a temporary protection regime for Syrian refugees,[40] although this renders them no less vulnerable.

Increasingly, measures of deterrence aimed at new arrivals and long-term stays have been adopted, such as the government demolishing old vacant buildings to impede people from using them as shelters.[41] Xenophobic discourse has increased due to job competition—large numbers of Turkish citizens were already unemployed or in precarious work before the Syrian refugees arrived,[42] and job opportunities have further diminished given the sheer number of Syrian refugees in lthe abor market. Discrimination against Syrian nationals in Gaziantep often translates into Turkish citizens not buying goods from Syrian-run shops or renting houses to Syrians. Reducing the amount of aid provided to refugees is commonly thought of as a way of encouraging their return to Syria.[43] Small and medium enterprises are increasingly unable to provide formal work permits to Syrian nationals.[44] Article 8 of the Regulation on Work Permits of Refugees under Temporary Protection, issued in January 2016, requires that the number of refugees holding a work permit not exceed 10 percent of the total number of employees at any workplace, leading employers to hire Syrians informally in a country where informal practices and economic vulnerability overlap.[45] In the absence of institutionalized and transparent policies addressing displacement—especially for non-camp refugees—people's situations are mainly left to the judgment of local authorities.[46] Most Syrian refugees work in textile factories, on building sites,[47] or in the service industry (restaurants, bakeries, stores), while a minority hold other professional and artisan jobs (accountants, carpenters, painters).[48] A large number of refugees have multiple employers who hire them for ad hoc jobs; as such, they are not tied to one employer for a year, as the Turkish work permit scheme would require.[49] As in the Lebanese case, the Syrian immigration process has caused unemployment and reduced internal migration of locally employable individuals.[50]

Despite a state-centralized response to the Syrian refugee crisis—unlike the Lebanese case—the state welfare system is insufficient, informal housing remains neglected, and population growth unaddressed. On the one hand, welfare provision and the social policy framework in Turkey have been based on "informal strategies, implicit social pacts, compromises and most importantly family ties and informal personal networks."[51] Turkey's welfare reform emerged from the 2000–2001 fiscal crisis, moving toward a minimalist welfare regime with the state seemingly retreating while increasingly subcontracting welfare provision to private actors and increasing public–private cooperation in the provision of basic services.[52] On the other hand, the deliberate neglect of informal housing—*gecekondu*s, literally "landed overnight" in Turkish—in urban areas was meant to ease the pressures of migration and integration in the cities.[53] Unlike in Lebanon, privatization and the retreat of the state in terms of service provision can exist side-by-side with the growing political reach and power of the state.

In the 1980s, Syria began to harbor militants belonging to the Kurdistan Workers' Party (PKK), which led to sporadic frictions between Syria and Turkey. Trade was largely nonexistent until the late 2000s, when Syria's economy was partly liberalized in the wake of Hafez al-Asad's death.[54] Turkey's export of goods to Syria—especially motor vehicles and electronics built or assembled in the Turkish southeastern provinces—finally took off in 2008, peaking at $1.8 billion in 2010. This was an important boost to the border economy and the regional development of Turkey. Moreover, for the first time, the southeastern region was exporting without relying on the Western Marmara industrial region. The exports continued during the Syrian conflict, and in late 2013, Turkish exports into Syria rose with the sale of wheat, sugar, cement, and other goods needed under wartime conditions (see Table 3.1). When, in 2015, Turkey-based rebels began to lose ground to the Asad regime forces, Turkey's exports began to teeter. Nevertheless, humanitarian organizations operating in Gaziantep and the government's Disaster and Emergency Management Presidency (AFAD) continued to purchase the needed resources from local firms. For instance, a Turkish export officer affirmed that she sold clothing and shoes to the UN agencies, as well as clean water-decontamination devices and plastic material for bags in Turkey and abroad.[55]

The number of Syrian-owned businesses in Turkey has increased. Between January 2011 and April 2017, the number of companies established in Turkey with Syrian capital stood at 5,797.[56] Syrian entrepreneurs who resettled in the southeastern provinces brought with them their familiarity with the border region and their market skills, as most of them came from the Aleppo region (referred to by Turkish and Syrian interviewees as "the sister city"), which already had robust trade relations with Turkey before the war. Local researchers have deemed urban economic growth as the primary reason for preserving the current social order,[57] which allowed for a more integrated economy across the border.[58]

Table 3.1: Exports from Gaziantep to Syria

Year	$US1000	Change (%)
2010	1.844.605	–
2011	1.609.861	–12
2012	497.960	–69
2013	1.024.473	105
2014	1.800.962	76
2015*	741.505	2.3

* January–June 2015.
Source: TÜİK; 2015 Gaziantep Chamber of Commerce Report, "Exports from Gaziantep to Syria."[59]

THE BORDERWORK OF HUMANITARIANISM

Humanitarian livelihoods programs in Lebanon and Turkey

Livelihoods have long formed an integral part of humanitarian programming. The concept of livelihoods, which came to prominence in the 1980s as an anti-development strategy,[60] gained ascendancy in international circles in the wake of the "sustainable development" and "resilience" mantras that now populate humanitarian reports and the scholarly literature engaging with humanitarianism. The technocratic use of the term "livelihoods" in humanitarian programming—not entirely translatable into the local languages of project-targeted regions—has been standardized across different geographic sites. Yet, it fits into the power discourse and the "construction of difference" that geographic borders are able to generate and that have widely influenced contemporary border studies.[61]

In the wake of the Syrian crisis, such programs in Lebanon and Turkey have generally been financed by UN agencies and INGOs and mostly implemented on the ground by local NGOs. Up against a highly compartmentalized humanitarian sector, livelihoods fits a broad and ungraspable scope of action, which has increasingly extended its arm from refugees to vulnerable local citizens: indeed, livelihoods are locally approached in the broader sense of "ways to improve life" (*sobol tahsin al-'aiysh*) in Lebanon and "possibilities of subsistence" (*Geçim İmkanları*) in Turkey, under the UN Development Program (UNDP)-coordinated umbrella of "livelihoods, employment and local economic development" (*Geçim İmkanları, İstihdam ve Yerel Ekonomik Kalkınma*). While most livelihoods programs in Akkar are rural-centered, in the Gaziantep region they focus on both urban occupations, such as the industrial sector, and rural activities like olive picking in Gaziantep's fields. In some cases, livelihoods strategies used to enhance people's capacity to make a living and render it sustainable consist of vocational training, such as: information technology classes; English- and Turkish-language classes in Lebanon and Turkey, respectively; and practical training in makeup, hairdressing, and chocolate-making. Other strategies include temporary work opportunities or income-generating home-based activities including cooking and sewing or embroidering. In other cases, livelihoods can be a component of the protection program—under emergency cash assistance or unconditional cash programs, or a component of food security.[62] Some of the livelihoods programs currently conducted in Halba and Gaziantep are a legacy of previous income-generating activities that, even though very small in number, were originally started to alleviate chronic poverty and to encourage women's empowerment in the Akkar region and in Gaziantep.[63]

Overall, humanitarian livelihoods programs in Lebanon and Turkey have increasingly revolved around cash transfers and small-scale forms of income-generating activities, leading refugees to hold temporary or seasonal jobs. The procedure is standardized, according to the INGO workers I interviewed in Halba and Gaziantep. Most programs are run by INGOs in Lebanon, while in Turkey, they are run by local NGOs and UN agencies in partnership with the government, continuing projects started by INGOs previously.[64] In Lebanon, most programs are designed on the basis of local and refugee interests and market skills gaps,[65] and, in Turkey, all programs are decided by the Chamber of Industry, which first conducts market assessments.[66] As a standardized procedure in both countries, potential beneficiaries generally register online after being classified as eligible. People's needs are mostly assessed according to the specific circumstances of vulnerability (e.g., types of food purchased, housing conditions, etc.) rather than merely on an income basis. In general, INGOs mostly align their needs assessments with the Survival Minimal Basket Expenditure for food and non-food items, which is based on national calculation methods.[67] As a common rule for all NGOs, beneficiaries are normally allowed to join livelihoods programs on a six-month basis, meaning that they must wait for six months to be eligible to enroll again in a new professional training.[68]

While cash for work is the most frequent livelihoods program designed for male refugees in Halba and Gaziantep, small-scale or home-based activities to self-generate income are designed for refugee women. Livelihoods centers have been built throughout the two border regions as a point of reference for refugees, and particularly vulnerable local populations increasingly look at these centers as recruitment agencies able to provide them with job opportunities.[69] Nonetheless, most of the livelihoods programs consist of self-employment and informal activities promoted to guarantee survival rather than entrepreneurship. Small-scale self-empowerment initiatives, in fact, challenge host governments to a lesser extent and are unlikely to raise local dissent.[70] The kind of work that is tacitly promoted in such livelihoods programs is therefore mostly informal and survival-driven and unable to liberate large segments of the refugee working population from everyday exploitation.

The original humanitarian purpose of providing refugees with livelihoods opportunities is accompanied by the delayed purpose of strengthening local municipal services, especially focusing on solid waste management and the construction of public areas. In Turkey, UNDP has been partnering with AFAD since 2015, while in Lebanon INGOs and UNDP have mostly dealt with local municipalities, under the central government's approval, to negotiate common endeavors. Nevertheless, due to the different stages of pre-crisis urban development in Halba and Gaziantep, only the latter has visibly upgraded its urban profile and benefited from the presence of the humanitarian system to improve pre-existing social services.

Interviews conducted with INGO workers in Halba and Gaziantep pointed to the use of refugee self-reliance as a back-route formula for social cohesion and regional stability rather than as a realistic strategy that pushes refugee lives toward something more than survival and restoration of normality.[71] Thus while humanitarianism attempts to promote inter-group programs and engender social cohesion and stability on each side of the border, the normalcy of livelihood-seeking was already configured across—rather than within—such borders before the Syrian crisis. Despite the small number of contentious incidents between refugee and local populations, livelihoods programs established on market-based recipes are analogously used as a means to guarantee secure regions and borders.[72] As a matter of fact, while it has not been possible to interview refugee beneficiaries of livelihoods programs in Gaziantep for security reasons, in Halba most beneficiaries emphasized the entertaining character of such livelihoods programs.[73] The latter programs led the refugees to look at humanitarian intervention as a way of providing leisure activities in a city with no social spaces, rather than guaranteeing their daily livelihoods and concretely providing them with sustainable jobs. Humanitarian aid provision, however, came as a delayed opportunity to develop the marginalized northern border regions of Lebanon, where segments of the local population did not even hold citizenship before the 1990s.[74] For instance, an increasing number of livelihoods programs nowadays involve city cleaning and infrastructural development in Halba and Gaziantep.[75]

Such programs have not managed to compensate for the strain under which the two cities have been put due to the demographic growth that has accompanied the arrival of refugees and humanitarian workers. In Gaziantep, exports fluctuated with a rise in sales in late 2013 during the Syrian war, although there is currently a significant decrease in the business volume toward Syria.[76] Also, local residents in Halba and Gaziantep highlighted that local competition has been on the rise over the last five years due to the jobs that INGOs offer, such as teaching and training in the humanitarian livelihoods programs, which are generally seen as ambitious, well-paid opportunities. In terms of refugee livelihoods, the Syrian refugees I interviewed in both

Halba and Gaziantep highlighted the fact that training people on the same tasks can also end up feeding local competition rather than creating new opportunities. As history has always shown, the "have-nots" find themselves in competition with poor newcomers. With the outbreak of the Syrian crisis, many local inhabitants do not believe that the presence of Syrian refugees in the region increases economic incentives "as they do not enlarge the market demand, but they rather steal water and electricity and do not work."[77] Moreover, the 2015 closure of the Lebanese and Turkish borders impoverished many border villages,[78] which used to make a livelihood out of smuggling and formal trade relationships. The World Food Program-issued smart cards in both countries not only allowed refugees to sustain their everyday consumption since the beginning of the crisis but also supported larger shops and businesses. Small businesses, according to the local inhabitants of both border regions, have been discriminated against by INGOs and consequently have lost their earnings over the last six years. Indeed, vouchers—and from 2013, e-cards—that are only redeemable at local businesses replaced direct food-aid in ways that created aligned interests between refugees and powerful local elitist lobbies, inherent to a hierarchical architecture of labor.[79]

In this context, humanitarian agencies and municipalities have started new joint projects in order to enhance citizen and refugee entrepreneurship initiatives while letting small and medium enterprises die out in local markets.[80] While the middle and high social strata of the Syrian refugee diaspora largely managed to reach the European coasts or third countries for resettlement, the most vulnerable refugees have no other choice but to remain in Lebanon and Turkey. These segments, among a diverse refugee community,[81] are left without sufficient resources to pay for a smuggler, or to provide skilled labor to qualify for sporadic humanitarian corridors to Italy and France,[82] which would privilege these refugee "profiles" as potential future neo-citizens in the Global North.

The ambivalent effects of the crisis on host urban economies have been overlooked in humanitarian accounts, which instead embed Lebanese and Turkish societies in discourses revolving around resourcelessness and hardships on the one hand, or flourishing and greedy economies taking advantage of the crisis on the other.[83] While Halba primarily lacks market demand, as its inhabitants generally have a "limited income and way of living" (*ma'iysh mahdud*),[84] the city of Gaziantep has flourished in terms of infrastructure, marketplaces, and entertainment spaces.[85] Although, on the whole, the presence of humanitarian agencies positively impacts the local employment of variegated middle classes,[86] the interviews conducted show that humanitarian livelihoods programs have not had a sizable impact on everyday refugee livelihoods either in Halba or in Gaziantep. In Halba, Syrian refugees affirmed that they are unable to rely on sustainable forms of financial support since they are unable to sell their handmade products in the local market. Alternatively, they work intermittently for low salaries. In the large urban setting of Gaziantep, most refugees I interviewed were not aware of UN- or INGO-initiated livelihoods programs or were not attending aid distributions on a regular basis even when living in particularly vulnerable circumstances.[87] This further demonstrates the limited impact of such programs. While Syrian refugees are not legally allowed to start businesses in Lebanon, the Gaziantep Chamber of Commerce counted twelve Syrian-owned companies registered with them before the Syrian war, rising to 738 during 2016.[88] In total, Syrians opened 4,456 companies operating in food, construction, and trade, and have invested US$666 million in Turkey since 2012.[89]

If training and workshops are unable to substantially integrate the refugee household's income in Halba, the percentage of refugee beneficiaries who have found stable forms of income in Gaziantep is deemed relatively high.[90] It is, however, worth noting that larger numbers of refugees are said to participate in such programs than in Halba, thereby leading to higher rates of success. On the contrary, Lebanese and Turkish residents, with the benefit of citizenship, approach livelihoods programs as a way to enhance one's own job opportunities. INGOs reject the locally produced configuration of new work agencies, although at present official humanitarian programming does address local unemployment.[91]

Deconstructing aprioristic identity categories of need

I now turn to discussing how local market actors maneuver practices and symbols to perform belonging or otherness, how humanitarian labeling creates and manages categories of need, and how this politics of labeling and allocating resources and services on an identity basis impacts the perceptions of the displaced self.

Most of the Syrian refugees and Turkish citizens I interviewed stressed their belief that Syrian nationals with Turkmen origins, or from mixed Turkish–Syrian families, were largely advantaged in finding sustainable sources of income and connecting to the host society. Moreover, overall, Syrian nationals living in Gaziantep expressed a greater connection with the city than did Syrian nationals in Halba, where, instead, the Syrian genealogy of menial labor kept Syrian newcomers particularly vulnerable. People's accounts therefore pointed to a fundamental relationship between personal identification processes, official identity politics, and local access to assistance regimes in times of crisis.

Türkmenler Caddesi is the main street of the İran pazarı neighborhood that, before the conflict broke out in Syria in 2011, used to be an attraction for Iranian pilgrims on their way to the Zeinab shrine in southern Damascus and a place where residents would accept foreign (i.e., Iranian, Iraqi, and Russian) currency.[92] Nowadays, the street market is populated by shops run—and less frequently owned—by Syrian nationals.[93] In the district, some buildings are falling apart, and the streets look unusual for a Turkish city, with religious symbols visible in public space. It is possible to hear the *adhan* (the Islamic call to prayer issued from mosques) or religious radio channels and see faith-related pictures on walls when entering Syrian shops. "All of this is quite unusual in Turkey, which tends to keep public spaces and commercial activities secular even in very religious cities," my Turkish research assistant noticed.[94] Also, the type of coffee and the style of apparel on sale do not reflect local Turkish habits.[95] Nonetheless, all shops present a Turkish flag, which local residents considered to be an attempt to attract Turkish customers, who are otherwise reluctant to shop there.[96] In parallel, a Turkish grocery owner affirmed that he began selling Syrian products to diversify and enhance his customer base, as business was otherwise declining.[97]

On the whole, Syrian shop assistants hang posters and public signs in Turkish primarily for two reasons: as an attempt to localize their shops and in compliance with the Turkish government's ban on using Arabic on public signs.[98] Some shops cover previous Arabic signs—which were mainly aimed at attracting Arab clients—with wooden planks. These shops would normally stock products that constituted the local market demand back in Syria.[99] All of them being located next to each other, they face great mutual competition: "We are not allowed to be located anywhere else in the city.... The choice is shutting down and remaining unemployed," said a Syrian national running a pet shop.[100] Refugees therefore find themselves competing with each other due to the difficulty of renting a shop or finding employment in the stores of upper- and middle-class neighborhoods. Moreover, since refugee influxes were halted, internal Turkish migration from Sanliurfa and Diyarbakir—and southeast Turkey in general—to Gaziantep has been providing a particularly cheap workforce.[101] Competition has emerged among refugees as much as among local Turkish residents.

In a realm where buyers and sellers seek to perform border-crossing market subjectivities, and strategically incorporate "the Other's" nationhood, Turkmens generally represent the comfortable zone between displacement from the Syrian conflict and resettlement in Turkey. The story of Ahmed is an example of the greater receptiveness of Turkish people toward Syrian Turkmens who are more likely to speak Turkish and know the local culture.[102] Living in a Turkmen village close to the border, Ahmed's grandfather and grandmother did not know Arabic at all when he was still living in Syria, telling me: "I learned Turkish at the university, but, as a Turkmen, Gaziantep's language and culture are very familiar to me."[103] Ahmed embodies a border-crossing identity that the humanitarian system would struggle to classify. The fluidity of the border partially determined his life: although not registered with UNHCR, Ahmed believes he is a refugee as he cannot go back to Syria. He is actually an earlier migrant who moved for educational reasons to Gaziantep and then returned to Syria before the conflict broke out. After the spring of 2011, he decided to undertake humanitarian work with a Qatari government charity organization. An analysis of Ahmed's identity therefore unfolds the constructed nature of beneficiary categories and (un)forced migrants, which the humanitarian apparatus tends to prearrange. Was the fact that Ahmed provided aid to his co-nationals evidence that he, in turn, did not need aid and care as a refugee? Did the fact that he *was* a refugee ever attenuate his capacity to undertake humanitarian work himself? Due to his previous time in Gaziantep, his ethnic origin, and his familiarity with the Turkish context, was he not classifiable as a local resident? Against this backdrop, Ahmed said: "If I had wanted, UNHCR would have registered me at the beginning of the crisis on the basis of my Syrian passport, even though I did not need anything from them."[104]

The case of Najwan in Halba similarly deconstructs normative accounts associating forced migration with nationality,[105] and the alleged—and exclusive—ethnic character of vulnerability. The paradox of such a predefined identity system of care emerges especially in border regions. Najwan is a Lebanese woman from Halba, and even though her mother is from Homs (western Syria), Najwan never inherited Syrian citizenship.[106] Against the backdrop of a regional migration flow primarily going from Syria to Lebanon, in 2003 Najwan and her husband decided to move to Homs where she worked as a hairdresser. After the 2011 uprising and its escalation to a complex international proxy war, Najwan and her family fled back to Halba by legally crossing the Lebanese–Syrian border. While they were lucky enough to be able to rely on relatives and acquaintances in northern Lebanon while escaping Syria, they had no sustainable sources of livelihood. After moving back to Lebanon, Najwan had been unable to find financial support to improve her professional skills and to open a beauty salon. Her husband, a Lebanese national, is now in the military; thanks to his modest salary, she was finally able to open a salon. She had been looking for micro-credit loans, but most of these UN- and INGO-financed projects were originally designed for Syrian nationals. Najwan and her husband—both Lebanese from Halba—had moved to Lebanon from Syria due to violence, shelling, and political persecution that began in the spring of 2011, but their passports did not allow them into the international humanitarian assistance regime for Syrian nationals. Nonetheless, this case shows how some displaced Lebanese citizens are ineligible to access livelihoods programs designed for Syrian nationals. In this case, Lebanese citizenship is a disempowering factor, despite Najwan's reliance on previous social capital networks.

The new social meaningfulness of borders

Both local residents and urban refugees described Halba as a city of *taʿaiyush* (coexistence), a city for all, where confessional identity politics has less significance than in other areas of Akkar or Lebanon. Unlike mono-confessional cities and villages, local inhabitants highlighted the "dignity" (*karame*) of Halba for being home to anyone, and for the presence of various political parties. This idea of local harmony contrasts with the local unease of living with the refugees, as they embody the historical specter of the *Pax Syriana*, which is locally perceived as the Syrian "occupation" of Lebanon (1976–2005). For instance, the *mukhtar*—a central state official—expressed his desire to introduce curfews for Syrian men by mentioning that he used to be stopped in the street by the Syrian army in early 2000: "We are now entitled to enact security measures against the refugees."[107] People from Akkar can still provide a tangible sense of the geography of the "Syrian protection" (*wikala suriyya*), mentioning the statues of Basel and Hafez al-Asad, checkpoints, and celebratory street names, which were removed immediately after the 2005 Syrian withdrawal from Lebanon. Moreover, the stifling of the once economically flourishing Akkar is locally attributed to the Syrian regime. Local residents often mention the fact that Syrian nationals, who oppressed them in the capacity of soldiers or as competitors in the labor market, can now leave for Europe much more easily than they can due to their refugee status. Up against the identity politics that underlies international humanitarian programming, a Lebanese resident finds such a legal differentiation unfair because "what is happening in Syria also occurred to us."[108] In the memories of a Lebanese resident, Waleed, the main street used to be called Basel al-Asad Street before 2005, in honor of the current Syrian president's brother.[109] Waleed still recalls the square where there used to be checkpoints, and where soldiers used to stop local people and control all movements. The Syrian regime used to forbid any commercial activities outside of its control.

The geography of the past Syrian presence in Akkar allows for an understanding of the anguish caused by the refugees' presence. Considering the paradoxical identification of the Syrian regime with the refugee newcomers—who, most of the time, fled political persecution—there is a deep historical wound that local people continue to carry and that several humanitarian agencies initially neglected.[110] In this sense, the refugee migration into Akkar has been experienced at a local level as a re-territorialization of the Syrian occupation.[111]

I define this local attitude toward prior inhabitants who become newcomer refugees in terms of "neo-borderization"—that is, the creation of in-city "borderscapes" of inclusion and exclusion,[112] according to which Lebanese people undercut the past presence of Syrians by highlighting the precarious character of their work before the crisis in the Akkar region. The presence of such borderscapes puts emphasis on the continuous burden on Akkar's people in managing the crisis and tackling rapid and unregulated population growth. In such a context, attributing new social fragmentation meanings to the border is a reminder of Akkar's past political and economic relationships, and an invitation to recognize local needs and support the local workforce while making the Other's presence temporary, as it was before the political crisis in Syria.[113]

Although southeast Turkey's political economy and human geography differ from Halba, local people in Gaziantep also tend to overshadow the common culture, habits, norms, and family ties with Syria. This particularly emerges as paradoxical when dealing with Syrian Turkmens, who are believed to be privileged among Syrian refugees of other ethnic origins due to the greater care provided to them by the Turkish government.[114] Despite the attempts to mark refugees out as outsiders, it is challenging to set a line of separation between refugees and local residents when they share the same language and culture. Najwan and Ahmed betray the normativity of refugee and citizen, guest and host, ideal-types. In this framework, humanitarian and national policies in the border cities make the Syrian presence "Other," even though Syrian migration, as mentioned, is certainly not unprecedented. The longstanding role of Syrian migrant work in local markets, even when not merely seasonal, is minimized in today's local accounts.

Local people also pointed to what I call a process of "Otherization" in Gaziantep—which was already home to Syrian workers—often expressing the desire to remain detached from Syrian city dwellers. For example, a Turkish national affirmed: "Syrians use parks intensively. When you go to the park, almost 60 percent of the people are Syrians. We used to go to Büyükbaba forest for picnics. I think we'll need to find another place.... Now *they* became the hosts and *we* are the guests."[115] In a similar vein, Ahmed, a Syrian Turkmen interviewee, describes the border as the only possibility, other than favorable governmental policies, of survival during war and as a means of slipping through national migration policies:

> After the border closure between Syria and Turkey, people needed to decide whether they should stay in Turkey or go back to Syria. Before then, we Syrians often said to ourselves—"Today I'm going to Syria" ... Then we find life difficult there, and we sometimes try to come back. When the border closed, we couldn't afford taking a definitive decision, as our families are spread all over the borders. Would you choose between your mother and your sister?[116]

Conclusion

Borders have been early sites of humanitarian action since the Syrian crisis broke out in 2011, when there was no expectation in the neighboring states that there would be large-scale spillover from Syria. That period saw the "reinvention of the border as a space of humanitarian government."[117] The border gradually became the unapproachable and irresolvable part of the crisis, where people coexist among outbursts of violence,[118] changing bureaucratic policies, and a humanitarian "minimalist biopolitics" that, so to speak, keeps border populations at the minimum of the "humanitarian reason."[119]

The longstanding process of human displacement that the Syrian conflict produced caused the local displacement of traditional points of call for livelihoods, sociality, and labor. This kind of displacement affected not only those who became refugees themselves but also local and migrant people living in border regions who did not move during the Syrian crisis. In this sense, it was not the Syrian refugee influx per se but rather the closure of the national borders in Turkey and Lebanon in 2015 that affected everyday life, social capital, and the work of local inhabitants. Indeed, mobility—of which conflict may be only one cause among many—has long been found to be a key livelihood strategy and a politico-economic rehabilitation tool for populations on the move.[120] Likewise, continued movement across borders, rather than home-making in the host country or return,[121] has historically served to effectively protect refugees.[122]

In the process of the "neo-borderization" of Halba and Gaziantep, the border has acquired new social meaningfulness, making local access to livelihoods a component of identity politics, which either grants or denies eligibility to assistance. The identity borderwork of humanitarianism has contributed to overshadowing the human and economic geography of the past Syrian "occu-pation" of Lebanon (1976–2005) as well as the longstanding hybrid market spaces of Gaziantep. In this sense, these new borderscapes produce new forms of spatial marginalization where the Syrian refugees reside. The first humani-tarian efforts in Akkar actively classified the emergence of new and old needs on a national basis—e.g., polarizing them between the needs of the Lebanese, those of the Turkish, and those of the Syrians. In contrast, today's humanitar-ian livelihoods programming acts through compensatory stability mecha-nisms meant to address social tensions, in a bid to pursue refugee economic survival and local empowerment. The present "inter-group" character of such programs shapes the identity politics of livelihoods programming. In this sense, humanitarian "modes of ordering" echo the scholarly and humanitarian ways in which local social groups have been thought of throughout Middle Eastern history.[123]

Before the Syrian crisis, what used to *constitute*—rather than *unite*—national identities was border livelihoods. At present, the borderwork of humanitarianism, acting through livelihoods programs, presupposes that identities are defined by nation-state politics, while producing eligible or ineli-gible subjects of care. It is therefore unsurprising that humanitarian liveli-hoods programming cannot help to restore everyday normality by any means, as it partakes itself in border governance. No durable solutions can be found without re-allowing human mobility across borders.

4

HOSTING AND BEING HOSTED
IN TIMES OF CRISIS

EXPLORING THE MULTILAYERED PATTERNS
OF SYRIAN REFUGE IN THE DAYR AL-AHMAR REGION,
NORTHERN BEKAA, LEBANON

Emma Aubin-Boltanski and *Leïla Vignal*

Introduction

This chapter aims to illuminate the dynamics and patterns of the Syrian refuge in Syria's neighboring countries, and its relations and interactions with the local host communities, in the broader context of the Syrian conflict and the massive exile of Syrians abroad that resulted from it. The chapter is based on in-depth fieldwork in the villages of the Dayr al-Ahmar *caza* (sub-district) in the *muhafaza* (district) of Baalbek-Hermel, in the north of the Bekaa plain in Lebanon. Our research focused primarily on the three villages that have the highest concentration of Syrian refugees according to a local census carried out in April 2016 by some of the *caza*'s municipalities: Dayr al-Ahmar city

(2,793 refugees in a community of 10,455 inhabitants); Btede'i (1,800 refugees and 859 inhabitants); and Beshuat, on the foothills above Dayr al-Ahmar city (300 Syrians; 1,114 inhabitants).[1] In 2018, 3,276 Syrians were registered by the United Nations High Commissioner for Refugees (UNHCR) in Dayr al-Ahmar city, 121 in Btede'i, and 72 in Beshuat.[2]

To examine the dynamics of hosting and being hosted, as well as contributing to a more nuanced understanding of the relations between Lebanese and Syrian refugees in Lebanon, we chose to study the Syrian refuge through a very local prism. Through this local prism, we rooted our inquiry in the host–guest relationship in time—the contemporary history of Syrian–Lebanese relations—and space—the Bekaa plain that combines dense social transborder interactions between Lebanese and Syrians, in particular, through the decades-long Syrian circular labor migrations to Lebanon—with memories of Syria's political and military domination over Lebanon. We consequently analyze the Syrian exile within local contexts of refuge. In Lebanon, these local contexts vary enormously from one place to another, although everywhere has been affected by insufficient economic development, the fragile organization of politics, the lack of consensus with regard to the Syrian conflict, and the inconsistencies of the Lebanese and international humanitarian response to the refugee crisis.

A situated ethnography is a powerful tool to articulate the experiences of a place to larger theoretical questions of what it means to host and be hosted in the context of a protracted situation of refuge. On the one hand, the fears and hatred expressed in some of the discourses of the hosts can be understood as reflecting the local population's own uncertainties and fragilities.[3] On the other hand, the Syrian refugees do experience harsh destitution, but they are not passive victims: they also display what Catherine Brun conceptualizes as an "agency-in-waiting."[4] In this chapter, we attempt to disentangle the different threads that are at the heart of a relationship that is more complex and ambiguous than the binary encapsulated in the host–guest approach. The first section of the chapter explores the socioeconomic and spatial dimensions of the relations between the Syrians and Lebanese, and the second section its multiple temporal layers. The third section focuses on the interactions and the two-way interdependency that organizes the relationship between the Syrians and Lebanese.

Our analysis is based on fieldwork in Dayr al-Ahmar that took place five to six years after Syrians began to settle there and hence at a time when the "temporary" had taken on various aspects of "permanence" for both the local population and the refugees.[5] We conducted three fieldworks in the *caza* of Dayr al-Ahmar in 2017 and 2018,[6] during which we carried out observations as well as interviews with more than eighty Syrian refugees and Lebanese inhabitants. We deliberately chose to meet with and interview the same people several times over this period in order to create a relationship of trust. In doing so, we were able to gain a deeper understanding of the local interactions and experiences, which were characterized by fluidity, contradictions, and complexity.

A local prism: Dayr al-Ahmar in the Bekaa Plain

The Bekaa Plain: an "intermediary" space between Syria and Lebanon

Lebanon was created in 1920 by the then mandatory power, France, out of the large Ottoman province of the Bilad al-Sham. It was formed of the Petit-Liban—the administrative area carved out in 1860–1 that was centered on the Mount Lebanon district and included Beirut—and the Bekaa Plain, to which it was attached at that time. Hence the Bekaa is a marginal region in the Lebanese historical construct: not only is this agricultural area less inhabited and developed than the coastal areas but it had also been administered by Syrian cities up to 1920, especially by Homs, one of central Syria's most important urban centers.

However, since 1920 and the establishment of an international border between Syria and Lebanon, the former social continuity between the Bekaa and the plain of Homs has endured. The open-border policy adopted between the two countries has facilitated dense transborder social ties and economic relations operating on different scales. Local cross-border family and kinship connections and trade routes (including illegal networks of smuggling in both directions) animated this cross-border space.

Lebanon's role as a labor market for Syrian workers also facilitated close transborder relations between the two countries. John Chalcraft showed that from the 1950s and 1960s onward,[7] Syrians were a key element in Lebanon's menial job market (in construction and agriculture mostly), representing between 20 and 40 percent of Lebanon's workforce in the early 2000s, when between 300,000 and 500,000 Syrians were employed. However, this important presence was not accompanied by permanent settlement and local integration: on the contrary, the Syrian workforce in Lebanon was characterized by patterns of circular mobility—going back and forth from one country to the other. Such practices of circular mobility had the effect of creating multi-sited social practices as well as transnational processes of production in space and place (e.g., the construction of homes in Syria with the money earned in Lebanon).

The porosity of this intermediary space was exacerbated by the Syrian occupation of the country from 1976, in the context of the Lebanese civil war, to 2005, in the aftermath of the assassination of Prime Minister Rafic Hariri. This occupation was to a large extent based on Syria's claim (but also of pro-Syrian parties in Lebanon) that Lebanon was part of a "Greater Syria" unjustly severed in 1920 by the French and their Christian allies.[8] Seen in this context, the Bekaa was a strategic territorial element of Syria's military occupation. Syrian troops remained posted en masse in the Bekaa until 2005, whereas in the coastal areas of the country, troops had partially withdrawn. For thirty years, checkpoints and military camps were part of the local environment.

These long-term historical processes have contributed to the transformation of the Bekaa into what Karine Bennafla calls a "territorial in-between" characterized by cross-border overlaps in economy,[9] trade, labor markets, formal and informal social institutions, and the private sphere. Transnational mobility shaped this space to a large extent. Before the current conflict, people would go back and forth across the border, especially in the northern borderlands,[10] mixing various transborder, family or tribal interactions, trade, and business relations with informal networks of smuggling or criminal activities—for example, the trafficking of drugs or weapons in a region where open conflicts resumed in the 2000s, in particular between Hezbollah and Israel in the July 2006 war.

Syrian workers have been important players in this transborder connectivity. Their mobility was part of the shaping of the territorial and social patterns of the Bekaa, as well as their insertion into the local low-wage labor markets. They would temporarily settle there, either in poor and crowded accommodation or under tents that were either isolated or part of an informal camp—which led the local population to call them "badû" (Bedouins), "Arab," or "nawar" or "nûri" (gypsies), although back in Syria these people were settled in villages originating from the regions of Aleppo, Hama, and Homs.[11]

Dayr al-Ahmar: a Christian Maronite enclave in north Bekaa

Dayr al-Ahmar is a Maronite Christian enclave located west of the town of Baalbek. The area comprises the eastern slopes of the Mount Lebanon mountain range, on which small villages are found, and a large section of the *sahel*, the agricultural plain of the Bekaa. The Dayr al-Ahmar *caza* is made up of fourteen villages, populated by families that have been established there for centuries. The village of Beshuat became an important interreligious pilgrimage center after an apparition of the Virgin Mary in 2004.[12] Every year since, Christian (mainly Maronite) and Muslim (mainly Shi'a) worshippers gather there in August, for Assumption Day.

Areas where the majority of the population is Shi'a surround Dayr al-Ahmar. Baalbek, the most important local city, is the cradle of Hezbollah. In this context, the population of Dayr al-Ahmar has always had to adapt to, cooperate, or negotiate with other confessional groups in its neighborhood. During the 2006 war, when Israeli planes bombed Shi'a areas in Lebanon, it is remarkable that the surrounding Shi'a population took shelter in Dayr al-Ahmar, which, as a Christian area, was excluded from the bombing campaigns. This event is still remembered and talked about by locals, who contrast this experience with the presence of Syrian refugees.[13]

It should be pointed out that, while Christians in Lebanon are estimated to make up about 36 percent of the population, in Syria before the war they represented only about 6 percent of a population that is mainly Sunni Muslim (70 percent). Mirroring this demographic situation, in the Maronite "bastion" of Dayr al-Ahmar, there is no connection between confessional belonging and refugee presence: the refugees are, in their huge numbers, Sunni Muslims. However, with the Syrian war, sectarian belongings and national politics reverberate in the local, underlying politics of hosting. As elsewhere in Lebanon, the refugee population has imposed costs on the host community, yet the local politicians have instrumentalized the Syrian refugee issue for political gains,[14] resulting in ambivalent and sometimes incoherent politics. In Dayr al-Ahmar, politics toward refugees is, on the one hand, shaped by the nearby presence of the ever-powerful Hezbollah, whose militia intervenes directly in Syria in support of the al-Asad regime. Since the beginning of the Syrian refugee influx in Lebanon, Hezbollah has adopted an ambiguous stance. Whereas it initially "branded itself a welfare agent for refugees,"[15] and emphasized "Lebanon's humanitarian duties and exhorted its fellow citizens to consider Syrians as guests in need of hospitality,"[16] after 2013, as the conflict in Syria worsened and tensions between refugees and host communities escalated, the "guest" became a "burden" and a "threat" for the Lebanese confessional demographic balance.[17] In June 2018, after the victory of the Syrian army over the insurgents in Deraa, Hezbollah's leader, Sayyed Hasan Nasrallah, declared that Hezbollah would work with the

Syrian state and Lebanon's General Security Agency to help the return of "the biggest possible number of Syrian refugees" on a "voluntary basis," a declaration that was met with concern by the UNHCR in the absence of a peace deal.[18] A twenty-five-year-old Syrian refugee we met in Dayr al-Ahmar told us that, as far as he and his family were concerned, they had chosen to settle in this area precisely because it was Christian and not Shi'a, and under the direct control of Hezbollah.[19]

In Dayr al-Ahmar, the political sphere is dominated by the Lebanese Forces (LF), a far-right nationalist Christian militia that was created in 1977 and became established as a party in 1990. The LF's leader, Samir Geagea (also spelled Ja'ja'), a longstanding opponent of the al-Asad regime, was imprisoned for eleven years (1994–2005) by order of the Syrian authorities. The LF has also adopted an ambivalent stance toward the Syrian refugees, either labeling them as victims of the hated al-Asad regime or developing a securitized rhetoric portraying Syrians as a threat to the security of the country in terms of the confessional demographic balance as well as a burden on Lebanon's economy.[20] Geagea has repeatedly asked for the establishment of border camps and has even suggested that displaced Syrians originating from areas liberated by the Syrian opposition groups should return home.[21]

"The little stone that supports the jar": hosting in an impoverished region

In the village of Beshuat, we met farmer Mikhayl.[22] He is in his forties, married, and a father of three. He inherited a few hectares on which he mostly grows tobacco and, recently, some grapes for wine. He drives the local school bus, and one day per week he works in Beirut for a micro-credit organization. His wife is a teacher who works at both the local primary and secondary schools in Dayr al-Ahmar. However hard they work, the farmer says that they are only just able to make ends meet. He expresses his feelings of precariousness in reference to a proverb: "My different jobs are like the little stone [bahsa] of the proverb bahsa btasnod khâbiya [the little stone that supports the jar]," meaning that each of these jobs (these little "stones") plays a vital role in providing a decent living. He also said he feels like the man in another proverb: ma thizzu wâqif 'alâ shwâr (do not push the man standing on the edge of the cliff).[23]

In the caza of Dayr al-Ahmar, people are not rich. According to the UN, it belongs to the second tier of the most vulnerable Lebanese caza-s (i.e., where an average of 12.8 percent of Lebanese are deprived and refugees make up 15.8 percent of the population).[24] Levels of unemployment are high, although no consolidated statistics exist. The absence of economic prospects has led to a huge out-migration—a situation replicated in other rural areas of Lebanon. The demographic profile of the *caza* of Dayr al-Ahmar is particularly depressed. Although a total of 22,169 people were registered in Dayr al-Ahmar in 2016,[25] the actual number of inhabitants is estimated to be one-fifth of this figure: above 5,000. Many Lebanese who have left the area remain attached to their home place, but the houses they built for the summer holidays that scatter the landscape (sometimes half-finished) remain empty for most of the year.

In Dayr al-Ahmar, the main sources of income for families are agriculture (mostly tobacco and grapes for wine), public sector employment (army, education), a few private semi-industrial enterprises (furniture and wood) or services (retailing, coffee shops), and pensions. As one of the main pilgrimage centers of the Bekaa, the economic situation in Beshuat is different. In the aftermath of the apparition in 2004, infrastructure, including hotels, restaurants, and devotional object souvenir shops, was developed to welcome pilgrims and tourists. This infrastructure was continuing to generate a significant income for the villagers as of 2018.[26]

Agriculture is mostly found on the plain and the lower slopes of the mountains. It is constrained by limited water resources, although several projects involving the provision of water tanks and the development of drip irrigation techniques aim to address the issue. Vegetables (potatoes, onions), wheat, and increasingly fruit (apples, grapes for wine) are grown in the foothills of the Lebanon range. The main crop is tobacco, which is heavily subsidized by the state in order to provide farmers with a regular income and to encourage the eradication of the cultivation of cannabis.[27] However, agricultural revenues are generally low. For instance, in theory each farmer owns one license (*rukhsa*) per year (equivalent to 330 kilograms of tobacco) that is sold to the state (*Régie des tabacs*) at an average price of $2,000. Although farmers usually farm with more than one license, and many of them rent unused licenses, this low price means that they are left with a modest net benefit when all costs of production are taken into account (they account for one-third to one-half of the sum of the final selling price according to farmers in Dayr al-Ahmar).[28] The local reactions to the presence of the Syrian population of refugees must be understood within this context of tight resources and the out-migration of the workforce.

At the national level, some economists estimate that 1.6 percent of the 2.4 percent GDP growth in 2014 should be attributed to the presence of

Syrians through rents, consumption, work,[29] and the contribution of humanitarian aid.[30] However, most Syrians in Lebanon are in an impoverished situation. In the Baalbek Governorate, 94 percent of households live below the poverty line.[31] Syrian households in Dayr al-Ahmar live in very variegated conditions. Some families have, for instance, regular access to food or "acceptable" conditions of shelter (including under tents) when others, more numerous, have to adopt coping strategies (e.g., reduction of number of meals, or poor quality food intake) or live in inadequate accommodation (overcrowding, insufficient basic equipment, poor-quality clothing, etc.).

Contrary to other places in Lebanon,[32] only four local organizations provide support to the Syrian refugees in the *caza*: the School of Good Shepherd Sisters offers a curriculum to some Syrian children with the support of the French NGO, Mission Enfance; the women's support-oriented WADA (Women Association of Dayr al-Ahmar) runs cooking sessions for Syrian women;[33] the Baalbek-based Shi'a NGO, Dirâsât wa tadrîb, implements vocational training classes for refugees in cooperation with UNICEF;[34] and Caritas, which has had its support center on the main road near Btede'i since well before 2011. Hence aid and humanitarian assistance is mostly provided through the UNHCR-coordinated humanitarian response: for example, for education, a second shift for Syrian children at the public primary of Dayr al-Ahmar city is provided, or financial assistance for the few families whose child is accepted at Beshuat's primary school; water distribution; waste management; protection implemented by Oxfam,[35] and other types of protection especially geared toward children;[36] and cash assistance.[37]

Even though external and local NGOs favor projects supporting the refugees and host communities,[38] the Lebanese population in Dayr al-Ahmar does not benefit from the sorts of direct aid provided to the Syrians, and with time it has come to resent this discrepancy. Many people in Beshuat told us about the drought in the summer of 2016, for instance, to highlight what they viewed as unfair treatment: during the drought, the Umam delivered the Syrian refugees with water tanks while they,[39] local Lebanese inhabitants, were offered neither support nor assistance from the Lebanese state (or the Umam), although they were experiencing regular water cuts. We also heard many descriptions of the supposed material comfort in which the refugees lived: "they are richer than us" we were regularly told; "you should see their tents, they have everything: television, fuel, washing machine, they are not poor" (no matter that our interlocutors had never been in a Syrian dwelling); "they get everything from the Umam for free, everything."

Contrasting landscapes

"Dayr al-Ahmar is a Christian Maronite region," and the ways in which the landscape is shaped reflect that claim of the inhabitants of this area: monumental churches, ex-votos, pieta dolorosa, and memorials serve as landmarks disseminated in the villages and in the foothills. The village of Safra is a good example of the will to apply a Christian footprint on the landscape. Safra is located in the foothills overlooking the plain where the Shiʿa town of Kneysseh stretches. Along the road leading to Safra, eight statues of saints are lined up. With fewer than 100 inhabitants, the village has two churches, one of which is monumental and can be seen from kilometers around.

The "biggest rosary in the world," whose construction started in 2013, is another example of the Christian shaping of the landscape: intended "to protect Lebanon against evil and war," according to an inhabitant of Beshuat, it is situated above Dayr al-Ahmar city. The rosary, still under construction in 2018, stretches across 625 meters, and when completed it will comprise fifty-nine beads made of concrete, each big enough to shelter five people. The Christian shaping of the landscape began in the 2000s and has accelerated since 2011, as if in response to the arrival of the Syrian refugees, whose presence drastically transformed the landscapes in the surroundings of cities and villages, especially in the *sahel* (see Fig. 4.1).

Lebanon's authorities have forbidden the establishment of official camps. However, small to very large informal camps now scatter the landscape of some of the regions of Lebanon, and especially the Bekaa. These informal camps are established on private lands, but they are materially supported by the humanitarian response coordinated by the UNHCR, which provides the families with wood for the structures of the tents, plastic tarpaulins to cover them,[40] water trunks, temporary sanitation, and so on.

In the region of Dayr al-Ahmar, there is a before and after to "the events" (*al-ahdath*), as the Syrian war is referred to by the local people. Indeed, spatially, the Syrian refugees' unofficial camps are often extensions of pre-2011 Syrian workers' settlements. In Beshuat "before," for example, during the harvest of tobacco, the seasonal Syrian workers—mainly women—were staying at a location some distance from the pilgrimage center. They were accommodated in two tents and a small, unfinished concrete room (*mazraʿa*, "farm") on the side of a small road crossing the tobacco fields. From 2011 onward, still remote from the gaze of villagers and visitors, two dozen tents now line that road. A third of them are "permanent," and their inhabitants stay there throughout the year.

Figure 4.1: Map of the Dayr al-Ahmar region

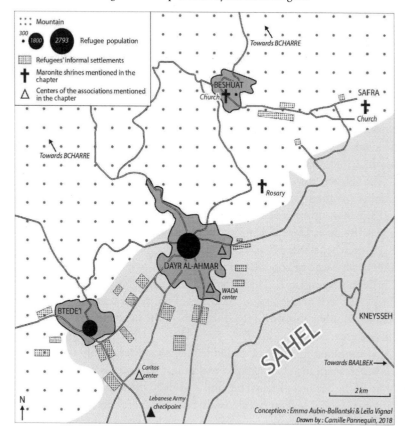

Conception : Emma Aubin-Bollantski & Leïla Vignal
Drawn by : Camille Pannequin, 2018

In the *sahel*, following a similar pattern but on a much bigger scale, the scattered tents that were set up on the edge of the fields during the harvest have now been replaced by an inescapable landscape of camps, one following another along the main road. Each of these camps is made up of several dozens of square structures made of concrete, wood, and plastic tarpaulins. The "tent" (*khaymeh*) has been replaced by the *barakieh* (a word that comes from the French *baraque*, i.e., shacks). It has become an "in-between" form of accommodation, one originally conceived of as temporary that, over time, acquires the features of a more permanent home. The flooring of these shacks is formed from a thick layer of concrete, while oil stoves (*subia*), as well as refrigerators, television sets, and washing machines are installed.

HOSTING AND BEING HOSTED IN TIMES OF CRISIS

Dayr al-Ahmar, a place of multilayered interactions between Lebanese and Syrians

Reminiscences of the Lebanese civil war

As a legacy of the civil war, the inhabitants of Dayr al-Ahmar share the feeling of being besieged by a hostile population. Before 2011, "here, wherever you turn your face or go to, you come across *metwali-s*" was commonly expressed. *Metwali* is a pejorative word used to designate the Shiʿa—especially the Shiʿa of the nearby village of Kneysseh—who are considered age-old enemies of Dayr al-Ahmar citizens. Since the arrival of the Syrian refugees, the "Sunnis" have replaced the Shiʿa in hostile discourses concerning "the other": "The Shiʿa we know them—the Sunnis, no. They are more aggressive," a woman from Beshuat told us in April 2016.

This sectarian, hostile discourse overlaps with the vivid and exacerbated anti-Syrian feelings of the local population. We have identified *discourses*—some of them extremely violent—against the Syrians, but also reminiscences and memories of the Syrian occupation from the civil war up until 2005, which are intertwined with the realities of the strong and complex long-term relationships that exist between the Syrians and the Lebanese in this region.

On the main road of Dayr al-Ahmar city stands a ghostlike abandoned building with a small guard shack on its left. Getting close enough to see through the window bars, one can distinguish a cell. This is where the Syrian *mukhabarat* (special services) were operating until 2005, and where many male inhabitants of the Dayr al-Ahmar region were imprisoned, interrogated, beaten, and sometimes tortured. The day after the Syrian withdrawal, graffiti appeared on the white walls: *quwwât lubnâniyya* (Lebanese Forces) written in black paint next to a triangle in a circle, the symbol of this nationalist, far-right party. It has remained on the wall ever since, untouched, a sort of material incarnation of the memory of the occupation.

"Because we have the reputation to be a Lebanese Forces stronghold, the Syrian occupation was particularly hard on us," explained Karam, an inhabitant of the city, adding: "Many were the men who had to flee to Beirut, and who returned here in 2005, after nearly thirty years of absence." At the entrance to the town, cars were stopped and checked by the *mukhabarat*. Karam said, "the driver was asked: 'Who do you love? Samir Geagea or Amin Gemayel?'[41] One had to answer: 'I love Hafez al-Assad!' By not doing so, you could be arrested and beaten."[42]

Another place embodies the memory of the Syrian occupation: the check-point of Shlifa, located at the junction of the plain and the foothills. The checkpoint controls the road to the village of Shlifa on the left and Dayr al-Ahmar on the right. This checkpoint was still there in 2018, although it has been operated by the Lebanese Armed Forces since 2005:

> To go shopping in Zahle or Baalbek, we had to go through the Shlifa check-point. On the way to and from there, we had to give something to the soldiers: cigarettes, or a kilo of apples ... anything ... something to eat mostly because ... *haram*,[43] they were starving,

remembers Rana, who lived all her life in Dayr al-Ahmar.[44] Starving soldiers on the one hand, and brutal *mukhabarat* on the other, were the two sides of the Syrian occupation from 1977 to 2005 in Dayr al-Ahmar.

From seasonal labor to labor in exile

The village of Izz al-Din lies northeast of Homs in Syria. Before the war, its population was about 4,000 inhabitants, most of whom engaged in agricul-tural activity: people grew grapes, almonds, olives, and vegetables, and raised cattle (goats, sheep, and cows). This remote and ordinary village—which has been heavily bombarded since 2012, and is now emptied of nearly all of its population—is tied by many links to Dayr al-Ahmar.[45] According to our esti-mates, most of the population of the al Foli camp in Dayr al-Ahmar city are from there, as well as about 50 percent of the 110 Syrians living in tents on the side of the agricultural road in Beshuat. We met people from Izz al-Din in most of the camps and villages we visited across the *caza*.

Indeed, many of the Syrians who have taken shelter in Dayr al-Ahmar since 2011 are the seasonal agricultural workers of the past. Before the war, many of them came in order to complement their annual earnings back home. According to the different crop cycles, in which tobacco dominated, Syrian workers were engaged in a circular migration between their homes in Syria during the winter (*shatwiyyeh*), and Dayr al-Ahmar during the agricultural season from April to November, with the summer (*sayfiyyeh*) harvest months being the busiest, in July and August. The cultivation of tobacco attracted a workforce that was dominated by women, in particular in the latter stages of the crop cycle.[46] Year after year, the same families would come for extended periods to work on the land of the same farmers, settling under large tents at the edge of the fields. Nowadays, the workers are doing very similar work, but with the difference being that they do not return home anymore.

In Dayr al-Ahmar, the seasonal presence of Syrian workers has consequently been a familiar feature of the local landscape since well before 2011, and the cheap labor the workers have provided has been key to the sustainability of this scarcely resourced local economy. For many Syrians, these former circular migrations provided the anchorage for organizing strategies of survival. Some families have settled on the land of their former employers, such as, for instance, the family of Abu Husayn who lives and works on the land of one of the families of the village of Btede'i. In another example, Umm Mohamad told us she received a message from farmer Mikhayl, in Beshuat, telling her to come there when the situation started to worsen in Izz al-Din.[47] Warda, a thirty-three-year-old single woman, has come to Beshuat to work on the lands of farmer George since she was a teenager. When it comes to tobacco, Warda knows her trade; and George trusts her and her skills. It is a form of relative security Warda values in such uncertain times. We learned in our interviews that those who did not come to Dayr al-Ahmar before the war often decided to go there because of the presence of fellow Syrians—family and friends generally from the same area, such as Izz al-Din—who had told them that employment could be found. These strong linkages between earlier episodes of labor migration and subsequent migration to seek refuge illustrate the continuum that exists between pre-conflict patterns of mobility and the current situation of refuge.[48]

Living in a "permanent temporariness"

> Before, we were putting all the money we were earning here, in Lebanon, into our house there, in Izz al-Din. We were working here, in Dayr al-Ahmar, but our life was there, in Syria. It took us years and years to build my parents' house. After it was finished, we built the houses of my brothers: first, when he got married, the house of my eldest brother, and after, the house of the second one. Now, everything is gone ... We lost everything. And they want us to go back there?

Warda exclaimed angrily. "Before," like many others who used to work in Lebanon—and in this case, always at the same place—Warda belonged to her hometown. As she put it, her "life was in Syria." Dayr al-Ahmar was experienced solely as a place of hard work during summertime. Since 2011, this temporariness has been "immobilized," and it is here that she must now "make home."[49]

Syrians in Dayr al-Ahmar "make home" by building shelters to live in, by getting married, giving birth, and even dying. Until 2017, as a way to prevent Syrians from thinking of the region as a place of permanence, they were not allowed to bury their dead in the Bekaa plain.[50] Syrians in any case prefer to transport the remains of their loved ones back to Syria, to be buried in their villages or hometowns. However, the heavy cost of the process of sending bodies back home ($2,000),[51] is an additional challenge on top of the fact that places of origin are sometimes completely destroyed, emptied of populations, or inaccessible, which means that Syrian refugees are often forced to circumvent the burial ban and bury their dead secretly in Lebanon. In March 2017, a few days before our arrival in Dayr al-Ahmar, a fifteen-year-old boy had died from a stroke. Because he had died at the hospital, the family had no choice but to send the body to Saraqib, from where they originate. "We had to pay the *mukhtar*,[52] the police, the ministry of health, the doctor. With the transport, it cost us $2,000 dollars," explained an uncle of the boy. He continued:

> It took us five days to gather the money, five days during which the remains were at the morgue, in a fridge with no electricity. To reach Saraqib, it took one more day. With all this, the parents were not allowed to accompany their son's remains: he was buried in Saraqib by remote relatives.

By the end of 2017, Buday, a Shi'a village, and two mixed villages in the plain—I'at (Shi'a, Maronites), Sha'at (Sunni, Shi'a)—had opened burial plots for Syrians. In 2018, a new space was created in the town of Baalbek at the instigation of the UNHCR and with the cooperation of the local Sunni authorities. Although this is a financial and logistic relief for Syrian refugees, people are nonetheless torn apart when it is necessary to bury their dead in Lebanon rather than at "home."

Life in refuge is also made of happy events, the most important being weddings. For many families, marrying inside the clan, and particularly between cousins (patrilateral or matrilateral), seems to be the most common and favored choice, in continuity with life before exile. We noticed that often, not only was the bride very young (around age fifteen) but in some cases the groom was young, too. During our first visit in his camp near Dayr al-Ahmar city, Abu Hamza proudly showed us the brand new *barakieh* of his recently married son. Like Abu Hamza's own, the new *barakieh* consists of a bedroom, a living/reception room (*madâfeh*), and a kitchen. The furniture and decor evoke an urban interior. In the bedroom, disproportionate wooden beds and cupboards occupied a large amount of the space. It is not uncommon for people in the camp to have a refrigerator, washing machine, and sometimes an oven. On a cement ground, kitchens display the basic equipment of modern houses—although there are not many other items. "This wedding cost me five years of savings: the *naqd* [dowry] was $2,600 and the new *barakieh* $1,000."

This *barakieh* reflects the social position of Abu Hamza, a former primary school teacher who left Syria in 2011 with his savings of $10,000 and made his way to the camps of Dayr al-Ahmar, from where he has not moved since. Like Abu Hamza, the refugees do their best to replicate the features of their lost homes and to ensure a form of continuity with their former social life by regrouping themselves according to familial and regional affinities.[53] Yet the majority live in much harder disrupted and unstable conditions.

Fûtû juwwa nashreb qahwa (Come in and let us have coffee together) is the way Syrians usually express greetings. Zeïna, a widow in her late thirties, also from Izz al-Din, invites us into her *ghurfa*, a one-room, unfinished concrete structure she had recently moved into with her nine children, aged five to thirteen.[54] Something in the tone of her voice stops us from accepting: she does not really want to show us the extreme misery of her life, and we have coffee in front of her house instead. In March 2018, when we met her, Zeïna was just back from the region of Tripoli. Like many other Syrians, Zeïna does not stay year-round in Beshuat. During winter (*shatwiyyeh*), because there is no work in the mountains, she moves to find work elsewhere. This year, she took part in the harvest of olives in the village of Kafer Zayn. While returning to Beshuat for the summer (*sayfiyyeh*), she had to renegotiate everything with a new landlord: a job and a place to settle. During her absence, her previous landlord and employer (*mu'allim*) had replaced her with another family from the governorate of Aleppo.

Hosting and being hosted: an ambiguous relationship

A local and private response to the Syrian refugee presence

The response to the influx of Syrian refugees in Lebanon is constrained by the weakness of the institutional and operational capacity of the state at all governance levels, and by the lack of a genuine coordinated national policy beyond the Lebanese Crisis Response Plan.[55] The response is therefore not organized by law (Lebanon is not a part of the 1951 Geneva Convention and does not have domestic asylum legislation), but by governmental decisions within which the UNHCR operates. The 2015 regulations have, in this regard, hardened the conditions of entry and residence for the Syrians. As a consequence, municipalities provide very diverse responses from one place to another.

What is common, however, is that in Lebanon the municipalities—the third level of local public administration—are the weakest level of governance,[56] and they do not have the political, financial, and administrative capacity to address the situation. In addition, municipalities are very much in the hands of the local families, and these are the real agents of local power onto which political affiliation is superimposed at a second stage.[57] When one family dominates, the municipality reflects the homogeneity of the village, such as in Beshuat, where all the inhabitants are from the Kayruz family, or in Btede'i, where four out of five registered inhabitants are from the Fakhi family. In villages where several influential families coexist, such as in Dayr al-Ahmar city,[58] the control of the municipality is an object of competition among them. In this context, Syrians have become part of electoral strategies as is illustrated by measures of firmness toward them.

For instance, the presidents of Dayr al-Ahmar's municipalities have taken different strands of sometimes erratic measures in order to address what they feel as the demand of their constituents: an arbitrary curfew has been imposed for Syrians,[59] and the use of motorcycles (an important means of transportation for Syrians) has been banned under the official guise of reducing road accidents.[60] In 2017, the Union of the Municipalities also decided to set its own system of registration for Syrian males over age fifteen,[61] based on the delivery of ad hoc ID cards, collecting name, date and place of birth, nationality, number of family members, sponsor's name, and plot number of the tent or address. The declared intent, to quote the president of the municipality of Beshuat,[62] was to "keep an eye" on the refugees and to control their influx in the region. In Dayr al-Ahmar city, Latif Quzeh, the president of the municipality elected in 2016, has established new procedures to control the presence of the refugees and their movements. On 16 July 2016, he published a thirteen-point administrative circular, among which were the following: the "split of the Syrian displaced in[to] groups and the designation of a representative for each group"; the "removal of all tents inside the village"; the "removal of the Syrians living in houses not equipped with sewage and electricity"; the "prohibition for Syrians to dwell in shops or commercial premises"; and the "total ban on motorcycles day and night." Another aim of the circular was to impose some duties on the Lebanese citizens renting lands or houses to Syrians: "the landlords have to keep the municipality informed of their tenants' names and the number of the members of their families," and "have to take responsibility for their conduct."[63]

However, we observed that these decisions had not been implemented systematically. For instance, attempts at keeping the Syrians on the outskirts of the villages are actually contradicted by the fact that some Syrians do live in villages, although in small numbers (e.g., seventy-eight families in the city of

Dayr al-Ahmar,[64] twelve in Beshuat, and several dozen in Btede'i); motorcycles do circulate on roads, although Syrians are always at risk of being reprimanded and having their motorcycles taken away. The only measure that seems to have been implemented (although, paradoxically, not listed on the Dayr al-Ahmar municipality's circular) is the extension of existing tents for growing families or the building of new ones for the recent arrivals. But this is a growing concern for the Syrian refugees settled in the *caza*, mostly for the many new households that are formed through marriage. But even in this instance we met with some exceptions to the rule in March 2018. In Beshuat, a few new tents have been de facto erected through ad hoc and direct agreements between landlords and refugees. In Dayr al-Ahmar city, Abu Hamza explained that he slowly and discreetly built the *barakieh* for his second son, who had just wed in February. He said he could do so without encountering trouble as he is well connected in Dayr al-Ahmar as a result of having worked there for many summers before the war.

The ability of municipalities to maneuver effectively is also constrained by the fact that, in the absence of formal camps or other public provisions, Syrians are mostly accommodated on private lands and in private dwellings. In exchange, landlords benefit from a regular income through the rents they receive. In the *caza*, the rent for a piece of land for one tent varies between $200 and $300 per year. The landlord of the seventy-five-tent "Caritas camp" (camp 002) in Btede'i collects $15,000 per year in rent.[65] Another Syrian pays $8,000 for the sixty-tent camp he manages near Dayr al-Ahmar city.[66] Also, and very much in continuity with pre-2011 times, the presence of Syrians provides landlords and local economic actors with a cheap, readily available workforce. Syrians engaged to work in the agricultural sector are paid $1.3 per hour (2,000 Lebanese pounds [LBP]) or $5.3 per day (8,000 LBP).[67] In this context, municipalities cannot go against the economic interests of their constituents, who are the members of the influential families in Dayr al-Ahmar city.

The contradiction between hostile discourses, restrictive regulations, and local economic interests is reflected in a project currently under study by the municipality of Btede'i. The project goal is to gather all Syrian tents onto one site, on municipal land. The objective is to rationalize land use and the provision of basic services (e.g., electricity, water, and solid waste management). It is also to create a much-needed source of revenue for the municipality, which has had to cope with the pressure that the additional population of refugees has placed on services. The farmers and village landlords have consistently refused to pay municipal tax on the rents they receive from the Syrians.[68] The municipal team is, however, aware of the fact that this project may never come to fruition as it is opposed by the landlords—an opposition that de facto acknowledges the embedding of the Syrians into the local political economy. The institutional and operational weakness of the municipalities is hence illustrated by the fact that their decisions are circumvented "from below," wherein they have to take into account the narrow interests of some of their constituents, as well as "from above": for instance, the union's 2017 initiative to provide Syrian males with local ID cards was dropped at the demand of the Ministry of Interior, itself under pressure from the international community.[69]

Discourses and measures of firmness can be understood as a way for municipal teams to mitigate the local population's feelings of frustration and fears of social demotion as the refugees stay for longer than expected, and with no end in sight. Expressions of firmness can also be interpreted as an efficient tool used to bargain for assistance from the international community, whose priority is to avoid expulsions,[70] as was illustrated by the delivery of a UNHCR aid truck to the municipality of Dayr al-Ahmar in 2017. Applying pressure on refugees is also a powerful way to "keep the refugees on their toes," a humanitarian worker told us: it makes them permanently aware of the temporary aspect of their stay.[71]

They are not refugees: the contested lexicon of the Syrian refugee presence in Lebanon

The ID cards prepared by the Union of Municipalities in 2017 had two options to select from: "displaced" (*nâzihûn*) or "worker" (*'ummâl*). These are the two words most commonly used to categorize the Syrians, and they are used to deny Syrians the status of "refugee." Legally, "refugee" refers to a status rooted in the 1951 Geneva Convention and its additional protocols. However, Lebanon is not part of the convention and has not developed domestic legislation on the protection of refugees. Since 1963, asylum-related issues are operated on behalf of the Lebanese state by the UNHCR. The UNHCR had been in charge of the registration of the Syrians from 2011 onward, until the Lebanese government suspended all registration processes for Syrian refugees in 2015 in order to discourage their presence in the country. As a consequence, the categorization of the Syrians who fled their country is extremely varied from one individual to another.[72] Indeed, since the ban on registration, UNHCR still considers most Syrians in Lebanon to be refugees. However, in practice, it has come to differentiate between registered, non-registered, and what it terms "recorded" refugees (i.e., those who have approached UNHCR after 2015). In Dayr al-Ahmar, we documented the fact that these different statuses can vary even within a family: some family members are UNHCR-registered, some are UNHCR-recorded (since 2015), some were once UNHCR-registered but are now illegal, some have no residency status (change in 2015) at all; they may cohabit with individuals who have a non-refugee status but are legal residents on (mostly work) visas, as well as with others who are and always have been present in Lebanon illegally.

In Lebanon, "to designate the Syrian is the subject of great controversy" the daily news service *al-Safir* wrote in a 2013 article entitled "Refugees or Displaced?"[73] Since 1948, for both Lebanese and Syrians, the category of "refugee" is indeed conceptually linked with the Palestinian question and displacement, and therefore with the idea of permanent loss of homeland and exile. The underlying figure of the Palestinian who never went back is a source of deep anxiety for all the people of the Middle East, based on historical experience. Moreover, because the word "refugee" is commonly associated with a "cause" (e.g., the Palestinian cause), its use in the context of Syrians in Lebanon is sometimes seen as a way to criticize the al-Asad regime by comparing it with Israel.[74] In that context, the term "displaced" (*nâzih*) is seen as less political and sensitive. The term "displaced" has become a sort of euphemism for "refugee,"[75] a consensual way to encompass the different facets of the issue without exposing the internal contradictions and sensitivities of the country.

During the first interviews conducted, we were not aware of these linguistic subtleties, and we used the word *lâji* (refugees) to talk of the Syrians. The reaction of the Lebanese was always the same: a denial, and exasperation at hearing the term and with having to utter it. However, the word *nâzih* was not employed by them either. The president of the municipality of Dayr al-Ahmar had a nervous reaction when we presented our research to him and said: "You say that they are 'refugees' [*lâji*]? I say that they are workers [*'ummâl*]!" *'Ummâl* is indeed the term most often used by Lebanese to designate the Syrians in Dayr al-Ahmar. Its use implies, as is sometimes openly expressed, that Syrians are not real "victims" of a war, but rather opportunists who come to Lebanon to flee poverty and to benefit from what is described as a luxurious humanitarian kit. "The UN gives them $30 dollars per month and they have everything for free: water, fuel oil, household cleaning products, clothes,"

Samira, a schoolteacher from Beshuat, told us. "On top of that, they make money by working in the fields and in construction," she said.

The Syrians had long provided a cheap workforce in agriculture and construction, two sectors being abandoned by Lebanese workers. As long as they were not permanently settled in Lebanon, and going back and forth to Syria, their presence was tolerated.[76] Since 2011, in the context of endemic high levels of unemployment, tension has started to build up across the country when Syrians moved from these two sectors into new ones.[77] In particular, in many regions of Lebanon, Syrians are running retail shops, barber shops, street food restaurants, and so on. These shops, run by Syrians and often (but not exclusively) catering for a Syrian clientele, are commonly called "Syrian shops" although their ownership officially remains within Lebanese hands. Syrians are also more frequently employed as workers in industrial ventures. In Dayr al-Ahmar, since 2016, the inhabitants periodically organize sit-ins to express their opposition to Syrian-operated activities that are viewed as a threat to their own economic activities.[78] This may be why one counts so few "Syrian shops" in the city apart from three secondhand clothes shops whose clientele is exclusively Syrian. However, in Dayr al-Ahmar, Syrians are working as employees in local shops and businesses such as falafel restaurants, garages, and grocery shops.

For Lebanese farmers, what is felt as a disruption to the system that prevailed before the Syrian war is the fact that, in some cases, Syrians try to negotiate salaries and the conditions of work. For instance, by the end of 2016, in Beshuat, a group of Syrians organized a "partnership" (*musharaka*) to grow tobacco with their boss (*mu'allim*) who was a farmer for whom they worked and on whose land they lived. The oral agreement, to be renegotiated every year, included the following: in exchange for their work and a share of the cost of seeds and chemical products, they would receive a percentage (between 37 and 40 percent) of the harvest income. This kind of partnership was not new. It was first implemented by "absentee" landlords (i.e., those working and living elsewhere in Lebanon), who found this system of tenant-farmed land to be in their best interest. But the attempts to extend such an agreement to those lands operated by local farmers were received with mixed reactions, in some cases rather negative, and even hostile. Umm Mohamed from Izz al-Din explained:

> When my son went to see the *mu'allim* to propose him the deal, at first he refused. We stopped working and the *mu'allim* removed us from his lands. For three weeks we had to live in the middle of nowhere, far from everything. Finally, the *mu'allim* came to find us and we started the *musharaka*.

Some farmers analyze this initiative as a perverse impact of humanitarian aid—a view that is widely shared, and often expressed in xenophobic terms. "Because of the assistance they receive, now they refuse to work. They prefer to sleep. They have lawyers who assist them. They organize themselves to claim their rights," said a farmer in Beshuat, who refused to enter a *musharaka* with his workers. "And they steal the jobs of the Lebanese. They kill, they rape,[79] and the Lebanese are unemployed," added his sister.[80]

Those discourses are indicative of tensions that can lead to outbreaks of violence. On 15 February 2017, for instance, a broken statue of Saint Charbel was found in a ditch at the entry of Dayr al-Ahmar city. A group of locals then blocked the road leading to one of the main refugee camps by burning tires. "What happened is a crime against the village. All the religions ban it and it is unprecedented here. It is why we have suspicions towards some refugees," explained a protester to the *Annahar* news service.[81] This complaint revealed anxiety about security, however, as it was mixed with grievances concerning work: "In addition, there is the employment issue, as there is no more space for us."[82]

Conclusion: between interdependency and separation

On a gray morning in April 2017, an important farmer from Beshuat, who wore a heavy moustache and a Borsalino-style hat, and kept a gun in his back pocket, offered to take us in his jeep to "tour his workers." Stopping near their encampment, from the window of his car he ordered them to come outside from their tents so that he could "show" them to us.

A few months later, in a nearby tent situated on the land of farmer Mikhayl in Beshuat, we met a young Syrian couple with their two little boys.[83] When we arrived, a Lebanese man was there. He had brought presents for the children. He lived in the house next to their tent, but he was neither a landlord nor a farmer. The family call him *ammo* (uncle), a familiar term that denotes both respect and affection. As neighbors in this remote place, they help each other, and a friendship has grown between them.

In a hamlet off Btede'i, in the mountains, tents of Syrians are settled in the middle of a dozen houses. The Syrians living there are all locally employed in the fields or in various construction and manual labor jobs. "Before, I would tend the vegetable plot myself," Mona told us. "Now, I can pay a Syrian a few thousand lira [Lebanese pounds]. Why would I tire myself?"[84] She is obviously relieved by the situation, but she complains at the same time that there are no more jobs for the Lebanese. When asked from where the people living for years nearby her house came, she replied: "Syria." She did not know more than that.

Karam and Rana live on the main road of Dayr al-Ahmar. Karam struck an informal deal with two young Syrians, Mashuhr and Imad.[85] Against a small percentage of the sales, Karam lets them use his cellar to store the secondhand clothes they import from Europe and resell to local secondhand shops. Rana, his wife, works as a volunteer with WADA and Caritas to help Syrian women, mainly with cooking classes. This couple are well known and well regarded by Syrians, some of whom come around to their house for a cup of coffee.

In December 2017, on our way back to Dayr al-Ahmar, the taxi driver tells us that "Our Lady [of Beshuat] did a miracle with 'them.'" Like the few others who told us about this event, "them" refers to Syrians, but he cannot remember their names or place of residence in Dayr al-Ahmar. The story of the miracle—a father and his disabled son came to pray at the church of Our Lady of Beshuat and the little boy miraculously stood up, moved, and talked—is in itself nothing new: other similar miracles have happened, and to "Muslims" as well. The only new thing is that the "beneficiaries" and "testifiers" invited by the parish priest to give a testimony in the church are Syrian refugees and Sunni.[86] These examples are representative of the various relationships that take place in Dayr al-Ahmar between Syrians and Lebanese that we have analyzed in this chapter. They mix proximity—and, more often than not, personal proximity rooted in long-term work relations—with distance, xenophobia, or fear.

These relations are shaped by interdependency. First and foremost, it takes the form of asymmetry between employer and employees, especially in the absence of any contractual formal employment, and, therefore, any possibility of recourse in cases of infringement of rights or abuse. This asymmetry is accentuated by the fact that, since 2011, most Syrians in Dayr al-Ahmar do not have many choices available to them: they cannot return to Syria nor can they move abroad to a third country for permanent settlement. They are a kind of captive workforce. In addition, the importance of earning a living—humanitarian aid being insufficient to meet basic needs—is coupled with the importance of securing an "acceptable" place to live. As such, the only option left to Syrians is to move elsewhere in the country to find better conditions of shelter and/or work—but moving comes at a cost.

The relations between Syrians and Lebanese in Dayr al-Ahmar can also be understood as a relation of mutual interest (*maslaha*). The Lebanese farmers benefit in many ways from the captive presence of Syrians, who are a cheap, disposable workforce that can now be employed year-round. Without them, however, the local economy would collapse. This is especially the case in tobacco farming, which does not produce huge benefits and requires experienced workers, especially during the harvest and for the threading of the leaves. It is hence in the interest of farmers to have a stable and trained workforce, although, in theory, the labor pool from which local farmers can choose is potentially limitless as there are plenty of Syrian refugees eager to work in the country. In return, this gives some leverage for the Syrians who are known, trusted, and skilled, such as the people who used to come "before" and their families ("the ones we know," said a woman from Beshuat). It is, for instance, workers from this group who succeeded in proposing the *musharaka* system to their *mu'allim*, and in doing so, they gained the possibility of securing their stay long term in the region. It is mostly Syrians from "before," such as Abu Hamza, who reinvested capital they brought with them from Syria to rent fields and grow their own vegetables. They are also the ones who ended up being *shawish*, intermediaries between workers and farmers,[87] who organize work teams (*warshat 'amal*) on demand. The workers of *shawish* teams also inhabit the camp run by "their" *shawish* on the basis of various arrangements. For instance, in Ahmed's camp, people do not pay anything for their tent but they give Ahmed 75 percent of their earnings,[88] whereas, in Caritas camp, the inhabitants pay $200 per year for the rental of their tent and give 50 percent of their earnings to the *shawish*.[89] While some refugees can reinvest their savings locally and leverage their former connections and skills to improve their situation in exile, most of the people we met are just trying to make a living and are in a much more precarious position.

In a few instances, the asymmetrical relationship is reversed and it is the Lebanese who are at the service of Syrians. For instance, there is one farmer who employs Syrians, but who is also Beshuat's primary school bus driver and is paid by the few Syrian parents whose children have been accepted at the school. In another example, the Lebanese teachers who teach the 385 Syrian children attending Dayr al-Ahmar's school—on a second shift in the afternoons—do so on a voluntary basis. They receive higher pay ($12 per period) for this than their average wage,[90] whose low level compels them to take the job. The teachers we met made clear to us that they did so reluctantly—they criticized the Syrian children as being unruly, dirty, not properly educated—perhaps in order to hide their unease at benefiting from measures taken in response to the refugee crisis and to work "for" Syrians by teaching their children.[91] Finally, as analyzed previously, interdependency stems from the revenues that Lebanese landlords extract from renting their land and flats to refugees.

The second feature of the relationship between Lebanese and Syrian refugees is that it is limited to a few interactions. It revolves around work (farmer–worker in agriculture, employer–employee in other jobs, and employee–client in shops and restaurants) and around the few local humanitarian aid projects. When not engaged in those interactions, Lebanese and Syrians generally do not meet. Hence, minimal numbers of Lebanese are in some sort of relationship with Syrians: the farmers, the police, the municipal employees, the teachers, and the few people involved in humanitarian aid. In these relations, money is always present and acts as a key mediator for interpersonal or collective interactions.

Features of separation therefore characterize the relations between Syrian refugees and the local Lebanese population. Separation translates physically into a segregated spatial organization. The Lebanese inhabit the urban space and the village, while the surroundings are left for the Syrians and their camps. However, this is not always as clear-cut as it seems, as some Syrians do live in villages, mostly those who are engaged in non-agricultural work, such as craftsmen or shop workers. Separation also translates into time, with, for instance, the imposition of curfews on Syrians that limit the hours they can be in public spaces or outside their homes. In this regard, interdependency and separation can illuminate the complex interactions taking place between two fragile populations forced into cohabitation, which then brings about the conditions for exploitation, and competition for space and resources.

5

DIASPORIC CIRCULARITIES

OMANI-ZANZIBARIS NARRATE EXPERIENCES
IN AND OUT OF THE ARCHIPELAGO, 1964

Rogaia Mustafa Abusharaf

I could not have believed, before experience taught me, how sad and solemn is the moment when a man sits down to think over and to write out a tale of what was before the last decade began. How many thoughts and memories crowd upon the mind! How many ghosts and phantoms start up from the brain—the shreds of hopes destroyed and of aims made futile; of ends accomplished and of prizes won; the failures and successes alike half forgotten! How many loves and friendships have waxed cold in the presence of new ties! How many graves have closed over their dead during those short ten years—that epitome of the past!

Sir Richard Burton[1]

Over a period of thousands of years, commerce had centered in the countries of the Indian Ocean littoral, particularly the Arabian Peninsula and the east coast of Africa. Trade networks were consolidated, and cultural exchange brought different cultures and languages together. [Omanis] settled in different areas and intermarried. Maritime trade broadened horizons, tolerance, and respect. Today so many Omani-Zanzibaris recall the incredible pain inflicted by Africans from mainland Tanganyika and by a Ugandan intruder, John Okello. We have good memories about our land. Omani people are Swahili-speaking and are proud of their Zanzibari identities. The ruling family built the most magnificent Stone Town and introduced electricity there, hence the name House of Wonders. Clove plantations employed large numbers of farmers.

Anonymous[2]

"Waarabu sio Wageni Zanzibar": Omanis are not visitors in Zanzibar

Africans and Arabs lived together and they would help each other with everything, they lived together in harmony.[3]

The experience of the Omani-Zanzibaris who were forced to migrate from Zanzibar to Oman in 1964 has received relatively little attention, particularly as seen from the arriving/returning Omani-Zanzibaris' emic perspectives. As we will see in this chapter, Oman's identity as a cosmopolitan empire offers a variety of pathways for understanding its present-day culture and politics, as well as its responses to the large wave of arrivals from postcolonial Zanzibar. The chapter seeks to arrive at a better understanding of the forced migrations by telling the story of this period from the theoretical stance of hybridity, which challenges the prevailing essentialism of the historical narratives of the 1964 events as an African uprising against Omani colonizers. To expound the experiences of Omani-Zanzibaris, this project gathered multiple accounts drawn from multi-sited ethnographic research carried out in the first round of fieldwork in Oman and Zanzibar together with extensive conversations held in Zanzibar and Muscat in 2016 and 2017.[4] Life-history collections, memoirs (both published and in private family possession in Arabic, English, and Swahili), archival materials in London and Muscat, and digital sources were also researched. I also reviewed a Swahili television program titled *Waliroudi*, which aired on Omani National Television during the lunar month of Ramadan between June and July 2017, and focuses on the returnees in Muscat. As an ethnographer, engaging with these media and the exchanges that took place with the arriving/returning Omani-Zanzibaris afforded me a chance to knit together the various strands of the tapestry of this forced migratory and diasporic Omani-Zanzibari story. In order to appreciate Omani exceptionalism, the chapter begins by providing some brief context of the Omani presence in Eastern Africa.

The Zanzibar archipelago's history, polity, and society have long captured the imagination of travelers, historians, anthropologists, and ethnomusicologists.[5] One of the most notable early forms of knowledge production is the travelogue *Zanzibar: City, Island, and Coast* (1872) by the Victorian explorer Sir Richard Burton. An equally important contribution was made by a plethora of ethnographic narratives on the Swahili coast at large, which was home to the Omani Wamanga communities.[6] More recent research in the field of visual arts and architecture has also enhanced our understanding of the ties that bind the Swahili coast's cultural production and political history of mobility to Oman, providing a greater understanding of the vernacular notions of self, space, and belonging among the Swahili coast's diverse inhabitants, including Omanis. Sandy Prita Meier, for instance, maps out the trajectories of identity formation on the coast and presents an account of the intricacies of spatial and social relations,[7] interweaving history, visual arts, and architecture in her book *Swahili Port Cities: The Architecture of Elsewhere* (2016) to present concrete examples highlighting how cultural fusions among the people of the Swahili coast were literally carved in stone. Meier provides evidence of these cultural processes in the built environment, such as monumental houses, tombs, mosques, and markets. Her work provides an architectural lens on what she calls "living with transoceanic things" and "things in motion":[8] "Swahili coast interior design and ornament invites an extended exploration of the meaning of objects when their 'life' is shaped by transoceanic circulation."[9]

Over the centuries, around 50,000 Omanis are estimated to have migrated to Rwanda, Burundi, Zaire, Congo, Kenya, Tanganyika, and Zanzibar, though no accurate censuses were taken at the time of these historic flows. This migration began in the ninth century and continues to the present day.[10] Many Omanis will tell stories about the historicity of their presence that spanned centuries,[11] hence the expression *Waarabu sio wageni Zanzibar* (Omanis are not visitors in Zanzibar).[12] Thus, while many associate the presence of Omanis in Zanzibar with the transfer of the capital from Muscat to Zanzibar by Sayyid bin Sultan of the Al-Busaidi dynasty, in 1840, during the period of Omani rule over Zanzibar, a significant number of migratory waves actually preceded this event. An Omani-Zanzibari interlocutor in Muscat provides further contextualization by explaining the environmental determinants of early migration, coupled with the masterly sailing and agricultural skills of Omanis, which opened up horizons and spawned a desire for travel, trade, and settlement in Eastern Africa:

> Two mistakes people make all the time. That the presence of Omanis in Zanzibar was associated with the Al-Busaidi. They do not count the power presence of the Nabhani and Yaruba, who expelled the Portuguese both from Oman

and then from Zanzibar. Our ties to Eastern Africa go back for centuries. It is hypocritical for those who colonized other communities to forget about their own history and call us invaders. The Africans who arrived in Zanzibar themselves formed associations such as the Association of Mainland Migrant Workers. They were the first to concede their identity as migrants.[13]

Nevertheless, the transfer of the Omani empire's capital from Muscat to Zanzibar did entail increased migration and an expansion of the territorial jurisdiction of the sultan who ruled over "all islets within a 12-miles radius of Zanzibar and Pemba."[14] William Ingrams notes that, according to a 1924 census, the population numbered about 186,000, of whom 16,000 were Arabs.[15] The sultan presided over a political entity comprising wide-ranging ethnicities and nationalities, including Europeans, Indians, Persians, Omanis, Washihiri Hadrami (low-status Arab immigrants from Hadramaut, Yemen), Comorians, Chinese, and mainland Africans belonging to different islets who were identified in terms of their residence, including the Wahadimu,[16] Wapemba, and Watumbatu.[17] According to Abdulaziz Lodhi, the mainlanders, known as Wabara, were "descendants of freed slaves but mainly from contract labourers brought to the clove plantations after the abolition of slavery."[18] Slave populations were also of great significance to the Sultanate in light of Zanzibar's recognition as the "last slave market."[19]

The transfer of the Omani empire's capital from Muscat to Zanzibar also played an important economic role in sustaining migrations across the Arabian Sea and the Indian Ocean. According to Abdul Sheriff, the

> economic unification of the ocean was facilitated by the paramount climatological factor in the Indian Ocean ... determining the rhythm of economic life ... not only in the provision of irrigation water for agriculture, but also by blowing the dhows across the ocean to redistribute goods and transport people.[20]

An early cosmopolitan imagination managed to transcend the barriers, borders, and differences that came to set Omanis and Omani-Zanzibaris apart. Both in terms of ethnological makeup and cosmology, this Omani exceptionalism made Zanzibar a place that radiated with cross-cultural interactions that were epitomized in the island's diversity, as demonstrated by early ethnographic records. When Ingrams joined Zanzibar in 1919 as district commissioner, he chronicled all facets of Swahili ethnology, in which he included "detribalized natives and natives of mixed descent [including Arabs]."[21] Lyndon Harries notes that the dispersed Arabs who migrated to Africa in the ninth and tenth centuries actually lost more of their Arab tradition and gave in to the African tradition.[22] "When we were ten or fifteen years old we had an idea, we could have either stayed in Oman under the same conditions or gone to Africa. We knew our relatives who moved to Africa had a different life, a better one," remembers an Omani-Zanzibari.[23] These migrations, both before and after the Al-Busaidi dynasty settled in the Zanzibar archipelago, helped foment an Omani-Swahili political and cultural subjectivity through an imperial expansion that brought populations of all sorts into its fold.

The relationship of Omanis in Zanzibar to those in Oman, particularly the ruling sultans, was one of economic commitment to kith and kin back home in the form of an annual payment made to the sultan in Muscat, as Zanzibar was relatively well-off at the time, particularly when compared with Muscat.[24] According to John Duke Anthony, the Zanzibar subsidy, as it came to be known, reached 86,400 rupees, equaling "the income of the two parts [of the Sultanate]."[25] While sending subsidies to the ancestral land, the sultanate also continued to receive people from diverse socioeconomic backgrounds, rich and poor. Most were landless Omanis who came to occupy the lowest echelons of the economy after arriving on the island and helped to create the economic base in Omani-Zanzibar that would contribute to the expedited process of Swahilization, through which Omanis became Swahili in language, culture, and outlook. Whether rich or poor, the Omani-Zanzibaris interviewed for this chapter argued that Omani migrants fully assimilated into Zanzibari society in language, kinship, and marriage. The structures in place were conducive to the openness of cultural, social, and political processes within Zanzibari society as a whole.

My interviewees also corroborated the interface between Swahili and Arabic, the shared Islamic culture, and Ibadist ethos that created an environment of tolerance.[26] "Let's not forget that most of the sultans and their descendants were of mixed African and Arab descent.... The most beloved, Sultan Barghash, was half-Ethiopian," an Omani noted in our conversation on Swahilization and cultural incorporation in Zanzibar.[27]

Further:

> There was a lot of intermarriage between Omanis and Zanzibaris, we were all considered the same. Africans and Arabs lived together both in Zanzibar and in other places in Eastern Africa. They always helped each other with everything, they lived together in harmony.

> Omanis were very easy to get along with, and so they interacted well with the Africans, there was a lot of intermarriage, they were together in everything, and the Africans really respected the Omanis.[28]

> My own father had multiple wives, Omani and Africans. We lived in the same households. I recall that he treated us children, and his wives equally. We were

not favored. In fact he relied so heavily on my half-brother from his African mother. Our life was free of conflicts. We led a happy life in a happy household that was Arab and African.[29]

Integration and the multidirectional acculturations between Arabs and Eastern Africans and the subsequent Swahilization of Omanis in Eastern Africa is Omani-Zanzibaris' main memory about life before the revolution, where this African identity became a frame of reference, a social and political subjectivity; Arabs became "Africanized."[30] However, during the period in which Zanzibar was a British protectorate from 1890 to 1963, identity became politicized due to British pseudo-scientific notions of race: Arabs, Africans, and Indians. It was on this basis that the British pursued a policy of ethnic bracketing. An interviewee in Muscat sheds light on the politics of divide and rule, the hallmark of British policies:

> Britain's involvement in segregating ethnicities in Zanzibar was critical. They pushed for segregation even during the time of food shortage, when they distributed flour to the Arabs, rice for Indians, and cassava for Africans. Food rations were ethnicized and politicized. Britain created the Afro-Shirazi Party to counteract Zanzibar National Party's agitation for independence from British dominance.[31]

Nowhere was this politicization challenged more than in the response of Ali Muhsin Al-Barwani in his exposé of the racist attitudes the British held toward the Swahili language, which, as an Omani-Zanzibari, was his first language.[32] Al-Barwani argued that there was an attack on the Swahili language by missionaries and colonials. He asked: "Why was it that Swahili, of all the languages, [was] subjected to this type of pushing and pulling by people who were not its native speakers?"[33] In his view, it was because colonialists found Swahili as an established language with institutions, administrations, governments, and laws. "The Swahilis were not naked barbarians, but a clothed civilized people":[34] "The colonialists did not like my trying to infuse that sense of unity among the Coastal people. About a decade later I was twice to be declared a 'prohibited immigrant' in British Kenya. My crime was in Kenya as it was in Zanzibar the preaching of unity and anti-racism."[35] The colonial destruction of communities as depicted by Al-Barwani is a thrice-told tale, one that colonial and postcolonial subjects intuitively recognize as identical to their own experiences with colonial violence, as an Omani-Zanzibari told me in Muscat in 2017.

Despite the colonial policies that destroyed communities, Omani-Zanzibaris' reminiscences about the period before 1964 invoke the social interdependence that marked their lives regardless of the views presented to the contrary in representations that heightened the rifts between rich land- and slave-owning lords and their subjects. Significant numbers of interviewees bemoaned the essentialism that continues to thrive to the present day and expressed their desire for a better understanding of the social realities of their society.

Governing issues

Omani-Zanzibari accounts of 1964 as a genocide are drawn from the realities of ethnic targeting. Invariably, the literature that was written on the subject during this period highlights the local African revolutionaries' intentionality as central to the concept of genocidal acts following the episode. Local African revolutionaries, however, perceived the episode as an act of decolonization from the yoke of Omani dominance. This view has been chronicled in the 1967 memoir *Revolution in Zanzibar*, written by the leader of the Zanzibar Revolution, John Okello.[36] To be sure, Zanzibar, like other societies, was neither an egalitarian conglomerate of communes nor immune to the perils of hierarchies and divisions drawn along race, class, and gender. These disparities, however, were relational rather than absolute. In Unguja (the seat of Omani power), the economic dominance of the Omanis deepened inequalities between the Arabs and the Africans, yet a different reality existed in Pemba, where the "integrative pattern of land relations, together with the consensual validation for Arab political supremacy, tended to keep Arab–African relations ... from invidious connotations of superiority–inferiority."[37] This is by no means a dismissal of mainland Africans' grievances, especially in relation to the abominable institution of slavery. Although critiques of essential representation of African societies abound, it is worth reiterating in the context of the Omani-Zanzibaris. According to Bill Ashcroft, Gareth Griffiths, and Helen Tiffin, "hybridity commonly refers to the creation of new transcultural forms within the contact zone produced by colonization ... hybridization takes many forms: linguistic, cultural, political, [and] racial."[38] The historical facts thus reflect the "transcultural forms" that fail to fit into the bifurcating narratives of "Arabs versus Africans" that marked the geopolitical representations mirrored in the Africanist literature.

A broader picture started to develop when my interviewees were asked some questions in light of the inextricability of method, theory, and memories. First, as competing ideologies under the Al-Busaidi dynasty, are Arabism and Africanism mutually exclusive categories, or can they be situated squarely in a dynamic society, the history, culture, and society of which capture the complexity of the event? Second, what opportunities can be found for individuals and communities in both Oman and Zanzibar to engage critically with their intertwined past and present? Third, how can this understanding help us listen to Omani-Zanzibari voices and perspectives on their Arabism and Africanism as once mutually inclusive, hybrid identities? Fourth, to what extent did the 1964 African revolution affect the standing of Omani-Zanzibari communities on the island, and to what extent did their forced migration influence their self-fashioning as Swahili communities in Omani society? And, finally, what were the most important obstacles they faced as far as integration is concerned? In other words, in what way were they transformed as Swahilis of Omani descent into "racialized sojourns"?[39] In asking these questions, I attempt to write against the grain, first by interrogating the perception that, after centuries of life in Zanzibar, Omani-Zanzibaris were and are still looked upon as invaders—a form of xenophobia that lent legitimacy to the revolution as an African triumph over Omani dominance. Against this prevailing Arab-phobia, I hope to amplify the hybrid identity of Omanis in Zanzibar as Eastern African people *par excellence*, whose forced migration served to solidify this identity yet further. To operationalize these questions, I stop at three stations of the life of Omani-Zanzibaris: before, during, and after the revolution/invasion.

Zanzibar's cosmopolitan and creole identity belies the monolithic characterization of its ethnology and opens up opportunities for understanding Omani-Zanzibaris' experiences as forced migrants rather than mere returnees to an ancestral home.[40] Today, how these entangled histories of political violence, revolution, and migration are told depends on whom you speak to, and how one's experience is imagined and re-imagined. Garth Myers' essay on the subject is of special relevance to this story. Calling the accounts of the revolution "excluded narratives,"[41] he examines the historical record of the revolution through various narrative texts, categorizing them as dominant and oppositional, with the latter further broken down into residual, emergent, and excluded based on how they portray the events of the revolution with an eye toward influencing (or understanding) the cultural landscape of Zanzibari society. Myers pays particular attention to how place/geography and race are used as a type of shorthand in the narrative texts to reinforce a representational ideological preference in the accounts produced on the revolution. The excluded narratives he refers to are of particular relevance to this study. These are the narratives that focus on the everyday existence and struggles for survival that those who directly experienced the revolution have had to face. They focus less on ideology and more on how it is possible for an average Zanzibari to embrace the cultural complexities of the society in which they live and recognize that politicians are actively attempting to manipulate their understanding of the revolution. But when faced with the struggle to manage the basics of daily existence and the loud voices of those in political power, in the "public realm" at least, "the voices" of average citizens "are silenced."[42] It is to the excluded narratives that I now turn in order to highlight the accounts gleaned from my own ethnographic fieldwork and archival sources.

Narrating invasion, ethnic cleansing, and dispossession

In *Revolution in Zanzibar*, Okello, a Ugandan migrant and the leader of the Zanzibar Revolution of 1964, proudly narrated the details of his call to arms and the "nine-hour revolution"—the shortest in African history—identifying the individuals involved and explicating the steps taken to overthrow the Omani dynasty:

> For the cause of freedom, gentlemen, I have no alternative but to ask you to act and to act now. I ask you to join your men with mine in a powerful team, capable of defeating the Arabs. If you are able to do this, I shall delay no longer, but commence immediately to overthrow by force this most vicious colonialist government. I have no doubt that we shall win, and that the sufferings of the African shall come to an end.[43]

According to Okello, 1,100 men were solicited, with General Ramadhan Haji designated to overtake the army headquarters. The tasks were divided among recruits who had been trained in coconut and clove forests and equipped with "sticks, tyre-levers, spears, bows and arrows, hammers and knives" to seize the radio station and the police headquarters.[44] The destinations and people to be targeted were also laid out by Okello. Absolom Amoi Ingen was designated to lead the Revolutionary Army, and Seif Bakari was designated to assemble forces in Zanzibar Town. Okello maintains that half the guards were either wounded or killed, while others surrendered to his forces immediately "when they realized what was happening."[45] After a short-lived battle, Sultan Jamshid bin Abdullah—who only governed the island for a few months after its independence from the British—fled to the UK, while others were killed and thousands fled to Oman or other African countries.[46] The first voice on the radio was that of Okello:

The most wanted of all is the Sultan and he is to be killed immediately upon being found.... Anyone in the age group from 18–55 must be killed without hesitation. Anyone older must be arrested only. This also applies to male children in the age group from 13–17.[47]

Zanzibar's previous sultan, Sayyid Jamshid bin Harib, his family, and other Zanzibaris of Omani ancestry immediately fled the island following the carnage that ensued. In his memoirs, Okello goes on to describe the so-called nine-hour revolution in greater detail, narrating how it unfolded on 12 January 1964. Hundreds of African insurgents attacked Unguja, armed with machetes, automatic rifles, and guns; an attack that lasted for nine hours, to destroy a centuries-old empire. He identified the individuals involved and the steps taken to bring Arab colonization to an end.[48]

In discussing the divisive role played by the British and Tanganyikan propaganda, the late Mohamed Ali Muhsin Al-Barwani claimed that the British and Tanganyika's alarmist narratives, suggesting Zanzibar's independence would bring a return to the slave trade, were used to heighten passions and incite violence.[49] As was to be expected, the revolution and its aftermath signify a moment of political emotionality.

Mohamed Ali Muhsin, who was born in Zanzibar and traveled to Cairo and then Muscat during the revolution, gives the broader context behind the revolution, suggesting the disruptive effects of its racialized politics. He comments on the fears for the future experienced by Omani, Zanzibari, and other multiethnic families during the revolutionary period. The heightening of difference within the context of racialized politics spawned communal rifts heretofore minimal in day-to-day interactions. In the words of Nasser bin Al-Riyami:

The so-called "revolution" was so replete with atrocities that its very depiction as Revolution is a misnomer for an event which represented "the most heinous and abominable crimes in the form of killings, beatings, flogging, rape, looting and confiscation of property as well as inflicting the worst types of humiliation, torture and opprobrium to anyone belonging to the African race; later on even they were not spared."[50]

To be an "Arab" living in Zanzibar between 1964 and 1972 was to live a more hazardous life than a rabid dog. Arabs in particular and many others in general were imprisoned without reason and/or due process, their property was confiscated. Many were flogged in public just to humiliate them.[51]

For many Omani-Zanzibaris, a certain paradox emerged in the aftermath of the revolution in that it was successfully executed by a Ugandan rather than

by an African Zanzibari. To many, Okello, who led the revolution, was a per-
fect "stranger and intruder," says an Omani interviewee from Unguja. In
Al-Riyami's words:

> The "revolution" was in actual fact an invasion by foreign elements which
> resulted in the merciless butchery of thousands of innocent Zanzibar citizens
> and non-citizens; women and young girls—many below the age of puberty were
> ruthlessly raped in front of their loved ones—before their bodies were dismem-
> bered with machetes and their limbs grotesquely severed or crushed with axes.
> Some were shot at close range with guns. This was, in all sense of the word, a
> genocide, an ethnic cleansing, that preceded both the Rwandan and Bosnian
> genocides. The brutal carnage was followed by mass imprisonment and torture
> forcing many Zanzibaris to flee their country.[52]

Omani-Zanzibaris' sense of their own Zanzibari-ness made them averse to
the foreignness of Okello and Abeid Karume, the first president of Zanzibar,
and they consequently rationalize the seeming impunity with which his
actions were carried out as being particularly evocative of the compounded
sense of violation.[53] During my conversation with Al-Barwani, I repeatedly
asked why Omani-Zanzibaris accept a narrative of invasion on a continent
with such blurred, undefined borders:

> These perpetrators were not African-Zanzibaris, they were mainly from
> Tanganyika. Zanzibari Arabs and Africans were too close to each other, that the
> Africans with whom they had a strong bond, would and could have never com-
> mitted senseless violence. The heinousness of the crimes committed were the
> work of invaders. I once confronted a prominent figure in the government by
> asking him, I said my great grandfather, grandfather, and father were buried here
> in Zanzibar, where is your father buried? Silence. He was so incensed that you
> see rage flying out of his eyeballs, but why shouldn't he be? He is a foreigner
> trying to mete out atrocities under false pretenses. I challenged his indigeneity,
> and he wasn't amused.
>
> This maneuvering, coupled with outside involvement from Tanganyika, led to
> the buildup of the tension and the war in Zanzibar. The seeds of conflict were
> sown and, in fact, I still believe that the conflict is still going on, except in the
> current day you don't see any bloodshed. With that said, I believe that main-
> land Tanzania until today does not want to grant Zanzibar its independence,
> even though the makeup of both places are completely different—in terms of
> Tanzania being divided by religion whereas Zanzibar is divided by race.
> Having political leaders in the mainland giving fabricated reasons such as: it
> will create Muslim extremists and Zanzibar will be considered a threat to the
> mainland, creating the propaganda that Zanzibar becoming independent
> would create trouble. Mainland Tanzania has more to lose if Zanzibar were to
> be granted its independence.[54]

He went on to explain:

It was the ASP which caused the massacre of sixty-eight innocent Zanzibaris in 1961. It was the ASP which caused the disaster of January 1964 and the massacre of thousands. It was the ASP which sold out Zanzibar to Nyerere in April 1964, and lost us our national flag, lost us our seat in the United Nations, closed down our foreign embassies, terminated the generous educational assistance Zanzibar was getting from Egypt and a number of other countries. It was the ASP which scrapped the would-be university which was to be put up at Kwa Mtipura in the outskirts of Zanzibar Town in 1964. It is the ASP which has been the cause for all the deterioration in education, healthcare, economy and morality that have been plaguing the country for the last thirty years. It is the ASP which has confiscated almost all properties belonging to Zanzibaris, including those of mosques and has handed them to aliens because they took part in, or supported, the mass murders of Zanzibaris.[55]

Michael Lofchie wrote with accommodation and satisfaction at the revolution, refuting the conspiracy theory behind the attacks, effectively believing that Okello's narrative of the revolution was in fact an accurate one. Okello's supporters were mostly members of the Zanzibar and Pemba Pain Workers' Union, the Afro-Shirazi Youth League, and "former policemen discharged by the government for being of mainland African descent."[56] Lofchie presents the prevailing accounts of the revolution's sympathizers, who portrayed it as a "righteous" act of "liberation."[57] The confluence of race and class figured centrally in what Lofchie calls "the African response" and the emergence of African nationalist agitation for change, beginning in 1951.[58] Overall, Lofchie seems to claim that economic class and location (urban versus rural) are the classifications that mean the Omani (or the Arabs) are different from the Swahili and more like the Europeans who came before and after them (namely the Portuguese and the British), despite similarities in religion or a shared location (i.e., Zanzibar). In 1964, confidential telegrams from the Foreign Office to Muscat noted its intention "to take action as feasible to discourage Zanzibari authorities from arbitrary deportation without-prior consultation with territory of intended destination."[59] A number of confidential notes addressed the humanitarian emergency relief efforts by the Red Cross and tackled the actions of the Zanzibar government that contravened international human rights and meted out violence against Omanis because of their ethnicity.

Archival British sources corroborate the narratives gathered in this research on the devastation caused to the Zanzibari-Omani communities. On 17 February 1964, a telegram from the Foreign Office to Muscat had as its primary subject: "Arabs Departed from Zanzibar":

It seems clear that those Arabs will have been reduced to effective statelessness by Zanzibari regime's unwillingness either to allow them to remain in Zanzibar, or it appears to retain Zanzibari status. To produce this situation and to add to the total of the world's refugees by expelling communities as such because of their race violates the recent United Nations Declaration on Racial discrimination and the Declaration of Human Rights which rules out racial discrimination, arbitrary arrest and deportation of nationalities.[60]

There was an increased recognition of the nature of the atrocities against Zanzibaris of Omani descent, and this in many ways lends credence to what may otherwise appear to be a subjective experience and a subjective retelling. Fleeing genocide, crimes against humanity, and ethnic cleansing are experiences that are by no means limited to Omani-Zanzibaris. Their memories of the 1964 episode reveal the persistent pain of a people who are now members of a Gulf society. The statements below, as reflected in interviews and as authored in memoirs, are illustrative of the emotionality that overwhelmed them.

What happened in the course of this episode? If genocide is defined by the intention of destroying a group by virtue of its race or ethnicity, then the voices chronicled below are an illustration of the reasons behind Omani-Zanzibari perceptions and their refusal to recognize the events of 1964 as a revolution.[61] Examples of ethnic cleansing and crimes against humanity provided in their narratives, memoirs, and newspapers abound.[62] These events, as we will see, had a significant impact on Omani-Zanzibari families as they sought asylum and reintegration in the Sultanate of Oman as Swahili-speaking Zinjibaris.[63] Al-Riyami captures the importance of this episode, which he terms "the massacre of the century" for Omani-Zanzibari political identities and their attendant memories when he notes: "the parameters for targeted torturing adopted by the new regime were the following: anyone bearded or light skinned or wearing the Arabian 'Kanzu' [*dishdasha*], which was well liked by the Arabs, the Comorians, African Muslims."[64] He provides numerous examples of the genocidal acts inflicted on Omani-Zanzibari families, most of whom were landless Arabs who occupied the lower echelons of the economy.

According to a female activist in Zanzibar, who resisted the Tanzanian authorities: "I was jailed in cells filled with feces. The security forces wanted to break me. I didn't keep quiet after my release. Most of the traumatized first generation resorted to silence, given their brutalization."

Almost all Omani-Zanzibaris lamented the obfuscation of their experiences in the midst of continental euphoria and jubilation vis-à-vis liberation movements in colonial Africa while Arabs were forced at gunpoint to dig their own graves and then shot dead. In keeping with the focus on the Omani-Zanzibari voices who reiterated this view was that of a man in his mid-sixties whose views were unequivocal, like those of a caravan of victims who resented the nature of the foreignness of the genocide's perpetrators. As these voices help historicize the events that led to the carnage, I take the liberty of citing them at length:

> I knew someone who used to own a restaurant for almost thirty years in Zanzibar, he was from Salalah. The man would have this Swahili neighbor, and during the revolution his own neighbor killed him. And that Omani man was very nice to him; he would give him food almost every day. For thirty years. And he killed him.[65]

The death toll ranged between 13,000 and 17,000 deaths—5 percent of the island's total population. The dead were mostly Arab. Arabs were also dragged in streets in the back of cars, Arabs in rural areas were killed or burnt alive inside their homes for no reason other than the misconception by the invaders and ASP supporters that they were the segment of Arab society possessing the most firearms.[66]

The unfortunate innocents who were victim to the bloody events were treated like animals and even worse. The methods of torture and humiliation were far beyond all human and ethnic boundaries. Pain and agony was the order of the day.[67]

Individuals were killed for having a picture of the sultan, the ZNP logo, and any objects relating to the toppled government such as postage stamps that had pictures of the sultans, and official headed paper with the sultans' emblem.[68]

The target of the violent revolution, which I see as invasion, were Zanzibaris of Omani-Arab descent whose ancestors lived on the island for centuries. To this day there is marked reluctance to call this event by what it really was, a genocide, pure and simple. A big deal was made about numbers. People say what was the number of those who perished during this episode? The answer was always reflective of subjective positions sympathetic to the insurgents. Generally, the numbers do not tell the whole story. The incontrovertible fact remains: people of Omani descent were killed, women were raped, and communities were displaced and dispossessed of their property. How can one describe these actions? Why aren't people talking about this as crimes against humanity?[69]

How many Brazilians of African slaves are in the world today, and how many are in Oman? I am not saying slavery is morally acceptable, I want people who dare to talk about us to soul search and scrutinize their own brutality and the havoc they wreaked in our continent, the virus they injected in our body politic, look what happened in America, in the Belgian Congo, and were they remorseful? Were they contrite? Of course not. These kinds of accounts about Omani slavery exude selective memory.[70]

In the context of the Eurocentric critique of colonialism in Zanzibar, the Portuguese and the British were largely exempted if not inoculated altogether from criticism and accountability. This acute sense of loss figured centrally in Ali Muhsin's memoir, which he authored after his release from a Tanzanian jail:

> The house which my wife and I had built with sweat and love for ourselves and our children and our children's children was confiscated by the usurping government and subsequently occupied by a number of usurpers. Some I know, and some I do not care to know. But all that I know is that everyone who has used that confiscated house and all other properties which have been confiscated are accursed by God. They are all doomed to perdition.[71]

After the coup and the devastation it caused, Okello disappears in the mire of history. Rendered redundant by Karume and Julius Nyerere, he was forced to return to Dar es Salaam only to be replaced by Karume, whose charismatic persona accrued significant political dividends. By that stage, it had become very clear that Okello was a mere pawn in a Tanganyika design rather than a mastermind of the revolution.

The Noda a Karume: on rape and the Marriage Solemnization Act of 1966

The rise of Karume, as the first African president of Zanzibar, opened up another period defined by what Omanis saw as racist governmentality and gender-based violence. Of the memories summoned in depicting the scale of political violence in Zanzibar, interviewees talked about the rape of women of Omani descent and the passing of the Marriage Solemnization Act of 1966, which came to be known as *The Noda a Karume* or *Karume's Marriage*. True to their conviction that what had happened involved the deliberate destruction of the Omani-Zanzibari community because of their ethnicity, the following statements were offered both in interviews and in the memoirs about the events and politics of Zanzibar.

Sexual violence figures prominently in this account:

> The ruffians' insatiable sadistic tendencies were not quenched by the torturing of ordinary men, but went further—as is the case with many coups and revolutions—to sexually assault women. Women were raped in front of their husbands and families, who were shackled or held at gunpoint to bear witness to this hideous act of fornication, this violation of their honour. In most cases these sexual assaults were committed in public areas where local residents including their close relatives were invited.[72]

[A seventy-year-old woman] narrated how the revolutionaries had raided her house and pulled her husband's clothes off him, stripped him naked in front of his grown up sons and daughters. They then threw him to the ground and beat him with a wooden club full of nails. The old woman, sobbing, described how the blood was seeping and bits of flesh were flying from her husband's skinny body.[73]

The old woman, cursing the Revolutionary Government and branding it with the most demeaning adjectives, went on to say that they had tortured her husband for no crime at all; he was a simple shopkeeper minding his own business who had no interest in politics whatsoever.[74]

A prominent Omani-Zanzibari in Muscat responded somewhat differently to my question about sexual politics in postcolonial Zanzibar and its impact on the family:

These mainlanders became fixated on the Arabs who, from their perspective, were primed for extinction. They also tried the tactic of raping women. They called it the Forced Marriage Code. Karume and his so-called revolutionaries wanted Arab women. They used their phalluses as daggers. Since humanity began, a man's mind is always occupied with "Ahhhh ... How can I get this woman in bed?" In their minds they had sexual fantasies about these women. These women were trapped in falsified matrimonies as they were seen as lacking affection and consent. A lot of bastards were born. Every general melted in the pleasure of sex, but it was forced.[75]

All members of the Revolutionary Council married Arab women. It must be remembered that as a Swahili, Omani, Zanzibari, marriage is a relationship that transcends the individual. When my own son wanted to marry an Arab woman, I refused on the basis of her father's rudeness. He asked: "Father, am I marrying her father?" I replied in the affirmative. I am married to a Tanzanian who is a relative of a Tanganyika nationalist. But we know that racialized politics was about post-1964 that brought about a union between Zanzibar and Tanganyika in the country Tanzania. This emerging Tanzanian Islamophobia was not about race, as many were led by their leaders to believe. To me marriage is not a problem if not forced against the will of the betrothed. Omanis married African women and gave birth to people like me, and if African men were to marry Omani women it didn't matter, they would still have given birth to someone like me.[76]

In the minds of many Omani-Zanzibaris, these acts were manifestations of the state's transgression and interference in the private realm of intimacy and kinship. The mobilization and weaponization of sex as a tool of dehumanization and ethnic cleansing also figured prominently in Omani-Zanzibaris' accounts of physical and moral harm to the community by reinforcing the distinction among ethnicities in the archipelago. *The Noda a Karume* added a new dimension to the politics of marriage and the "contestation over consent and coercion" in this Afro-Arab society.[77] Rape and forced marriage as sanctioned by Karume were conceptualized by the Omani-Zanzibaris as morally equivalent, as both involved asserting power over women without their consent. Large numbers of girls and women were forced into marriage, sometimes at gunpoint. During this time, no one was allowed to refuse a marriage proposal. Parents who resisted or refused to let their daughters be married were subject to imprisonment, hard labor, beating, and lashes. Many officers, mostly in the hierarchy of the Zanzibar government and members of the Revolutionary Council, were reportedly involved in these actions. This was done under the shield of protection against moral and social decay and a campaign against racism.

There is a sense that the forced marriage in this era was taken as a form of revenge for past acts of slavery and concubinage. As Karume reportedly declared at a public rally, "in colonial times the Arabs took the African concubines without bothering to marry them. Now we are in power, the shoe is on the other foot."[78] The law also provided punishment for any person acting in contravention of the act. The government claimed that the law was formulated as part of the government's campaign against immorality and to protect young girls from *mambo maovu* (evil things). Others said that the president wished not just to ensure that everyone in Zanzibar was living in harmony but also to encourage inter-ethnic marriages between people living in Zanzibar. "Karume's marriages" were part of a process designed to create a new, multiethnic population. During this period, invocations of the practices of concubinage and slavery, perpetuated by the sultans and slaveholders, served as grounds for the African state to exact revenge, and in so doing bestow legitimacy on forced marriage and gender-based violence in Zanzibar.

One interviewee, who maintains a home in Muscat and one in Zanzibar, is proud of his mixed heritage. However, he also feels a sense of unease with this, as he is concerned that it sanctions the *Noda a Karume*.[79] An elderly Zanzibari asserted:

> When a sultan takes a concubine and marries her, she was granted not only automatic manumission, but a place in the throne. The only wife who is buried next to her sultan husband Maatooqa [meaning manumitted] was his favorite wife. Everyone knew that she was the real power behind the throne. Men didn't refer to their concubines or slaves as *Wahadimu* as the Europeans want people to believe, they called them the mothers of kings.[80]

95

In our conversations about forced marriage, Omani-Zanzibaris seized the opportunity to draw distinctions between the state's coercion and concubinage, as the latter practice was by no means consistently followed in Omani-Zanzibar. To them, forced marriage was yet another act of sexual violence given the non-consensual nature of the unholy matrimony, a spoil of war, as it were:

> Forced marriages, the violent rapes of women and men that went on and on, the mass confiscation of properties, the utter destruction of the educational system, the judiciary system, the health service, everything that the sultans and the British ever created was torn into shreds by the vandals who have taken over control of the country. The Larimjee Hospital built by a philanthropic Zanzibari family for all people irrespective of race, nationality or religion, has been allowed to rot under the name of the Communist demi-god, V. I. Lenin. Zanzibar and Tanganyika for that matter have hit the rock bottom of poverty and backwardness, a high price indeed to pay for the mere satisfaction of "exterminating Arabs."[81]

Women and girls disproportionately suffered the wrath of mainland aggression, as communicated in a confidential telegram sent by the Red Cross to the Foreign Office on 2 February 1964.[82] In the patrilineal system, in which lineage is reckoned by the father's ancestry, Omani-Zanzibaris saw the state's law as an attempt to reconfigure the prevailing kinship structure and, in so doing, commit ethnic cleansing by forced marriage. This law has further prompted forced migration in postcolonial Zanzibar.

In the Sultanate: 140 years later

The issue of forced migration, from the outset, was one of the most difficult and emotionally charged subjects I encountered in this ethnography. When I began an interview in Muscat with an Omani-Zanzibari in his early seventies by asking about the subject of returnees, he stated that I had asked the wrong question:

> The correct question from now on, is to ask me—and all Zanzibaris of Omani descent for that matter—the following: When did you arrive in the Sultanate? I was born in Zanzibar. It is my home and the home of my forefathers, from which we were forced to leave.[83]

The criticism of my question animated my recalibration of this subject and my overall understanding of what Pierre Bourdieu calls *doxa*, meaning scheme of thought, and the grasp of the world.[84] This corrective has another advantage methodologically—not only did it help enrich my views on the genocide narrative but it also helped me to reconfigure the ways in which the questions of loss, associated with forced migration, home, and belonging, are articulated. The memories told and retold in this ethnography are clearly reflective of how political-violence events were remembered and were by no means woven out of some hallucination or wild imagination. After the 1964 revolution, the memories harbored by Omani-Zanzibaris speak to an undeviating loss and enduring dispossession:

> We are Zanzibaris, Swahili-speaking Omanis. We belong to a land where our great grandfathers were buried. Where was Karume's grandfather or father buried? How come our Swahili-language shares a significant portion of Arabic? *Akhabar* [news in Arabic], for example, is *harabari* in Swahili; *asante*, or thanks in Swahili, is *ahsanta* in Arabic; *Mualim* in Arabic is *Mualimo* in Swahili! Would you like me to go on and on and on? So many influences let me conclude that Swahili is 60 percent Arabic and 40 percent Bantu. Let people deny all they want about the accuracy of this number. Today, Zanzibaris of Omani descent who left, were forced by the devastation of Zanzibar by the so-called revolutionaries. The losses are the kinds you feel so deep in the marrow.[85]

Upon arrival in the Sultanate, forced migrants acquired the appellation Zinjibari to signify their African heritage in their Swahili language, mixed ancestry, and even physical appearance. Most of them relocated to Muscat and Ibri.[86] Others, speaking on condition of anonymity, describe the trauma of the first generation of displaced Omanis, and of secondhand memories that are only recently being transmitted from one generation to the next. Forced displacement from Zanzibar resulted in complicated grief and loss. A member of an aristocratic Omani-Zanzibari family recalled his experiences:

> We left Zanzibar when I was four. Therefore, my memories are rather faint. Only a few I will never forget. I recall that my father was in Pemba Island for work. I heard loud noises and screams and my mother pulled me back from the window. My family told me that when we left my father was unable to join us [because] he had an aunt who had raised him after the death of his mother [and who] was too sick to leave. So he decided to stay behind. We moved to Egypt during Nasser's days. Although my mother spoke Swahili only, she was happy to be in Egypt. When the 1967 conflict started in Cairo, we moved to Yemen, which itself was in the throes of war. It seemed like there was no peaceful spot on earth. War was there, wherever we went. Things changed for the better after 1970 when His Majesty Sultan Qaboos invited Omani-Zanzibari families to return to Oman. At that point they were all over the world, in Egypt, the Gulf, and London. [When we arrived] at the port, old relatives who never left the Sultanate were asked to vouch for us and attest to our Omani descent.[87]

I have not encountered anyone who returned to Ibra or Sur as the primary sending provinces to Zanzibar. "Through the end of 1964, Oman accepted some 3,700 Zanzibari Omani refugees."[88] The stories that unfolded demonstrated that the forced migration of Omani-Zanzibari families to Oman was much more than a mere homecoming: it was a passage to self-fashioning and soul-searching as family identities were reinforced and new ones constructed. A marked diasporic consciousness was thus formed as Omani-Zanzibaris reckoned with their new experience in an ancestral locality from which their forebears hailed. Another interviewee, a seventy-four-year-old member of the Al-Busaidi ruling dynasty, who was born and raised in a royal palace in Zanzibar and now lives in Muscat, voiced similar views about Omani-Zanzibari political history, kinship, family, and social organization. He was able to contextualize the historical ties between Oman and Zanzibar going back to ancient times, addressing subjects as diverse as maritime trade networks, patterns of Omani settlement, intermarriage with Africans, slavery, the arrival and defeat of the Portuguese, and British colonization under the guise of protection:

> Zanzibar represents something very dear to Omani-Zanzibaris in Muscat. No amount of racist rhetoric against the Arabs can wipe out our intertwined lives and experiences. I descend from the royal family in Zanzibar. I left for Egypt before the revolution in 1963 then later went to Muscat. I was certainly luckier than my own parents, who didn't.

And unlike the statement above, some returnees demonstrated a deep sense of ambivalence vis-à-vis their dislodgment from Zanzibar:

> Coming back to Oman was one of the biggest struggles. If someone went through that, I promise you, they wouldn't want to come back.[89]

> When I got to Oman, I didn't like it. I felt like the life I had back in Africa was better, but I was already here, and didn't have enough money to go back.[90]

Instability and the quest for permanence in transience remained a persistent quandary for the thousands who voiced dissent at the violence and displacement they had to endure. The returnees sought asylum in Muscat and elsewhere because of the 1964 revolution—a term they resent. Omani-Zanzibari families endured political violence and forced migration from the island.

The call and responses to the new arrivals

> The Sultan called Omanis to return in 1970 after he ascended to the throne. The first wave to return were those from Zanzibar, Pemba, and the Gulf states. The

second wave were those coming from Tanzania, Burundi, Rwanda, etc. There are now 1.2 million residing in East Africa [Tanzania mainly] and others scattered around Europe.[91]

[Even without the Omani identity] I am thankful for this country, and that there is no segregation, because when I land, I still feel like an Omani, regardless. Maybe until you personally say that you aren't Omani. Also the language, because then they automatically know that you originally came from Zanzibar. Of course everyone here says Zanzibar, but they don't understand that some people came from different parts.[92]

I thank Qaboos for everything, and may god give him health; we are originally Omani, we get so many benefits.[93]

I also ask Omanis to visit their hometown, because Oman and Zanzibar can both be your home. And we should always thank Qaboos for all his efforts and support.[94]

The arriving/returning Omani-Zanzibaris to Oman were grateful for the refuge Oman had offered. The sultan's call to Omani-Zanzibaris to return had garnered tremendous admiration for him personally. The point here is to recognize how Swahili-speaking families are an intrinsic part of Omani society, as they are part of the larger history of diaspora:[95]

So there was an announcement from the Omani government asking the people in Africa to come back, and luckily my daughter was one of them. This was in the '80s, so here a lot of people came from Africa to Oman, and they were given the passport.[96]

During the 1970s, I got news from family that said if you want to come to Oman, we are ready to take you. By then I already had my business, and was already married. I sold my shops and came to Oman. I came in 1975.[97]

In the words of one of those interviewed on *Waliroudi*:

So people told me that I need to send my passport to Oman and then get it changed under the sultan's reign passport. So I gave it to an Arab man. I don't remember his name but he managed to get it to the immigration place in Muscat. So when that man got there he said "the person with this passport, wants an Omani passport, the sultan one." So the immigration [Omani] sent me a letter. I left my address, so they sent me a letter saying I needed to pay two pounds to send the passport.[98]

What we wanted to do after the revolution calmed was to head back to Oman, but we had a choice to either go back to Oman or Burundi. Because, you see, if we headed back to Oman we wouldn't have anything. So we decided to go to Burundi. We had no capital in Oman; in Zanzibar we had a little bit of income from here and there. Going back to Oman would take us to zero.[99]

Interviewees demonstrated that Omani families were involved in ongoing dialogue about self-fashioning and identity formation, processes emanating from their interwoven past and present. This draws on Omani-Zanzibaris' understanding of their family dynamics, grounded in their knowledge of the historical context that shaped it and the cultural and political logic underpinning it. Through an "intertextual" reading coupled with ethnographic research, this study demonstrates the convergence of ancestral genealogies and political concerns.

The narratives I gathered in Muscat from a prominent Omani-Zanzibari, speaking on the condition of anonymity, shed further light on the Omani-Zanzibaris' experiences following the forced migration and deportation. At the outset, forced migration, it was argued, affected their identity as a Swahili-speaking community in the Sultanate of Oman, whose ancestors left centuries ago as Omani-Arabs and returned as Zanjibaris—"Zanzis," so nicknamed.[100]

According to sociolinguist Nafla Kharousi, the ethnic label "Zinjibari" is used in Oman to describe "individuals associated with any part of the East African region"—regardless of whether they speak the Swahili language or not.[101] Those labeled as "Zinjibaris" are recognized as having previously lived in East Africa, where they adopted different social and cultural norms from native Omanis.[102] Today, "Zinjibaris" are often recognized for being highly educated and hold positions in the government due to their lack of previous political and tribal tensions. This was part of Qaboos's prerequisite for working in governmental positions during his modernization process.[103]

Whether the label "Zinjibaris" has indeed created a sense of an outsider identity was not clear from my research. Instead, there was an emphasis on the significance of Sultan Qaboos's welcoming of the Omani diaspora. What Omani-Zanzibaris addressed, however, was how their identity as Swahili-speaking "communities of memory" acquired new significance as far as their belonging and reintegration are concerned. Overall, the interviewees in this ethnography articulated their Swahili Africanity with pride and solemnity, as any African would.

Conclusion: after the fact

The foregoing accounts of Omanis in Muscat and Zanzibar have amply illustrated the characteristic energy of various social processes, of "borrowing ... a remarkable capacity to adapt, create, rebound, and collectively remember and forget."[104] This study has sought to emphasize Omani exceptionalism, as expressed in the manner in which the Sultanate handled the absorption and integration of Zanzibaris. An African-Gulf experience apart, Omani-Zanzibaris' representations of society, identity, diaspora, and political violence were narrated with a sense of yearning to maintain their ties to Zanzibar, while cherishing Oman, which at the state level did not mitigate their own yearning and self-fashioning as a Swahili in Omani society. These narratives lead me to concur with G. Thomas Burgess, who wrote: "how Zanzibaris remember the revolution—as either the original sin or the triumph of the independence era—often determines whom they call their friends, with whom they share a cup of coffee, or whom they welcome to their homes as in-laws."[105]

Given the conflict between how communities remember transformative experiences—i.e., liberation or genocide—we ought to consider their views as emblematic of the complexities at stake in the production of the "signifying debates" over an event that transfigured the lives of those who left Zanzibar. This episode engendered competing narratives—typical of ethnographies of political violence—as revealed in historical scholarship, personal narratives, and memoirs. Their forced migration led to the emergence of paradoxes in which they had to reconcile new ways of "being in the world." Their experiences remain unmatched elsewhere in the Gulf region. Navigating a new sociopolitical terrain in the Sultanate of Oman did not obliterate their Africanity or Arabism. Instead, it presented an opportunity for soul-searching and reflection. "You can be an Arab and an African at once, this is who we are," says an interviewee in Muscat. Ties with Zanzibar, as violence started to taper off after the revolution, also strengthened their transnational identity in the form of purchasing property and splitting time between Oman and Zanzibar. "I go to Zanzibar frequently, visit my relatives in Pemba, and maintain very strong relationships with them," I was told by a third-generation Omani-Zanzibari in Muscat, whose parents had a great deal to teach him about his Zanzibari identity. Another added: "our case as refugees is among a very few examples where we ended much better than we started," speaking of the tolerance and accommodation they found in Omani society.

6

AFGHAN MIGRANTS IN TEHRAN

TOWARD FORMAL INTEGRATION

Pooya Alaedini

Introduction

Persistent upheavals in Afghanistan since 1978 have resulted in the exodus of a large number of its citizens,[1] with neighboring Iran and Pakistan becoming host to most of these forced migrations. According to Iran's census figures,[2] there were 1,452,513 documented Afghans living in the country in 2011. The United Nations High Commissioner for Refugees (UNHCR) has given a figure of 951,142 for documented Afghan refugees in Iran as of May 2015.[3] In addition to this, UNHCR also reported 620,000 Afghan visa holders[4] and from 1.5 to 2 million undocumented Afghans. The Iranian government has emphasized repatriation as a policy goal vis-à-vis Afghan migrants and has carried out voluntary return initiatives with the assistance of international organizations. However, the voluntary return of 902,000 Afghans from Iran between 2002 and 2012[5] appears to have been offset by fresh migration that has maintained their overall population in the country.

Furthermore, considering the continued security, nation-building, and economic challenges in Afghanistan, there has only been a very small number of voluntary repatriations in recent years.[6]

Amayesh cards and long-term visas are the two legal means for Afghans to reside in Iran.[7] *Amayesh* cards, with their associated benefits, have been issued for refugees, while visas carry other benefits such as the possibility to get a driver's license or the freedom to travel out of the country. However, in practice, the functional distinction between the two is not without ambiguity. This appears to reflect a gradual change of status for Afghans in the region, from refugees to migrants.[8] In reality, many Afghan residents of Iran are likely to be economic migrants—with this type of mobility between Afghanistan and Iran having significant historical precedence.[9] Migration and migrants are thus the general terms used here, without any attempt to downplay their forced nature against the backdrop of major political and security issues in Afghanistan.

All formal barriers to the education of Afghan migrants at primary and secondary levels have now been removed by the government, notwithstanding the myriad trials and errors and persisting practical issues.[10] Theoretically, health insurance also became available and mandatory for all documented Afghans in 2016.[11] Furthermore, there has been significant upward mobility in terms of education and employment between first- and next-generation Afghans in Iran.[12] Second- and third-generation Afghans with higher levels of education are better adapted to the host society, with cultural and behavioral attributes more akin to those of Iranians.[13] At the same time, there remain significant sociocultural barriers, which are related to the legal and economic challenges faced by the migrants that prevent the integration of second- and third-generation Afghans in Iranian society.[14]

There are reportedly over 2 million Afghans present in the Iranian labor market—more than 85 percent of the total migrant labor—accounting for around 10 percent of the active labor force in the country.[15] Nearly 40 percent of Iran's foreign migrants, mostly from Afghanistan, are active in the labor force. This is higher than the overall labor force participation rate, and the Afghan labor force in Iran has a 7.3 percent unemployment rate—lower than the country's overall rate. Many Afghan residents of Iran, especially the undocumented, are engaged in manual labor and work in difficult and hazardous occupations. While this is partly a reflection of their low levels of human capital, official regulations also restrict Afghan employment in four categories of occupation: manufacturing construction materials, construction, agriculture, and miscellaneous blue-collar occupations. Many Afghans in Iran may, however, hold more skill-intensive occupations, especially due to labor shortages in some regions in particular occupational categories. At the same time, the types of jobs performed by Afghans in Iran are in most cases not in direct competition with those of Iranians—despite the occasional outcry to the contrary, which has also permeated other issues such as healthcare.[16] For example, the contribution of Afghans to Iran's construction sector and other labor-intensive activities has been pervasive and highly positive.[17]

Most of Iran's Afghans live in towns and cities, with only 3 percent of their estimated total population residing in settlements.[18] Based on government regulations,[19] Afghan refugees are permitted in certain provinces or territories—fifteen provinces are designated as no-go areas, while full access is allowed to the provinces of Tehran, Alborz, and Qom.[20] Iran's 2011 census reported the largest number of registered Afghans—474,687 persons—residing in the province of Tehran.[21] Furthermore, the overwhelming urban primacy of the national capital located within the province makes Tehran particularly important in the study of migrants—whether from other areas of Iran or from Afghanistan. In fact, much of Tehran's population growth is attributed to migration—over 88 percent was due to migration between 2012 and 2017.[22] While the more affluent migrants have no specific geographic concentration in terms of their origins, poorer entrants into the city are likely to form enclaves in less expensive neighborhoods to benefit from existing social networks, more affordable housing, and jobs. Afghans in Tehran are more likely to fall within the latter group and are especially concentrated in several neighborhoods. Against this background, the present study focuses on the capital city of Tehran as a significant area of residence for Afghans in Iran. The next section provides a brief review of important discussions on the marginalization and integration of migrants in urban areas in order to justify the study's urban focus and to formulate its approach. This is followed by a section on the fieldwork methodology and selection of three case study neighborhoods. Other sections shed light on the demographics, housing, social structures, and occupation of Afghans in the three neighborhoods.

Migrants in urban areas: integration versus marginalization

Notwithstanding repatriation and resettlement initiatives, the main debates concerning refugees, displaced persons, and other migrants revolve around marginalization and integration. Marginalization occurs when a combination of socioeconomic, cultural, legal-political, or spatial inequality, together with various characteristics of the migrants themselves, acts to prevent their positive adaptation to and integration into the host society.[23] Addressing these issues, an oft-cited integration framework proposed by Alastair Ager and Alison Strang covers ten domains under four categories: markers and means (employment, housing, education, and health); social connection (social bridges, social bonds, and social links); facilitators (language and cultural knowledge as well as safety and stability); and rights and citizenship.[24] These domains become especially important in urban settings. In fact, alongside the unprecedented growth in refugees, displaced persons, and migrants globally,[25] migration has become an increasingly urban phenomenon and is progressively recognized as such in the academic literature and by international and advocacy organizations.

Large cities such as Tehran—where shelter is costly and other expenses tend to be equally high—are not easy places for domestic or international migrants in terms of livelihoods. Migrants can further face hostility and discrimination in urban settings, although these issues can be monitored more carefully in comparison with more remote areas. In the Iranian context, anecdotal evidence suggests better adaptation of Afghan migrants living in rural areas in comparison with their urban counterparts.[26] Yet, urban areas offer an array of opportunities, not limited to subsistence, that continue to attract migrants, including Afghans in Iran. The likelihood that there are already large numbers of domestic migrants living in urban areas, especially in developing countries, confronts those coming from outside the country with tough competition for decent jobs, affordable shelter, and other resources, but also affects their ability to blend in or hide their potentially undocumented stays.

Since 2000, UNHCR's approach to refugees and displaced persons has evolved to embrace the increasingly urban aspect of their migration. In its 2012 report, "State of the World's Refugees," one chapter is devoted to "Displacement and Urbanization." It explains how the organization's policy shifted after 1997 from giving priority to placing refugees in camps to adopting a new policy on refugee protection and solutions in urban areas in 2009, and further evolved to striving—through a community-based approach—to address various protection risks that refugees face in urban areas. These risks include restrictions on movement and residence, lack of residency documents and illegality, inadequate housing and food, lack of access to healthcare and education, as well as harassment, sexual exploitation and violence, and trafficking—which are further addressed in the 2016 New York Declaration.[27] The new community-based paradigm has nonetheless been criticized for its out-comes—e.g., in the Middle East, where most refugees live in urban areas rather than camps—and for its temporariness against the backdrop of the protracted migration situations at hand.[28] This state of temporariness has, for example, been recorded for the case of refugees in urban Cairo.[29]

On the urban policy side, the UN's New Urban Agenda embraces the con-cept of "the right to the city" for refugees and displaced persons,[30] as Article 28 commits to support "local authorities in establishing frameworks that enable the positive contribution of migrants to cities and strengthened urban–rural linkages." Likewise, a 2016 report by UNESCO,[31] "Cities Welcoming Refugees and Migrants," provides a checklist for enhancing effective urban management in relation to migrants. The measures called for in the checklist include pursuing a deliberate approach based on values and rights; ensuring effective and multi-level city governance alongside the right to the city; pro-viding urban services to all, with the associated implications for finances; engaging all stakeholders; ensuring accountability at all levels; facilitating integration and social cohesion; and campaigning against discrimination, racism, and xenophobia while celebrating cultural diversity, which also includes the appropriate use of the media. Another publication worth men-tioning is "Global Migration: Resilient Cities at the Forefront,"[32] which offers a similar checklist of measures, including planning for a dynamic future by embracing migration and incorporating migrants into designs for the provi-sion of services and infrastructure; ensuring adequate opportunities for the realization of migrants' potentials, including access to income-generating activities, financial services, and entrepreneurship possibilities; embracing newcomers by addressing their fundamental needs and by promoting their interactions with others together with narratives that emphasize common visions; and leading for change by seeking the participation of various public, private, and non-profit-sector stakeholders at local, national, and international levels in terms of both funding and policy direction.

Given the above discussion, this chapter treats the issue of the integration and marginalization of Afghan migrants in the context of Iran's largest metrop-olis, Tehran. It shows that the Afghan migrants in Tehran have actively strived to carve out spaces on the fringes of the society through various livelihood strategies based on the available resources. However, their presence is treated as temporary by the national and municipal authorities, and to some extent them-selves. As such, while they can access some of the benefits that help their adap-tation, they are also excluded from a host of others that can ensure their integration. They have joined the urban poor as basic laborers, informal settlement residents, street vendors, street children, and the like. Afghan migrants in Tehran are thus marginalized in a number of ways, despite the significant contributions they are making to the city. The central argument of the chapter is that, given the reality that most Afghan migrants will not be repatriated or resettled, it is best that the city embraces them in full—which will have significant benefits for both the migrants and their host communities.

Selection of neighborhood case studies and fieldwork methodology

Based on preliminary explorations as well as communication with municipal authorities and nongovernmental organizations (NGOs), Tehran's Districts 20, 12, and 2 were identified as major areas of residence and work of Afghan migrants. Furthermore, after additional field observations, Farahzad, Harandi, and Aminabad (in Districts 2, 12, and 20, respectively) were chosen as neighborhoods of focus. Figure 6.1 shows the location of the selected districts and neighborhoods. All relevant national, city, district, and neighborhood-level documents were accessed and studied. Field activities commenced through observation alongside individual and group interviews with Afghan and Iranian residents, urban management entities,[33] NGOs, and Afghans active in culture and/or media in Tehran. A list of these is provided in the Appendix. GIS software was used to create maps based on secondary information as well as the results of fieldwork.

The neighborhoods and their Afghan demographics

Tehran's District 2, with a population of around 620,000,[34] is one of the more developed areas of Tehran. According to "Characteristics Document of District 2,"[35] while the majority of its neighborhoods have some Afghan population, most Afghans in the district live in Farahzad (see Fig. 6.2). With a rural past and facing the mountains to the north, Farahzad is reportedly several hundred years old (in contrast to the rest of District 2) and has attracted migrants from various corners of Iran as well as from Afghanistan since the 1970s. As a result of these migrations, there are now recognizable Khorasani, Kermani, and Quchani areas in the neighborhood, but Afghans are scattered across Farahzad. In parts of Farahzad, unresolved land tenure issues, and especially makeshift construction and physical deterioration of buildings, have gradually resulted in the exodus of some of the older resi-

Figure 6.1: Location of Aminabad, Farahzad, Harandi, and their districts in Tehran

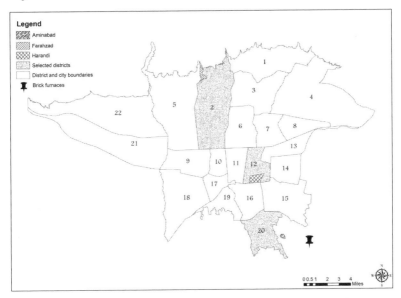

dents of the neighborhood and their replacement by lower-income groups. At the same time, due to the favorable climate of Farahzad, the area has become an important destination for Tehran residents seeking to engage in leisure activities. There are a large number of cafés and restaurants that provide some employment opportunities, in particular for manual labor. According to the 2011 census, the population of Farahzad was 19,407.[36] Yet, in 2015, Farnahad Consulting Engineers carried out a survey in Farahzad that counted around 14,000 persons in the neighborhood in 3,412 households—including 694 households with Afghan nationality, comprising close to 20 percent of the population.[37]

District 12 comprises the older part of Tehran where a number of historic buildings are located. It has been rapidly losing its residential character and increasingly becoming a major commercial zone of the city.[38] In fact, over one-fifth of commercial units and micro and small workshops in Tehran were reported to be in District 12.[39] Many of the housing units next to Tehran's Grand Bazaar in the Emamzadeh Yahya neighborhood have become depots at the service of the nearby commercial outlets. The 2011 census indicated a population of 236,679 persons and 76,329 households for this district.[40]

Figure 6.2: Map of Farahzad

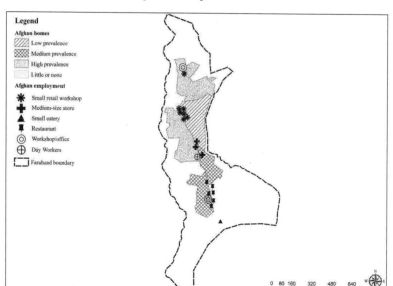

According to the Deputy Office for Social Affairs of the District 12 municipality, Harandi (Fig. 6.3), along with Emamzadeh Yahya, is host to the largest number of Afghan migrants. Despite the commercial nature of the districts, Harandi is a poverty-stricken neighborhood with high rates of drug addiction and crime. The 2011 census indicated a population of 22,808 for Harandi.[41] Furthermore, the municipality carried out a door-to-door survey of Harandi residents in 2015, which indicated a population of around 24,000 persons in 6,607 households—of which 1,069 households had Afghan nationality.[42]

District 20 is the southernmost zone of Tehran. It has five sub-districts inside Tehran's official municipal boundaries and two outside, with a total of twenty-two neighborhoods.[43] The district includes the old Silk Road town of Rey (ancient Ragae) with its historic sites. Land prices in the area are relatively low, which has translated into more affordable housing as well as the continued presence of manufacturing workshops, cement and other factories, and depots. There are also relatively significant agricultural lands on the fringes of Rey that provide some employment opportunities. According to Tehran's "Neighborhood Profiles," the city's District 20 had 324,372 inhabitants in 2008, of whom 32,204 persons were migrants from outside the country.[44] Yet,

Figure 6.3: Map of Harandi

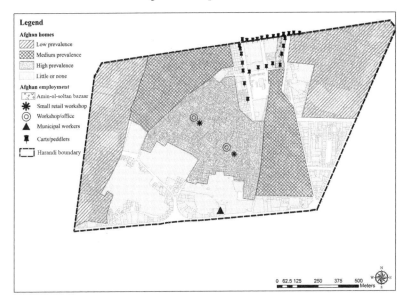

Figure 6.4: Map of Aminabad

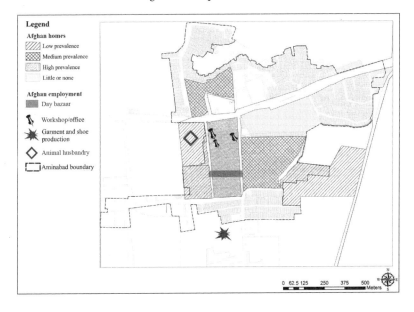

the 2011 census indicated 5,582 migrants from outside the country among a total population of 363,570 and 111,691 households recorded for District 20.[45] As a reduction in the number of migrants despite the growth of the district's total population is unlikely, the smaller census figure is possibly due to the undercounting of foreign nationals.

Based on interviews with officers of the District 20 municipality, Afghan migrants are scattered across various parts of the district but may be divided into two groups. Members of one group are engaged in construction work or agriculture on the urban fringes. Many of the second generation are attending institutions of higher education in Rey and other colleges and universities in Tehran. Yet, a smaller, poverty-stricken group of Afghan migrants lives and works where the brick furnaces exist (see Fig. 6.1). The study mainly focuses on the Aminabad neighborhood in sub-district 6 of Rey (see Figs 6.1 and 6.4) in light of the economic opportunities it has provided for migrants, but it also briefly addresses those families who work at the brick furnaces. As shown in Figure 6.1, Aminabad is in fact an urban village with a somewhat ambiguous municipal position. It comprises 700 hectares, of which 500 are used as agricultural land. The population of this neighborhood was 13,815 persons in 4,357 households in 2011.[46] Yet, according to a council assistant of the Aminabad village who was interviewed for this study,[47] around 12,000 Iranians and from 2,000 to 2,500 Afghans live in the neighborhood, while more recently the population of the latter group has decreased due to the sudden opening of opportunities to migrate to Europe.

Housing

After income and wealth, the length of stay in Iran, kinship relations, and occupation are the most important determinants of housing conditions for Afghans. In Farahzad, housing tenure insecurity along with the deterioration of the housing stock has created a set of push-and-pull factors. Many original residents have been replaced by Afghans, who are likely to find employment either within the neighborhood or nearby. Many of the older Afghan residents first found makeshift shelters in the valley in Farahzad before "gradually moving up the slope to reach higher grounds," in the words of one Afghan man, to homes in the middle of the neighborhood. Furthermore, those Afghans who have lived in Farahzad for a long time may have been able to buy homes using promissory notes. Rental prices in the poorer areas of Farahzad are relatively high given the housing conditions. Owners of these units make a handsome profit, yet they do not feel obliged to invest in property upkeep or renovation. Afghan migrants accept these prices since the houses may be close to their places of employment and may further allow them to bring an entire extended family under one roof without the usual disturbances or complaints. The average size of housing units for an entire family is in the range of 50 to 70 square meters.

Although Harandi has a central location in Tehran, it is also considered a high-risk neighborhood in terms of crime. As such, real estate prices are lower in Harandi in comparison with similar inner-city areas of Tehran—and there is no major real estate tenure issue in the neighborhood. Harandi's location, and low real estate prices, especially for rent in the older buildings, has attracted a large number of Afghans to the neighborhood. Some of them may have invested in the nearby Amin-ol-soltan bazaar. Many of the earlier residents of this neighborhood have relocated elsewhere in the city and have rented out their housing units to migrants. Although the area has been a target of municipal renewal activities through a dedicated facilitation office (which will be discussed later), and some of the dilapidated buildings have been replaced, few of the original Iranian residents have returned. Some Afghan migrants have been able to purchase homes in Harandi, either through promissory notes or under the name of an Iranian whom they trust, as revealed to us by the real estate agents active in the area. Younger migrants often rent homes using a one-time lump sum that will be returned to them once they move out.[48] The average size of homes is about 70 square meters. Older homes in the area typically have a number of rooms around a courtyard, which are rented separately to different households. Sometimes an Afghan individual rents the whole building and then rents out the rooms to separate families who likely do not possess proper residency permits. There are also some very small two-story buildings, and each story is rented to a separate household. Both types of housing tend to be in poor condition, and have shared toilets and kitchens.

Aminabad is designated as having village status. It is nevertheless an old neighborhood of Tehran with a rural fabric. The Afghan presence in the neighborhood may go back fifty years. This, in addition to the rural aspects and low real estate prices, continues to attract Afghan migrants. Some Afghans with construction skills have been able to acquire land—likely through the informal market—and build their own shelter. Others have purchased homes using promissory notes or under the names of Iranians whom they trust. The housing stock is generally dilapidated. The average size of homes occupied by Afghan families is around 50 square meters. Larger homes are usually occupied by more than one family. There are also two-story buildings, with one story used as the living space and the other turned into a home-based commercial workshop for the production of garments, shoes, or bags. There are other such workshops set up by Afghan migrants in other types of building.[49] Afghans may also reside in some of the newer apartment buildings. Rental price as an up-front full payment—which is preferred by Afghans—is around 600 million rials (US $20,000 in 2017).[50] As the up-front payment will be returned after move-out,[51] this is also a form of saving for Afghan families, who are officially unable to own any property. Many of these types of home are nevertheless occupied by an extended family or several families, which makes them affordable. It appears that, given the circumstances, landlords prefer Afghan residents to Iranians, especially since the former can be evicted rather easily.

Real estate agents in the neighborhoods under investigation have significant interaction with Afghans. In Aminabad, a few real estate agents even specialize in Afghan clients. Some Afghans lease homes in the name of these agents. For this reason, several agents have Afghans in their employment who also act as nodes of an information network in the Afghan community, providing guidance to the community in terms of housing. In all three neighborhoods, there are Afghans active in moving furniture, home repairs, and supplying basic home needs.

Education and social structures

Across the three neighborhoods, the number of college, university, and seminary students is small, and almost all of them are based in Farahzad and Aminabad. Furthermore, nominal human capital, as demonstrated by education, is generally quite low among the Afghan migrants in Tehran. For example, in Harandi, while children and teenagers have access to schooling, the older generation is mostly illiterate or barely literate. In Farahzad, there are a number of young Afghans raised in Iran who have received tertiary-level education. Some are involved in activities such as teaching or working for NGOs or other service providers. Aminabad appears to have the best-educated youth in comparison with the other two neighborhoods.

There are a number of Afghans active in the cultural arena, especially in Rey. Most appear to be Hazara or other Persian-speaking Shiʿa, while very few are Sunni Pashtuns. It appears that traditional mores persist among the latter while the former have encountered more opportunities to enter modern life, including modern cultural activities. In fact, many among the second- and third-generation Hazaras or other Shi'a believe that they must educate themselves in order to advance in Iranian society. Many of them must endure hardship to study, although they are often too proud to perform hard manual labor. They may, however, work in shops as apprentices or as tailors. Some of these educated individuals have initiated various cultural activities. For example, the Afghanistan Literature House was established by a few younger individuals who were friends and classmates in childhood. Another example is the work of some Afghan students who have created educational centers, operating since 2000, for Afghan children who have not attended school. There is little support for these cultural or educational initiatives from the public sector, according to our interviews with those involved in these activities. Some have tried in the past to create cultural bridges between Iran and Afghanistan, but this has proven difficult due to the situation in Afghanistan. There have been a few media-related successes in the form of programs produced in Iran and broadcast in Afghanistan. According to our interviewees, the presence of a large number of Afghans in Iran means that there are also jobs for educated Afghans—including in education and media.

Low levels of human capital among Afghans appear to be associated with low educational attainments in Afghanistan, the average nominal human capital of the population in each respective neighborhood in Tehran, and restrictions placed on the education of Afghans in Iran in earlier times—some of which most likely continue in an unofficial manner to this day. Another inhibiting factor seems to concern religious denomination, with Sunni Afghans possibly being concerned about the Shi'a-dominated curricula in primary and secondary schools. This is likely why the Hazaras seem to enjoy higher levels of education compared with other Afghans. While, in theory, the restrictions placed on the education of Afghan children before 2014 have been removed, available curriculum choices and cost still limit educational access for Afghans. Furthermore, because of the earlier restrictions, many Afghan children had faced major difficulties with enrollment; their meager financial situation, they had to enter the job market and were never able to continue their education despite the eventual removal of restrictions. In Harandi, notwithstanding the scarcity of Afghans with tertiary education, the presence of NGOs has had a positive impact on improving literacy and basic education. That said, many of the younger Afghans recently arriving in Iran may be illiterate or at very low literacy levels.

Legal restrictions on some aspects of Afghan life in Iran have given impetus to the formation of enclaves in these three neighborhoods. This does not mean that social networks are of the same type across or within the three neighborhoods. Notwithstanding the prevalence of single Afghan men, the mean household size for Afghans appears to be larger than that of Iranians. Average age for a first marriage is also low among the studied communities— fifteen for women, and twenty for men. Endogamy is prevalent within Afghan ethnic groups, especially among newcomers to Iran. Those who have stayed in Iran longer may marry outside their ethnic groups but still within the Afghan community as the first priority, and religious denomination as the second priority. Thus it is more common to observe Shiʿa–Sunni couples than mixed couples in terms of nationality. Furthermore, our interviews with the younger, second-generation Afghans reveal that they are open to marriage outside of their communities, and there are indeed some marriages between Afghans and Iranians. Most of these appear to be between Afghan men needing residency permits and Iranian women who may be from extremely poor and/or vulnerable backgrounds. Love affairs between Afghans and Iranians seem to be discouraged by both communities. Children of mixed marriages—specifically between Afghan men and Iranian women—may be denied Iranian citizenship, although this is now being addressed by the government.[52] Marriage customs mimic those of Afghanistan but are also influenced by those in Iran. More affluent families look for eligible brides for their sons from an early age, among families with similar backgrounds. Boys and girls are aware of these preliminary arrangements, although decisions will be finalized when they grow up. Marriages within the extended family are therefore quite prevalent. This also means that many marriages occur between those residing in Iran and those living in Afghanistan, which results in further migrations to Iran. Divorces are rare and remarriage for widows is not common, even when the woman is quite young, if she has children. There are some cases of polygyny in the Afghan communities across the three neighborhoods.

In Farahzad, there are significant interactions between Afghans and Iranians, facilitated especially through the local economy and employment in the neighborhood's retail businesses. Based on these interactions, mutual trust has developed such that Afghans may hold some of their assets under the name of Iranians. Conversely, there are local Afghans who are highly trusted by Iranian residents and with whom they have strong employment or familial interactions. Yet, Afghan women interviewed in Farahzad told us that they were restricted in their interactions by cultural norms dictated by men and elders. Yet, overall, it appears that Afghan residents of Farahzad are satisfied with social interactions in their lives. According to a sixty-year-old, long-time resident of Farahzad: "the nice thing is that any step I take I must say hi to lots of people. I feel I am in Afghanistan. Everybody here knows me."

Social relationships are not as strong in Harandi, although migrants have interactions with providers of Afghan ethnic services in the neighborhood through which they also interact with others. In fact, Harandi is highly heterogeneous in terms of the ethnic origins of Afghans. Because of this, Afghans tend to interact mostly with their own extended families. Some of the interviewed residents in Harandi—especially among Hazaras—stated they were not happy with their children's friendships with Iranians. They thought they would be discriminated against now or later because of their different Inner Asian features. There is some anecdotal evidence for this: football teams tend to be mixed Iranian and Afghan for younger children but not for teenagers and older youth. Also, one Afghan retailer in Harandi complained of bullying of Afghan children in school by Iranian kids. That said, some Afghans interviewed in Harandi stressed the importance of neighborhood relationships, which was not the case in other areas. Afghan families with relatives in the neighborhood, and in other areas of the city, have significant interactions with them and host gatherings for each other in turn. These types of interaction with non-family members are uncommon. However, religious gatherings—especially for the Shi'a Hazaras in Harandi—may be held with non-family members.

Aminabad is not much different from the other two neighborhoods in terms of community acceptance of Afghans. At the same time, according to some Afghan residents, they have felt some hostility from Iranian residents who may think of them as interlopers. Yet, interactions through employment in the area have also created friendships among younger Afghans and Iranians. Some Afghan teenagers interviewed said that they are not looked down upon in the neighborhood, but that is something that they feel is prevalent in other areas. However, the participation of Afghan community members in various affairs of the neighborhood does not appear to be well received by Iranian residents. For example, Shi'a Afghans stated that their desire to volunteer in organizing Shi'a ceremonies was met with resistance from Iranian community members. At present, they can only be present at such ceremonies. This situation is similarly observed at women's cultural events. According to one Afghan woman, a socially active Aminabad resident, they can attend such events, but the overall atmosphere dissuades them from repeat visits. Furthermore, while some Iranian women interviewed pointed to beauty salons as places where Afghan women like to work and where Iranian women are receptive toward them, Afghans in general think that Iranians do not want Afghans to establish any businesses in the area. Many Iranian residents disagree with this perspective. According to one resident:

> I had someone working for me in the beauty salon who returned to Afghanistan. There was no work for her husband. They stayed there for one year and faced poverty and unsanitary conditions. They came back to Iran after losing everything to start from zero. The bazaar businessmen took them in and helped them to rent a home.

Overall, despite some resistance or envy on the part of Iranian residents toward the activities of Afghans in public places—including sports facilities—the latter group is slowly gaining access to such spaces. For example, the neighborhood park in Aminabad is an important space that connects Afghan residents.

Across the three neighborhoods, Afghans with a longer record of residence in Iran have *amayesh* cards, more recent migrants have visas, while those who work in agriculture or animal husbandry and live as single men may lack documentation. Yet, even those with legal documents do not feel completely secure. For one thing, they have to renew them every year. Furthermore, an Afghan migrant must have an Iranian partner in order to open a bank account or start a business, even if they hold the proper residency documents. Another restriction is placed on Afghans' travel and place of residence, with some areas considered off limits.

Yet, migrants in each of the neighborhoods under investigation exhibit a degree of attachment to their current places of residence. Most do not desire to change location, especially since they are familiar with the place. Naturally, the sense of attachment is stronger among those who were born or grew up in a neighborhood, while many Afghan children are second- or third-generation migrants. Furthermore, few people desire to return to Afghanistan, especially given the lack of security there, though older people have a sense of nostalgia for the country. Overall, migrants prefer to stay in Tehran, as the city is quite cosmopolitan and multicultural and they easily blend in. Some say that their situation is not unlike the Iranian migrants that have come to Tehran from the rest of the country. It is not possible to distinguish Afghans and Iranians (except by their accents) in terms of appearance. Even Hazaras, who may have more Inner Asian features, can mostly blend in, since Iran is an ethnically diverse country.

Subsistence, employment, and business activities

Afghan families may have additional expenses in comparison to Iranian families. They have to pay fees as foreign residents, and, furthermore, they must pay in full for many of the services that are subsidized or free for Iranians. For example, Afghans pay tuition to attend public universities in Iran, which are free for Iranians in most cases; health services are the same. Afghans do not receive the government cash transfers that every Iranian has been receiving over the past few years. They must also renew their driver's licenses every year, for which they pay fees. Those Afghans who have lived in Iran for a long time have found ways to manage these expenses. There are many families with more than one breadwinner, many single Afghans live in groups, and those who work for municipal contractors may get to sleep in allotted dormitories (see below). While there certainly are some rich Afghans living in Tehran—including some traders and businessmen—finding them was not easy, especially since this study's focus was on specific areas. Findings in this section are therefore in reference to average Afghan migrants in the three neighborhoods.

Employment permit cards given to Afghans are not indicative of their skills or actual occupations. The reason has to do with the limited number of occupations allowed; some listed on the permits no longer even exist (e.g., chimney cleaner). Many people we encountered were ashamed to show their cards. Notwithstanding, some of the key occupations that Afghans hold are similar across the three neighborhoods, including construction, municipal services, and other manual labor. Unskilled Afghan workers earn wages in the range of 10–15 million rials per month and skilled technicians earn about 20–30 million (as of 2017). Until a few years ago, most construction workers active in Tehran's Districts 2 and 3 were Afghan migrants, and they often lived in Farahzad. There was a construction boom at the time, which meant that their wages were similar to those of Iranian workers. Their hard work was in demand and most employers preferred to hire them, especially as they required almost no additional expenses, even for injuries. Construction was no longer booming in 2017, but one could still see seventy persons daily at Farahzad Circle waiting to be picked for construction or other labor-intensive jobs. Similarly, Moallem Square in Aminabad receives around 150 Afghan— but also some Iranian—day workers seeking jobs in construction. Those who are not picked up by midday may try to make money by offering to move home furniture. Construction workers make 500,000 rials for a day's work, but it is not always available. Relationships between Afghan and Iranian construction day workers are not always amicable, especially since the latter group is likely to think that Afghans bring down wages.

Afghan migrant workers provide various municipal services, especially in gardening, street cleaning, and garbage recycling, which are outsourced to contractors who are likely to be former municipal employees. Unlike Iranian workers who are hired on short-term contracts in accordance with the Iranian Labor Code, Afghans usually work for fixed wages based on a certain amount of work rather than by the hour—and without any other benefits. Since the municipality tends to meet its financial obligations irregularly, contractors prefer to hire Afghans who are willing to cope with this situation, while they are also more readily available, do not request vacation time, and are willing to do any job. Garbage recycling is an important occupation associated with the municipality in which Afghans are engaged (discussed below). Yet, the municipality in District 20 allows a contractor to only hire Afghans for up to 30 percent of its workforce, which must be reduced over time. Workers for contractors of District 2 are mostly single young men and sometimes teenagers—about seventy to eighty in each sub-district—who can sleep in dormitories supplied by the municipality. A similar situation prevails in District 12, including in Harandi, which has about eighty such persons. Workers often share the same area of origin in Afghanistan—mostly from Badakhshan villages—which is reflective of migration decisions made at the clan level rather than individually. Clan structures endure in Iran, as some influential and trusted individuals manage the travel of other clan members in terms of finances and illegal border crossing. Compensation comes from the wages the migrants receive. The influential clan members work in association with heads of every sector of work. They further maintain discipline among the workers by devising regulations and procedures, including on workers' relations, tidiness of dormitories, food programs, relations with Iranian supervisors, remittances, as well as managing logistics for individual or group returns to Afghanistan together with their replacements, and in other activities.

Each of the three neighborhoods further provides unique work opportunities for Afghan migrants. Farahzad and Aminabad offer work in the groves and gardens and in other agricultural activities. While the owners of Farahzad's agricultural lands, which are rapidly being broken up and lost to other land uses, are the original natives, they are not likely to reside in the neighborhood any longer. These employers prefer Afghan laborers who are mostly single and sleep in the gardens at night; few Iranians are enthusiastic about this type of work. Afghans have worked on agricultural lands and in animal husbandry in Aminabad over the past forty years. The more successful workers have entered into partnerships with Iranian landowners, where they receive half of the harvest in exchange for their labor. They may in turn hire day workers, employ workers on a monthly basis, or recruit their relatives who come to Iran on a seasonal basis. Many of the workers in agriculture and animal husbandry in Aminabad are single men from the agricultural areas of Herat who are likely to domicile at the workplace. Some have improved their skills over the years in relation to the use of more advanced machinery and technology. Afghans raised in Iran are often unenthusiastic about agricultural work; therefore employers prefer to hire newcomers from Afghanistan.

Some migrants have been successful at starting retail businesses. In Farahzad, several of the retail stores on the main commercial street, Farahzadi Avenue, are run either by Afghans or in partnership with Afghans, including the corner supermarket.[53] There are a number of female-operated dress shops located on Emamzadeh Davud St, half of which are managed or rented by Afghans. A few sell Afghan clothing items and accessories imported to Iran by Afghans holding import permits. The customers are mostly Afghans but there are also a few Kurds, who come here because the products are cheaper. The female-operated stores in Farahzad also act as nodes for the Afghan women's local network. Furthermore, some of the women managing or working in these stores were previously street vendors who saved enough money to acquire a retail store. Stores selling shoes and bags or kitchenware—some made in Afghanistan—as well as shoe-repair shops, are mostly run by Afghan men, who may also sell chewing tobacco on the side. Some stores in Farahzad require special skills—e.g., motorcycle repair, carpentry, and cabinet making. The few run by Afghans are often family businesses and are likely to face additional costs compared with similar Iranian-run businesses—especially as related to permits and licensing. For Afghans, running food-related businesses requires Iranian partners, who may not do any of the actual work. Farahzad is a recreational area of Tehran kown for its garden restaurants. A significant number of Afghans work in these restaurants at various levels, including as managers. Some are likely to have been established by Afghans or in partnership with Iranians. However, almost all hide their Afghan ownership or management, as these job categories are not officially recognized for migrants.

In Harandi, the Mowlavi bazaar and especially the Amin-ol-soltan bazaar (increasingly known as the Afghan bazaar) are important for Afghan employment. Many of the basic laborers and street vendors do not have identity documents appropriate for staying in Iran. They must secure the trust of the retail businesses where they work, often through introduction by others. Furthermore, the few Afghan-run retail stores (outside the main bazaars) in Harandi sell fruits and vegetables. A number of Afghans in Harandi run shoe-repair and second hand shoe businesses. In the Harandi fabric bazaar, many of the apprentices are also Afghan. Many shopkeepers in the Amin-ol-soltan bazaar are from Kabul, mostly Pashtuns; some of the business partnerships are with Iranians. In other cases, the store is rented from an Iranian. Their customers are both Afghan and Iranian. Afghans have slowly built these businesses—most having started in other activities—by first becoming shop apprentices and saving enough money to share or start a business. Some of the shops exhibit the Afghan flag. Many of the apprentice workers are young and some have recently come to Iran. Children as young as eight or nine are in Iran with their families and they are also working.

Apprentice workers make around 10 million rials per month (about US $330 in 2017), sometimes plus tips, but with no health insurance or work protection. Young Afghans working in the bazaar are likely to have completed primary education and then joined the workforce at a young age. Iranian employers prefer Afghan apprentices since they are perceived as more hard-working and with fewer expenses. Furthermore, since a large number of customers are Afghan, it makes sense to have Afghan workers in the shops. Afghan merchandise is brought to the bazaar by small-time Afghan businessmen who carry 30 kilos of merchandise each trip from Afghanistan. These include dresses, handkerchiefs, and prayer hats—which are also bought by Iranians—as well as certain shoes that are sold along with Iranian and Chinese items. Some decorative items and suitcases are also sold to mostly Afghan customers. Other items of interest to Afghans are sold next to the mosque. These items are sometimes purchased by those who will carry them to other parts of Iran to be resold. Those working in the mosque are also Afghan. One interesting item sold in the bazaar, apparently made by Afghan women in Afghanistan, is a vest with four pockets. Single Afghan men who sleep in dormitories or in temporary places buy these to keep their items next to them at all times. Yet, some of those wearing the vest in the bazaar are informal money exchangers.

Furthermore, there are a few stores that sell traditional Afghan outfits and similar Pakistani and Indian items. Their customers are not only Afghan but also Iranian—including some Lors, Kurds, Baluch, and Khuzestanis, as well as those belonging to the artistic community in Tehran. One of the stores also makes custom cloth, with claims to have also produced this specialized fabric for TV programs. Yet, most of the outfits or at least the fabrics are imported from Afghanistan by Afghan traders. They may be worn as regular outfits but are more likely worn on special occasions such as weddings, according to a shopkeeper. The Amin-ol-soltan bazaar seems to be among the few places in which work and social interactions among Iranians and Afghans and various ethnic groups within the Afghan community are relatively common. This is apparent in the presence of both Shi'a and Sunni Afghans at the mosque as well as their contributions to its upkeep.

Aminabad is more a locus of production by Afghans, although it also has a Monday bazaar in which Afghans are highly active. In Aminabad workshops, which employ both men and women, Afghans produce dresses as well as men's suits, bags, and crystal ware. Many of these businesses are managed or owned by Afghans and are usually acquired after years of work and/or in partnership with Iranians. Producing crystal ware is a difficult job as it involves working with a furnace. As a result, few Iranians work in the workshops. They employ mostly young Afghan men, many of whom are related. The products are sold across Iran and are even exported to Afghanistan and Iraq. This line of business is relatively profitable, although Afghans who run these workshops are sometimes harassed by the Iranian authorities, which is dealt with through under-the-table payments.

Producing menswear—suits in particular—is an important occupation for some Afghans in Aminabad. The workshops are mostly managed by Afghans, who may be Hazara, Tajik, or Pashtun. Afghans must work in partnership with Iranians, as a work permit alone is not sufficient for opening a workshop. Within each workshop, the workers are usually related. Women and men work side by side in these workshops. Some workshops are based in an apartment or in the basement of a building. They are of differing sizes: the larger ones are about 300 square meters and can have around fifty sewing machines, although during our visit only a few people were working at any time. The reason was a general decline in the market as well as a recent fire that destroyed one of the most important buildings in Tehran—Plasco[54]—that bought their products. Retail and wholesale stores in the Plasco building used to give the clothing workshops large orders. These workshops receive checks when they sell their clothing and bags to wholesalers.

Many partnerships between Afghans and Iranians establishing and running workshops operate in this way: material and equipment are provided by Iranians and the work is done by Afghans. The former appear to get a larger percentage of the profits. Yet, according to many Afghans working in or running workshops, it is better to work with Iranians since it is easier to get paid. An interviewee who previously ran a menswear workshop compared his situation to that of an Iranian worker who started in the business at the same time. The Iranian is now a rich businessman, in contrast to the meager income the Afghan earned. Some tailors claimed that their own designs are copied by others, but there is no recourse. Others indicated that their suits are sold in Afghanistan.

The Monday bazaar in Aminabad is an important place for Afghans. Many of the sellers are Afghans, who may be from the neighborhood, from elsewhere in Tehran, or even from nearby towns such as Varamin. Some are traders from Afghanistan who sell their products in the day markets in various neighborhoods and purchase other products to take back to Afghanistan. There are those who offer products that they produce themselves, such as farm produce or plastic items made from recycled materials. Various items are sold in the market to Iranian and Afghan customers. There are a few sellers who offer Afghan items such as Afghan cloths.

There are some differences among the three neighborhoods under investigation. According to residents of Farahzad, more migrants have been able to start their own businesses in the neighborhood over the last decade, especially those who have been there for longer periods. Given the high expense and risks of running retail businesses that Afghans experience, their earnings do not amount to much more than those who work for others. Business owners do enjoy a sense of prestige and independence, however. It should also be noted that living expenses in Farahzad are higher compared with the other two neighborhoods, which means that residents must have access to more stable and higher-paying jobs. In Harandi, most occupations are unskilled, earning workers no more than 10–15 million rials per month. Aminabad is similar to Farahzad in terms of being more conducive than Harandi to the development of Afghan businesses.

Brick furnaces of Mahmudabad

Around thirteen brick-manufacturing furnaces are located on the outskirts of Aminabad in an area referred to as Mahmudabad. Each is worked by ten to thirty households who live there mostly from April to November. The workers come from Mashhad, Tabriz, and from various places in Afghanistan. The latter group, in contrast to the Iranians, tends to remain in the same place year-round—comprising around two-thirds of the total population. Households associated with one of the furnaces were approached for this study. Their living spaces—comprised of one mostly makeshift room for each average-size household—are right next to the furnaces. Shared toilets are in the yard, while potable water is accessible from a tank that must be refilled weekly. Most families are young and are likely to have three children or more. It is a very long walk to the school, where girls and boys, who must also work on the side, mostly complete the ninth grade before becoming full-time workers.

Most of the residents have minimal interaction outside of Mahmudabad, except for visiting health centers in Rey; they have little knowledge of the city of Tehran. The reason is that their work hours—performed by men and women, children, and the elderly—are between early morning and 6:00 p.m. They get paid by the number of bricks they make—300,000 rials (around US $10 in 2017) for 1,000 bricks. Depending on the number of working members, families may make anywhere between 800 and 3,000 bricks per day during the furnaces' working months, some of which must be saved for other times. Unlike their Iranian counterparts, Afghan workers in the furnaces do not have health insurance. Considering the working conditions, health issues are common, especially for females, and with their treatments come cost burdens. During the months when the furnaces are inactive, family members may find jobs in agriculture or perform other labor-intensive, home-based work— for example, shelling pistachios—with extremely low remuneration. There are plans to establish an industrial estate in the area of the brick furnaces in Mahmudabad, and apparently the land has already been sold for this purpose. This means that the Iranian and Afghan families working in the furnaces will lose their jobs and residences in the near future.

Afghan street children and those engaged in Tehran's solid waste recycling

Many Afghan residents of Tehran are among the lowest-income groups in the city. Because of this general poverty, a disproportionate share of child labor and street children is associated with them. For example, in a report on the issue by the Imam Ali Society—a national NGO that provides extensive activities in the poorer neighborhoods of Tehran—58 percent of the pubescent children, adolescents, and teenagers they served were Afghan.[55] Additionally, more than 90 percent of those working for solid waste recycling contractors or engaged in informal recycling in Tehran are Afghan. Every district has several places where plastics and metals are transferred from dumpsters for eventual recycling. The formal part of this recycling operation is performed by trucks and motorized tricycles, whose drivers may be Iranian or Afghan. Alongside the formal recycling activities, there is also an informal operation, perhaps employing more people, which sells collected materials to the stations. A large number of the workforce collecting items from dumpsters by hand are children and teenagers. Apparently, many come from the Herat region and are without immediate family members. They are likely living collectively in appalling conditions. Their earnings are proportional to the amount of material they collect. Since these informal operations are illegal, their collected items can be taken from them if they are caught by inspectors. Given their circumstances and ambiguous domicile, the few NGOs providing services to working and street children are unable to do much for them. Overall, the recycling operations, which are contracted out by the municipality, are highly ambiguous with regard to Afghan labor conditions.

Services provided to Afghans by the municipality, NGOs, and neighborhood centers

Master plans or other spatial plans prepared for Tehran, its metropolitan region, or the province have little to say about Afghan or other migrants. Migrants. and more specifically Afghans, are not considered in any of the detailed plans prepared for the three districts, and are only briefly mentioned in some municipal documents prepared for the three neighborhoods. As an example of the latter, the "Sustainable Development Vision Document of Harandi Neighborhood"only touches upon the presence of Afghans when discussing one of the NGOs active in the neighborhood.[56] In fact, the only urban regulation directly affecting migrants in Tehran has to do with special fees to be collected from Afghan nationals when they apply for renewal of their residency cards and employment permits.[57]

In our interviews with Tehran municipal councilors, they stressed that all residents of the city are considered citizens, no matter their ethnic or religious background. At the same time, they appeared quite unfamiliar with the challenges faced by the city's Afghan residents. This has much to do with the fact that Afghan residents are not represented anywhere in the municipal management. Tehran's neighborhoods, including Farahzad, Harandi, and Aminabad, also have municipal council assistants (*showrayari* in urban areas; and *dehyari* in Aminabad, which is designated as a village) together with neighborhood centers (*sara-ye mahalleh*), where they meet, and which usually have a social officer. The main interaction between local council assistants and Afghan residents is for issuing residency cards, for which the latter must verify residence in the neighborhood. The neighborhood centers also provide cultural and social services, some of which are of interest to Afghans. In Aminabad, remedial educational classes for students have attracted a large number of Afghan children. In Harandi, more than 80 percent of the beneficiaries are Afghans, who access services such as religious classes, personal and psychological counseling, literacy classes, remedial classes for primary-level students, and workshops on drug abuse. English-language and computer classes, which are attractive to a large number of people, entail a tuition fee that is likely beyond the means of many Afghans. The kindergarten is more readily accessible to Afghan families, whose children make up about half of the beneficiaries. In Farahzad, Afghan women especially benefit from the life and skills training classes that are free. Other educational classes that require a fee have not been sustainable. The kindergarten, which is attended by a few Afghan children, also charges a tuition fee.

Harandi and Farahzad have urban renewal (regeneration) facilitation offices for the purpose of renovating the neighborhoods' dilapidated building stock using a combination of financial incentives and social activities; Aminabad does not have this. As the facilitation offices mostly deal with home/property owners, their interactions with Afghan residents—who are either renters or lack official titles in their name—are minimal. While these offices have little to offer renters, including Afghans—who could get pushed out as a result of gentrification—they may see the dynamics of the Afghan presence as a hurdle to renewal. For example, in Farahzad, because the deteriorated buildings can be rented at relatively high prices to Afghans by owners living outside the neighborhood, enthusiasm for renovation is dampened. Yet, in areas where renewal efforts face major hurdles due to tenure ambiguities, the Farahzad facilitation office has opted to concentrate more on community enabling activities by forming work groups. One for teenagers is focused on environmental issues in the neighborhood and has mostly Afghan members. Another, also focusing on environmental issues, has both Afghan and Iranian members, but the two are not integrated and have quite separate activities. The activities of a third work group, which is supported by the municipality and is mostly composed of Afghan women, concern the organization of a local self-employment bazaar. A fourth work group, involving interaction with the municipality in preparing a local development document, does not include

Afghans. This is despite the significant presence of Afghans in Farahzad, who certainly have a sense of attachment to the neighborhood.

Several NGOs are active in Harandi and Farahzad and provide a number of services to Afghan migrants. Harandi appears to have the largest number of NGOs of any neighborhood of Tehran—around sixteen, plus others that provide services on an occasional basis. They work on child welfare, addiction, empowerment, and local development. Based on our interviews, Afghans comprise a significant target group for these NGOs, especially since these migrants lack full access to many of the urban and social services available to Iranian citizens. The NGOs provide training and education, basic necessities for families such as healthcare, clothing, household appliances, and sometimes cash transfers, and also drug rehabilitation. Except for the last service, most of their beneficiaries are Afghans, who may access the services of more than one NGO. Few Afghans, other than those involved in cleaning or cooking, work in these NGOs. A large number of Afghan children and adolescents receive educational services through these organizations. Farahzad has about four NGOs and some employ Afghan personnel including trainers. One of these has been especially active in the past five years in providing literacy and basic education classes for Afghan children. This NGO also employs trainers, some of whom are Afghan women, to provide literacy classes and practical training to Afghan women. The women are engaged in producing goods that are paid for and marketed by the NGO. Another NGO has worked in Farahzad for close to fifteen years, concentrating its activities on working with street children. This NGO also employs a number of Afghan women, and the children served are mostly Afghans. Furthermore, skills training is provided to their mothers, with the hope that they can eventually engage in income-generating activities.

Conclusion

Due to political and economic turmoil in Afghanistan, a large number of Afghan migrants have resettled across Iran's urban areas over the past four decades. Yet, their migration has significant precedence given the two countries' historical ties. This study has probed various livelihood aspects of Afghan migrant communities in Tehran. The metropolis has rapidly grown over the last decades—especially due to the influx of migrants, of which Afghans are but one group. Like other migrants, Afghans have been attracted to Tehran in light of the diverse economic opportunities it offers, as well as its cultural diversity. This is despite its high expenses, especially associated with housing, with which they are able to cope by finding shelter in low-income neighborhoods with significant stocks of older buildings affordable to migrants. This study's three neighborhood case studies have allowed an investigation of how urban spaces are perceived and used by Afghan migrants in Tehran, and how these spaces are transformed by their presence and influence.

Afghan migrants in the three neighborhoods mostly hail from traditional backgrounds in rural areas or small towns in Afghanistan. Like other migrants from small towns and rural areas in Iran, they tend to rely on traditional social networks for support. Given this and their different legal status in comparison with domestic migrants in Tehran, their presence in the studied neighborhoods is often in the form of enclaves—mostly based on their various ethnic origins in Afghanistan. It nevertheless appears that interethnic relations among Afghans have expanded, and in many cases Iranians and Afghans have developed strong business relations. In fact, many Afghans have developed feelings of attachment to their current neighborhoods, especially since a large number of them are second or third generation. Yet, they are likely to also feel nostalgic about Afghanistan, as they are routinely reminded of their differences from other migrants in the city. As many Afghan families strive to maintain their culture, they are also heavily influenced by their surroundings. Their religious denomination and specific ethnic background in Afghanistan may impact the extent of these influences and their adaptation to the host communities. Furthermore, as Tehran is quite diverse, some Afghans can conceal their identities to overcome some of the legal restrictions placed on them, or just blend in.

Although human capital levels are generally low among Afghans in the studied neighborhoods—which is both a reflection of their starting point at migration, and the average level of human capital of their current communities—there has been significant mobility among second- and third-generation Afghans in terms of education. Their occupational mobility, however, is restricted, partly due to the national regulatory framework to which they are subjected. This, together with the low or extremely low levels of human capital associated with the earlier generation, as well as for the most recent migrants, means most Afghans hold manual jobs. Yet, some have succeeded in starting their own businesses, especially since each of the neighborhoods also offers unique occupational opportunities: in Farahzad, there are restaurants and small stores; in Harandi, there are large bazaars; and in Aminabad there are small manufacturing workshops and agricultural activities. Many of the other manual-type occupations are, however, common across the three neighbor-hoods, including construction and municipal services. Afghan labor in Tehran is quite important for both activities, as much of the construction as well as the gardening, street cleaning, and garbage recycling for the municipality is performed by them. Furthermore, some Afghans fall within the poorest income strata in Tehran, which means that they are over-represented among street children, families working the brick furnaces, and those working in informal garbage recycling.

Overall, the study of the three neighborhoods shows that Afghan migrants are undergoing informal integration in the city. This is evident across many of the integration domains mentioned in the literature, including housing, employment, and social relations as well as language and culture. Despite this, the municipal management in Tehran does not have any significant interaction with Afghans as residents of the city. It is true that Afghan families have been able to receive some services from NGOs active in their neighborhoods and through the neighborhood centers. However, urban plans for Tehran, including those prepared specifically for the three neighborhoods, pay little attention to the significant presence of migrants, whether internal or from Afghanistan. Part of the reason for this is the generally non-participatory nature of urban planning and management in Iran. Yet, Afghans are more affected by this since they cannot access, or they incur higher costs for, many of the services received by Iranians. More importantly, their presence in the city is generally perceived as temporary. Some of these challenges have to do with national-level regulation, including the residency registration and work permit processes of Afghans, and restrictions placed on their mobility inside the country. That said, there have been some positive developments concern-ing Afghans in Iran, especially the removal of legal and financial barriers to their primary and secondary education. There have also been limited efforts to give nationality to children of mixed marriages (with Afghan fathers) as well as to those recruited in military operations abroad.[58] Most Afghans in Iran, however, cannot benefit from these initiatives, and their presence on the fringes of Iranian urban society remains insecure. Furthermore, Afghans are not only affected by regulations limiting their employment opportunities but they also face significant hurdles in conducting business, which seriously ham-pers their entrepreneurial activities.

All these challenges have long-term effects on Afghans, most of whom will continue to live in the city or in Iran, which will have significant implications not only for the migrants but also their host communities. It is easy to come up with a strong argument claiming that the restrictions placed on Afghan lives in Iran and Tehran are in fact counterproductive. The government and the municipality allocate significant resources to alleviate poverty and reduce inequality, which are inherent in the development dynamics of the city. Creating obstacles to the upward mobility of one group of residents only makes the job much more complicated. There is thus a need for a paradigm shift with regard to Afghan residents. The first step in this direction would be to accept the reality of their permanent presence in Iran and in the city of Tehran. Two follow-up steps would involve removing the restrictions placed on the upward economic mobility of Afghans and rethinking Iran's nationality laws. The latter can be reformed to grant citizenship to those meeting certain eligibility criteria that are aligned with other policies of the Iranian government, including those concerning additional migration from Afghanistan, border and internal security, and relations between Afghanistan and Iran.

Yet, to fully realize the potential of Afghan migrants in Tehran, it is necessary that they are embraced as fully-fledged residents by urban planning and management systems—that is, to aim for their formal integration. Some of the initiatives to ensure this, which are endorsed by international organizations and advocates, were reviewed at the beginning of this chapter. For Tehran, the city can at minimum include a rights-based, inclusionary approach to Afghan migrants and fight against any form of discrimination against them. It can acknowledge the presence of Afghan migrants in urban planning and in the provision of urban services and infrastructure, and ensure their access to income-generating—including entrepreneurial—activities. To achieve such aims, there is a great need for a cultural and media campaign that promotes the integration of Afghan migrants in urban society. There are some positive signs in this direction. For example, the television program *Vatandar* not only deals with the lives of Afghans in Iran but also introduces success stories among them. Yet, there is a long way to go.

APPENDIX

List of study interviews

In Farahzad, the following interviews were conducted: forty individual interviews with Afghan retail businesses, Afghan men/women/youth, and Afghan construction workers; seventeen interviews with Iranian residents and retail businesses; one group interview with Afghan women together with the office manager at Mehr NGO; and one interview at Ruyesh-Nahal NGO with its manager and its Afghan female officer. In Harandi, the following interviews were conducted: thirty-eight individual interviews with Afghan businesses at Amin-ol-soltan bazaar and other Afghan businesses in the neighborhood as well as porters and street vendors; two group interviews with women and teenage girls; seven interviews with Iranian residents and retail businesses; one interview with each of the five major NGOs active in the area. The activities in Aminabad included: thirty-one individual interviews with Afghan residents and retail businesses together with thirteen interviews with Iranian residents and retail businesses. Further interviews were conducted with urban service providers and twelve municipal cleaners—for a total of twenty-one interviews—and Afghans working the brick furnaces in the vicinity of Aminabad. Also, a group interview was conducted with Afghan cultural activists in Tehran. Other than these, interviews were conducted with Tehran's municipal council representatives, municipal council assistants, and municipal officers.

7

LIVING WITH UNCERTAINTY

THE STORY OF SUB-SAHARAN MIGRANTS IN LIBYA AND TUNISIA

Mustafa O. Attir, Mohamed Jouili, and *Ricardo René Larémont*

Introduction

Migration across the Sahara from the Sahel to North Africa is a longstanding practice. Its origins can be traced to 1500 BCE when three routes were established to traffic goods and people: the Ghadames road (from Gao in present Mali to Ghat, Ghadames, and Tripoli); the Garamantean road (from Kano and Lake Chad to Bilma, Murzuk, and then Tripoli); and the Oualata road (from what is now Mali to Sijilmasa in Morocco—see Fig. 7.1).[1] Traffic increased significantly from the eighth to the seventeenth century CE when the principal commodities in trade were salt, gold, and slaves.

These trading routes have continued to be used in the twentieth and twenty-first centuries, with people and commodities in continuous movement from the south to the north and vice versa. These contemporary patterns of mobility are examined in this chapter. Migrants are arriving in Libya and

Figure 7.1: Map of trans-Saharan trade routes: medieval era

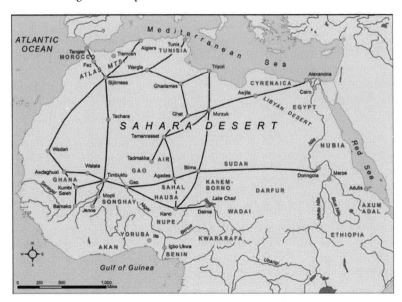

Source: map created by the authors.

Tunisia, for the most part, from the neighboring countries of Egypt, Sudan, Chad, Niger, Burkina Faso, Mali, Côte d'Ivoire, and Cameroon. Migrants from these countries frequently settle in Libya or Tunisia, or are engaged in circular migration between Libya and Tunisia and their home countries.

Since the 2011 Arab revolts, there has been a considerable increase in the number of migrants moving from North Africa to Europe. Media accounts and academic articles have focused primarily on trans-Mediterranean flows of migration and tend to view North African countries as mostly transit states through which migrants pass on their way to Europe. These analyses ignore one of the more important emerging mobility trends that increasingly places North Africa as a migratory destination rather than a location that migrants use to continue onward to Europe. Our research demonstrates that in the case of Libya there is a historical precedent of sub-Saharan African labor migration, primarily linked to jobs in the petroleum industry and construction. Sub-Saharan labor migration is also occurring in Tunisia but is more recent. Sub-Saharan Africans began arriving in greater numbers in 2004 when the African Development Bank moved its headquarters from Côte d'Ivoire to Tunis. (The bank returned to Côte d'Ivoire in 2014). Furthermore, travel to

Figure 7.2: Map of western, central, and eastern migratory routes: twenty-first century

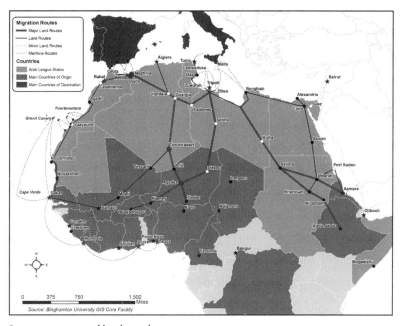

Source: map created by the authors.

Tunisia for sub-Saharan Africans is made easier by the fact that Tunisia does not require them to obtain visas prior to entry, which facilitates migration.

This study was conducted between June and August 2017, and its purpose is to examine clandestine migration to Libya and Tunisia. The inquiry was undertaken by the authors with the assistance of graduate students. With research funds provided by Georgetown University in Qatar's Center for International and Regional Studies (CIRS), we interviewed 609 migrants in Libya in five different cities, and 152 migrants in Tunisia, principally in Tunis and its environs. Since it is not possible to know the size of the population or the characteristics of its units, we used an accidental sample. A copy of our questionnaire can be found in the appendix to this chapter.

In our study, we tried to ascertain whether Libya and Tunisia were countries of ultimate destination for migrants or whether they were simply jumping-off points to Europe. Overwhelmingly, we determined that most migrants were not interested or did not have the means to continue onward to Europe. Instead, they saw Libya and Tunisia primarily as places to work and secondarily as places to settle. We also wanted to determine which countries contributed migrants to Libya and Tunisia. Our findings were interesting in that migrants from states bordering Libya and Tunisia were more likely to be involved in circular migration whereas migrants from farther afield (especially Nigeria, Cameroon, and Côte d'Ivoire) were usually more intent upon continuing onward to Europe. Since most of our migrants were intent upon residing in Libya and Tunisia for a while, we were interested in the social networks they created (with friends or family or resident nationals) to survive. In this context, we inquired substantially about their daily lives, their capacity to work either legally or illegally, and their encounters with employers, neighbors, the police, and other representatives of the state. We dug deeply, inquiring about satisfaction with living conditions, income, capacity to meet expenses, and the ability to send remittances back home. Finally, we asked about aspirations: What lives did they envision for themselves and their families?

Background to the study in Libya: a brief history

Migration—especially labor migration—to Libya is not a new phenomenon. Since petroleum was discovered in the country in the 1960s, Libya has attracted migrant labor mainly from neighboring countries. In the 1960s, the figures were not large, numbering in the few thousands, and most labor migrants were from Egypt, Sudan, Tunisia, Algeria, and Morocco.[2] Libya's phenomenal GDP growth during the 1960s, at an average annual rate of 14 percent, continued to fuel migration, primarily from North Africa. Although petroleum production and revenue fluctuated during this period (see Table 7.1), the Libyan government nevertheless endeavored to design consecutive five-year socioeconomic plans to develop the country and, in doing so, it recognized that migrant labor would be needed to implement these plans. Libya has a small population of 6.4 million people,[3] making migrant labor essential for its economic development. With this constant demand for labor, communities of both legal and illegal migrants grew larger and became more diversified in the country.

At the onset of the discovery of petroleum, most migrant labor to Libya came from neighboring countries in the Maghreb. After his 1969 coup, given his pan-Arab inclinations, Muammar Qaddafi emphasized that "Libya was the land of all Arabs." Because of Qaddafi's orientation toward pan-Arabism, Arabs could enter Libya easily, often obtaining visas at official points of entry and frequently without passports.

Table 7.1: Oil production, revenue, and population

Year	Oil production (Millions of barrels per day)	Revenue (Million Libyan dinars)	Population (Millions)
1956–7	–	0.06	1.22
1961–2	0.018	2.0	1.43
1966–7	1.501	139.0	1.63
1971–2	3.318	469.6	2.25
1976–7	1.455	2681.2	2.56
1989–90	1.600	6826.4	4.05
1995–6	1.400	3455.5	4.80
2000–1	1.300	3633.0	5.12
2005–6	1.525	4266.0	5.32
2010–11	1.600	5571.3	6.20
2015–16	0.400	1997.6	6.60

Source: Central Bank of Libya, the Economic Bulletin; Government of Libya, Bureau of Statistics and Census, different population censuses.

During the mid-1990s and in the first decade of the twenty-first century, as Libya became increasingly isolated in the international community in the wake of the 1988 Lockerbie aircraft bombing and other bombings in Europe, Qaddafi reoriented his foreign policy from one that had emphasized pan-Arabism to one that stressed pan-Africanism.[4] Qaddafi undertook this strategy in a conscious effort to develop allies at a time when he was being made a pariah in Europe and the United States. To further this pan-Africanist strategy, in 1999 he became the prime mover in the creation of the African Union (which, not coincidentally, was established at a conference in the Libyan city of Sirte). This strategy was effective and earned him much support in Africa. As he was promoting pan-Africanism, Qaddafi also encouraged migration from the Sahel, West Africa, and East Africa, which led to the emergence and establishment of new communities of sub-Saharan Africans in the country.

While these developments were taking place in Libya, other sub-Saharan Africans who aspired to transit to Europe usually traveled along the western Mediterranean route to Morocco or the Canary Islands and then onward to Europe, rather than using the central Mediterranean route through Libya. The Figure 7.3 provides outlines of both the western Mediterranean and central Mediterranean migration routes.

Figure 7.3: Map of western Mediterranean and central Mediterranean migration routes: twenty-first century

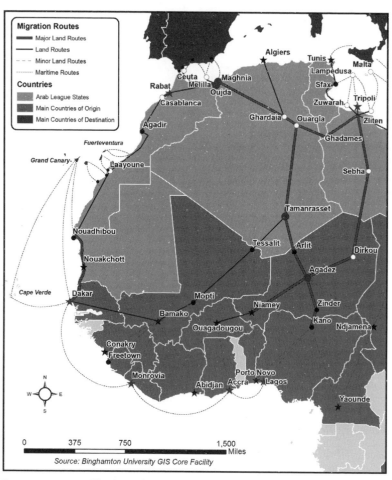

Source: map created by the authors.

During the mid-1990s, the member states of the European Union, because of relatively stagnant economies and a declining need for lower-skill manual labor, negotiated agreements and developed relationships with the governments of Morocco and Algeria to reduce migration from those countries to Europe.[5] Those efforts at curtailment, particularly in Morocco, have been effective, leading to the partial closing of the western Mediterranean route. As a result of these efforts, migrants began using the central Mediterranean route, which made Libya the pivotal state in this migratory corridor. In addition, during the 1990s, Qaddafi intermittently threatened European states (particularly Italy) with unrestrained African immigration, which intimidated the government of Silvio Berlusconi to pledge $5 billion in assistance so that Libya would "cooperate" on migration issues.[6]

From the mid-1990s until the fall of his regime in 2011, Qaddafi held and played the migration card to his advantage. Additionally, during the first decade of the twenty-first century, several towns along the Libyan coast became quite active in directing clandestine migration toward Europe. Thousands of migrants left Libyan shores each month in attempts to reach Europe, with many losing their lives in the effort. When the Qaddafi regime was ousted in 2011, Libya's security forces disintegrated and Libya became a failed state. Insecurity ran rampant. In this context of civil instability, significant numbers of migrants left the country. According to figures from the International Organization of Migration, more than 181,000 persons arrived on Italian shores in 2016. The number in 2017 dropped to 119,000. The data in Table 7.2 provide detail for those years.

Table 7.2: Irregular migrants arriving in Italy by sea (2004–17)

Year	2004	2005	2006	2007	2008	2009	2010
Total	13,635	22,939	22,016	20,455	36,951	9,573	4,404

Year	2011	2012	2013	2014	2015	2016	2017
Total	62,692	13,267	40,304	170,664	153,843	181,436	119,000

Source: Frontex, https://frontex.europa.eu/along-eu-borders/migratory-routes/central-mediterranean-route.

Surprisingly, despite the persistent state of insecurity and the unstable economy in Libya, many migrants from sub-Saharan and other countries continue to come to Libya, primarily to look for work. One of the key aims of this chapter is to provide some empirically based insights on the aspirations, experiences, and living and working conditions of sub-Saharan migrants in Libya.

Conducting the field research

Migrants can be found everywhere in Libya, in urban and rural locations, in large cities as well as small towns. There have been several estimates of the number of undocumented migrants in Libya, with a great deal of variation found between different sources. For example, in 2006, Human Rights Watch suggested that the number of migrants stood at between 1 and 1.2 million, but just two years earlier an expert had suggested a number almost double that amount when he reported that Libya had between 2 and 2.5 million migrants in 2004.[7]

This chapter presents an analysis of a sample of migrants in Libya, who were interviewed in five localities (Tripoli, Beni Walid, Tarhuna, Garyan, and Sebha) between 19 June and 15 August 2017. These cities are known for having large numbers of undocumented migrants, and Sebha, Beni Walid, and Tarhuna are among those most commonly used by human traffickers. All interviews were carried out by Mustafa Attir, Mohamed Jouili, and Ricardo René Larémont along with graduate students who had previous fieldwork experience and who were familiar with their localities.

In our sample, we decided not to include migrants in detention centers, where Libyan authorities keep those who were intercepted at sea, or migrants who were in the custody of human traffickers. We deemed that conducting interviews in these locales would put us and our assistants at risk. Consequently, the participants in our study were drawn from documented and undocumented migrants in the general population.

Our research assistants were instructed to approach migrants politely, usually in street locales where daily migrant workers were known to congregate. They introduced themselves and asked whether the subjects would voluntarily participate in our study. Interview subjects were then read this standard statement:

> The aim of this study is to develop a better understanding of the circumstances that lead someone to leave their country and become a migrant, the problems faced from the point of departure to the point of the final destination in Libya, and problems encountered while in Libya. The goal of the research project is to produce information to be presented to officials to help them develop better ways to mitigate problems encountered by migrants in Libya.

After the introduction, each individual migrant was asked whether he or she would agree to participate in the study or not. Only those who provided consent were interviewed.

Our research in Tunisia was limited to the capital and its environs. In Tunis, we interviewed 152 migrants in three age brackets: eighteen to twenty-nine, thirty to thirty-nine, and forty to forty-nine. Our locations for interview in the capital region included Laouina, Sokra, Les Berges du Lac, Lafayette, and La Place de la République. We used the same interview questions that were used in

Libya, and we were assisted by graduate students from the University of Tunis. The interviews took place between 2 and 31 August 2017. Our questionnaire was written in Arabic, English, and French. In Libya, the principal language used in interviews was Arabic and secondarily English or French, while in Tunisia it was primarily French followed by Arabic. The interviews were conducted in relatively private places (including quiet cafés or homes and working places) to ensure the privacy of our subjects. As in the case of Libya, our objectives were to ascertain reasons for migration to Tunisia, problems faced while traveling to and living in Tunisia, aspirations, and future plans.

In the wake of the Arab uprisings, migrants came to Libya and Tunisia not only from North, West, and East Africa but also increasingly from Bangladesh, Syria, Yemen, and the Philippines. There were thousands of workers from the Philippines and Bangladesh in Libya before the 2011 uprising, who were working in different government departments and for foreign companies. Many of those who had been working with the government did not leave. It seems that some of their relatives who planned to go to Europe made use of the situation in Libya and decided to cross to Europe using the North African route.

Background of members in sample

In Libya, our interviews were conducted with 640 migrants. Thirty-one interviews were excluded because of incomplete answers or when we believed that the subjects' privacy would be compromised. Consequently, 609 cases were accepted for analysis. In Tunisia, we had 152 respondents. Data from our completed interviews were entered in an Excel spreadsheet for quantitative analysis. The following are the main results:

- 74 percent of our respondents in Libya had been in the country for one year or longer. From this group, 10 percent had been living in the country for more than six years.
- 90 percent of the total sample arrived after the 2011 Arab Spring revolts.
- Many respondents had traveled to Libya several times, being involved in circular migration between Libya and their home countries.

Gender

Most of our respondents in Libya were young males and only thirty-four females were interviewed. This was partially due to the fact that it was much easier for the research team to meet with and interview male migrants in public spaces. By contrast, it was much harder to set up meetings or interviews with female migrants, as these women tended not to frequent public spaces very often and worked primarily in the domestic sector, as nannies or house-maids. In Tunisia, we obtained a sample that was divided between the sexes almost equally, with eighty-three males and sixty-seven females being interviewed.

Age

Fifty-five percent of our Libyan sample were in the eighteen to twenty-nine age bracket and 28 percent were age thirty to thirty-nine, resulting in a number wherein 83 percent of our respondents were under forty years of age. There were twenty-six respondents in the fifty to fifty-nine age bracket and fourteen were sixty or older. In the Tunisian sample, in the eighteen to twenty-nine age cohort, 55 percent of respondents were male and 45 percent were female. In the thirty to thirty-nine age cohort, 59 percent were male and 41 percent were female. In the forty to forty-nine age bracket, 25 percent were male and 75 percent were female.

Nationality

The Libyan sample comprised twenty-two nationalities. Chadians represented the largest group (21.5 percent), followed by Niger (16.6 percent), Egypt (13.3 percent), and Sudan (10 percent). All four countries share borders with Libya. Next we interviewed Nigerians and Bangladeshis, with 6 percent representation for each.[8] We also encountered Syrians and Yemenis in smaller numbers. The percentages represented in our sample did not necessarily represent their shares in the general population, but they nevertheless demonstrate how easy it is to meet migrants from diverse nationalities (see Table 7.3).

The Tunisian sample comprised sixteen nationalities. Migrants from Côte d'Ivoire represented the largest group with fifty-seven respondents, followed by Cameroon with twenty-four, then Mali and the Democratic Republic of Congo/Kinshasa with fourteen each. The Republic of Congo/Brazzaville had fourteen representatives, Gabon and Senegal each had seven, and Burkina Faso, Guinea, Angola, and Equatorial Guinea had three each. Last we had Niger with two, and Benin, Chad, Ghana, and the Central African Republic with one each.

Table 7.3: Libya–Tunisia: distribution of the sample by nationality

Country	Libya			Tunisia	
	Frequency	%	% prefer going to Europe	Frequency	%
Chad	131	21.5	0.05	01	0.6
Niger	101	16.6	0.06	02	2.0
Egypt	81	13.3	0.1	00	00
Sudan	59	9.7	0.05	00	00
Bangladesh	38	6.2	0.03	00	00
Nigeria	34	5.6	0.35	00	00
Ghana	24	3.9	0.29	01	0.6
Senegal	18	3.0	0.1	07	5.0
Syria	15	2.5	0.45	00	00
Guinea Conakry	15	2.5	0.33	03	2.0
Mali	14	2.3	00	14	9.3
Morocco	14	2.3	0.07	00	00
Côte d'Ivoire	13	2.1	100	57	38.0
Togo	9	1.5	00	00	00
Cameroon	8	1.3	0.50	24	16.0
Yemen	8	1.3	00	00	00
Gambia	7	1.1	0.57	00	00
Benin	5	0.8	0.40	01	0.6
Ethiopia	4	0.6	100	00	00
Gabon	3	0.5	00	07	5.0
Mauritania	1	0.2	00	00	00
Burkina Faso	1	0.2	100	03	2.0
Equatorial Guinea	00	00	00	03	2.0
Angola	00	00	00	03	2.0
Congo Brazzaville	00	00	00	14	9.3
Central African Republic	00	00	00	01	0.6
Democratic Republic of Congo	00	00	00	14	9.0
Missing information	6	1.0	–	00	00

Family size

Most of the migrants interviewed in Libya came from large families in their home countries, which, given the limited economic opportunities in their countries of origin, often requires that one member of the family journey abroad to obtain work and send remittances to their families. Only 28 percent of those within the Libyan sample came from families with fewer than five

Table 7.4: Libya: variables by nationalities for selected countries (percentages)

Variable	Egypt	Sudan	Chad	Niger	Nigeria	Bangladesh
Age: 18–29 years	38	34	61	67	67	42
30–39	36	20	26	18	29	37
50 and above	20	22	4.0	6.0	0.0	2
Education: None	7	7	35	30	25	9
Elementary diploma	14	24	7	10	12	49
High school and above	50	37	5	6	32	20
Living in Libya: less than six months	6	5	11	6	18	0
Less than one year	27	24	25	16	45	6
Two years and more	42	41	41	51	12	60
More than six years	14	32	2	3	2	11
Work at home: agriculture and grazing	20	22	56	44	12	2
Construction and technical	63	41	16	20	33	81
Economic reasons for leaving	94	92	92	97	65	100
Plan to go to Europe	1	1	0.05	0.06	35	0.03
Perception of Libyans: the majority are nice	39	66	44	45	29	44
The majority are not nice	10	7	3	8	6	8
Treatment of Libyans: majority treated me nicely	47	61	45	44	22	51
The majority did not treat me nicely	5	5	3	2	7	2

individuals, while 54 percent belonged to families of between five and nine individuals. A smaller minority, 18 percent of migrants, came from families of more than ten persons. The migrants interviewed in Tunisia presented very similar results in terms of their family size. Of those in the eighteen to twenty-nine age cohort, around 50 percent belonged to families of five to ten individuals, while 19.4 percent of this group belonged to large families of ten individuals or more. Within the thirty to thirty-nine age cohort, 27 percent came from families of five to ten individuals, while 47.9 percent came from families of ten or more. Of those in the forty to forty-nine age cohort, 75 percent came from families of five to ten individuals, while 25 percent came from families of fewer than five individuals, and none came from families of ten or more individuals.

Looking only at female migrants interviewed in Tunisia, we found that 24.4 percent came from families of five to ten individuals, while nearly half the migrants belonged to larger families of ten members or more. Twenty-six percent of female respondents belonged to families of fewer than five individuals.

Education

In the Libyan sample, almost one-fifth of respondents (18 percent) reported not having obtained any formal education; 12 percent attended primary school but did not finish; 18 percent completed primary school; 20 percent attended Koranic schools. Seventeen percent had completed their secondary education, while another 9 percent had attended vocational school. Six percent had attended university. The migrants in our Tunisian sample were better educated. Of those in the eighteen to twenty-nine age cohort, 54.6 percent had successfully completed university education, 25 percent had completed secondary school, and the remainder had completed elementary school. In the thirty to thirty-nine age cohort, 39.6 percent successfully completed university; around 25 percent had successfully completed secondary school; while only 4.2 percent had failed to complete their elementary school education. In the forty to forty-nine age cohort, around 25 percent had successfully completed university education, 50 percent had successfully completed secondary education, while the remaining 25 percent did not mention any educational attendance. Attendance at purely religious schools was very low (from 3.1 percent to 8.4 percent).

In Tunisia, taking women into account as a separate category, 4.5 percent attended primary school for some years, 10.6 percent had completed their primary education, 27.3 percent had completed secondary education, while 45.5 percent had successfully completed their university education. A total of 1.5 percent attended technical schools and 4.5 percent attended religious schools; 6.1 percent did not mention any school attendance.

What was clearly observable in comparing our Libyan and Tunisian respondents was that the community of respondents in Tunisia was much better educated. Their higher level of education and generally higher income status when viewed in tandem with Tunisia's ease of entry regarding visas meant that this category of migrants had the income to travel by airplane to

Tunisia rather than traverse the desert, which was most often the case in Libya. Our respondents in Tunisia had more education, had greater access to money, and, given Tunisia's comparative security, more humane conditions under which to live as migrants.

Libya and Tunisia as destinations for migrants

As mentioned earlier, Libya has been a destination country for undocumented migrants since the early 1970s, and for increased numbers of sub-Saharan migrants since the mid-1990s. The case of Tunisia is rather different, with the surge in sub-Saharan migration emerging since the 2011–12 Arab Spring, and particularly during 2016 and 2017.

We asked our respondents why they chose Libya or Tunisia as destinations. In the case of Libya, the majority of respondents in Libya (80 percent) reported economic reasons for migration. Also, among our Libyan respondents, only 15 percent reported that they were planning to go to Europe. Four percent reported war or political reasons for leaving their home country, while the remaining 1 percent reported other reasons. In Tunisia, the majority of respondents mentioned economic reasons for migration: 29.6 percent in the eighteen to twenty-nine age cohort, 45.8 percent in the thirty to thirty-nine age cohort, and 25 percent in the forty to forty-nine age cohort made this claim, while 5.1 percent in the eighteen to twenty-nine age cohort and 4.2 percent of those in the thirty to thirty-nine age cohort aspired to travel to Europe. Two percent in the eighteen to twenty-nine age cohort fled because of threats to their lives, while 1 percent in the eighteen to twenty-nine cohort and 4.2 percent in the thirty to thirty-nine age cohort fled because of civil wars. It is equally important to note that 62.2 percent of respondents in the eighteen to twenty-nine age cohort, 37.5 percent of respondents in the thirty to thirty-nine age cohort, and 75 percent of respondents in the forty to forty-nine age cohort refused to disclose their reasons for leaving their countries.

In Tunisia, taking women into account as a separate category, 41.8 percent left their country of origin for economic reasons, 1.5 percent because of personal threats, 4.5 percent were escaping civil war, 4.5 percent aspired to migrate to Europe, and 47.8 percent reported having left for other reasons.

For those migrants coming from countries sharing borders with Libya, most reported that they migrated to Libya to obtain better income. From this group, 13 percent said they had relatives in Libya, and 7 percent had friends. Generally, respondents who said they had relatives in Libya were from Chad,

Niger, Sudan, and Egypt. Most of these people had migrated to northern Libya, but they were also well represented in southern Libya. In some cases, persons within this group had relatives who held Libyan nationality. Acquiring Libyan citizenship became easier when Qaddafi reoriented his foreign policy from one that focused on pan-Arabism to one that focused on pan-Africanism. When Libyan foreign policy changed in that direction, residents of Niger, Chad, and Mali moved to Libya in their tens of thousands, with many eventually acquiring citizenship.[9] Furthermore, during Qaddafi's war with Chad, considerable numbers of sub-Saharan Africans chose to fight for Libya.[10] Upon the conclusion of the war, many of these fighters stayed in Libya. They often settled in Libya's southern towns because they had become accustomed to the environs and had freedom of mobility. Only 15 percent of respondents admitted that they planned to go to Europe.

Data from Table 7.4 show that while a large percentage of migrants from certain countries of origin did admit that their objective was to migrate to Europe, other migrants with different nationalities expressed little desire to do so. In our Libyan sample, all the respondents from Côte d'Ivoire, Ethiopia, and Burkina Faso expressed a desire to migrate to Europe. The second tier of migrants expressing a desire to migrate to Europe were from Gambia, Cameroon, Syria, Benin, Nigeria, and Ghana. By contrast, our respondents from Morocco, Chad, Niger, and Sudan expressed little interest in migrating to Europe (less than 1 percent). This contrasting result for Chadians, Nigerians, and Sudanese is explicable because migrants from these states that border Libya have been engaged in longstanding circular migration for decades. As for Moroccans, we consider this finding an outlier that warrants further research. Of those who expressed a desire to migrate to Europe, 75 percent had been in Libya less than one year. And from this group, 47 percent had been in Libya less than six months. These data reveal that those who aspired to migrate to Europe were newcomers to Libya and they were principally from Côte d'Ivoire, Ethiopia, and Burkina Faso. The data also reveal that most of those who aspire to migrate to Europe come from countries that do not share borders with Libya, while migrants from countries that do share borders with Libya are more likely to consider Libya as a destination or are involved in circular migration between Libya and their home countries.

Closer analysis of the data reveals a number of different trends. For example, all respondents in Libya who were from Côte d'Ivoire admitted their intention to migrate to Europe, while 35 percent of Nigerians in Libya expressed the same desire. However, we believe from our on-the-ground observations that a much higher percentage of Nigerians aspire to migrate to Europe. We draw these interpretative conclusions based partly from responses to our survey and partly from insights obtained from the contexts of our interviews.

In Tunisia, most of the respondents stated that they had migrated for economic reasons. Travel from the Sahel or West Africa to Tunisia is comparatively easy. Visa requirements are low or nonexistent. In contrast to Libya, the majority of our respondents traveled to Tunisia by air rather than motor vehicle, which made their journeys easier and more comfortable. For a long time, illegal migrants from sub-Saharan Africa have traveled to southern Libya by large trucks suitable for desert terrain. The trucks are managed by traffickers, who know how to move easily on unmarked desert roads and cross the international borders through uncontrolled points.

Another significant finding of our study was that existing networks of support from family and friends within Tunisia facilitated migrants' travel to the country. These relationships resulted in faster integration into Tunisian society despite sometimes surreptitious or clandestine entry. Of those in the thirty to thirty-nine age cohort, 21.3 percent had relatives in Tunisia who encouraged or assisted them to travel to Tunisia, while 50 percent of those within the forty to forty-nine cohort had the same. As far as respondents in the eighteen to twenty-nine age cohort were concerned, 46.9 percent had been supported by acquaintances, 26 percent were supported by friends, 5.2 percent resorted to traffickers, and 21.9 percent resorted to reputed travel agencies.

Our third question in this section was about length of stay in the host countries of Libya or Tunisia. In Libya, the length of stay was usually dependent upon the migrant's desire to stay in Libya or use it as a transit country to Europe. Because our cohort included subjects who generally desired to stay in Libya for reasons of employment, it was common to find migrants who had been living in Libya for many years. Most of the respondents in our sample (73 percent) had been in Libya for one year or longer. From this group, 10 percent had been living in the country for more than six years, 29 percent had been in the country for two to six years, 35 percent had been in Libya one to two years, 12 percent had been there from six months to less than one year, while 10 percent had arrived between one and six months before the interview. Only 2 percent had come within less than a month prior to being surveyed.

Our research reveals that the composition of the sub-Saharan African migrant communities in Libya and Tunisia is quite different. In Libya, the migrant community is considerably more diverse, with representatives not only from the Sahel, West Africa, East Africa, and North Africa but also from the Levant, and South and Southeast Asia (particularly Bangladesh and the Philippines). In Tunisia, the clandestine migrant community is primarily represented by sub-Saharan Africans and the regularized migrant community is represented by Algerians and Libyans. The surge in the arrival of sub-Saharan Africans to Tunisia became more noticeable between 2015 and 2017, with the arrivals in our sample coming principally from Côte d'Ivoire, Cameroon, and Mali. In Tunisia, the majority of our respondents had been living in the country for less than two years. In the eighteen to twenty-nine age cohort, 15.3 percent had been in the country less than one year, and 25 percent had been living there less than two years. In the thirty to thirty-nine age cohort, 16.7 percent had been in Tunisia for less than a year, 22.9 percent had been there for less than two years, and 33.3 percent had been living there for two to six years. In the forty to forty-nine age cohort, 25 percent had been living in the country for less than one year, while 50 percent had been living in the country for less than two years.

As far as our female respondents in Tunisia were concerned, 38 percent had been in the country more than two years, 26.9 percent reported having been in Tunisia for less than two years, while 17.9 percent said they had been in the country for less than a year.

The fourth question in this section dealt with travel arrangements. Migrants in Libya come from as far afield as South Africa, the Philippines, Yemen, and Bangladesh, although the majority of our respondents were from four countries that share borders with Libya: Egypt, Sudan, Chad, and Niger. Other nationalities that were strongly represented among the interview cohort were Nigerians and Bangladeshis.

During their interviews, migrants were asked how they had been put in contact with the person responsible for arranging their transport to the Libyan borders, as well as the person who had taken care of their transportation within Libya. Respondents were also asked whether there were particular ethnic groups, tribes, or clans in Libya that were involved in transporting migrants into and across the country. Of the respondents, 82 percent said that someone from their country of origin arranged for their transport to the Libyan border. Only 8 percent of respondents relied upon Libyans to get them there. This predominant reliance upon non-Libyans may reflect how the ownership and management of the transport system has been taken over by non-Libyans as a result of the instability created by the ejection of the Qaddafi regime. Of the respondents, 41 percent said that they got to know their middleman through a friend; 29 percent knew the middleman; 15 percent did not have previous acquaintance or knowledge of the middleman.

Migrants were asked to identify their means of transportation. In Libya, as expected, 91 percent had traveled via motor vehicle, a few had arrived by air, and fewer than 1 percent said they reached the Libyan border on foot. Regardless of the mode of traveling, the trip to the Libyan border involved crossing the desert, which could sometimes be as dangerous as crossing the Mediterranean Sea. The first stage involved the journey from the country of origin to the Libyan border. The number of days spent before reaching the Libyan border depended on country and city of origin. Because the majority of our respondents originated from the bordering countries of Chad, Niger, Egypt, and Sudan, these trips to the border did not take more than three days and were undertaken by truck or sport utility vehicle. After arrival in Libya, 55 percent of our respondents said it took them one to three days to arrive at the city of destination. Those coming from more distant countries (like Yemen or Bangladesh) talked about journeys of one week or more. From this group, 10 percent of respondents said it took them seven days to reach the Libyan border, while 3 percent said it took them ten days, and another 8 percent said the trip required eleven days or more. We asked respondents for the name of the first Libyan city they entered. Those from Algeria usually entered at Ghat, while those arriving from Chad or Sudan entered at Matan as Sarah or Kufra.

Traveling arrangements in Tunisia are distinct from those we found in Libya. Most migrants to Tunisia arrive by air rather than motor vehicle, and migrants to Tunisia mostly do not use human traffickers. Just a small percentage of our respondents in Tunisia (2.7 percent) in the thirty to thirty-nine age bracket claimed that they traveled to Tunisia by motor vehicle. Air travel to Tunisia is easy for two reasons: Tunisia often does not require visas for visitors from many sub-Saharan countries; second, what becomes clear from our study is that sub-Saharan migrants to Tunisia are comparatively "better off," meaning that they can afford air travel. Our research reveals that the amounts paid for travel to Tunisia were considerably higher than the amounts paid in Libya. The higher amounts paid reveal both the higher income of migrants to Tunisia and their higher levels of education.

To understand these details, we asked our respondents about travel costs. In the case of Libya, the largest percentage of respondents (36 percent) reported paying between $500 and $1,000 per person for transportation. Further, 25 percent reported the cost of their journey to be less than $500, and 24 percent said their costs were between $1,000 and $2,000. Only 12 percent indicated that their journey cost more than $2,000. Of our respondents, 4 percent did not provide accurate information about costs. The total cost of the trip to Tunisia ranged from $500 to $2,000 or more. Costs varied depending upon country of origin and means of transport. In the eighteen to twenty-nine age cohort, 41.7 percent paid amounts ranging from $1,000 to $2,000, while those in the thirty to thirty-nine age cohort reported paying similar amounts. Of migrants within the forty to forty-nine age bracket, 75 percent reported paying less than $500, while 25 percent paid between $1,000 and $2,000.

The fifth question in this section was about the problems migrants faced while journeying to Libya or Tunisia as well as problems encountered while in these countries. We expected that security would be a primary concern because of the fact that militias exercise control over security rather than a state-sponsored police or military. To our surprise, 64 percent reported that deterioration of income was their most pressing problem. After income, 25 percent said they were homesick, and 8 percent mentioned theft and robbery.

We also expected that travel to and within Libya would be dangerous and full of unknown and unpleasant surprises due to the ongoing conflict. Migrants may face all kinds of problems during their journeys, including exploitation, being captured by armed militias, imprisonment, and even death.[11] Yet the majority of respondents did not mention major harm inflicted by Libyans during their journeys. Such an answer within our interview sample perhaps was understandable because most of our respondents paid for their travel to Libya and came via middlemen whom they knew and trusted. Other migrants who have had bad experiences have faced these either in militia- or army-controlled detention camps. It is in these camps that most incidents of physical and psychological abuse take place. However, despite the generally positive responses obtained in our surveys, conditions faced during the journey were far from easy, as 12 percent of the migrants reported being beaten, 11 percent said that they did not have enough food and had experienced hunger for many days during their journey, another 6 percent reported being insulted and spoken to poorly, and there were also a few cases of sexual assault and imprisonment.

Because most migrants arrive in Tunisia by air rather than motor vehicle, incidents of abuse during the journey to Tunisia were rare. In terms of conditions within Tunisia, among all age cohorts, 30 to 50 percent of all respondents reported that they had never experienced any kind of physical or psychological aggression during their period of migration. Of those in the eighteen to twenty-nine age cohort, 10.2 percent reported being assaulted in

Tunisia and 22 percent reported not being paid for work. In the thirty to thirty-nine age cohort, 12.8 percent stated that they had been insulted, 17 percent claimed that they had been beaten, 6.4 percent stated that they had not been paid for work performed, and 40.4 percent said they had never been assaulted or harassed. In the forty to forty-nine age cohort, none reported being assaulted, and 25 percent reported either not being paid for work or being paid less than was promised. Few respondents reported being sexually assaulted.

Another important question was related to migrants' experience with work in their home countries and their sector of employment in the host country. According to our sample, most migrants arriving in Libya desired to stay and work in Libya. Only a minority (15 percent) expressed a desire to travel to Europe. Most of our respondents (30 percent) in Libya said they were employed as blue-collar workers and mostly worked as plumbers, painters, electricians, and mechanics. Those in the second largest group (25 percent) were daily manual laborers. Members of this second group tended to be younger, physically stronger, and able to work very long hours at manual tasks. Daily wage manual laborers can be found in many cities, with groups of migrants often gathering at street corners waiting for potential employers to stop by. Libyans who need some manual labor can go to these locations and hire a few of the migrant workers for a whole day or for a few hours. Afterward, these workers return to their street corners and await the next job. Of our respondents, 9 percent reported that they worked in construction, and 8 percent said they were sanitary and domestic workers. Other areas of work, which were less significant, included pasturage, agriculture, shopkeeping, trade, and working for government or private employers.

We expected that the majority of those who left their countries had not been employed in their home countries. However, much to our surprise, only 16 percent of the respondents in the Libyan sample reported that they were unemployed in their home countries. Most were either regularly or intermittently employed prior to migrating to Libya. On-farm labor and employment were the main areas of employment for the migrants in their home countries. Of those who said they worked regularly or had been fully employed, 25 percent said they had been working in agriculture and 7 percent had been working in pasturage. Of those who worked intermittently, 25 percent were engaged in technical work, 11 percent said they were daily manual workers, and 9 percent were engaged in trade. But regardless of the type of work they had in their home countries, all migrants expected that their incomes in Libya would be much higher.

Within our Tunisian sample, in the eighteen to twenty-nine age cohort, 56.4 percent said they were unemployed in their country of origin. In the thirty to thirty-nine age cohort, 35.4 percent said they had been jobless. Interestingly, 100 percent of those in the forty to forty-nine age cohort said they were fully employed in the homelands but that the salaries were inadequate. Of those who said they had employment before coming to Tunisia, most had worked in construction, commerce, domestic service, and agriculture. Considering the female respondents in our Tunisian cohort, 50 percent said they had been unemployed before their arrival. Of those who had been working back home, 16.5 percent worked in commerce, 1.5 percent worked as housemaids, 1.5 percent worked as technicians, and 1.5 percent worked in agriculture.

Most migrants who arrive in Tunisia seek work so that they can send remittances home. In Tunisia, however, obtaining work for migrants is a challenge given the country's declining economy since 2011. In the eighteen to twenty-nine age cohort, 61.5 percent reported that they were unemployed compared with 47.8 percent in the thirty to thirty-nine age cohort, and 75 percent in the forty to forty-nine age cohort. Men who did find work often worked as day laborers in painting, house construction, and as waiters. Of our female respondents in Tunisia, 60.3 percent said they were unemployed. Those who were working were mostly employed as housemaids, nannies, and waitresses. With respect to this section of the study, we must acknowledge parenthetically that our data may be inaccurate because, given their irregular legal status, many of our respondents may not have been entirely candid in their responses regarding employment.

Wages, banking, money transfers, and the Libyan economy

Migrants who travel to Libya, especially those from Egypt, Sudan, Chad, and Niger, arrive with the objective of working, saving money, and sending that money home to their families. Because many are undocumented migrants without legal status, they often cannot transfer their money through official banking systems. To solve this problem, a new kind of entrepreneur has entered the market to facilitate money transfers in an informal, unregulated banking network that is capable of transferring money around the world.

Migrants are paid in Libyan dinars but must convert this money into US dollars. The official exchange rate in Libya remained stable for many years with 1 dollar equaling 1.32 Libyan dinars. Migrants usually preferred to exchange their Libyan dinars into US dollars on the black market, where they obtained a rate of 1.40 and 1.50 Libyan dinars for the dollar. However, with the start of the Libyan civil war in the second half of 2014, the Libyan dinar has considerably weakened. In June 2014, the exchange rate on the black market rose to 1.72 dinars for 1 dollar. The trend continued over the course of the civil war and deteriorating political and economic conditions in Libya, reaching 6.20 dinars by the end of 2016. It even reached 10 Libyan dinars on 11 April 2017. Since June 2017, the exchange rate has varied between 8.30 and 8.50 dinars to the dollar. Many entrepreneurs buy the US dollar on the black market to import goods to be sold in the Libyan market, thereby obtaining sizable profits. Prices for basic goods have become very high, making life difficult for everyone.

Historically, Libya has relied on the extraction and export of hydrocarbons as its primary source of GDP. Fluctuation in oil production or in its price has had negative consequences for the country's GDP and inflation rate over the years. Before the 2011 Arab Spring, and with very high global oil prices, the government was able to subsidize the costs of major essential goods (especially food and other necessities), making life affordable for most Libyans and migrants. Both Libyans and foreigners benefited from the subsidies, and during those years migrants were able to save substantial income from their salaries to send back to their families. The deterioration of the Libyan dinar has made life difficult for everyone and has certainly had an impact on the ability of migrants to save and remit money home.

Because the majority of the Libyan sample had been living in Libya for one or more years, they were asked about their income during two time periods: presently and prior to 2014. Our respondents in Libya were asked whether they were satisfied with their income, satisfied to some extent, or not satisfied. As expected, only 18 percent of respondents said they were "satisfied" with their income. By contrast, when asked about the period before the start of the civil war, the percentage of those "satisfied" with their income jumped to 50 percent.

When we asked the same question in Tunisia, all those in the forty to forty-nine age group said they were dissatisfied with their income. Those in younger age groups expressed various degrees of contentment, with 21.2 percent of those in the eighteen to twenty-nine age cohort saying they were more or less contented, and 25 percent saying they were contented. In the thirty to thirty-nine age group, 25 percent said they were contented with their income, while 51.5 percent were discontent. Furthermore, because those in younger age cohorts were less likely to send remittances home, they were under considerably less financial pressure and were more likely to express contentment regarding income. Regarding female respondents in Tunisia, 69 percent were not satisfied with their income, 14.3 percent were satisfied, and 16.7 percent said they were more or less satisfied.

We then inquired about remittances. Most sub-Saharan migrants to Libya or Tunisia are expected to send remittances to their families back home. In our Libyan sample, 21 percent answered that, at the time of the survey, they sent remittances to their families back home. By contrast, before the onset of the civil war and ensuing economic crisis that accelerated from 2014, 54 percent of the respondents had sent remittances. At the time of the survey, 56 percent said that they did not send anything home, while only 22 percent had not done so before 2014.

When we inquired about the ability to send remittances in Tunisia, 33 percent in the forty to forty-nine age cohort said that they did. Our research revealed that it was this age group that was most likely to support their families back home. That percentage declined to 14.3 percent when the same question was asked of the thirty to thirty-nine age cohort. What was additionally striking was that 81 percent of migrants in the eighteen to twenty-nine age cohort admitted never having sent remittances to their families.

When we segregated answers from female participants of the survey in Tunisia, we learned that 86.7 percent said they did not send remittances, 11.1 percent said that they did, and 2.2 percent said they sent remittances intermittently.

Living conditions and relations in the host country

The living conditions of clandestine or even documented sub-Saharan migrants in Libya and Tunisia are poor relative to those enjoyed by residents or citizens. Examining the details of daily living, even within the community of migrants, reveals differences in living conditions. For example, in Libya those working as craftsmen, technicians, domestic workers, or in government or private companies had the highest standards of living. Furthermore, 26 percent of those within the Libyan sample said they were living with family members, cutting the cost of living expenses; 12 percent reported living alone; and 62 percent reported sharing living quarters with friends or strangers. Although many of our respondents were living in what most Libyans would describe as substandard housing, 45 percent of our respondents nevertheless described their living conditions as good or excellent, while only 23 percent said their living conditions were bad or difficult, which meant that most of those who were surveyed indicated they were relatively content with their living conditions.

In Tunisia, our respondents lived in the center of the capital or nearby suburbs. Of those in the eighteen to twenty-nine age category, 85.7 percent lived in the city, and 14.3 percent lived in the suburbs. In the thirty to thirty-nine age group, 77.1 percent lived in the town center, and 22.9 percent lived in the suburbs. In the forty to forty-nine age category, 75 percent lived in the town center and 25 percent lived in the suburbs.

The majority of migrants shared houses or rooms with other individuals. In fact, the survey disclosed that 87.3 percent of respondents in the eighteen to twenty-nine age category, 83.3 percent of those in the thirty to thirty-nine age cohort, and 77 percent of those in the forty to forty-nine age group share dwellings with other people. Migrants were asked if they shared dwellings with their relatives. In response to this question, 100 percent of respondents in the age cohort forty to forty-nine answered yes; 42.6 percent of respondents in the age group thirty to thirty-nine answered yes, and 57.4 percent answered no. In the age cohort eighteen to twenty-nine, 41.7 percent answered yes and 58.3 percent answered no. It is clear that most migrants share houses with their relatives so that they can share costs, save money, and have networks of solidarity.

Another question in this section dealt with migrants' relations with individuals of the host country. As mentioned earlier, migrants, with or without legal documents, have been arriving in Libya since the early 1970s and have become an important component of Libyan society. Migrants are important economically because they constitute around one-third of the population and they have been contributing to the development of the country for a very long period of time. Overt racism in Libya and Tunisia is not generally expressed because of the long period of miscegenation between indigenous peoples and sub-Saharan Africans, which dates at least from the tenth century, making skin color a less prevalent basis for social or economic discrimination.[12] However, it has become more noticeable that, since the 2011 uprisings, cases of tension between Libyans and sub-Saharan migrants have arisen. By contrast, during the Qaddafi era, and even before, incidents of racial tension or violence were rare. Since 2011, however, more incidents of racial discrimination and violence have occurred, and the security situation has disintegrated to such an extent that Libya is now a failed state where physical security cannot be assured. Well-armed militias and criminal gangs are active throughout the country, launching attacks on individuals and terrorizing both Libyans and migrants alike. Migrants, as newcomers, are even more vulnerable. News of such attacks is well recorded, documented, and circulated by international organizations dealing with refugees, illegal migrants, and human rights.[13] These reports have varied in accuracy, depending on the context and the quality of investigation and reporting.

When a CNN report on slavery in Libya was made available in November 2017, it stirred a great deal of discussion worldwide.[14] Within Libya, many claimed that the report was non-contextual.[15] In Libya, social and commercial relations between Libyans and migrants are commonplace. Libyans seeking day laborers often go to certain well-known street corners where migrants congregate to seek employment. After exchanging words with one migrant or more, a deal is usually struck, and the migrant or migrants join the employer in his vehicle. This activity takes place every day in cities, both large and small. Before the fall of the Qaddafi regime, slavery in Libya was nonexistent. The emergence of human traffickers since the fall of the regime, however, requires a different commentary. The persons engaged in this illegal, nefarious trade may indeed be involved in human trafficking, in which considerable sums of money may be exchanged. Undeniably, this is tantamount to slavery. Nevertheless, despite this reported activity by some traffickers, slavery is still not commonplace in the country.

Migrants' perceptions of Libyans and Tunisians

In our research, migrants were asked how they perceive Libyans and Tunisians according to three options: most are nice; only some are nice; most are not nice.

In our Libyan survey, 38 percent said most Libyans were nice, 51 percent said some Libyans were nice, and 9 percent said Libyans are not nice. In answer to our second question, "How has the average Libyan treated you?" 39 percent said most Libyans treated them nicely, 51 percent said only some treated me nicely, while another 9 percent said the majority of Libyans had not treated them nicely at all. Interestingly, few respondents admitted to having been robbed by Libyans despite the fact that robbery and theft is commonplace in post-Qaddafi Libya. Our third question inquired about the treatment of migrants by government officials, which elicited the following responses: 79 percent said government officials followed regular formal procedures; 13 percent said they were not friendly; and 6 percent said they were treated badly by government officials.

In Tunisia, respondents were given the following options: most Tunisians treat us nicely; only some are nice; most are not nice. Taking into account all age cohorts, almost 25 percent of our respondents said that Tunisians were nice. Looking solely at the eighteen to twenty-nine age cohort, approximately 50 percent said that most Tunisians were nice, and approximately 25 percent said they were not nice. In the age thirty to thirty-nine age cohort, 27.1 percent said the majority were nice, 47.9 percent said some were nice, and 25 percent believed that the majority were not nice. In the forty to forty-nine age cohort, approximately 25 percent said that Tunisians were nice, another 25 percent said they were somewhat nice, and the remainder, approximately 50 percent, said they were not nice. Looking only at female respondents in Tunisia, 22.4 percent declared that the majority of Tunisians treated them nicely, 43.3 percent stated that only some Tunisians treated them somewhat nicely, while 34.3 percent said that the majority of Tunisians treated them badly.

In response to the question "How have government officials treated you?" 37 percent of our respondents in the eighteen to twenty-nine age cohort in Tunisia said that government officials dealt with them in a professional manner, and 29.9 percent reported cruel behavior by police officers. Among those in the thirty to thirty-nine age cohort, 37.7 percent claimed that police officers treated them in a professional manner and 29.2 percent declared that they were dealt with roughly. Among female migrants in Tunisia, 37.9 percent declared that they were dealt with in a professional manner, 25 percent said they were dealt with brutally, and 30.3 percent said that officials were cruel.

The third question in this section dealt with the migrants' relations with other sub-Saharan Africans. From our observations in Libya and Tunisia, individuals from the same country often congregate together, especially considering choice of residence and places to assemble for work and recreation. On occasion, the workplace may bring together individuals from different ethnic or political groups. In Libya, there has not been significant reporting of fighting or conflict between different groups of migrants despite differences in nationality or language. The majority (66 percent) classified their relations with other Africans as normal, 19 percent described their relations as friendly and warm, and 14 percent did not answer the question.

In response to the question about migrants' relationships with other sub-Saharan Africans in Tunisia, three options were available for response: normal, close, or tense. For those in the eighteen to twenty-nine age category, 85.6 percent said their relationships with other sub-Saharan Africans were normal, while 89.4 percent of those in the thirty to thirty-nine age cohort responded the same way. For those in the forty to forty-nine age cohort, 75 percent declared that their relationships with sub-Saharans were normal. Further, 13.4 percent of those in the eighteen to twenty-nine age cohort and 25 percent of those in the forty to forty-nine age group said their relationships with other sub-Saharan Africans were close. Incidents of conflict with other sub-Saharan Africans were very low, registering 1 percent in the eighteen to twenty-nine age group, 4.3 percent in the thirty to thirty-nine age group, and 0 percent in the forty to forty-nine age group. In Tunisia, migrants were asked about other problems they faced. Most often mentioned were homesickness, insufficient income, and physical or psychological aggression.

Aspirations

The last two sets of questions were about aspirations, and whether migrants were planning to return to their home countries. When asked "Do you plan to go back to your country?" 73 percent of those in Libya said they hoped to return permanently to their homes, while another 9 percent said they would be involved in circular migration between Libya and their home country. In Tunisia, 74.5 percent in the eighteen to twenty-nine age cohort declared an intention to return home, and 25.5 percent aspired to travel to Europe. In the thirty to thirty-nine age cohort, 79.5 percent intended to return home, and 20.5 percent hoped to travel to Europe. In the forty to forty-nine age cohort, 100 percent of the migrants told us they intended to return home after their sojourn in Tunisia. Taking account of the female respondents in Tunisia separately, 87.7 percent declared their intention to return to their home countries, while the remainder admitted that they aspired to migrate to Europe.

Conclusion

The most important result of this study is the clear evidence that Libya is a destination rather than a transit country to Europe, involving tens of thousands of irregular migrants. While many migrants to Libya come from the neighboring countries of Egypt, Sudan, Chad, Niger, and Algeria, we also discovered migrants from more distant regions and countries, first from Nigeria and Bangladesh and secondarily from Somalia, Eritrea, and Ethiopia. Migrants from these countries were less likely to be involved in circular migration and were more likely oriented toward planning onward voyages to Europe.

Although the director of Frontex (the European Border and Coast Guard Agency) and others have claimed that there were 1 million migrants in Libya ready to leave for Europe,[16] that assertion is not accurate. It is alarmist. Our research reveals that most migrants in Libya (around 85 percent) either want to stay in the country or are engaged in circular migration between Libya and their home countries. The data again reveal that approximately 15 percent plan to go to Europe. In other words, the data and analysis provided in this study correct that misperception. The civil war that commenced in Libya in 2011 caused 790,000 foreigners to leave the country during that year alone.[17] Many of those who left that year would have preferred to stay and work in Libya if the country had been at peace. The civil war that has ensued in the country since 2011 has caused considerable grief and has rent the country asunder. Nevertheless, and quite surprisingly, migrants continue to arrive in Libya to work, and the country continues to attract and sustain migrants, as our research reveals.

In Tunisia, what has emerged from our research is that there has been a significant increase in migration from sub-Saharan countries, especially between 2015 and 2017. The primary motive for migration has been economic. Most migrants see Tunisia as a final destination or they are involved in circular migration between Tunisia and their home countries. A minority aspire to migrate to Europe. Employment opportunities in Tunisia are better than their home countries, even though the Tunisian economy has been in decline since 2011. When these migrants do find jobs, they are most often in the informal sector and occasionally they are not paid for their work. Our data in this survey also reveal comparatively high levels of education among migrants to Tunisia, which contrasts considerably with the population of migrants in Libya, who are less educated.

Future research directions for Libya and Tunisia

In the present study, we questioned migrants in five Libyan cities, who were chosen in a series of rolling interviews. We interviewed our subjects without regard to nationality, which led to a situation where some nationalities were overrepresented and others were underrepresented. Nevertheless, the data we have assembled are informative. They reveal considerable disparities in the migratory experience and eventual goals (whether to stay in Libya or move onward to Europe). These goals seemed to be informed by country of origin, with nationals from the bordering countries of Egypt, Sudan, Chad, and Niger more likely to settle in Libya, while nationals from countries farther afield (like Yemen, Bangladesh, Nigeria, and Ghana) were more likely to express desires or plans to emigrate to Europe. In the next iteration of this research project, we intend to account for nationality in our research design given what we have learned from this research program. Probing deeper into motivations based on country of origin, level of education, and prior work experience before arrival in Libya will provide better indices that will help predict which groups are more likely to settle in Libya and which groups are more likely to plan to move on to Europe.

APPENDIX

Immigrant questionnaire

1. Sex: Male Female
2. Age ....
3. What is your country of origin?
4. What is the name of your village or city?
5. What were the reasons for leaving your country?
    a. Economic
    b. Threats to personal security
    c. Civil war
6. Why did you choose Libya or Tunisia as a destination?
    a. Some of my relatives living there
    b. Other reason
7. Where did you enter Libya/Tunisia?
8. How did you enter Libya/Tunisia?
9. Did you leave your home country before?
    a. No, this is the first time
    b. Yes, more than once
10. Why are you here?
    a. To work and send money home
    b. To work and collect enough money to pay for the trip to Europe
    c. To go directly to Europe
11. Is your father alive? Yes No
12. Is your mother alive? Yes No
13. How many members are in your family?

14. Did you go to school? Yes No
15. If yes, indicate what type of education?
    a. Religious
    b. Vocational
    c. Few years of elementary education
    d. Finished elementary school
    e. Finished secondary school
    f. Finished university
16. Did you work in your country? (farming, fishing, trade, construction, technician, et cetera?) Yes No
17. What was the nationality of the individual who helped to arrange your journey into Libya/Tunisia?
18. How did you get to know the individual who helped you to travel to the border of Libya/Tunisia?
19. How many days did it take to reach the border of Libya/Tunisia?
20. How long did it take to travel within Libya/Tunisia?
21. How much did it cost for the trip?
22. How long have you been in this country?
23. Do you return to your home country from time to time?
24. How have you survived financially during your journey?
25. Are you working now? If yes, what type of work?
26. Are you satisfied with your income here?
27. Do you send money to your family back home?
28. Please describe your living experiences in Libya/Tunisia.
29. Describe your living conditions
    a. Where?
    b. Do you live with others?
    c. How many?
    d. Are members of your family with you?
30. Do you plan to return to your home country?
    a. No. Why.............
    b. Yes. Why...........
31. How do you perceive Libyans/Tunisians?
32. How have average Libyans/Tunisians treated you?
33. How have government officials (especially the police) treated you?
34. When you meet other sub-Saharan African migrants, what have been their countries of origin?
35. How are your relations with sub-Saharan Africans in Libya/Tunisia?

36. Have you been physically or emotionally harmed during your journey? How?
37. What have been your greatest problems?
38. What are your aspirations?

8

INTEGRATING AFRICAN MIGRANTS?

GAUGING CITIZEN OPPOSITION TO MIGRANT RESETTLEMENT IN MOROCCO'S CASABLANCA REGION

Matt Buehler and *Kyung Joon Han*

Introduction

In one of Morocco's most central neighborhoods, Casablanca's Ain Diab beach boardwalk, two landmarks face each other. The first is the Borj al-Arab Hotel, built in the 1960s and adorned with an Arab architectural façade. The second is an artistic mural of an African queen, with colorful robes commonly found in some sub-Saharan African cultures. These landmarks symbolize two key ethnicities that help to constitute Morocco's national identity—Arab and African. Morocco's first constitution in 1962 declared that the country had not only "Arab and Islamic" roots but also "African" origins. Generally, relations between Moroccan citizens of Arab and African descent have been historically harmonious and integrated. Intermarriage and social intermixing exist; little discrimination disenfranchises Black Moroccans (i.e., citizens of sub-Saharan African descent who speak Arabic natively and follow Arab cultural traditions, but whose families came to Morocco centuries ago mostly as soldiers or slaves). Ethnic relations are fluid and flexible, resembling countries like Cuba or Brazil. Morocco's multiethnic national identity is not exceptional, as such diversity also appears in neighboring North African countries—Algeria, Tunisia, and Libya.

Given historically amicable relations between North Africa's native citizens of Arab and African descent, it is counterintuitive that prejudice against foreign African migrants from sub-Saharan countries seems to be rising.[1] Discrimination seems to be intensifying against African migrants who have recently arrived from Congo, Nigeria, Senegal, Cameroon, Mali, and elsewhere. Where conflict and poverty proliferate in these countries, migrants flee to North Africa seeking clandestine access to Europe by boat across the Mediterranean, or by foot through Spain's North African enclaves of Melilla and Ceuta. In response, Spain, Italy, and North African countries have increased border and maritime security.[2]

Thus, as an alternative, many sub-Saharan African migrants have decided to resettle in North Africa. Previously, articles have appeared depicting North African states as "sender" countries of migrants.[3] Yet, more recently, they have also become "recipient" countries of African migrants. Given the clandestine nature of such migration, it is difficult to know how many African migrants have resettled. According to Hein de Haas, about 65,000 to 120,000 African migrants arrived annually in the 2000s. Whereas about 70 to 80 percent went to Libya, about 20 to 30 percent—or 24,000 to 36,000 African migrants—traveled to Morocco and Algeria.[4] By 2015, this statistic ballooned to nearly 45,000 in Morocco alone, per a government estimate.[5] One report noted that hundreds of thousands of African migrants have integrated into Moroccan society without residency permits since 2000.[6] African migrants primarily integrate into Morocco's largest cities, such as Casablanca, Rabat, Tangiers, and Oujda.

Since Morocco has traditionally been a diverse, multiethnic society in which its native citizens of African origin have integrated easily, conventional wisdom suggests new African migrants should similarly integrate seamlessly. Yet, unexpectedly, African migrants resettling often face opposition from native citizens. Some Moroccans vocalize discrimination toward African migrants. Ugly, racist jokes have emerged mocking the idea of "having a black baby" or "having black smell."[7] Frequently, in Casablanca, apartment buildings will refuse tenants who are African migrants, occasionally posting signs reading: "It is strictly prohibited to rent to Africans."[8] Many citizens oppose

African migrants' resettlement as they feel they have poor chances for integrating into society successfully.

Some native citizens voice the opposite attitudes, however. They have supported African migrants' resettlement and believe they have good chances of integration. Several civil society organizations have mobilized to help African migrants, providing food, clothing, and other forms of assistance. In 2016, they organized peaceful marches to sensitize Moroccans to problems of discrimination. Countering the despicable, racist epithets that some Moroccans call African migrants, they shouted the slogan: "Neither Slave, Nor Negro — Stop, That's Enough!"[9] Whereas some Moroccans oppose African migrants' resettlement into their society, others support it. Hence this study investigates the question: Under what conditions do native citizens either express opposition or support for African migrants' integration into society?

The chapter addresses this question by using an original survey of 1,500 native citizens in Morocco, completed in September 2017. Our public opinion poll is statistically representative for Morocco's largest, most populous region (the Casablanca–Settat Region), and was undertaken with a professional survey firm that works regularly with the Arab Barometer, Afrobarometer, and World Values Survey. Through a variety of correlative tests, this study subsequently uses the survey's data to isolate the sociological and economic conditions that either raise or dampen attitudes of opposition or support for African migrants' resettlement. Responding to the survey's main dependent variable statement, "Black African refugees and migrants have good chances to successfully integrate into Moroccan society," 17 percent of Moroccans disagreed strongly with this prompt, 28 percent disagreed, 40 percent agreed, and only 7 percent strongly agreed. This variation in negative and positive opinions toward African migrants' integration is important and puzzling. It signals new, rising opposition toward African migrants, controverting Morocco's legacy of interethnic harmony.

This study argues that a multiplicity of factors related to native citizens' sociological concerns and economic well-being affects variation in their opinions about migrants' resettlement. Moroccan citizens' religious identity, their anxieties about employment competition, and their ethnic background influenced their opinions toward African migrants' integration. That is, not all Moroccans expressed opposition to African migrants' integration. Moroccans who have lower education and income levels, those who think that most African migrants are Christians, and those who are troubled by competition with African migrants for jobs, were more likely to believe such migrants would have poor chances for successful integration. By contrast, respondents who self-identify as Black Moroccans believe foreign African migrants have good chances for successful integration.

This study's results confirm and confound preexisting studies of public opinion toward migrants' integration. Confirming the findings of studies in Western industrialized countries, the results herein reinforce the centrality of immaterial, cultural variables in encouraging anti-migrant attitudes.[10] Yet the results also highlight economic considerations, specifically labor market competition. This is unanticipated for two reasons. The first is that it confounds studies of Western industrialized countries that question labor market competition as a source of anti-migrant sentiments.[11] The second is that immaterial, cultural factors (e.g., religion, ethnicity) have historically shaped the contours of public opinion, specifically, and politics, more generally, in the Arab world. Although this study's results indicate such immaterial factors do matter greatly in Morocco, its finding on labor market competition also shows that more proximate economic concerns carry influence in this developing society, where many native citizens struggle to make ends meet.

This study advances in four sections. Section 1 sets the baseline by explaining how Morocco became a multiethnic society with native citizens of both Arab and African ancestry. It also describes the crisis created by the arrival of new, foreign sub-Saharan African migrants. Next, drawing on extant literature, the second section posits six theories explaining variation in citizen attitudes on African migrants' integration. The third section describes the survey and its results and identifies the theories that most accurately predict which Moroccans oppose or support African migrants' integration. The conclusion discusses generalizability and avenues for future research.

A political history of sub-Saharan African migration to Morocco

From pre-colonial times to the contemporary period, African individuals have migrated to Morocco and successfully integrated into its society. What resulted, as Mustafa O. Attir, Mohamed Jouili, and Ricardo René Larémont suggest in this volume, is that discrimination based upon race or skin color was rare because race or skin color was not considered important in social relations. Migrants came to Morocco, in part, because of its military, cultural, and commercial ties with sub-Saharan Africa. These relations began during the pre-colonial periods, were sustained during European colonialism, attenuated between the 1970s and 1980s, and reemerged in the 1990s, 2000s, and

2010s. Before the consolidation of control by Morocco's current royal family, the Alaoui dynasty, local kings and warlords ruled. Morocco's Almoravid kings commanded a trans-Mediterranean territory extending from Spain to sub-Saharan Africa. Caravans traversed the Sahara northward from West Africa, bringing gold, ivory, and local nuts, whereas caravans going southward carried cloth, salt, and weapons. The most important trade item was sub-Saharan African slaves, however. Slave markets first emerged in the seventh century and continued until French colonialism was established in 1912.[12] One of slavery's centers was Marrakech, a nexus of trade routes of tribes from sub-Saharan regions, Saharan territories, and northern Morocco. Stronger sub-Saharan African tribes captured and enslaved people below the Senegal River and traded them to Arab and Amazigh tribes, who transported them northward.[13] Regular interactions between these tribes meant that Moroccan kings had alliances with African tribes. Religious ties reinforced southward links, and Morocco's Sufi order (the Tijani) was brought to West Africa by a Mauritanian Islamic sheikh, who had been educated in Fès.

African slaves were forced laborers, but slavery did not work in Morocco as it did in the American South or the Caribbean. Plantation-style chattel slavery did not exist, and slaves' descendants were not presumed slaves. In wealthy Moroccans' homes, female slaves worked as wet-nurses, cooks, and other domestic servants, whereas male slaves worked as store clerks, doormen, boatmen, and private librarians.[14] Slaves became prominent as servants of Morocco's monarchy. In the 1670s, Sultan Mawlay Isma'il ibn al-Sharif recruited the *'abid al-bukhari*, what became known as the "black army."[15] Generals deemed these African soldiers more loyal and courageous. By 1727, the army grew to 150,000 fighters, achieving success in helping Mawlay Isma'il solidify his rule.[16] This provided the foundations for today's Alaoui dynasty. African slaves were also in the harem; numerous kings were rumored to favor African courtesans. The association of African slaves with Morocco's monarchy meant they had unique status in pre-colonial society. Any form of slavery is unjust, yet enslaved Africans in Morocco seemed to fare better than elsewhere.

Although Morocco's monarchy never outlawed slavery, it became de facto illegal when French colonialism began. While Africans continued to serve in the king's palace as his guards, servants, and concubines, slavery diminished elsewhere. Colonial officials banned slave markets and trading in 1923. Thereafter, as Eric Ross relays: "clandestine trading in persons continued for another two decades. Cases involving slave ownership and inheritance were still being heard in courts in 1950. By this time the slaves were almost exclusively female domestics and concubines."[17] This was an informal unpaid work arrangement—called *at-talit*—between descendants of African slaves and their erstwhile masters' families.[18] Former slaves and their descendants— known as the Haratine—gained their freedom and integrated into Moroccan society as fully equal citizens. Descendants of African slaves assimilated into society, adopting the Arabic language and Arab culture. The term "Haratine" is not widely used and no official designations separate such Black Moroccans from Moroccans not of distant sub-Saharan African origins. Morocco's census does not track ethnicity, so it is difficult to know how many citizens are Black Moroccans today. Nearly 15 percent of native citizens self-identified as Black Moroccans in our survey.

During the colonial era, relations continued between North African populations and sub-Saharan African populations. Colonialists facilitated commercial relations, maintaining land trade routes across the Sahara. In the First World War, North African and African soldiers—the Tirailleurs Sénégalais and Tirailleurs Marocains—fought alongside each other in Europe; 70,000 perished. For their sacrifice, Paris's Great Mosque was constructed in 1926.[19] However, after colonialism, Morocco's regime favored stronger relations with Arab countries in response to rising pan-Arabism symbolized by Gamal Abdel Nasser. This emphasis on Morocco's Arab identity led to the Arabization of newspapers and street signs, and the concomitant decline of emphasis on its African identity. While Morocco remained a multiethnic, diverse society of native citizens with Arab, Amazigh, and African origins, these events discouraged new migrants from sub-Saharan Africa in the 1970s and 1980s.

By the 1990s, the number of new African migrants to Morocco increased markedly. Following Spain's entrance into the European Economic Community in 1986, its economy improved. Similarly, after Mohammed VI became king in 1999, liberalization spurred Morocco's economy. New "rags to riches" entrepreneurs emerged, generating unprecedented economic growth, especially in Casablanca.[20] The booming Spanish and Moroccan economies generated "pull" factors, drawing sub-Saharan African migrants northward. "Push" factors also emerged, including the Cold War's end in 1989. Many sub-Saharan African autocracies—once bolstered by the Soviets—collapsed. Whereas democracies sometimes emerged, as in Senegal, elsewhere they collapsed into war, ethnic conflict, and coups.[21] Africa's democratization produced instability, slowing economic growth. Ecological crises also drove African migrants toward Europe.[22] Yet, rather than seeing

African migrants as victims of oppression, instability, or poverty, most European governments considered them "desperate invaders" or "poor victims of smuggling networks."[23]

In 1996, the next phase of African migration began. Many African migrants travel (often by foot) across Morocco seeking to access Europe via Spain's two enclaves, Ceuta and Melilla (first captured in the fifteenth century). That summer, 103 African migrants had gained access and were awaiting processing in Melilla. "Since the infrastructure and reception facilities in Melilla and Ceuta were grossly inadequate for receiving many migrants," as Luisa Martín Rojo and Teun A. van Dijk noted, "tensions ... sometimes rise high."[24] Protesting their unacceptable living conditions, several dozen African migrants rioted and attacked the local city hall with sticks and stones. They demanded an audience with local officials.[25] The Spanish authorities arrested all 103 African migrants and transported them to mainland Spain, where they remained incarcerated. Even though many of the African migrants did not riot, they were all deported collectively without court hearings. Several were drugged to ease expulsion.[26] Shocked Spanish citizens were concerned that using such tactics contradicted their country's image as a new EU state.

Because forceful security measures against African migrants became politically unpalatable, Spanish and other European leaders began to externalize border enforcement to Morocco, Algeria, Libya, and Tunisia. They were given millions of euros in security funds and military equipment to stop African migrants.[27] Some of the high-tech security equipment provided to Morocco included advanced radars, heat-sensing cameras, speedboats, and helicopters.[28] Moroccan and Spanish naval ships began collaborating in intelligence and joint patrols in the Mediterranean.[29] Spain provided air support to track African migrants moving northward.[30] Although few European politicians would admit it openly, their governments externalized more vigorous border protection practices to their southern autocratic neighbors, who had few qualms about using such methods. European governments enlisted Arab autocracies to help meet "demands for the creation of a migration 'buffer zone' to keep out African migrants."[31]

The upshot was that Europe became more inaccessible for African migrants. Many became, as Joris Schapendonk notes, trapped between the "desert and the sea" in Morocco.[32] They were unable to reach their European "El Dorado," but also could not return to their homelands.[33] Increased border security resulted in higher numbers of deaths and conflicts. Many incidents occurred throughout the 2000s and 2010s, but one particularly tragic event took place in 2005, when 700 migrants clashed with Moroccan border police. They tried to climb the 10-foot, razor-wired border fence, which led to six deaths.[34] Similar conflicts occurred in 2017 and 2018.[35] In January 2018, 209 African migrants scaled the security fence between Morocco and Spain at Melilla, overwhelming and injuring a Spanish border officer.[36] As Amnesty International details, Morocco's police exhibit a "disturbing pattern of breaches of national and international legal standards" when dealing with African migrants.[37] Consequently, prices for clandestine migration increased, costing African migrants between $800 and $1,200 for passage across the Mediterranean (Moroccans paid between $500 and $800).[38]

Given the growing dangers and costs of entering Europe, more and more African migrants began to resettle in Morocco by the 2000s. It became an attractive runner-up destination. Indeed, as Pedro Marcelino and Hermon Farahi note: "African migrants are nowadays a conspicuous sight" in some of Morocco's "largest urban areas." They are "becoming part of a fluid ethnoscape facilitated by a new geopolitical paradigm encompassing West Africa, the Maghreb, and the Mediterranean."[39] In Casablanca, African migrant entrepreneurs cluster in the Senegalese market, where they sell traditional food and crafts. They have also contributed to the informal economy, working as unlicensed street vendors, taxi drivers, building guards, domestic servants, and restaurant staff. Thus, as Emily Pickerill notes, African migrants have developed "creative livelihood strategies in the informal sector" to integrate successfully.[40]

Besides these economic benefits, many African migrants find Morocco—and particularly Casablanca—a freer environment. Indeed, as Kristin Kastner writes, they see Casablanca as a place "where it is possible to move more freely," which is "linked to the image of cool places."[41] Morocco is not fully democratic politically, but perhaps Casablanca's open, liberal atmosphere feels freer compared with many African migrants' home countries, which suffer from ethnic conflict, civil war, and entrenched poverty. Although African migrants reside in numerous areas of Casablanca, they cluster in specific neighborhoods. The Firdous neighborhood, in particular, hosts several blocks of housing primarily occupied by African migrants whose children play with Moroccan children, speaking the local Arabic dialect—*darijah*—fluently. Many African migrants seem to have integrated fully into Moroccan society. Indeed, of the 1,262 African migrant minors registered with the Moroccan government, about 73 percent have been enrolled in public schools.[42] Interviewing migrants, Schapendonk found that some see themselves as having "a role to play in Moroccan society" as long-term residents and, perhaps, someday citizens.[43] For instance, one Congolese migrant who gained legal status in the 2000s became a civil society leader to improve Moroccan society.[44]

In the early 2000s, Morocco introduced legislation to help improve the status of African migrants trying to integrate into society. Promulgated in 2003, Law 02–03 founded an office in the Interior Ministry to deal with migrants. It banned the expulsion of migrants who are minors and pregnant women. It also outlawed refoulement, or the forcible return of migrants to their homelands.[45] The reality, however, was that abuse of migrants continued and often de jure laws did not get enforced fully. Moreover, the regime's bureaucracy moved slowly to implement the new laws. For example, the office dealing with migrant affairs was only established in 2010, though it had been legally approved in 2003. Further, sections of Law 02–03 are written ambiguously, suggesting criminalization of African migrants. Ultimately, Morocco's branch of Doctors Without Borders, working on migration aid, ceased its operations citing ongoing "daily violence" meted out against African migrants.[46] Much of this violence comes from native citizens who oppose the integration of African migrants.

In part, the Moroccan regime's efforts to improve conditions for African migrants came from renewed relations with sub-Saharan African countries. These were reminiscent of trade and political interactions from bygone centuries. Between 2000 and 2010, Morocco's exports to African countries increased from $248 million to $849 million.[47] In the 2000s, Morocco's government-owned airline opened numerous routes to sub-Saharan African countries, expanding to over thirty by 2016. Today, 55 percent of the airline's traffic goes southward.[48] Morocco's government-owned Attijariwafa Bank has the most branches of any bank in fourteen francophone West African countries.[49] After leaving the African Union thirty-three years earlier over regional disputes, Morocco also rejoined this pan-African organization in 2017. Given the stronger ties between Morocco and sub-Saharan African countries, the former's regime sought to improve treatment of African migrants to enhance its image in the latter. This process climaxed in 2013 and 2017, when the regime launched two regularization campaigns that gave legal residency to about 40,000 migrants and refugees.

Theory: explaining opposition and support for African migrants' integration

Although Morocco has a storied status as a multiethnic, integrated country with native citizens of both Arab and African descent, the arrival of new, foreign African migrants has provoked mixed reactions. Six distinct, rival theories hypothesize which citizens should be more (or less) likely to oppose or support African migrants' integration. That is, the theories predict which Moroccans are most likely to either disagree or disagree strongly with this study's main dependent variable statement as it appeared on the survey: "Black African refugees and migrants have good chances to successfully integrate into Moroccan society." The six theories relate to issues of racism, crime, religion, persecution status, job competition, and native citizens' ethnicity. Table 8.1 identifies the survey's main outcome question and questions used as proxies to operationalize and test these theories.

Theory 1 hypothesizes that racism will encourage some Moroccans to oppose African migrants' integration. Racists believe race relations are a hierarchy and see their own race as superior to other inferior races. Cognitive values related to racism include nationalism and a belief that one's own country is superior to others, nativism as the combination of xenophobia and nationalism, and opposition to multiculturalism and the harmonious coexistence of cultures.[50] It is reasonable to theorize that racism shapes attitudes toward migrants, particularly those who are racially, culturally, and ethnically different from native citizens. In sum, people's views on racial hierarchy—regardless of whether they are acquired by education or social construction—could likely predict their opposition to migrants' integration.[51] Those citizens who view migrants as members of inferior races will be more likely to oppose their integration into society.[52] In a survey, it is difficult to gauge a respondent's level of racism, as few people will openly admit to considering some races inferior. Yet, we maintain that the question prompt used herein (see Table 8.1) serves as a reasonable proxy to measure a respondent's personal level of racism. It is a sad (and alarming) fact that nearly 24 percent of Moroccan native citizens either agreed or strongly agreed with our survey item stating that Black Africans' cognitive abilities resemble animals or small children more than adults. Because such Moroccans see Black Africans as inferior human beings, theory 1 hypothesizes that survey respondents holding such intrinsically racist beliefs will be more likely to think such refugees and migrants will have poor chances for successful integration.

Theory 2 concerns criminality, even though the relationship between migrants and crime is not clear and direct. Because of migrants' lower rates of labor participation, lower work skills, and linguistic barriers, some theorize they are more likely to become involved in criminality.[53] Conversely, other studies suggest that low-skilled migrants have equal employability to low-skilled native citizens, and sometimes find labor niches like construction and food processing in which they achieve higher employability.[54] Thus, no scholarly consensus exists on how much migrants may actually be drawn to crime.[55]

Table 8.1: Theories explaining Moroccans' opposition to African migrants' integration

Question prompt (read to respondents)	Do you Agree Strongly, Agree, Neither Agree nor Disagree, Disagree, or Disagree Strongly with these statements about refugees, migrants, and displaced persons who are Black Africans from sub-Saharan African countries?
Outcome statement (dependent variable)	"Black African refugees and migrants have good chances to successfully integrate into Moroccan society"

Explanatory Theories	
Racism	"Black African refugees and migrants have trouble understanding things. They are more like animals or small children than adults."
Criminality	"Black African refugees and migrants increase crime in Morocco."
Religion	"Most Black African refugees and migrants are Christians."
False victims of persecution	"Most Black African refugees and migrants from sub-Saharan Africa do not face real persecution in their home countries."
Job competition	"You are bothered by competing over a job with a Black African refugee or migrant."
Ethnic background	"Which of the following expressions best describes your family's origins?" (Possible Respondent Answers: Arab; Amazigh, Mixed Arab-Amazigh; Black Moroccan)

However, many surveys indicate that native citizens misperceive migrants as exacerbating crime, which is mainly attributable to negative media coverage.[56] This means citizens' concern about crime has become one determinant of attitudes of opposition to migrants' integration.[57] Numerous Moroccan newspaper articles appeared in 2012—notably two entitled "Le péril noir" (The black danger) and "Al-jaraad as-aswad" (The black locusts)—speculating that

African migrants were increasing crime rates. While it is difficult to verify whether African migrants cause more crime than ordinary Moroccans, the unfortunate fact is that many citizens believe that they do. In our survey, around 54 percent of Moroccans agreed or strongly agreed that migrants exacerbate crime. Thus, theory 2 hypothesizes that respondents who perceive African migrants as increasing crime will be more likely to think they have poor chances for successful integration.

Theory 3 relates to religion. Aside from a 3,000-person Jewish community, almost all Moroccans are Sunni Muslims. Islamic celebrations are official holidays, and the king claims religious authority as *amir al-mu'minin* (generally translated as prince of the believers or commander of the faithful). Because African migrants are mostly clandestine, it is difficult to know the true distribution of their religious affiliations. One small and non-representative survey of 154 African migrants (completed in the cities of Rabat, Casablanca, Tangiers, and Fès) found that 74 percent were Christians, 20 percent Muslims, and 5 percent adherents of traditional religions.[58] While the empirical reality is that Black African migrants in Morocco come from numerous countries, and many are in fact Muslims, many Moroccans perceive them to be non-Muslim. And in our survey, Moroccans confirmed this notion with 59 percent of respondents agreeing or strongly agreeing that most African migrants are Christians. Such attitudes hinge upon social identification theory, which posits that individuals sympathize more with individuals with whom they share background characteristics, including religion. Hence, theory 3 hypothesizes that respondents who perceive African migrants as being non-Muslim—most likely Christian—will be more likely to think migrants have poor chances for successful integration.

Theory 4 links to migrants' status as victims of persecution. Many native citizens of recipient countries question whether migrants and refugees are genuine, and whether they fled from real persecution in their home countries. Some allege that they do not face real persecution, but migrate to recipient countries in order to exploit economic opportunities and welfare programs.[59] Native citizens' perceptions (and misperceptions) about whether or not migrants escaped persecution play a critical role in determining attitudes.[60] If native citizens see migrants as escaping real risks of persecution in their homelands, then they will likely become more sympathetic, and thus support their integration into society. However, if they see migrants as not fleeing genuine danger, then they are more likely to oppose their integration.[61] While this study does not distinguish between different types of displaced peoples—

whether economic migrants or political refugees—differences do exist between them. Although often inaccurate, both Arab and European media portray African migrants as simply "economic migrants" who are "masquerading as refugees."[62] This lessens the compassion of native citizens, who become more likely to perceive Africans as economic competitors rather than forcibly displaced peoples. In our survey, 32 percent of Moroccans questioned whether African migrants came to Morocco fleeing real persecution in their homelands. In general, Moroccans may express more sympathy toward African migrants who are perceived to have faced persecution than those who did not. Therefore, theory 4 hypothesizes that respondents will be more likely to think that African migrants have good chances for integration if Moroccans believe migrants fled bona fide danger.

Theory 5 connects to labor competition. However, like the link between migrants and criminality, the relationship between migrants and labor competition is not conclusive. Some studies say new migrant workers increase the labor supply, depressing the wages of native workers. This is particularly true for those who directly compete for jobs with migrants (e.g., low-skilled native workers and low-skilled migrants).[63] Conversely, other studies claim native workers who do not directly compete with migrants over jobs may benefit from their presence. They earn higher wages from firms' lower marginal production costs that boost total output.[64] In an open-economy model, the inflow of low-skilled migrants to recipient countries helps them overcome comparative disadvantages, increase outputs of goods (that need low-skilled workers), and improve exports.[65]

Nonetheless, at least a segment of native citizens in recipient countries directly competes with migrants over jobs and feels economically threatened by their arrival. They thus express opposition to their integration into society. In Western industrialized countries, people with lower skill levels generally oppose migrants more strongly.[66] However, native workers with high skills are not invulnerable to migrant labor market pressure and sometimes express opposition to highly skilled migrants, particularly in high-technology industries.[67] Generally, unemployed native citizens also have negative views toward migrants, blaming them for their struggles in the labor markets.[68] Unemployment in Morocco hovers at 10 percent nationally; greater numbers of African migrants increase competition in the labor market. In this survey, 44 percent of Moroccans were concerned by the possibility of African migrant labor competition. In sum, theory 5 hypothesizes that respondents concerned about African migrants competing with them over jobs will be more likely to think migrants have poor chances for integration.

Theory 6 relates to native citizens' ethnicity, which shapes how people self-identify in society and their opinions toward migrants. Generally, native citizens are more sympathetic to migrants who are similar to them ethnically. Thus native citizens' ethnic backgrounds and also those of foreign migrants could matter in shaping attitudes toward integration.[69] Whereas native citizens who belong to the mainstream culture of a society may sympathize less with migrants, those with social identities closer to migrants may be more sympathetic to them.[70] Although the families of Black Moroccans typically came to Morocco many centuries ago, their ancestors likely came from sub-Saharan African regions originally. Phenotypically, many Black Moroccans also resemble African migrants more than they do Arab or Amazigh citizens. For these reasons, it is possible that Black Moroccans may believe that African migrants have better prospects for integration than non-Black Moroccans. Hence, theory 6 theorizes that respondents who are Black Moroccans will be more likely to think that African migrants have good chances of integration.

Methods and results: a survey on citizen attitudes toward African migrants' integration

To assess these six theories, we conducted a survey of 1,500 native citizens in Morocco's Casablanca–Settat region. Case selection of this site for the survey is justified. Casablanca–Settat is Morocco's most populous region (nearly 7 million citizens). It includes nine different provinces that have urban and rural areas and varying levels of socioeconomic diversity. It includes heavily urbanized areas, such as Casablanca's Ain Chock, Anfa, and Sidi Ma'arouf quarters, as well as rural areas like Mediouna and Sidi Bennour. Casablanca–Settat also has a large number of African migrants. During the 2013 regularization campaign, Casablanca–Settat recorded the second-highest number of migrants at nearly 24 percent of the total of those applying for legal residency status; only the Rabat region exceeded it at nearly 30 percent.[71] This means that Moroccans answering survey questions in the Casablanca–Settat region will provide information based on real, past experiences of interacting with African migrants. If the survey had been conducted in a region with fewer African migrants, respondents' answers may likely have been based on media information or hypothetical scenarios.

The survey was conducted from 12 to 28 September 2017, in collaboration with a professional public opinion polling firm. This firm is equivalent to Morocco's version of the Gallup or Pew organizations in the United States.

The polling firm's president is a local academic who serves as the local director for all major international polling initiatives occurring in Morocco, including the Arab Barometer Initiative, the Afrobarometer Initiative, and the World Values Survey. Since the firm works regularly as the exclusive local partner of these three international polling initiatives, it is considered to be the country's most reliable and meticulous firm. Although other survey organizations exist, they focus primarily on less rigorous market research and are not led by university-trained scholars.

A multi-stage probability sampling design was used with random selection methods at all levels of sampling. This ensured that a representative, randomized sample was obtained. Province served as the strata for the sampling design. Within the provinces, housing blocks were selected randomly by way of a random number generator. Each block had a number assigned to it and was selected randomly. To randomly select houses for administration of the survey, the random walk method was used. This is where the survey interviewer attempts to administer the survey at a randomly selected home along a pre-established randomly selected street route within the housing block. For example, the interviewer will go to every tenth house along the route. Population source data for weighting and other demographics were taken from the Moroccan census and obtained through the National Institute of Statistics (Haut Commissariat au Plan). All efforts were undertaken to ensure quality data collection and survey administration. One of this study's authors oversaw data collection directly in the field, observing nine out of ten of the interviewers who administered the surveys door-to-door. The questionnaire was translated professionally into local Arabic dialect and confirmed by one of the authors, who is professionally fluent in Arabic, and the survey firm president, a native Arabic speaker.

To prepare the interviewers to administer the survey, a pilot survey was conducted and a training workshop was held. These two activities helped refine Arabic translations of questions and enhanced understandability for respondents. They also familiarized the interviewers with the survey questionnaire. Our survey's sampling strategy replicated those successfully used in Morocco by Lindsay Benstead,[72] though our sample was limited to the Casablanca–Settat region. Funding constraints prohibited using a nationally representative sample.

Generally, the survey's results show that native citizens' attitudes toward the integration of African migrants are negative. These trends become especially clear when compared against their positive attitudes toward the inte-

Figure 8.1: Divergent support for the integration of Black African and Arab migrants

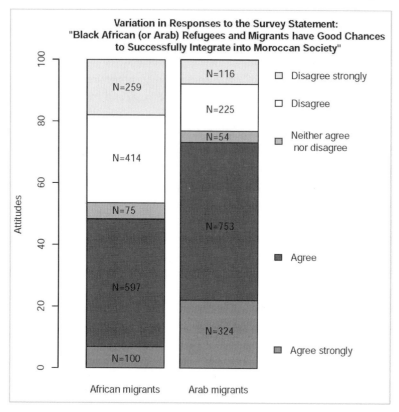

Note: N = Number of survey respondents.
Source: Authors' survey.

gration of Morocco's second major foreign-migrant group: Arab migrants (e.g., Syrians, Iraqis, Algerians, and Libyans). Moroccans support the integration of Arab migrants more than that of African migrants, and they oppose the integration of African migrants more than that of Arab migrants (see Fig. 8.1). Whereas 73 percent of Moroccan citizens support the integration of Arab migrants (i.e., either agree or agree strongly), only 48 percent of them support integration for African migrants.[73] Moreover, although 23 percent of Moroccan citizens have negative views (i.e., either disagree or disagree strongly) on the integration of Arab migrants, 46 percent hold such negative attitudes toward African migrants.

Next, we analyzed what determines Moroccan citizens' opposition or support for the successful integration of African migrants. Utilizing an ordered logistic regression, including basic demographic variables, we obtain the following results (Table 8.2). First, people with a higher level of education support integration of African migrants more than those with less education. Studies find that higher education helps people to develop more cosmopolitan views and tolerance toward migrants by enhancing their knowledge of foreign cultures, strengthening their critical thinking, and diversifying their social networks.[74] Thus it is found that more educated people have weaker nationalistic sentiments,[75] stronger tolerance of outgroup people,[76] and less restrictive attitudes toward migrants.[77]

Second, income level also matters: richer people are more supportive of African migrants' integration than poorer people, who are more vulnerable to exogenous shocks in the economic system and are more likely to believe that their economic status will be badly affected by broader, structural phenomena occurring in society, such as the sudden arrival of new migrants. Consequently, such citizens typically hold more negative views of migrants than those with higher incomes.[78]

Table 8.2: Determinants of the support for the resettlement of African migrants

	(1)	(2)	(3)	(4)	(5)	(6)	(7)
Female	0.16	0.17	0.11	0.16	0.15	0.16	0.11
	(0.10)	(0.10)	(0.11)	(0.10)	(0.11)	(0.10)	(0.12)
Age	0.00	0.00	0.00	0.00	0.00	0.01	0.00
	(0.00)	(0.00)	(0.00)	(0.00)	(0.00)	(0.00)	(0.00)
Education level	0.08**	0.08**	0.10***	0.09**	0.05	0.07**	0.08**
	(0.03)	(0.03)	(0.04)	(0.03)	(0.03)	(0.03)	(0.04)
Income	0.39***	0.39***	0.43***	0.39***	0.40***	0.45***	0.45***
	(0.06)	(0.06)	(0.07)	(0.06)	(0.06)	(0.06)	(0.07)
Unemployed	0.18	0.18	0.20	0.19	0.18	0.17	0.18
	(0.11)	(0.11)	(0.12)	(0.11)	(0.12)	(0.11)	(0.13)
Religiosity	0.07	0.07	−0.06	0.08	−0.09	−0.01	−0.20*
	(0.10)	(0.10)	(0.11)	(0.10)	(0.10)	(0.10)	(0.11)
Racism	0.00	–	–	–	–	–	0.00
	(0.00)						(0.00)
Criminality	–	−0.01	–	–	–	–	−0.00
		(0.01)					(0.01)

Religion	–	–	–0.24*** (0.04)	–	–	–	–0.06 (0.05)
Persecution	–	–	–	0.00 (0.00)	–	–	–0.00 (0.00)
Job competition	–	–	–	–	–0.44*** (0.04)	–	–0.41*** (0.05)
Black Moroccan	0.50*** (0.15)	–	–	–	–	–	0.29* (0.18)
Constant cut1	0.31 (0.42)	0.26 (0.42)	–0.73 (0.51)	0.32 (0.43)	–1.85*** (0.49)	0.23 (0.42)	–1.96*** (0.55)
Constant cut2	1.72*** (0.43)	1.68*** (0.43)	0.72 (0.50)	1.73*** (0.43)	–0.35 (0.49)	1.66*** (0.43)	–0.43 (0.55)
Constant cut3	1.96*** (0.43)	1.91*** (0.43)	0.96* (0.51)	1.96*** (0.43)	–0.10 (0.49)	1.89*** (0.43)	–0.17 (0.55)
Constant cut4	4.52*** (0.44)	4.47*** (0.44)	3.48*** (0.52)	4.52*** (0.45)	2.59*** (0.49)	4.45*** (0.44)	2.46*** (0.56)
Observations	1,276	1,276	1,107	1,276	1,240	1,276	1,081

Note: Positive coefficients denote support for the integration of African migrants. Standard errors in parentheses.
*** $p<0.01$, ** $p<0.05$, * $p<0.1$.

Among the six theories hypothesizing the determinants of attitudes toward African migrants, Moroccan citizens' perceptions of African migrants' religion, their concern about competition with migrants over jobs, and the ethnic background of native citizens shape their opposition or support for integration. Fundamental religious and ethnic characteristics of most Moroccan citizens' social identity affected their opinions toward the integration of African migrants. Respondents who believed that most African migrants are Christians, and those who did not have Black Moroccan family origins, were less likely to support resettlement. The substantive effects of these religious and ethnic characteristics are not trivial. As a respondent's belief in the statement "most Africans refugees and migrants are Christians" changed from "disagree strongly" to "agree strongly," their predicted probability of affirming support for integration of African migrants decreased from 0.49 to 0.31.[79] Similarly, whereas respondents who self-identified as Black Moroccans had a 0.49 predicted probability of affirming support for integration, those who did not had a 0.40 probability (Fig. 8.2).

These results imply that despite the ostensible "modernization" of many societies, including many areas of Morocco over the last thirty years, traditional religious, cultural, and ethnic factors remain deeply embedded and influential in people's minds. They continue to shape how people define their national identity and their attitudes about other foreign people in their society.[80] Such factors are found to shape people's opinions even in the highly modernized and "postmaterialist" societies of Western Europe, where they

Figure 8.2: Predicted probabilities of expressing support for the integration of Black African migrants

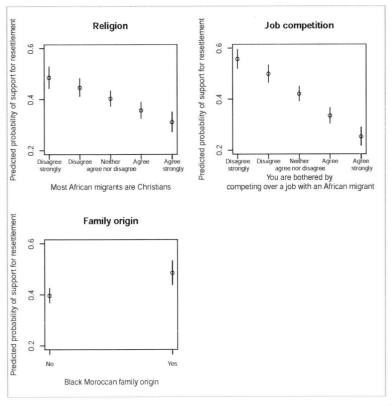

Note: The circles are the predicted probabilities of support for the integration of African migrants (lines denote 95 percent confidence levels). These are calculated with Table 8.1 results (models 3, 5, and 6). The response scale to the question of the support for resettlement of African migrants is: 1 (disagree strongly); 2 (disagree); 3 (neither agree nor disagree); 4 (agree); 5 (agree strongly).

play a significant role in formulating native citizens' attitudes about the integration of foreign migrants.[81] For example, Jan Pieter van Oudenhoven, Karin S. Prins, and Bram P. Buunk find that Dutch people with Moroccan or Turkish ethnic backgrounds have more positive views on the integration of migrants who share the same ethnic backgrounds as themselves, compared with foreign migrants who do not.[82] This coheres with this study's finding that Black Moroccans are more favorable to African migrants' integration than Moroccans who do not self-identify as Black.

Yet basic material issues, such as increasing job market competition, also raise people's opposition to African migrants' integration. As a respondent's answer to the statement "you are bothered by competing over a job with an African refugee or migrant" changed from "disagree strongly" to "agree strongly," their predicted probability of affirming support for African migrants' integration slumped from 0.56 to 0.25.[83]

Despite evidence questioning the role of economic factors in shaping public attitudes toward migrants in Western industrialized countries,[84] this study emphasizes that economic concerns—particularly those about labor market competition—still serve as a significant factor provoking anti-migrant attitudes. This trend from Morocco aligns with other studies.[85] Neil Malhotra, Yotam Margalit, and Cecilia Hyunjung Mo, for example, find that American native citizens working in the high-technology sector who are in direct labor market competition with certain types of migrants (e.g., highly skilled Indian migrants) want to decrease the number of the migrants more than other native citizens do. Similarly, Colleen Ward and Anne-Marie Masgoret also find that the threat of job competition leads to negative views on the integration of migrants in New Zealand.[86] In conclusion, this study's results indicate that both cultural and economic factors influence public opinion toward migrants not only in Western industrialized countries, which comprise the majority of studies on the subject, but also in developing societies, like Morocco, that have become recipient countries of migrants.

Conclusion

Given the danger migrants face when traveling from sub-Saharan Africa through North Africa to Europe, and Europeans' opposition to them entering their countries, this migration route has, as Schapendonk notes, become one of the "most stigmatized forms of migration of the 21st century."[87] Hence, whether intentional or not, more and more African migrants have chosen to resettle in Morocco, without entering the European Union. They have also had a greater number of interactions and conflicts with Morocco's native citizens, who have expressed tremendous variation in how much they oppose or support these migrants' integration into their society. This attitudinal variation is puzzling, especially given Morocco's legacy of interethnic harmony between native citizens of Arab and African descent. Indeed, for centuries, sub-Saharan Africans have migrated to Morocco and integrated into its predominantly Arab and Amazigh society. This helped Morocco—like neighboring North African states—develop into a multiethnic, integrated society. This study used a survey of 1,500 Moroccans to identify the determinants of citizens' opposition and support for African migrants' integration. A number of cultural and economic variables seem to combine to shape these attitudes: Moroccans who believe most African migrants have a different religion (Christianity) from theirs, those who do not have Black Moroccan family origins, and those who are concerned by employment competition with African migrants are less supportive of resettlement.

These findings are reasonable because public attitudes toward migrants are typically found to be shaped mostly by immaterial values (e.g., nativism and racism) and identities (e.g., ethnicity and religion), even in Western industrialized countries.[88] There is, however, an unexpected and interesting aspect in these results because Moroccans' attitudes toward migrants are also shaped by their material concerns (competition for jobs). Some of the literature questions the role of labor market competition in shaping public attitudes toward migration in Western industrialized countries, however.[89] Hypothetically, we might expect it to be more difficult for material factors to determine people's attitudes toward migrants in Arab countries like Morocco, because immaterial factors such as ideology, culture, religion, and ethnicity often seem to hold great importance. However, our results indicate that economic insecurity and material considerations also greatly influence citizens' attitudes, which may derive from Morocco's status as a developing economy with entrenched poverty.

This study's constraints highlight the need for future research. Since the study's survey was conducted solely in the Casablanca–Settat region, it is difficult to know whether its results apply to other Moroccan regions or neighboring North African countries. Follow-up surveys can assess whether these dynamics also appear in other countries with numerous sub-Saharan African migrants, like Algeria, Libya, Tunisia, and Egypt. Doing so could also provide insights about non-Arab migrants and refugees, like Afghan migrants in countries like Iran. In particular, our survey results highlight the challenges and obstacles that non-Arab migrants—especially sub-Saharan Africans—encounter from some native citizens of Arab countries when they depart their homelands in search of work opportunities or safety from persecution.

9

GENDERING THE TRIANGULAR RELATIONSHIP BETWEEN VULNERABILITY, RESILIENCE, AND RESISTANCE

THE EXPERIENCES OF DISPLACED SYRIAN REFUGEES IN JORDAN

Aitemad Muhanna-Matar

Introduction

Since the beginning of the Syrian crisis in 2011, the total number of Syrian refugees who have fled to Jordan and registered with the United Nations High Commissioner for Refugees (UNHCR) was 655,624 as of 2 January 2018.[1] Most Syrian refugee families in Jordan have lost all sources of livelihood and face increasing vulnerability. The majority have become reliant on cash and food assistance from international humanitarian organizations.[2] The continuing household vulnerability and the insufficient support provided by the international humanitarian community have forced many refugee families to accept humiliating and "negative" coping mechanisms. Some of the negative coping strategies are based on Syrian refugees' patriarchal culture, such as early marriage for girls and child labor. Others go beyond the moral virtues of patriarchal culture, such as women's involvement in "survival sex" (e.g., exchanging protection or housing for sexual favors) and socially and culturally unacceptable jobs outside the home.[3] Literature on gender-differentiated coping mechanisms undertaken by Syrian refugees provides evidence of the reconfiguration of gender, in which women act as the primary family providers through reliance on humanitarian assistance, while the men work in casual menial jobs, or are jobless and helpless.[4]

Within this context, international humanitarian aid organizations (IHOs) have intervened intensively to develop Syrian refugees' resilience by providing them with economic and social resources as well as psychosocial support, enabling them to replace "negative" coping strategies based on patriarchal and gender inequitable culture with "positive" coping strategies based on the Western international standards of gender equality.[5] International humanitarian organizations perceive situational gender reconfiguration as a window of opportunity for resisting patriarchal culture, which is considered to be the driving factor for Syrian refugees' gendered vulnerability. Yet, the approach of resilience introduced by the international humanitarian community has not succeeded in replacing the mode of resilience initiated by Syrian refugees based on gender and age. Instead, Syrian refugees combine the two opposing modes of resilience for the sake of family survival. They accommodate what works for them and resist what does not work, and they abide by some governing rules and resist others.

This research fills a gap in the gender literature on Syrian refugees in an attempt to understand the relationship that Syrian refugees, through their experience of displacement, have developed between gendered vulnerability, resilience, and resistance. The chapter frames its analysis on a triangular relationship between the three terms. The term *gendered vulnerability* refers to men and women's loss of all sources of power that allows them to fulfill their socially and culturally constructed gender roles. The term *resilience* refers to their ability to cope with the socioeconomic consequences of war and to recover from shock and stress through the reconfiguration of normative gender. And, finally, the term *resistance* refers to the refusal to fully acquiesce to the principles and rules of the gender-based resilience approach introduced by international humanitarian aid organizations. The three entities do not operate in a sequential manner but in a processual relationship and with mutual assistance.[6] Through a triangular relationship, vulnerable masculinity and femininity are negotiated, renegotiated, and contested through different modes of everyday acts of resilience and resistance, or resilient resistance. According to Caitlin Ryan, "enacting a resilient resistance means finding a way to get on with daily life without acquiescing to the prevailing political, economic, or social situation."[7]

In the following section, the chapter engages with some of the existing literature on vulnerability, resilience, and resistance in order to shape the conceptual framework of analysis. Next is a contextualization of the gendered vulnerability of Syrian refugees, how they cope with it, and the response of the international humanitarian community. Following this is a description of the research methodology. The chapter concludes with an analysis and discussion of empirical data drawn from the personal narratives of sixty Syrian refugees.

Conceptual analytical framework

In a situation of displacement, gendered vulnerability is an expected result when both men and women have lost all their socioeconomic sources of power to fulfill their gender roles within normative gender relations of power. In such situations, both resilience and resistance become inevitable acts, and they most likely interweave for the sake of survival on the one hand and re/gaining power on the other. This is contrary to the argument that resilience cannot be concurrently associated with resistance because "the resilient subject is forced to put all its effort into mere survival."[8] However, resilience and resistance do not necessarily operate in the same directions and with similar intents. One may precede or follow, produce or reproduce, enhance or possibly suppress the other, but neither acts as completely and constantly competitive with or opposed to the other.[9]

With the same logic, gendered vulnerability, as an intersectional entity, is influenced by different factors, or layers, of power based on differences in class, sect, gender, age, geography, history, state politics, and subjective and intersubjective factors.[10] These different forms of power that a person experiences in his/her life generate different types and layers of vulnerability, and, as a result, generate different modes of resilience and resistance, or resilient resistance. Resilience and resistance amalgamate in their everyday practices in ways that may simultaneously undermine a particular form of power and recreate another.[11] The relationship between gendered vulnerability, resilience, and resistance acts in a triangular manner in which each is influenced by and influences the other, but with unpredictable gendered outcomes. Gendered outcomes—progressive, regressive, or in-between—may not only depend on an individual's capacity to make change, but also what form of change is desired to create or recreate power. Within this triangular and dynamic process of interaction between the three entities, vulnerable people are always a subject of acting and being acted upon.[12] They accommodate and resist power, produce and resist vulnerability, and govern and are governed.

This chapter does not present gender resilience as contrasting with gender resistance, or as merely a governing tool used by those in power to impose a particular form of gender and gender relations according to neoliberal gender and development ideology. The neoliberal ideology calls for the burden of tackling gendered vulnerability to be shifted from state agencies to individual vulnerable women and men by enhancing their resilience.[13] Rather, gender resilience is defined as an integral component of gender resistance and an engine that produces and provokes resistance. Gender resilience is by itself a form of resistance when its act does not fully comply with or rely on principles of gender governance imposed by institutions in power.[14] Resilient resistance may be visible and invisible, loud and silent, straightforward and maneuvering, and pure and contaminated. Although actors of resilient resistance do not always act with a prior articulated and conscious intent to resist, the association of "a subjective account of oppression" with "an express desire to counter that oppression" is sufficient to count their acts as resistance.[15] Resilient resisters may act spontaneously as they reflect on their previous knowledge and life skills to survive, solve a certain problem, follow a particular gender desire, or gain and regain power.

Resilient resistance, as it is presented in this chapter, is a form of gender governmentality that vulnerable Syrian refugees shape on their own. Resilient resistance overlaps with some of the techniques of gender governmentality introduced by humanitarian organizations based on international standards, yet it also contrasts with them in a number of other respects. The modes of resilient resistance revealed in this research are analyzed within post-structural theories of everyday resistance, which challenge the inevitable relationship between resistance and the disturbance of power structure.[16] Everyday resistance is understood as part of daily activities, or tactics undertaken at a certain time and under certain conditions, that may or may not disturb the existing order of power.[17] Theorists of everyday resistance debate its relationship with power; however, this chapter seeks to go beyond that debate to argue that everyday resistance is definitely connected to power but does not necessarily aim to subvert it. Everyday resistance may aim to restore or regain power,[18] even symbolically.

According to James Scott, everyday acts of resistance are a hidden transcript, or "infrapolitics," which seek "tacit, *de facto* gains" but without complying with, or legitimizing, the ideology of those in power.[19] Such everyday resistance is marked by "passive noncompliance, subtle sabotage, evasion and deception."[20] In everyday resistance, the line between resilience and resistance is obscure and depends on the changing context of power, such as when visible or public resistance is too risky and takes a lower profile or an invisible form in order not to jeopardize necessities for living.[21] Within everyday resistance theories, coping for survival and coping for resistance are not mutually exclusive concepts but are spaces within which some aspects of power move back and others move forth.[22]

This chapter bases its analysis on the concept of everyday resilient resistance to challenge the dominant neoliberal discourse of resilience adopted by the international humanitarian community.[23] The neoliberal project of resilience and resistance aims to reshape gendered subjectivity and agency to visibly and publicly operate within the universal principles of gender equality,[24] without recognizing the everyday forms of resilient resistance that are undertaken by vulnerable people and mostly labeled as "negative coping strategies." Gendered vulnerability is conceptualized by international humanitarian organizations in relation to patriarchal culture, and thus the dynamics of resilience and resistance have to operate within the intent and goal of tackling patriarchal culture and gender inequality based on international standards.[25]

This chapter will discuss and analyze Syrian refugees' modes of resilient resistance as ways of intentionally or unintentionally delegitimizing the international humanitarian organizations' discourse of gender resilience and resistance as well as the gender ideology that underpins it. Resilient resistant acts described in this chapter challenge the binary gender presentation of vulnerability, resilience, and resistance and emphasize that the three entities operate in a dynamic interactive process. Each contributes to shaping, reshaping, undermining, or strengthening the other depending on the changing context of power and the opportunities that everyday resilient resistance generates. Within this process, masculinity and femininity act as mediators to push resilient resistance forward (a higher profile of resistance) or backward (a higher profile of resilience), with unpredictable gender outcomes.

The context of Syrian refugees

The context through which gendered vulnerability, resilience, and resistance triangularly operate includes three dimensions: the legal and socioeconomic aspects of gendered vulnerability, how Syrian refugees have coped with it, and how the international humanitarian community has responded to strengthen Syrian refugee families' resilience.

Legal and socioeconomic aspects of vulnerability

Over two-thirds (78.5 percent) of displaced Syrian refugees live in urban and semi-urban areas and the rest live in camps. They are distributed primarily in four Jordanian governorates: 26.4 percent in Amman, 20.9 percent in Irbid, 23.9 percent in Mafraq, and 16.2 percent in Zarqa.[26] Many Syrian refugees who live in urban and semi-urban areas still experience difficulties documenting their refugee status and obtaining government-issued identity cards and birth and marriage certificates. Refugees with no documentation legalizing their stay in urban areas are mostly those who have left Syrian refugee camps in Jordan, such as Za'tari and Azraq, without following formal bailout procedures required by the camp authorities.

Documentation for Syrian refugees living in urban areas is necessary to prove their legal status, identity, and family relationships in Jordan.[27] In early 2015, the Jordanian government introduced new regulatory procedures for Syrian refugees who live in urban areas. Every Syrian refugee living outside the camps must be registered with UNHCR and obtain an updated Ministry of Interior (MoI) card. Syrian refugees without updated MoI cards or UNHCR Asylum Seeker Certificates are subject to risks of deportation either to refugee camps or to Syria. Their access to basic services including health, education, and the labor market is also at risk.[28]

Lack of documentation also risks refugees' ability to obtain work permits. Until March 2016, the Jordanian government did not allow Syrian refugees to have a work permit, and, as a result, 99 percent worked illegally.[29] With few opportunities available in formal labor markets, refugees are often pushed to accept informal work with low wages and poor safety standards. If Syrian refugees are caught working illegally, they are sent to the Za'tari and Azraq refugee camps.[30] In view of insufficient funds to meet the humanitarian needs of Syrian refugees, the international humanitarian community put pressure on the Jordanian government to ease its market regulations for Syrian refugees in order to reduce their dependence on humanitarian aid. As a result, starting from March 2016, the Jordanian government eased Syrian refugees' access to work permits. Nonetheless, most Syrian refugees, particularly men, have been reluctant to take advantage of this policy change.[31] There are two interlinked reasons for their reluctance: (1) Syrian refugees are aware of the fragility of the Jordanian market and believe that attaining a work permit will not allow them to compete with Jordanians, who dominate the best jobs;[32] (2) Syrian refugees do not want to risk their access to emergency cash and humanitarian food support, which is more secure than working in the fragile Jordanian market.[33]

The 2015 UNHCR Vulnerability Assessment Framework Baseline Report indicates that Syrian refugee families live below the Jordanian national poverty line of 68 Jordanian dinar (JoD) ($95.91) per capita a month. According to a 2016 Care International assessment report, the monthly income of Syrian refugee families has declined from 209 JoD ($294.78) in 2015 to 185 JoD ($260.93) in 2016. Most families need to spend more than they earn in order to meet the needs of their household, which accumulates high levels of debt.[34] More than one-third (39 percent) of surveyed households were headed by females, an 11 percent increase from 2015.[35]

In terms of Syrian refugee health and education conditions, up to 30 percent of Syrian refugees in Jordan have specific physical or intellectual needs, and one in seven refugees is affected by chronic illness.[36] The Jordanian government opened additional schools and classes to absorb Syrian refugees of school age. Yet, around a third of Syrian children aged seven to eighteen are not currently attending school. Although Syrian refugees' health and education services in urban areas are subsidized by the Jordanian government, accessing healthcare and education generates other expenses such as fees, transport, medicines, clothes, and books that are often unaffordable for many Syrian refugee families.[37]

The vulnerability of Syrian refugees has negatively affected all segments of the Syrian refugee population in Jordan, with some differences based on gender, age, education, ethnicity, geographic location, and previous sociocultural and economic background. In regard to some aspects of vulnerability, some Syrian men appear more vulnerable than women and children. For example, men were more exposed to torture from the Syrian regime than women, and this has left many of them with signs of trauma and other psychological problems, as well as physical injuries resulting in chronic disability.[38] The majority of employed Syrian refugees are men who work in the informal economy and thus are subject to police surveillance and harassment and are more at risk of deportation to Syria or refugee camps.[39] Teenage males are more likely than females to drop out of school to earn an income—37 percent of males aged fifteen to seventeen years are economically active compared with 3 percent of females of the same age group.[40]

As commonly occurs in situations of war and displacement, refugees are exposed to sexual and gender-based violence (SGBV). Almost all reports on SGBV produced by international humanitarian organizations confirm that livelihood vulnerability of Syrian refugee families generates more sexual and domestic violence against women.[41] Other reports indicate that women in female-headed households are more exposed to SGBV than those living in male-headed households because they are forced to leave home to search for sources of income, whether from humanitarian organizations or the private sector.[42] Yet, the available data on SGBV against Syrian refugee women does not provide sufficient and accurate evidence that Syrian refugee men have become more violent as a result of displacement and vulnerability.

How do Syrian refugees cope with household vulnerability?

Although many Syrian families fled to Jordan with no possessions, particularly those whose houses and properties were destroyed by aerial bombardment, others escaped the war with money, jewelry, or other assets of economic value. The latter group relied on their savings in the first phase of their displacement to cope with the crisis of livelihood, while the former became completely reliant on humanitarian aid from international charity and humanitarian organizations, mosques, and individual donors. However, with the high housing and living expenses in Jordan compared with Syria, families' savings were exhausted and most refugee families soon became exposed to extreme poverty and thus reliant on humanitarian aid.[43] Rent, for example, has been a major financial burden for Syrian refugee families, as it is estimated to make up around half of families' monthly expenditures.[44] To cope with the high cost of rent, many refugees followed their tradition of living in extended families, where several siblings and their spouses share the same accommodation with their parents. Syrian refugee families also cope with their household vulnerability by reducing food intake in general, particularly expensive food items such as meat, vegetables, and fruits.[45]

Child labor has risen as a household coping strategy, particularly in female-headed households. In a 2014 International Labor Organization (ILO) assessment, only 11 percent of employers reported that they had recruited children during the past three to four years, while 84 percent said that they had employed children in 2015 and 2016.[46] Child labor, particularly among boys, is more common among households that were poor and that had little or no education before the conflict.[47] Child labor is also used as a response to the threat that adult men face by working illegally.

Another coping mechanism based on gender is early marriage for girls, which is one form of SGBV, according to UN agencies. Although early marriage in Syria before the war was recorded at 13 percent, and the official age of marriage was eighteen, early marriage among Syrian refugee girls is presented in almost all international humanitarian organizations' reports as a culturally accepted practice for displaced Syrian refugees. Parents, particularly those who came from rural areas and have little or no education, believe that marriage might secure a better future for their daughters and ease the financial burden faced by families that depend on humanitarian aid. Early marriage has increased rapidly since the conflict began—the figure rose to 18 percent in 2012, 25 percent in 2013, and 32 percent in early 2014.[48]

In addition, gender roles among adult men and women have reconfigured. Reports confirm that men take the risk of working in illegal and informal jobs with sometimes humiliating and exploitative conditions, where they work six days per week for an average of ten to twelve working hours per day.[49] Along with the precarious working conditions for men, many women, both in female- and male-headed households, are forced to leave home and spend long hours searching for humanitarian assistance or for jobs in the informal sector to cover gaps in family expenditure. They work in harvesting in the agriculture sector; in private schools, kindergartens, or other organizations; and as hairdressers, secretaries, house cleaners, and salespersons in shops.[50] Other women use their traditional domestic skills to generate income for their families by making crafts or food items for sale to neighbors, or selling fruits or vegetables from home or in the streets and local markets.[51]

Gendered resilience-based humanitarian response to Syrian refugees

To tackle the above-mentioned negative coping strategies initiated by Syrian refugees, based on their patriarchal and cultural views on gender and age, the international humanitarian community introduced a resilience-based approach to the Syrian crisis. It aims to build the capacity of Syrian refugees to self-regulate and acquire attitudes and skills that enable them to replace negative coping strategies with positive ones.[52] This is part of the global neoliberal project of resilience that focuses on self-sufficiency—Syrian refugees invest in their displacement situation by learning how to become self-sufficient and not reliant on the state or international humanitarian aid. According to the international humanitarian community, one element that significantly contributes to addressing the root causes of vulnerability is gender and gender relations of power within the household and in the community. While women are often considered strong and capable in situations of war and displacement, they are also regarded as belonging to the most vulnerable group of people. This is explained by such factors as women often lacking access to and control over resources, being economically dependent on men as the breadwinners, being exposed to reproductive health dangers due to pregnancy and child-birth, being restricted in their mobility because of gender stereotypes and domestic responsibilities, and being exposed to SGBV due to a lack of safe accommodation and social infrastructure.[53]

Resilience from the international humanitarian aid perspective also requires women to have equal access to that enjoyed by men in the formal labor market and in vocational training, facilitating their competition in the open market. From the neoliberal perspective of resilience and resistance, Syrian refugee women need to act as responsible subjects able to manage their own lives and make rational choices. Being autonomous and self-regu-lating is a precondition for women to challenge their gendered vulnerability, which is basically caused by patriarchal culture.[54] International humanitarian organizations in Jordan also give high priority to SGBV prevention efforts. These efforts draw on the assumptions that Syrian refugee women and ado-lescent girls are at high risk of SGBV because they have no access to educa-tion and are culturally restricted in their participation in the labor market. Therefore, they need to be protected and provided with vocational training, psycho-social support, support from self-reliance programs, and financial support to set up their own businesses.[55] International humanitarian organi-zations have started to place more emphasis on the importance of engaging men in SGBV prevention efforts, which focus on changing men's attitudes about gender inequality and supporting the empowerment of women to become socially and economically autonomous.[56]

Despite hundreds of thousands of Syrian refugees being targeted based on the resilience approach of international humanitarian aid, Syrian refugees' socioeconomic conditions of vulnerability have not improved and have actu-ally deteriorated. The Care International assessment report of 2017 indicates that early marriage has declined by only 1.8 percent compared with the 2016 assessment. Additionally, there were declines in child labor by 2.1 percent, removal of children from school by 4.3 percent, and reliance on humanitarian aid by 2.5 percent. This context of vulnerability and resilience gives an indica-tion that Syrian refugees combine the two opposing strategies of resilience: the ones initiated by Syrian refugees based on their patriarchal culture, and those adopted by the international humanitarian community based on Western international standards. Does this combination only reflect an actual further need for coping at a material level, or might it reflect acts of resistance to cope in a particular way, or perhaps both? The research presented below seeks to answer this question by reflecting on Syrian refugees' everyday experiences of gendered vulnerability, resilience, and resistance.

Research methodology

Research methods

The research relies on the ethnographic qualitative methods of personal narrative interviewing (PNIs), focus groups (FGs), and key informants interviews (KIIs). Although six FGs with Syrian refugees (three with women, three with men), and nine KIIs were conducted (with case managers from one international organization responsible for assessing Syrian refugees' eligibility for humanitarian assistance following the organization's gender criteria of vulnerability), this chapter largely relies on empirical material collected from sixty PNIs with Syrian refugees (thirty men and thirty women). Data from FGs and KIIs are used to cross-check, or support, the data of PNIs. Some PNIs were conducted only with one person (a wife, a husband, or a female head of household) and others were conducted with a couple. On a few occasions, three to four female and male friends were interviewed together (sex segregated), but each narrated his or her personal experience. The group PNIs were useful for participants to share memories, emotions, practices, and meanings. I purposely facilitated the personal narratives to go beyond accounts of the present situation in order to encourage participants to give expression to their memories of the past and their anticipations of the future—their experience before and after displacement. The use of PNIs facilitated a free and relatively informal process of storytelling.[57]

In all personal narratives I conducted with individuals and groups, I asked one general question: "Can you please tell me how your style of life after the war and displacement has changed from your style of life before the war?" During research participants' narration, I intervened to elicit further clarification, or interpretation, by asking sub-questions such as: "What did you do in response to that event? How did you manage to do that? What were the consequences of doing things this way? Why did you select this path of action? How did your husband, wife, or other family members respond?" The average time of each PNI was between ninety minutes and two hours. Each group

PNI was conducted once, and about half of the individual PNIs, particularly the ones with women, were conducted over two sessions. Female interviewees were more open in narrating their stories and experiences than men, and thus one interview was not sufficient to generate a holistic narrative. A second session of an interview was often conducted to cover the information gaps in the first session.

Research sites and sample

Research participants were equally distributed between three governorates in which Syrian refugees are concentrated: Mafraq, Zarqa, and Amman. Participants were purposively selected to vary in terms of where they fled from in Syria and when, their socioeconomic backgrounds before displacement, and their age, social status, employment, location, size of household, and sources of livelihood. The great majority of research participants fled from the most marginalized urban and rural areas of Syrian provinces. Most fled from Daraa and Homs, and the rest fled from Ghouta (a suburb of Damascus), Aleppo, Deir al-Zor, Raqqa, and Hama. The vast majority were between twenty-seven and forty-five years of age. The majority (forty-five out of sixty, 75 percent) had completed their schooling between grades six and nine (or lower), and the rest were highly educated, with college and university degrees. In terms of their employment before the Syrian war, only five women had worked (one doctor, three teachers, and one business owner). The men had worked in different jobs before the war: some in the public sector and the majority in the private sector as laborers, business owners, and technicians. At the time of the field research, two women were working as cleaners, two as volunteers with international organizations, and one as a salesperson in a pharmacy. The majority of men (twenty-four out of thirty, 80 percent) worked without permits in different jobs, mostly in packaging, construction, and restaurants, and the rest did not work for medical reasons. I purposely conducted individual and group PNIs with married men and women, and female heads of households who are widows, divorced, or separated. The reason for such a selection is to focus on the roles of men and women in providing for the family and how their dynamics of resilience and resistance for the sake of family survival differ. I also purposely selected my research participants to be reliant on humanitarian aid, whether the regular financial support came from UN agencies or other international and national humanitarian organizations.

Empirical analysis and discussion

The personal narratives of Syrian refugees challenge the predominant mainstream perception of gendered vulnerability that has been adopted by the international humanitarian community, which is based on women and men's different access to material sources of power after displacement. Syrian refugees appeared more passionate in their personal narratives to present their feelings of gendered vulnerability not just in relation to what is lost: "What is lost is lost and will never return."[58] Their feelings of vulnerability are strongly connected to their successes and achievements and the lifestyle they had before the war. They were more fluent and emotional when talking about their past than their present conditions—several women cried during the interview. When they were asked to compare their lifestyle after and before displacement, the answers of the majority of men were "can't be comparable," or "not comparable."[59] The answers given by most of the women were similar to that offered by Nehal,[60] a woman in her mid-thirties who fled from Damascus and lived in Amman: "whatever we do, we will not have the same life we lived in Syria." I observed that the common saying, "we have nothing here,"[61] was not necessarily about what they currently have, or do not have, but a comparison with what they used to have and how they used to live before the war, as their memories were still fresh.

What men and women had achieved in terms of living standards, education, employment, social status, and prestige before the war determined the level of bitterness concerning the loss they experienced after displacement. This dimension of gendered vulnerability contributed critically to how men and women interdependently responded to their present vulnerable conditions and the different dynamics of resilient resistance they developed. I classified the personal narratives of the Syrian refugees into three categories based on differences in their socioeconomic and cultural backgrounds, experienced modes of masculinity and femininity, and the modes of resilient resistance they undertook, as follows.

1. *Resilient resistance through silence, avoidance, and being in-between two rejected opposing gender discourses.*

Men and women in this category had succeeded in achieving a certain gender position and image of power that was based on the moral virtues of patriarchy. Most came from relatively wealthy families, had a good level of education, and had prestigious work positions and status in their local communities prior to displacement. However, due to the distribution of origins of Syrian refugees, with the majority fleeing from rural areas and with a low level of education, the number of people in this category was much smaller than in the other two categories. They were between thirty and forty-five years old and most of them had finished their schooling or university education. Most of the women described their husbands as authoritative, reliable, decisive, responsible, and as having had a strong sense of masculinity before the war and having remained the same after displacement. Men who had established a good standard of living for their families also confirmed that their marital relationships were ideal before displacement, when they were committed to fulfilling their gender responsibilities and maintaining their social status, both for themselves and their families. According to the women's narratives, after displacement, gender relations between wives and husbands remained tolerant and cooperative.

Although this group withstood the effect of losing material power by war and displacement, they rigidly resisted losing the constructed moral image of the gendered subjectivity (masculinity and femininity) they experienced before the war. They were keen to talk about their lifestyle and to glorify the structure of gender relations of power they experienced before the war. Resistance in this category was largely symbolic, relying on idealizing and moralizing a structure of gender relations of power—in which a man is the primary family provider and protector of women and children—which was no longer functioning after displacement.

Syrian refugees in this category reconfigured their gender after displacement but in a selective and limited way. According to the narratives of wives in this group, their husbands coped with their household vulnerability in different ways: accepting work in illegal, insecure, and demeaning jobs that were inferior to their employment in Syria; and reducing their personal expenses to a minimum to provide for the family, for example, by quitting smoking and reducing the quality and quantity of their food intake. Men in this group confirmed that they avoided socializing with other Syrian refugees in their local community, engaging in activities organized by humanitarian organizations, and negotiating with their employers to improve their working conditions. They also avoid obtaining a work permit, as explained by Abu Haider, a thirty-seven-year-old man from Amman, because: "We paid fees for the government to obtain the permit and the government did not guarantee us secure jobs. With or without permits, we will end up doing the same demeaning jobs." Avoidance here has a resilience and a resistance dimension. The resilience dimension was exemplified in their attempt to adapt to the existing conditions to avoid the risk of losing their jobs. They also tried to avoid the expenses of socializing and engagement. The resistance dimension of avoidance was presented in several ways by different men: "not to feel dishonored by the police if they capture us working illegally";[62] "not to be fooled by government promises";[63] "to restore my dignity in front of those providing humanitarian support";[64] and "escape daily humiliation from my boss."[65]

The majority of men in this group emphasized that they overlooked daily abusive behaviors or not being paid their wages by their employers, and preferred to stay silent to ensure the continuity of their work. When asked why they stayed silent against these abusive acts, the answers varied. Abu Anwar, a thirty-nine-year-old man who used to be a business owner in Syria, employing several laborers, said:

> What result will I have if I argue with my boss? He is a Jordanian, he will take me to the police and the police may send me to Za'tari camp, or deport me to Syria for any alleged security reason. By staying silent I keep my job and do not put myself in an encounter with the police.

Avoidance and silence according to these quotations imply a conscious intent to delegitimize the humiliating existing system of power that governs the lives of Syrian refugees in Jordan, whether by the Jordanian government or international humanitarian organizations.

Another aspect of gender reconfiguration that men of this group used for coping with their household vulnerability was accepting the idea of visiting organizations to seek humanitarian assistance. According to interviews conducted with the case managers, men of this group are more silent and not confrontational when they present their need for assistance. Most of them go to the assessment appointments without their wives, as several men in the focus groups recounted: "our wives have never been in a position to seek assistance. We do that ourselves."[66] Another man in his early forties who was a teacher in Syria and used to have a prestigious social position before the war said angrily: "this is what international humanitarian organizations want, to change our culture, as presumably we came from an animal shed."

Men and women in this group reciprocally presented themselves as sacrificing to rent a decent house for their children, to obtain good quality food for them, and to provide care and love in order for them not to feel bad about their conditions. Their children's education was a priority. None of the parents in this group had asked their young sons to work, nor had they married off their daughters at a young age. They emphasized that they treat girls and boys equally. The gender relations between men and women in this group are intimate, negotiable, and not discriminatory, but they are not equitable either. During the conversation with men and women of this group, they confirm that they are committed to their religion (Islam) and believe that according to Islam, men and women are not equal but complement each other's roles and responsibilities.

Abu Hasan, a forty-year-old man with a university degree, viewed Syrian culture as not being oppressive against women and girls. He rejected the association of Syrian culture with the negative coping mechanisms used by Syrian refugees, as presented by humanitarian organizations. He said:

> In Syria, education for girls and boys is obligatory, including in rural areas. Marrying off young girls is not a Syrian culture, but it is greediness of some Syrian parents. This is a moral not a cultural act. Those who did it in Syria are the same who are doing it here. For me, this is not a big story. Early marriage for girls is exacerbated by international organizations and western media to distract attention from important issues.

Men of this group tried to present their Syrian culture as morally superior to resist the post-displacement dismantling of family relations caused by men and women's involvement in coping strategies. They also considered physically able Syrian men who allowed their wives to leave home to search for jobs or humanitarian assistance to "have no sense of manhood."[67] Although the majority of men in this group, according to their wives' narratives, were more authoritative toward their wives and children, they were also more loving and caring. This is the model of masculinity that is considered ideal by the wives of this group. Um Kamal, a thirty-seven-year-old woman, criticized men who have become careless and irresponsible after displacement, saying: "I am happy that my husband has not changed. He is still the man of the family and we rely on him. He endures humiliation at work but did not let us feel in need for anything."[68]

Um Ahmed is a thirty-two-year-old woman residing in Amman. She criticized international humanitarian organizations that encourage women to search for jobs outside the home when these organizations are aware that there are no appropriate services available for children:

> Of course that would be ideal for both men and women to work in good jobs. But we know that would not happen. Syrian men do not mind their wives working if there are good services for children. If not, international organizations have to give the priority to provide good jobs for men and let women take care of children. This is how violence against women is reduced.

The three tactics that men and women in this category used—namely avoidance, silence, and being in-between two opposing gender discourses of resilience—are indications that they reject compliance with the rules and discourses introduced by institutions in power: the Jordanian government and the international humanitarian organizations. Some members of this group have an ideological and political intent behind their "invisible" means of resistance, as reflected in one narration: "We are aware that international organizations want to distance us from our religion and our national cause by providing us humanitarian aid."[69] However, positioning themselves in-between two opposing gender ideologies has another implication that goes beyond moral, ideological, and political aspects. It is the intent of this group to regain the power that they had attained prior to displacement by not show-ing a complete hostility to the gender discourse introduced by organizations in power, as is demonstrated in Um Ahmed's quote above.

2. *Resilient resistance through maneuvering with the gender resilience discourse of humanitarian assistance.*

This mode of resilient resistance is more common among Syrian refugees who came from poor and marginalized backgrounds and who had a low level of education prior to displacement. It is particularly common among female heads of households but is not exclusive to this particular socioeconomic group. According to the narratives of some of the married women who fell into this category, their husbands' modes of masculinity were characterized as weak. Eight out of thirty female research participants who fled from rural areas characterized their husbands before displacement as indecisive, irrespon-sible, unreliable, and controlled by their mothers or fathers. Some also reported that their husbands were violent.

This group of men was described by their wives as having become more resilient to gender reconfiguration and was responding positively to the gen-der discourse of international humanitarian organizations. Men of this group invested in the opportunities available in their displacement and the gender resilience discourse introduced by humanitarian organizations to hide their weak masculinity, or to renegotiate it.

According to interviews conducted with case managers, men in this cate-gory, who fled from rural areas and had a low level of education, did not mind their wives going out to search for humanitarian assistance, and they joined their wives when they did so. Suad, aged thirty-three, who had only finished grade nine schooling, analyzed the characteristics of this group of Syrian refugee men, reflecting on her previous knowledge of men from her rural community in Syria and her personal experience with her husband.

Suad resides in Mafraq after having fled from a rural area of Homs in 2013. She presented her married life before displacement as full of misery because her husband was financially reliant on his mother and was not able to protect her from her mother-in-law's daily mistreatment and oppression. Describing him after displacement, she said:

> My husband, who did nothing in his previous life, counts himself as equal to those who hold weapons and sacrificed their life for their nation, or equal to men who work day and night to feed their families. Syrian refugee men like my husband are not few.... One day he said to me: "I am not different from other Syrian men who fled Syria: doctors, teachers, lawyers. We are the same now, refugees and reliant on humanitarian aid." He does not mind visiting humanitarian organizations several times to show that he is eligible for assistance. Not only that, he comes and informs me about organizations that provide assistance, and asks me to go on my own because he knows that these organizations prioritize women.

Suad added:

> OK, I don't deny that he has changed after displacement. He is no longer interfering in my life, he even does not ask me where I go. He is quieter now. Why not to be quieter? He does not do much to improve his and his children's lives. I am the one who does everything. I receive *basmet e'yn* from UNHCR to pay for the rent.[70] Sometimes I feel it would be easier to live without him, but I don't want my children to grow up without their father.

Suad's narration implies an overlapping between two forms of resistance. While her husband maneuvers within international organizations to hide his weak masculinity, she invests in her husband's resistance to gain power and free her mobility without necessarily taking revolutionary action against him, even though she has the power to do so. Resilient resistance here is intersectional and depends on the particular context created by displacement. In a context of displacement that socially and economically recognizes men's vulnerability, and morally legitimizes their reliance on humanitarian assistance for the family's survival, the weak masculine characters of men before displacement became invisible within the overall contextual vulnerability of displaced Syrian men. As Suad's husband told her: "We are the same now—refugees and reliant on humanitarian aid." Men with weak masculinity feel empowered by equating themselves with other men who came from better-off socioeconomic and cultural backgrounds and used to fulfill their socially and culturally constructed masculine role before the war. This group of men also realizes that searching for humanitarian assistance is a humiliating and unpleasant task for many Syrian refugee men, and thus they invest in it to gain power through more engagement with the humanitarian organizations' activities.

Most wives of these men described themselves before displacement as passive and weak, and living in conflict with their mothers-in-law during their married life before the war. These women also invested in the context of displacement to renegotiate their femininity. They invested in their husbands' renegotiation of their masculinity to gain freedom of mobility and to live without violence. They also developed new life skills and knowledge that made them able to protect themselves within the new context. Most interviewed married women of this group confirmed that the gender relations of power between wives and husbands had become more tolerant after displacement. The reason given for this change is related to how men and women have to act with international humanitarian organizations to gain material support, but it is not an actual change in the attitudes of men. Safa, aged twenty-eight from Zarqa, said: "My husband wishes to prevent me from going out but he can't. He knows that it is me who brings money and humanitarian assistance."

Sana is thirty years old and resides in Amman with three young children. She fled from Ghouta, a poor suburb of Damascus, with her husband and his family. She and her husband did not finish their schooling. Previously, her husband worked in construction as a daily casual laborer, and she worked in a textile factory but quit after marriage. Before the war, Sana lived with her husband's family in very poor conditions and had daily problems. She described her husband as lazy and reliant on his mother. He was unable to provide for her, and sometimes he beat her to satisfy his mother. When asked how things had changed, she said:

> Things have changed so much, some changes are good and some are bad. My husband is still lazy and does not want to search for a job, but he is so good when it comes to humanitarian aid. Now, he presents himself outside home as the head of the family, and he has become active with humanitarian and charity organizations. He helps them distribute aid to Syrian refugees. He becomes a man outside the home. I am not angry about that. What I am angry about is that after he retrieved his manhood, he cheated on me with one of the young Syrian refugee women.

When Sana was asked how she responded to her husband's cheating, she said:

> I don't trust him anymore. I also do whatever I want to do and don't inform him about everything. For my family to survive, I go and visit organizations and ask

for support. I had several incidents of sexual harassment from men who call themselves donors for Syrian refugees. The first time, I told my husband that a wealthy man offers JoD 5,000 [around $7,000] to have me. He said jokingly: "OK, ask him to give you the money" ....Since then I stopped telling him anything because I don't trust him to protect me. I protect myself. I know how to deal with such cheap men. I *bullef we ba dour* [maneuver] until I get what I want without letting them do anything wrong against me. By the way, those cheap men are so weak ... they are afraid of a cat. Though I always try to be careful. I wish I can rely on my husband to protect me.

Although the characteristics of men of this group are mostly narrated by their wives, two men presented their personal experience. Jamal is twenty-nine years old and resides in Zarqa. He came from a Bedouin family with a rigid tribal culture. He said that he used to have a weak personality and was controlled by his father and uncles. During the focus group, he said: "International humanitarian organizations helped to bring myself back. Since I worked as a volunteer with them, I learned so much about life." When Jamal was individually interviewed at home, I discovered that he got married to a young girl, aged sixteen. When I asked him about the reason for this marriage, he gave a moral reason related to his tribal culture: "She is a relative and I married her to support her desperate family."

In male focus groups conducted in Zarqa, Mafraq, and Amman, many men who had been committed to participate in activities organized by international humanitarian organizations for the sake of gaining humanitarian assistance and/or volunteering jobs admitted that they had not achieved any success. One man from Amman said: "Nothing works. Organizations do not want to listen to us. They always give the priority to women."

Femininity and masculinity in this group are negotiated and renegotiated, shifting back and forth to contribute to survival of the family on the one hand, and to resist the modes of masculinity and femininity that were undesirably experienced before displacement on the other. Syrian refugees in this category maneuver with the two opposing gender discourses—patriarchal and non-patriarchal—to turn "the actual order of things" to their own ends.[71] When things do not work out as they wish, they change their tactics depending on the opportunities available. Unlike the first category, members of this group do not intend to delegitimize a certain ideology or discourse of power, but strive to gain power. Thus, they have more potential to be acculturated to humanitarian organizations and to attain their desired outcomes through their discursive practice of maneuvering.[72]

3. *Resilient resistance through deceiving and circumventing institutions in power.*

Deception, or *tahayul* in Arabic, as it is used by research participants, may not have a negative connotation. Some interviewees presented deception as a tactic of circumventing the rules and providing misinformation to hustle in order to receive humanitarian assistance. According to the experiences of the interviewees, access to humanitarian aid is not straightforward due to the rigid standardized criteria of humanitarian assistance, or lack of institutional transparency. Some Syrian refugees admitted that they deceive humanitarian organizations by presenting fake documents or information that meets the gender criteria of humanitarian assistance in order to guarantee essential humanitarian support. Although they may be able to gain humanitarian support without deception, some deceive in order to avoid an encounter with organizations in power and the discourse of gender they use.

For example, some interviewees think that international humanitarian organizations condition the provision of financial assistance to vulnerable men and women on their regular attendance of activities organized by these organizations. The activities focus on psychosocial counseling on the issue of domestic and sexual violence against women. Through my observation, some men and women tried to avoid attendance by calling organizations at the right time, for example, an hour before the event starts, and apologizing for their inability to attend, giving false reasons, such as sickness or child care. When I asked: "Why do you have to call to apologize ...?" Abu Ayman, a thirty-one-year-old man living in Mafraq, said: "If I don't attend for no reason, the organization will not trust me and will not put me on the list of beneficiaries whenever assistance is available." In order to avoid attendance, Abu Ayman acknowledged that once, he apologized by phone; a second time, he sent his wife with their her baby to attend in order to leave early. A long conversation with Abu Ayman shows that he is well equipped with knowledge about humanitarian organizations' criteria of assistance and knows how to deal with them. He confirmed the practice of deception by Syrian refugees, saying: "Of course, some Syrian refugees deceive organizations because if they are straightforward, no one will listen to them."

According to several discussions conducted with Syrian refugee men, deception may be related to how Syrian refugees think of the politics of humanitarian aid. For some, humanitarian aid is intended for Syrian refugees and so should be used by them. This argument is drawn upon a belief among some Syrian refugees that a large amount of international funding allotted for Syrian refugees is stolen by the Jordanian government to pay its employees, or by the humanitarian organizations themselves. Several interviewed men said: "They [humanitarian organizations] are all *haramyya* [thieves]."

In the case of some Syrian refugees in Jordan, resilient resistance through deception is not enacted by a particular group who are completely different from those in the above two categories. Rather, it cuts across the groups. However, material from the interviews suggested that men who used to be more authoritarian and abusive tend to be more deceptive of humanitarian organizations than men who were described as having passive or weak personalities before the war. Those in the first category are interested in regaining power by delegitimizing both the oppressive patriarchal actions undertaken by some Syrian refugees and the Western gender ideology introduced by humanitarian organizations. This group positions itself in between the two opposing ideologies, while those in the second category—who do not have any intention of resisting politics or ideologies but only seek to get what they need—are more interested in regaining power by disturbing the operation of organizations in power and undermining their effectiveness. The narratives also showed that the act of deception occurred in cooperation between wives and husbands. Each negotiates and renegotiates his/her gender to serve the purpose of deception and finds ways to circumvent the humanitarian organizations' rigid criteria of assistance—except in two cases that only involved women as the heads of their households. However, some of the reported cases of deception were practiced by the research participants themselves as well as by their relatives, friends, and neighbors.

I interviewed Hamid, a man in his early forties who resides in Amman, in the presence of his wife, who also contributed to the discussion. He said:

> Syrian refugees have changed so much by displacement. They deceive to gain what they want. There are several families I know who deceived international organizations to gain assistance, including my sister-in-law. You know the most important support that Syrian refugees receive from international organizations is *basmet e'yn* that is provided by the UNHCR. Families rely on it to pay for rent, while any work income is used to pay for other expenses. What do those families do? When UNHCR called them to make an appointment to assess their eligibility for *basmet e'yn*, on the day before the social worker comes, they emptied their house of all furniture and appliances in order for the social worker to give them a higher score. Deception worked with several families I know.

Hamid did not completely condemn deception, but excused it. Yet, it is hard to know if this meant that he himself also deceives. He explained that some families received good furniture as a donation from friends, neighbors, or charity, but they did not actually have enough money for rent. In Hamid's view, it is the need for rent that forces families to deceive, because men's work is irregular and does not cover the rent, bills, and food. Hamid's wife confirmed her husband's view, saying:

> We have *basmet e'yn* of 120 JoD [$169] and my husband works twelve hours a day in a food packaging factory for 200 JoD [$281], and we are still in debt. In Syria, the state used to pay our water and electricity bills, here we have to pay for everything, how can we manage?

In another interview, Ahmed, a forty-two-year-old man from Mafraq, recounted two stories about married couples who split to improve their situations. In both cases, the wife applied for *basmet e'yn* as a female head of household with a large number of children, which, according to UNHCR criteria, is given the highest score of vulnerability assessment. Research participants also mentioned several cases of women registering themselves as widows on the Syrian–Jordanian borders in order to register with UNHCR as female heads of household and to be eligible for *basmet e'yn*. The husbands of those women either joined their families later, or remained in Syria. Syrian refugees who used this type of deception were informed about the harshness of life in Jordan and often had prior knowledge about the criteria for humanitarian assistance recounted by relatives and friends who fled before them.

Another form of deception was noticed in a few interviews with women. Salwa is a forty-four-year-old woman from Zarqa. She is a widow and the head of her household. Her son, aged fourteen, dropped out of school to work in order to support the family. After Salwa heard about the UNICEF child grant for children to go back to school, she applied for it and registered her son. When I visited her at home the second time, I coincidentally met her son and was surprised to hear that he was still working. Hadeel, a thirty-seven-year-old woman from Amman, did the same. She registered her fourteen-year-old daughter in school as a precondition to receive the UNICEF child grant, but her daughter had not been attending school during the time I conducted the field research. When I asked both Salwa and Hadeel why their children do not go to school, Salwa said that she was in severe debt, and that she had to rely on her son's work to repay it. Hadeel said that she encouraged her daughter to go to school, but the girl refused because she said her teacher abused her. In both cases, the women were aware that UNICEF would withdraw the grant if it found out that the children did not go to school, but it seemed that they were prepared for that.

Another example of deception was also discovered during the field research. During individual interviews with women in their thirties, I noticed that a considerable number of married women were benefiting from humanitarian organizations either because their husbands do not work or because they are physically or mentally ill, as it was reported by the wives. When I tried to cross-check this information in the male focus groups, several men mentioned that in order not to work in demeaning jobs, or for abusive employers, some paid doctors to give them medical reports confirming that they are unable to work. With these fake medical reports, the men were eligible for humanitarian assistance.

The last example is not simply deception by means of providing misinformation. Rather, it is a purposive reshaping of the family structure in a way that fits with the criteria of humanitarian assistance, while the actual functioning of the old structure of the family remains the same. This includes parents marrying off their sons at a young age (seventeen or eighteen), which is consequently associated with early marriage for girls, in order to remove working sons from their family records with humanitarian organizations and to become eligible for humanitarian assistance. I conducted informal group interviews with several members of three families who married off their late-teenaged sons. The narratives show that this pattern of early marriage is arranged between families who know each other's circumstances, as relatives or neighbors. The marriage happened with almost no cost, which is against the traditional customs in Syria. While fathers mentioned that the main reason for marrying off their young sons was to prevent their frustrated boys from returning to Syria and exposing themselves to possible death, mothers gave other reasons related to the economic survival of the family.

Um Mohammad, from Zarqa, has two sons who were married at the ages of seventeen and eighteen, and they all live together in a big house, but in very poor conditions. Um Mohammad divided the big house into three small houses, one for the parents and their twelve-year-old son, and another for each married son. Keeping to cultural norms, the big family still cooks and eats together as one extended family to reduce expenses. According to my observation, the whole family uses the parents' kitchen, and as narrated, the married couples only go to their houses to sleep. Um Mohammad said:

> We did not use to marry off sons at this young age in Syria, but the situation here is different. If we have single sons aged seventeen or eighteen who work, we would not have *basmet e'yn*, or humanitarian support from charity organiza-

tions. So we selected two girls from a respectable family that we knew from Syria to marry my two sons. Since my sons got married, my husband and I and the young boy applied for *basmet e'yn* and we have received it. We pay for the rent, and my married sons work to cover other expenses.

These different examples of deception simultaneously act as means of resilience and resistance. Deception helps this group of Syrian refugees, albeit in a very small way, to escape negotiation, cooperation, and alliance with institutions in power. It also helps some men to escape humiliation in the workplace. As is apparent in personal narratives, some Syrian refugees used deception with a high level of caution, and they were ready to give up, or go back to, deceptive practices, depending on the opportunities available.[73]

Resistance through deceiving humanitarian organizations is an everyday practice occurring on "a small scale," is "relatively safe," and has a "promise" of "vital material gain," which "requires little or no formal coordination" with those in power.[74] Deception is a tactic of resilient resistance that remains associated with "continuous tentativeness," and it is thus unreliable.[75] Through deception, this group of Syrian refugees guarantees financial support for the sake of family survival, but at the same time is used to delegitimize and undermine institutions of power. A man from the first category of Syrian men and women, discussed above, who was angry with his living conditions in Jordan, said sarcastically: "I wish I can do it [deception], at least I empty my feeling of oppression from everything around."

Conclusion

Although it is true that most Syrian refugees reconfigure their gender roles, whether to directly cope with household vulnerability, or to respond to the gender criteria for international humanitarian assistance, gender reconfiguration is not a smooth process devoid of resistance. Personal narratives reveal that gender reconfiguration, as a situational mode of resilience, moves back and forth with different levels, scales, and intents of resistance, to restore a moral image of gender relations of power, or to gain or regain power. The ways in which gender is reconfigured, and the ways reconfigured gender is resisted, are not only influenced by Syrian refugees' present conditions of vulnerability in socioeconomic and material terms. Rather, they are also influenced by the historical experience of gender—the models of masculinity and femininity experienced before displacement, based on differences in class, education, geographic location, and sociocultural background.

In the context of Syrian refugees' displacement in Jordan, the three entities of gendered vulnerability, resilience, and resistance operate in a triangular manner, and each acts fluidly in relation to the other to score a temporary victory within the constraining structure of power.[76] The three modes of resilient resistance undertaken by Syrian refugees are the outcome of negotiation, renegotiation, and contestation between the desired image of gender and its situational performance. Yet, resilient resistance is not based on a conscious intent of all Syrian refugees. Some selectively and subtly maneuver within the gender discourse of resilience introduced by Western humanitarian organizations to meet their ends. This is done without actually changing their ideological beliefs or applying the Western gender discourse in their day-to-day life;[77] and others turn "the actual order of things ... to their own ends," regardless of the morality of the act or the ideology it targets.[78]

The three modes of resilient resistance discussed above show that the different groups of vulnerable Syrian refugees, with their different gender characteristics, position themselves in-between two opposing gender ideologies, whether through pure or contaminated means of resistance, aiming to meet their ends without losing their desired gendered subjectivity. Although, for Michel de Certeau, while these modes of resilient resistance are a creative way of meeting ends without obeying the rules (determined by institutions in power) that govern their lives, they can also be a hidden way of undermining the structure of power and its function.[79]

However, being in-between two opposing gender ideologies, or systems of power, provides an opportunity for using and reusing the discourses or systems of power in non-hegemonic ways. For example, Syrian refugees' acts of maneuvering within and deceiving international humanitarian organizations require them to be in a continuous interaction with a different culture that would provide an opportunity for some Syrian refugees to combine their maneuvering and deceiving tactics with an acquisition of new knowledge and skills. The repetitive practice of this combination may change attitudes, perceptions, and relations, or, as argued by de Certeau, create "acculturation" to these organizations.[80] To make this change possible, institutions in power need to understand the intersectional intents and motivations behind the different acts of resilient resistance each group undertakes, and to reshape their strategies accordingly. For example, if the intention of regaining power by some Syrian refugees, as in the case of men and women belonging to the first category, is recognized by institutions in power and translated into responsive actions—i.e., integrating their views and interests into the design and implementation of humanitarian programs—this group would have more potential to shift from the in-between gender ideological position, and from being silent and avoidant of social interaction, to visibly resisting the backwardness of patriarchal attitudes that are used by the less educated and more conservative displaced Syrian refugees.

10

"THE WORLD FORGOT US AND EUROPE DOESN'T WANT US"

THE SITUATION OF YAZIDI, CHRISTIAN, AND BABAWAT INTERNALLY DISPLACED PERSONS AND REFUGEES FROM SINJAR AFTER THE GENOCIDE OF 2014

Thomas Schmidinger

Introduction

When the so-called "Islamic State" (IS) attacked Iraq's Nineveh Governorate, the region's religious minorities became victims of genocide and displacement. This chapter focuses on the region of Sinjar (Kurdish: Şingal) and the displacement of the Yazidi (Kurdish: *Êzîdî*) along with other religious minorities living there.

The displacement of these groups directly resulted from their vulnerability as religious minorities. IS targeted them as religious minorities, and their current problems as internally displaced persons (IDPs) also resulted from their status as relatively small communities without a historically strong political lobby or military force.

The region of Sinjar in Iraq was the largest region inhabited by adherents of the Yazidi in the Middle East. Other regions have a large Yazidi population, and Shekhan (Kurdish: Şexan), to the east of Mosul, has the Yazidi's main religious center; however, during the twentieth century, Sinjar grew to have the largest population of Yazidi. It was not only the Yazidi living in Sinjar but also a Christian minority and the historically heterodox Shiʿite of the Kurdish Babawat tribe. Thus, the whole region became a focus of IS jihadist aggression in August 2014.

While the Yazidi have long faced accusations of being "devil worshippers," IS also intensely hated Shiʿites. Despite Christians' official status as wards of Islam (*dhimmī*) if willing to pay the *jizya* (a per capita yearly tax historically levied on non-Muslim subjects), most Christians also had to leave all territories occupied by IS in 2014. Several international and regional observers called the atrocities against the Yazidi and other religious minorities in the region a genocide; undoubtedly, the systematic deportation, enslavement, and rape of women, and mass executions of men, was "committed with intent to destroy, in whole or in part, a national, ethnic, racial or religious group" (i.e. genocide as defined by the UN Convention on Genocide). However, the question of whether this genocide should be characterized as a genocide against the Yazidi or as a genocide against the Kurds remains a disputed issue in the new order of Iraq.

When IS conquered Sinjar after the Peshmerga of the Democratic Party of Kurdistan (PDK) hastily withdrew on 3 August 2014,[1] the local Yazidi, Christians, and Babawat fled along with the Turkmen Shiʿites from Tal Afar, who had already been forced to flee to Sinjar when IS took over their town in June 2014. Thousands of people found sanctuary in Iraq's Kurdish territories; more than 50,000 could only flee to the Sinjar mountains, where they joined nomads and herders who already lived on the mountain and defended themselves with the support of self-organized militias. The Syrian-Kurdish People's Protection Units (Kurdish: Yekîneyên Parastina Gel, YPG) and their female comrades, the Women's Protection Units (Kurdish: Yekîneyên Parastina Jin, YPJ), with the support of US air strikes, finally opened a corridor from Syria (Rojava) on 10 August that year.[2] This enabled about 35,000 civilians to flee to Syria, while about 15,000 stayed on Mount Sinjar. The fighters from YPG, YPJ, and the Turkish Kurdish People's Defense Forces (Kurdish: Hêzên Parastina Gel, HPG) kept the corridor open for two weeks until the second siege of Mount Sinjar. In October 2014, IS failed in another offensive against the remaining positions held by the Yazidi militias; only a joint offensive of

YPG/YPJ and Peshmerga, with US air support, ended the siege in December 2014. While the north of Mount Sinjar was liberated by the end of 2014, the city of Sinjar was not liberated until November 2015. IS controlled Yazidi villages south of the city of Sinjar until May 2017, when Yazidi Popular Mobilization Forces (PMF) took over these villages with the support of the Iraqi Army and the Shiʿite PMF.

Many towns on the northern edge of Mount Sinjar regained their populations after 2015; however, the city of Sinjar and most villages and towns south of Sinjar remain destroyed or largely empty. Most people from this region still live in IDP camps in the Kurdistan Autonomous Region of Iraq, in refugee camps in Syria (Rojava), or as refugees in Turkey and in Europe. Additionally, up to 5,000 IDPs still live in tents on the plateau of Mount Sinjar.

Many survivors are highly traumatized.[3] Nearly every family lost some members. Many women captured by IS were raped and held as slaves, and children were brainwashed and forced to become Muslims. Since the liberation of the Sinjar region, forty-seven mass graves have been found.

Research with such a highly traumatized group presents challenges for research ethics, in both conducting and analyzing the interviews. To respect their privacy, the interview participants are not named in this chapter, and only general information will be shared about the background of the people who courageously shared their experiences and opinions.

This chapter analyzes the living conditions and political framework in which these IDPs and refugees must survive and presents their personal perspectives from inside and outside of Iraq. Interviews were centered on the following questions: What conditions prevent Yazidi, Christians, and other groups from returning to Sinjar? What are their perspectives on building a future in the region? What would they need in order to return and rebuild their homes? And how do the displaced adherents of the different religious groups interpret the 2014 genocide within a longer history of perceived genocidal acts against religious minorities in the area?

In this context, we face a fundamental problem: many survivors of the genocide of the "Islamic State" consider the atrocities carried out by the jihadist fighters as crimes committed by all "Muslims" or "Sunni Muslims" and not just as crimes of a specific political and terrorist movement. This fits the narrative of IS, which defines its own position not as a specific ideology but as "pure Islam," and as the only form of real Islam. Of course, millions of Muslims, both Shiʿite and Sunni, decisively reject the IS claim to represent Islam and absolutely oppose jihadist ideology and practice. Nevertheless, the perpetrators and the victims share the view that Islam—as a religious confession—inspired the brutal aggression. The self-presentation of IS as "purely Islamic," and the fact that the Yazidi became the victims of different groups who legitimized their crimes against them with religion, led to a confessional interpretation of this violence. In other words, although it would be ahistorical to interpret the violence against these religious minorities simply as confessional violence, confessionalized violence leads to a confessional perception of violence.

We must avoid two traps: first, we should not accept the self-perception of the perpetrators and should not simplistically attribute social relations, political and military struggles, and crimes to a religious confession. On the other side, we should seriously respect how victims of genocide interpret their suffering. This does not necessarily mean that we should completely accept their narrative. An outsider's scholarly perspective necessarily differs from that of a victim and a survivor. However, we should not ignore their perspective or reinterpret the victim's experience according to our own ideas of how such atrocities should be interpreted. This chapter nevertheless takes the victim's viewpoint seriously, without limiting its analysis to factors considered important from their perspective.

This research involved extensive fieldwork in IDP camps in Iraq, in refugee camps in Syria and Turkey, and with the IDPs on Mount Sinjar. In 2015 and 2016, the author conducted fieldwork in refugee camps in Syria and Turkey, and in some of the IDP camps in Iraq. Additional research was done in 2017 in the IDP camps of Xanke, and with the IDPs on Mount Sinjar.[4] This chapter is based on four field trips to IDP camps in Iraq, between 2015 and 2017;[5] four field trips to the IDPs on Mount Sinjar in 2016, 2017, 2018, and 2019;[6] three visits to the Newroz refugee camp in Syria in 2016, 2019, and 2020;[7] and a 2015 visit to the refugee camp in Fidanlık Park near Diyarbakır in Turkey.[8] All interviews in this chapter were carried out by the author unless indicated otherwise.

Difficult research conditions

Almost no research has been conducted on the consequences of the IS genocide against the Yazidi. This chapter is based on the author's own fieldwork and not on secondary literature.

Research in such an area of political conflict is difficult and requires great patience and sensitivity to unexpected concerns. Research ethics must ensure that IDPs who share information about their problems and political pressures will not suffer negative consequences from their honesty. Therefore, most interviews with the IDPs could not be recorded. Field-notes from the interviews could be written only after the talks in the camps. This was especially difficult in Xanke camp in June 2017, as the ruling PDK party openly exerted strong political pressure and many interview partners were afraid to share their problems. Several times, the author had to avoid people who obviously wanted to monitor his actions. However, after three days in the formal and informal IDP camp in Xanke, forty-two interviews were obtained with IDPs from different towns of the Sinjar region, which provided a good sampling of the problems and opinions of IDPs from Sinjar.

It is especially difficult to meet directly with the IDPs on Mount Sinjar, as the Kurdish police (Asaysh) limit access to the region. In the months before the Kurdistan independence referendum on 25 September 2017, the police refused to grant permission for most researchers and journalists to visit. Earlier, some journalists could visit the region if accompanied by people of the ruling party, PDK. Despite many efforts, this researcher never received official permission to visit. The only way to enter Mount Sinjar was through personal contacts with people within the PDK, who unofficially could bring me to Mount Sinjar. However, the limited time available without their company resulted in few opportunities to talk freely with IDPs. However, these opportunities were important moments to ensure that the information collected was not simply propaganda. On at least two occasions, random IDPs on Mount Sinjar could be interviewed for up to thirty minutes without any presence of the ruling party's monitors. Most of these interviews were conducted in Arabic, although some were in English; and some interviews were conducted with women with the help of a female Kurdish translator.[9]

The interviews conducted in Xanke and on Mount Sinjar, and the talks with refugees in Syria and Turkey, do not provide proper quantitative research findings. However, they offer qualitative insights on the problems and living conditions of IDPs from Sinjar. Additional to these interviews, a Christian family from Sinjar and two men from the Babawat ethno-religious community separately and openly engaged in long conversations about their perspectives on the conflict. They also preferred to remain anonymous.

Sinjar as a retreat for religious minorities

Kurdistan's mountain ranges end with Mount Sinjar overlooking the southern expanses of the Mesopotamian plains. The region consequently has a strategic significance, including its importance as a retreat for religious minorities. Already,

> before the Yezidi population became dominant in Sinjar, it was home to Christian communities. It was in the middle of [the] thirteenth century that Sinjar became important for Yezidi immigrants. Its mountainous features offered an ideal shelter to the Yezidi community [that] fled Sheikhan after Badr al-Dīn Lu'lu' the Atabeg of Mosul, began to massacre the Yezidis.[10]

In the late medieval era, Sinjar was one of several regions with a strong Yazidi population. The expanding Ottoman Empire destroyed other Yazidi settlements, forced conversions, and repressed their cultural identities, leading Yazidi from other parts of Kurdistan to migrate to Mount Sinjar.[11] Dominated by a non-Sunni population, the mountain became a retreat not only for the Yazidi but also for various religious minorities. Until the 1970s, a distinctive culture of Yazidi mountain farmers and semi-nomadic transhumance existed on Mount Sinjar. Although the Yazidi from Mount Sinjar only partially supported a revolt in 1965,[12] the then Arab-nationalist—but not yet Baathist—regime retaliated by displacing many Yazidi villagers. In the 1970s, a centralized move toward collectivization forced Yazidi from Mount Sinjar, as well as from the Shekhan region, to leave their remote mountain villages and their historically developed, irrigated terrace fields, to live in collective towns (Arabic: *mujamaʿat*).[13]

The city of Sinjar has an ancient history. The museum in Dohuk exhibits the Roman ruins of old Sinjar. During the late Roman period, the city of Sinjar must have had a significant Christian population. Although the population and cultural identities of Sinjar in that period remain unknown, many documents exist from an important Syrian Orthodox Christian scholar from Sinjar in the seventh century: Gabriel, who originally belonged to the Nestorian Church of the East[14] and played an important role in the inter-Christian rivalries in the Sassanid Empire under the rule of Khosrau II.[15]

The *Apocalypse of Pseudo-Methodius*, once believed to be authored by Bishop Methodius in the fourth century, mentions in a preamble that Methodius received the revelations contained in the text on Mount Sinjar. However, scholars currently believe that the text was actually written in the seventh century,[16] and no other evidence has been discovered of early Christianity in Sinjar. Most probably both Nestorian (Assyrian) and Syrian Orthodox Christian communities existed in the region, and adherents to Christianity have probably lived in Sinjar from the time of early Christianity in Iraq until 2014.

According to Nelida Fuccaro, the "available sources do not clarify whether the Christian community of Sinjar survived the first centuries of Ottoman rule. However, by the end of the 19th century a rich Christian urban elite whose interests were mainly linked to trade had clearly emerged in Jabal Sinjar."[17] In 1915, when the İttihat ve Terakki government of the Ottoman Empire committed genocide against Armenians and Assyrians, the Yazidi in Sinjar protected and gave refuge to both Armenians and Assyrians.[18] Raymond Kévorkian claims that Chechens saved the lives of 400–500 Armenians by bringing them to Sinjar from the Armenian death camps in Ras al-Ayn (Kurdish: Serê Kaniyê) in present-day Syria.[19]

Christians from Sinjar recall that "500 Christian families lived in Sinjar"[20] 80–100 years ago. However, during the twentieth century, most left the impoverished and isolated region for Mosul or Baghdad, or went abroad to Sweden, Canada, or the United States.[21] When IS attacked Sinjar, about fifty-two Christian families still lived in the city, which had three churches—a Syrian Orthodox, a Syrian Catholic, and an Armenian Catholic one. Christians from Sinjar remember that for fourteen Christian families living in Sinun (Kurdish: Sinûnê) and five Christian families in neighboring Khanasor—towns on the northern edge of Mount Sinjar that are without churches—a Syrian Orthodox priest from Sinjar sometimes performed services in private homes.[22]

These remaining Christian families fled with their Yazidi neighbors to Mount Sinjar when IS attacked the region in August 2014. They now live in IDP camps in Iraq or as refugees in Europe. A Syrian Orthodox family from Sinjar interviewed in September 2017 said that they do not see any future for Christians in Sinjar or Iraq. Many Christians from Sinjar have already left for Europe or other continents, and this family also intended to leave Iraq.

Besides the Christian minority, a small Jewish community also existed in Sinjar. However, like the Christians, no evidence has been found that shows that the small group of Jews who lived in the city of Sinjar in the twentieth century had any continuity with an older Jewish community. Christians from Sinjar say that their Christian cemetery has two Jewish graves. Like most Iraqi Jews, the last Jews from Sinjar also left in 1950 after the establishment of Israel and never returned.

Finally, Sinjar was also a retreat for heterodox Shi'ites of the Kurdish-speaking Babawat ethno-religious community. The Babawat community has a disputed religious affiliation. While most present-day members of the Babawat consider themselves ordinary Shi'ites, the Babawat practiced a certain degree of heterodoxy at least until the end of the twentieth century.

Fuccaro considers the Babawat to be Ali Ilahis and reports about their relationship with the Yazidis during British rule of Iraq:

> Although the Babawat's veneration for 'Ali placed them in direct doctrinal opposition to the Yazidis (whose cult for Yazid b. Mu'awiya was particularly strong in Sinjar), they made offerings to the Yazidi men of religion living in Balad, and to the sacred image of Malak Tawus when it was paraded in the district of Sinjar. They also participated in Yazidi religious ceremonies. Furthermore a contemporary observer noted that generally the Babawat tribesmen could not be distinguished from the local Yazidi population on the basis of their clothing, language or eating habits, the last point probably indicating that they had adopted Yazidi food taboos.[23]

As well as taking part in certain Babawat ceremonies, the Yazidi also accompanied them on their pilgrimage to Bier Zakar.[24]

However, the close relationship between the Yazidi and Babawat in the Sinjar region changed after 2003. After the destruction of the Baathist regime in 2003 and the growing politicization of religious confessions, various heterodox groups of Iraq came under pressure. Similar to the Shabak in the Nineveh Plains east of Mosul,[25] the Babawat also felt the need to ally with one of the large ethno-religious groups in Iraq. A Yazidi described this development: "In the past, they [the Babawat] were with us. They had a close relationship with us and were not very religious. In the last years, they became religious. Now they don't want to take part in our ceremonies and celebrations anymore. They are with the Shi'ites now."[26]

The Babawats have a different perspective. One member of the Babawat community from Sinjar told me:

> We were always Shi'ite Muslims. However, during Saddam Hussein, we were oppressed. You know that Saddam hated the Shi'ite and he oppressed the Shi'ite ayatollahs and even killed some of the most important Shi'ite leaders. At this time, the Shi'ite clerics would not dare to come to us and teach us the religion. We were ignorant about our religion and did things that were not according to our religion. After Saddam's regime was gone, we were free to practice our religion and we could also learn our true religion. Now the Shi'ites are not oppressed anymore. So, we can learn about our religion and we can practice it like other Shi'ites in Najaf or Karbala.[27]

However, other community members have different narratives about the religious development of the Babawat ethno-religious community. Another member of the Babawat, who lived in Sinjar until August 2014, told me:

> I am sorry that we are losing our local tradition. Yes, we are Shi'ites, but not like in the south of Iraq. We had our local version of Shi'ite Islam and we were

very close to the Yazidi. We respected the Shi'ite imams but we also respected Tausî Melek. This changed. You know, the people who rule Baghdad are different Shi'ites. And in 2014 we also had to leave Sinjar. We had to leave the graves of our ancestors and our religious men. We are not living with the Yazidi anymore. Our people live in Dohuk, Baghdad, or Najaf now. Now we lose our traditions.[28]

Heterodox Shi'ite groups could only survive for centuries because they practiced *taqqiya*, a precautionary denial or camouflage of religious belief used when endangered by persecution. Therefore, all confessions of orthodoxy from (former) heterodox groups have to be treated with caution. However, the Babawat community experienced internal changes, also witnessed by their (former) Yazidi neighbors.

The scope of this chapter does not include a proper study of these Babawat changes, which would involve intensive field research and interviews with members of the Babawat ethno-religious community. However, from this researcher's initial observations, the Babawat could be experiencing similar developments to those that Michiel Leezenberg observed with the Shabak communities of the Nineveh Plains.[29] Under the pressure of confessionalism and nationalism, heterodox groups tend to become mainstream and integrate into one of the bigger and less ambiguous "identities" of Iraq. Not only the Shabak but also other heterodox groups such as the Bajalan, Sarli, Kakai,[30] as well as the Babawat, seem to be under such a pressure against heterodoxy and ambiguity and might become part of the orthodox Shi'ite community of Iraq.

From a historical perspective, the city of Sinjar had been one of the most multiethnic and multi-religious municipalities in Iraq. In the 1930s, the town consisted of 1,950 Sunni Muslims, 476 Shi'ite Muslims (most probably the majority of the Babawat), 660 Christians, 485 Yazidis, and 15 Jews.[31] While Sunni Islam had a relatively strong influence in the city of Sinjar, many villages and towns on the mountain and to the north of the mountain were nearly entirely Yazidi or mixed with Babawat and Christians. The Sunni population around Sinjar was either Kurdish or Arab from the Shammar ethno-religious community.

Muslim animosity toward the Yazidi

Many of the Yazidi's Muslim neighbors have falsely accused them of being devil worshippers or being unclean,[32] accusations that existed long before the so-called Islamic State. IS used these existing prejudices for its own propaganda and as a justification for its genocide against the Yazidi (and other religious minorities) of Sinjar.[33] Similar to fascism, which absorbed and radicalized already existing resentments against Jews, IS used and radicalized large-scale anti-Yazidi sentiments held by both Kurdish and Arab Muslims in northern Iraq.

Even today, the Muslim populations of northern Iraq generally believe that Yazidi are unclean; hardly any Muslim Kurd or Arab in Iraq would willingly eat in the house of a Yazidi. Likewise, the region's Muslims generally believe that Yazidis worship the devil. Although twentieth-century Kurdish nationalism tried to portray the Yazidi as the "real Kurds," and their religion as an ancient, original Kurdish religion existing before the Islamization of the Kurds with connections to ancient Zoroastrianism,[34] this nationalist reinterpretation of Yazidism did not overcome popular prejudices and resentments. International organizations remove Yazidi women from training courses for food production because Muslims would not buy bread or fruit from them.[35] Marriages between Muslims and Yazidi are still prohibited by both sides. Some of this animosity also exists between Christians and Yazidi. However, the Christian and Yazidi's common experiences of persecution also led to alliances and to solidarity between the two minorities. However, in Sinjar some of the tribal identities softened these confessional differences. Some of the tribes of Sinjar, who play an important role to this day, had not only Yazidi members, but also Shi'a and Sunni families. Such tribal connections played an important role for the survival of some Yazidis from mixed tribes in 2014.

Political and military situation in Sinjar after 2014

Diverse militias—and not the official Iraqi Army—recaptured Sinjar.[36] This chapter does not retell the history of the recapture of Sinjar but simply provides an overview of the region's different military and political actors. Understanding the situation in Sinjar helps to clarify why refugees and IDPs hesitate to return to their homeland and why many Yazidi want to leave Iraq. In fact, Sinjar became the focal point of tensions between diverse militias affiliated with rival Kurdish and non-Kurdish parties.[37]

When Haydar Şeşo and his uncle, Qasim Şeşo, returned from their German exile in August 2014 to help their relatives in their struggle against IS, they helped create two Yazidi militias to defend the civilians on Mount Sinjar. Haydar Şeşo—then a member of the Patriotic Union of Kurdistan (PUK) of Jalal Talabani—established his own militia called Singal Protection Units (Kurdish: *Hêza Parastina Şingal*, HPŞ).[38] However, his uncle started to cooperate with the fighters with the Peshmerga of the PDK, the party of President Masoud Barzani. Although Qasim Şeşo harshly criticized the PDK-Peshmerga for leaving Sinjar in August 2014, he put his troops under Peshmerga command and agreed to fight in the framework of the Kurdish Peshmerga.

Haydar Şeşo tried to maintain a degree of independence from Barzani and his PDK. As a result of the alienation between them, police forces loyal to Barzani's PDK arrested Haydar Şeşo on 5 April 2015 and detained him for a week. Renaming the Singal Protection Units to Êzîdxan Protection Units (Kurdish: Hêza Parastina Êzîdxanê, HPÊ) in November 2015, Haydar Şeşo tried to focus on a specific Yazidi identity, distinct from (Muslim) Kurds. However, in March 2017 PDK political pressure forced Şeşo to announce that his Baghdad-registered militia would join the Peshmerga.

In August 2014, a second militia formed, the Sinjar Resistance Units (Kurdish: Yekîneyên Berxwedana Şengalê, YBŞ). A nucleus of an armed Yazidi militia had worked with the PKK and its allies since 2007; however, it only became an effective militia in August 2014 when defending Yazidi civilians against IS. In January 2015, a female sister-militia was also established as the Women's Defense Unit of Singal (Kurdish: *Yekîneyên Parastina Jin ê* Şengalê, YPJŞ). The Iraqi government in Baghdad had registered YBŞ and the HPÊ as Popular Mobilization Forces (Arabic: *al-hashd ash-sha'abi*).

The YBŞ controlled the northwest of the region with the town of Khanasor and the villages of Bara, Kerse, Sikeniya, Majnuniya, and Jidale. Qasim Şeşo's PDK-Peshmerga controlled the northeast with Sinun as its new center, and the city of Sinjar. Surrounded by Peshmerga-held territory, Haydar Şeşo's HPÊ controlled the villages of Ghobal, Şerfedîn, Borik, and Zorava. A few PUK-Peshmerga held positions in the city of Sinjar; the PDK placed some Rojava Peshmerga close to the border of Syria in the north to hamper pro-PKK forces from crossing the border from Syria. The Rojava Peshmerga served as the militia of Syria's Kurdish National Council (ENKS), an umbrella organization of Syrian–Kurdish parties with a close relationship to Barzani's PDK. Strictly opposed to Rojava's ruling party allied with the PKK, they seemed to be useful border guards at the Syrian border north of Mount Sinjar.

In between the territories controlled by PDK-Peshmerga, YBŞ, and HPÊ, about 5,000 civilians still live in tents and other forms of temporary housing on the Serdast plateau. No single militia controlled this plateau. Although the YBŞ controls the northern road to the plateau, and the Peshmerga of Qasim Şeşo controls the southern road, the Serdast plateau has no checkpoints. Off the road, both sides have some small bases with a handful of fighters. The two sides maintained civil institutions, such as the PKK's women's center and a "Mala Êzîdiya" (Yazidi house), and the PDK's office and compound of the Barzani Charity Foundation. The two main rivals tried to avoid each other and have found a precarious *modus vivendi*—at least most of the time.

These different militias have never had an easy relationship. However, the YBŞ on one side have had particular difficulty with the Peshmerga on the other. The worst incident between the pro-PKK and pro-PDK militias did not happen between Yazidi militias, but between YBŞ and so-called Rojava Peshmerga on 3 March 2017. As outsiders and Muslims, they did not have local ties with other Yazidi in the region. Unsurprisingly, the tensions in the region escalated between them and the pro-PKK YBŞ. On 3 March, the Rojava Peshmerga and YBŞ were involved in a skirmish with each other in Sinun and Khanasor that led to several casualties and caused further political conflict between the pro-PKK and pro-PDK forces in the region.[39]

The conflict escalated in May 2017. Neither the Peshmerga nor the YBŞ advanced against IS, which still controlled the villages south of the city of Sinjar. Therefore, villagers from towns like Koço, Qahtaniyah, Ger Zerik, Tal Qasab, Tal Banat, and Qabusiye lost their patience with the rival Kurdish militias and started to connect with the PMF and the Iraqi government in Baghdad. In early May 2017, they established two brigades (Lališ and Koço) of the PMF. Between 12 and 29 May, these Yazidi PMF liberated the southern part of the Yazidi settlement area with the help of Shi'ite PMF and the Iraqi army. As a result, three to four rival alliances (depending whether the HPÊ and the small number of PUK-Peshmerga count as allies with the PDK-Peshmerga or as separate groups) now controlled the region of Sinjar.

This situation continued until September 2017. The government of the Kurdistan Region insisted on including Sinjar in its Kurdistan independence referendum on 25 September, which increased the tensions between the PDK-ruled territories of Sinjar and the territories controlled by Yazidi PMF. International journalists did not have any access to the region during the summer of 2017. Only by using all personal contacts to different militias and parties in the region could this author have any chance of entering the Sinjar region. Finally, when the Kurdistan regional government conducted the Kurdistan independence referendum in Sinun and in other areas under its control, many local Yazidi started to fear that the region could split between Iraq and Kurdistan along the existing frontlines between the militias. However, after the PUK-Peshmerga withdrew from Kirkuk, the PDK-Peshmerga also left Sinjar on the following day, 17 October 2017.

While all the Muslim PDK-Peshmerga and Rojava Peshmerga left the region within a few hours, Qasim Şeşo left the city of Sinjar and fled with about 1,000 Yazidi Peshmerga to the positions of Haydar Şeşo's HPÊ in Şerfedîn. Both Haydar Şeşo and Qasim Şeşo announced that they wanted to stay in the region and would take responsibility solely for the security of the local Yazidi people. Both of them stayed in the region, but they do not control territory beyond the village of Şerfedîn.

When the Iraqi army and Iraqi PMF took over most of the territory formerly controlled by the Peshmerga of the PDK, then the YBŞ also advanced. The YBŞ gained control over the town of Sinun—the biggest Yazidi settlement to the north of the mountain—as well as the village of Duguri. In 2018 both Sinun and Duguri were under shared control of the Iraqi army and YBŞ.

Yazidi refugees from Sinjar in Turkey and Syria

After the attacks on Sinjar, more than 30,000 Yazidi found temporary refuge in the Kurdish-inhabited regions of Turkey. Many towns administrated by the pro-Kurdish Peoples' Democratic Party (Halkların Demokratik Partisi, HDP) became hosts of spontaneously erected camps. With the return of some of the refugees to Iraq, and the further escape of others to Europe, the remaining Yazidi refugees were offered a better-organized camp in a park in the town of Çınar near Diyarbakır. The camp in Fidanlık Park still hosted about 4,000 refugees in the summer of 2016.[40] However, by the end of that year, most refugees living there somehow managed to travel to Europe. Some reached family members in Germany; others still wait in camps in Greece. The 1,000 or so people who remained were forced to move to an official refugee camp near Midyat in January 2017. Sources close to the Kurdish movement in Turkey reported that Turkish soldiers transported the refugees and confiscated most of their household goods.[41]

During the field visit in the camp in Çınar in November 2015, nearly all refugees that spoke with this researcher desperately asked for help to get to Europe. A large group had already undertaken an arduous trip to the border of Bulgaria and tried to force entry into the European Union. However, they failed and had to return to the camp. Interestingly, most of the refugees had an open conflict with the HDP and their Yazidi member of the Turkish parliament, Feleknas Uca, with whom this researcher went to the camp. Uca—who grew up in Germany and "returned" to Turkey after two terms in the European parliament to become a politician of the HDP—tried to persuade the refugees to stay in Kurdistan. However, most refugees desperately wanted to find a way to Europe. It has become increasingly difficult to reach the EU, and the remaining refugees generally do not have enough savings to pay professionals to facilitate undocumented travel to Europe.

Refugees in Syria faced a different situation. In September 2016, this researcher visited the Newroz camp near Dêrik in the Kurdish part of Syria (Rojava). At that time, the camp's administration had counted up to 5,000 refugees from Sinjar. In June 2016, UNHCR had registered only 2,214 refugees in Newroz camp, and recorded about 3,000 in 2015.[42] Many camp residents had relatives fighting with pro-PKK militias in the Sinjar region. Most of the 35,000 people rescued via the corridor established by pro-PKK militias in August 2014 continued on to the Kurdistan Region of Iraq or through Turkey to Europe. However, families with political and personal ties with the PKK stayed in Rojava.[43] The well-structured camp seemed highly politicized with many images of Abdullah Öcalan, the leader of PKK, and flags and symbols of the Sinjar Resistance Units (Kurdish: Yekîneyên Berxwedana Şengalê, YBŞ). This camp clearly had many sympathizers with the PKK. Most people I interviewed in the Newroz camp did not speak about dreaming of migrating to Europe; instead, they wanted to fight for an autonomous canton for the Yazidi in Sinjar. The UNHCR and Kurdish organizations such as the Kurdish Red Crescent (*Heyva Sor*) provided healthcare and food to the camp. In early 2019 only very few families were left in Newroz camp. When the Turkish invasion in October 2019 against Northern and Eastern Syria started, the camp was finally reused for IDPs from Tal Abyad and Ras al-Ain.

IDPs in Iraq's Kurdistan Region

Most Yazidi civilians from the Sinjar region still live as IDPs in the Kurdistan Region of Iraq, mainly in camps in the Dohuk Governorate. In February 2016, the Board of Relief and Humanitarian Affairs (BRHA), responsible for administrating IDP camps in Dohuk Governorate, released data about these camps in Iraq's Kurdistan Region. At that time, 189,321 IDPs lived in formal camps in Dohuk Governorate while only 32,306 IDPs lived in formal camps in the governorates of Erbil and Suleymania.[44] The BRHA reported that 325,178 IDPs live "off-camp" in informal camps,[45] rented apartments, or in building shells. Therefore, many more IDPs were living outside the organized camps than inside. The largest IDP camp was Xamişko (Chamishko) with 26,314 people (4,679 families), followed by

Shariya with 17,547 people (3,348 families), and Xanke (Khanky) with 16,511 people (2,902 families).[46]

These numbers only reveal part of the picture. Many non-camp IDPs live close to IDP camps, especially in regions with already existing Yazidi populations, like in the Shekhan and the Simele (Kurdish: Sêmêl) districts. According to the BRHA, in the town of Shekhan (Arabic: Ain Sifni), where the Baba Şex (one of the two highest religious representatives of the Yazidi) resides, 13,152 IDPs lived off-camp in 2016. In Ba'adre—the traditional seat of the other most important traditional leader of the Yazidi, the Mîr— another 6,921 IDPs lived off-camp. The district of Shekhan has a total of 47,106 IDPs living off-camp and the Simele district has 56,001.[47] This means that the IDPs from Sinjar outnumber the local Yazidi living in the Shekhan and Simele districts.

The Yazidi IDPs from Sinjar logically sought refuge in the Kurdistan areas where other Yazidi already lived. They felt safer and more welcome in Shekhan and the Yazidi villages in the districts of Simele and Dohuk than they felt in purely Muslim regions. However, the Yazidi from Sinjar and those inside the Kurdistan Region have cultural, tribal, and economic differences. Even the Yazidi villages in Dohuk and Simele, and those in Shekhan, perceived themselves as different from each other.[48] These regional distinctions between Yazidi do not necessarily lead to mutual suspicion, but along with the socio-religious divisions between the Pîr, Şex, and Murîd groups (often referred to as castes), family and regional divisions also play a significant role in Yazidi political culture. Normally, Yazidi do not move easily between Sinjar and Shekhan; mutual solidarity for those threatened with genocide does not mean that regional distinctions suddenly disappear. Every Yazidi from Shekhan could immediately identify a Yazidi from Sinjar because of habitus and dialectal peculiarities.

This researcher visited several formal and informal IDP camps in the Shekhan and Simele districts on five occasions between 2015 and 2017.[49] Most observations are from Xanke, both from the official IDP camp and the IDPs living off-camp in tents or rented rooms inside the village. Xanke is a traditional Yazidi village that was removed from the Tigris valley to a location near Simele in 1986, when the Mosul dam flooded the original village. Villagers from Xanke told the researcher that about two-thirds of its original 3,000 inhabitants had left for Europe since 2014. Yazidi from regions not conquered by IS also lost hope for a secure future in Iraq. Unlike IDPs from Sinjar, people from Xanke could afford professional assistance with undocumented migration to Europe. If they were not an IDP, they did not lose all their property, and by selling their houses they could afford the costs of undocumented migration to Europe (in 2017, about $10,000 per person). Houses that had been abandoned by locals were rented to IDPs from Sinjar.

It is not only Xanke's residents who have lost their hope for a future in Iraq—so,too, have the IDPs. In late May and early June 2017, this researcher interviewed IDPs from Sinjar in Xanke. Of thirty interviews with people and families inside the camp and twelve with those outside of camps,[50] only five interviewees wanted to return to Sinjar. Two wanted to stay in Xanke and twenty wanted to leave for Europe. However, at least fifteen interviewees said they would be willing to return to Sinjar under certain conditions. When asked for reasons for not returning to Sinjar, twenty-seven interviewees cited lack of security and thirty-four explicitly mentioned the rivalry between parties and militias. Two interviewees said that the main reason they could not return was because their villages had been destroyed; four mentioned the lack of infrastructure. This researcher used a simple, random walk through the camp and to off-camp areas to talk with different people and to develop a sample of perspectives, and a proper quantitative study cannot be based on forty-two randomly sampled interviews. However, some common views clearly emerged when almost all interviewees declared they wanted to leave Iraq. Nearly half of the interview partners only stayed in Iraq because they had not yet found a way to pay for undocumented migration to Europe or any other way to leave Iraq. Most of the others would only return to Sinjar if certain conditions were fulfilled. Although this researcher did not systematically ask what conditions would assure a return to Sinjar, many interviewed said that some kind of autonomy for Sinjar—for example, a Sinjar governorate—would be an important step toward a safe return; some interviewees also asked for international armed protection.

Interestingly, most of those who were concerned about the rivalry between militias did not hold a specific group responsible for the insecurity resulting from armed conflicts between political groups. These interviews occurred after the armed incident between YBŞ and Rojava Peshmerga in March 2017 and after the PMF took over south of Sinjar, but before the independence referendum. Nevertheless, most interview partners did not take a clear side in this conflict and accused all actors of being part of the problem. Only one interview partner explicitly accused "the PKK" of being the problem in Sinjar. At the same time, despite the difficulties in conducting fully confidential interviews, nine interview partners directly accused the PDK of putting strong political pressure on them inside the camp.

The PDK's political pressure around the camp was easy to notice. Some interview partners explicitly expressed fear, while others hesitated to answer questions that allowed for the expression of negative opinions on Kurdistan's ruling political party. There was a large PDK poster with a huge image of Masoud Barzani at the camp's entrance. While doing research in the camp, a PDK party meeting could be observed inside the camp administration's official building, where a party official gave a long and furious speech against the PKK and the PMF. Party flags and a large picture of Barzani loomed above the stage, where a Yazidi PDK spokesperson angrily condemned all rival Yazidi forces.

Despite official permission to conduct interviews inside the camp, the camp security official did not want this researcher to speak freely with IDPs inside the camp. Outside the camp, I could talk more freely with IDPs, and some interview partners also openly expressed their sympathies for the PKK. The political rivalries in Sinjar have direct consequences for the IDPs in Kurdistan. When the Lališ and Koço Brigades took over the south of Sinjar in May 2017, families with links to these two PMF faced problems in the IDP camps in Kurdistan. A group of IDPs was expelled from the Kurdistan Region and forced into territories controlled by the central government of Iraq.

Although the official camp's infrastructure had improved after my first visit in January 2015, other problems became more pressing. In January 2015, the Xanke camp still had severe sanitary problems, and the sporadic schooling that was offered took place in tents. By 2016, a container campus sheltered schools, and new sanitary facilities prevented more outbreaks of cholera (a previous outbreak occurred in 2015). However, the families' tents and the food supply had not improved. A thirty-year-old man from the city of Sinjar said: "The situation in the camp is even worse than in 2015. We receive less food supplies than before and our old tents are rotten after three years. The world forgot us and Europe doesn't want us."[61]

IDPs on Mount Sinjar

Another group of up to 5,000 IDPs still lives on the Serdast plateau on Mount Sinjar. No single militia controls this vast plateau and its widely scattered camps; the different armed militias regard it as non-militarized territory. Until October 2017, this neutrality endured between YBŞ and YJÊ on the one side and the PDK-Peshmerga on the other. Both groups had their positions staked out on the plateau, but the open streets did not have any militia checkpoints. Except for occasional small acts of violence, the two groups mostly tried to avoid each other. At the same time, both groups had their own civil infrastructure. The PDK had a large office of the Barzani Charity Foundation (where the World Food Programme distributed food for the IDPs), a party office, and a healthcare station. The PKK provided institutions like a women's center, a "Mala Êzîdiya" as a religious and cultural center, and the office of the council of reconstruction for the Yazidi of Sinjar (Kurdish: Meclisa Avaker a Êzdiyên Şengalê) that coordinated different infrastructure projects for the IDPs.

The territory is a high-security zone and very difficult to enter. This is one reason why very limited news coverage emerges and almost no research has been done in the region. However, this researcher was able to enter it twice, in June 2016 and September 2017. Since those visits, only small things have changed. The most obvious change was that people started more gardens and tried to produce as much food as possible for their own needs. Some IDPs also started to build houses, but most still lived in the tents they had been given in 2014. As in the IDP camps in Kurdistan, these tents have deteriorated. One young man repeated complaints almost exactly as were heard in the Xanke camp: "Our tents are meanwhile in a very bad condition. For three years, they are under the sun and the snow and they get worse and worse. And we receive only little food here. Very little international help arrives here on the mountain. I think the world forgot about us."[52]

Until October 2017, the Barzani Charity Foundation only operated one school for the IDPs. Some IDPs complained that they did not have an Arabic school. Until 2014, children in Sinjar did not attend Kurdish schools but attended schools with the Iraqi general curriculum that had Arabic as the language of instruction. Additionally, their Kurdish dialect differs significantly from the Kurdish used in the Barzani Charity Foundation school. The IDPs living amid the turmoil of the different militias lamented the lack of security and the problems with the armed rivalries. As in Xanke, most interview partners did not accuse a specific militia, but generally stated that one of their biggest problems was the partition of Sinjar and the militias' rivalry. Surprisingly, even here, where people stayed in their region and did not flee to Kurdistan, many IDPs wanted to go to Germany, with its growing Yazidi diaspora and its political and religious freedom. People noted their frustration with the lack of possibilities to flee to Germany.

One woman, while baking bread in a clay oven, told me: "We will never have a quiet life in Iraq. Even if Kurdistan would become independent, they will never accept us. The Kurds are Muslims, too, and they do not accept us Yazidi. For us, no freedom exists in Iraq, only in Germany!"[53]

"THE WORLD FORGOT US AND EUROPE DOESN'T WANT US"

Christian perspectives from Sinjar

Both the Syrian Aramaic and Armenian Christian minorities of Sinjar fled the attacks of IS in August 2014. Most Christians from Sinjar could escape, but IS captured four young men: Najeeb Mallah, George Ibrahim, Saad Botrus, and David Hannah, who are all still missing. It is possible that their remains may lay together with Yazidi men in one of the mass graves of the region. However, most Christian minorities did not join the Yazidi IDPs in the camps in Dohuk Governorate, but found refuge in a Christian settlement in Kurdistan or went as quickly as possible to Europe, Canada, the United States, or Australia. Some now live in Dohuk in Christian villages in Dohuk Governorate or in the Christian town Ainkawa—a suburb of Erbil.

The Christians from Sinjar who remain in Iraq do not have different perspectives from the Yazidi. However, they connect their history with the general decline of Christianity in Iraq. A Syrian Orthodox man who lives in Dohuk Governorate said that he would like to return to Sinjar. However, he does not find continuing to live under a Muslim rule a realistic option:

> I would like to go back to Sinjar, but this mentality of people around me, and this misunderstanding of regarding me as an unbeliever.... So now let's take the people of the Quran: In the Quran it says, "and whoever desires other than Islam as religion, is a kafir."[54] We do not have such an understanding. If Muslims have such an understanding, that means we cannot live together. If it was this way: Jesus came to find the salvation for the humans; that means Jesus is for me and for the Muslim and the Yazidi and for the whole humanity. With this understanding I could live with them. But it is quite difficult because these guys do not agree. Christians get their heads cut off for no reason. So, they want to emigrate from this county to find a safe area to settle and establish a family. It is because of our love to the Lord Jesus why we are still staying here because he says: You will be in all the world. We are waiting for the Lord, we have stayed all our life here.[55]

He directly connects the atrocities committed by IS with the history of the genocide of 1915, where IS and the Young Turks of 1915 become the same perpetrator:

> One hundred years ago, this family, my father was in Turkey. In Tur Abdeen, they killed our fathers and grandfathers. From the Armenians, one and a half million; 650,000 Syriacs, 150,000 Chaldeans. Not to mention the Assyrians who revolted against them. Here in Simele next to Dohuk in the year 1933, they killed about 5,000 Assyrians and the rest dispersed around the world. In Tel Tamer in Syria near to Qamishli, ISIS has attacked them there, and the dams in Turkey flooded them. All the problem came from Turkey, the Ottoman state. From the beginning of the time till now, it is an enemy to the Christians. So, Mr. Thomas, our life is so harsh.[56]

233

This narrative connects the genocide in the late Ottoman Empire with the massacres against the Assyrians in Iraq in 1933 to the atrocities committed by IS. Although the Christian from Sinjar interviewed belongs to the group that had not yet left Iraq, he hardly sees any future for Christians in Iraq. He has limited hopes of returning to Sinjar:

> We don't know how the situation will be in the future. It is harsh. Sinjar is divided in three parts. One in PMU's hands, one in PKK's, the other in PDK's hand. So, the Christian people have an unknown destiny. This Iraq that you can see, from Zakho to the south had once been all Christian. As a result of the persecution, it had started from the south and slowly, slowly ... We had thirty-nine churches in Najaf. In Baghdad, we had almost the oldest church in Iraq ... but where are they now? They all have disappeared, Mr. Thomas. And we are still uncertain about our destiny, part of us have arrived in Australia, others in Germany, Sweden, Canada. We, those who remained—about thirty families—are still here in Kurdistan. Some in Zakho or here or in Fish Khabour, some in Kirkuk ... I mean the simple, poor families have remained. We are powerless.[57]

A Christian woman whose family also fled from present-day Turkey to Sinjar similarly connects the massacres of IS with the history of genocide in the late Ottoman Empire:

> One hundred years, exactly 100 years after we came to Sinjar, they applied another *ferman* [massacre] on us. Nine of my father's family were killed and only he survived. He was four and a half years old. Thanks to God, and he lived here among the Yazidi. He lived wisely and thanks to God, we are the children of God and his children [of the father].[58]

Using the same terminology as the Yazidi for the massacre (*ferman*) offers an example of the close relationship between the Christian minority and the Yazidi majority in Sinjar. From clothing to food and habits, Christians in Sinjar became acculturated into the Yazidi world of Sinjar. Most Christian men even wear the same kinds of moustaches as Yazidi men from the region and, if they speak Kurdish, they use the same Sinjari dialect of Kurmanji.

Finally, the two groups share overlapping narratives of Muslim atrocities against Yazidi and Christians. Both seem to share a common fear of the end of their existence in Iraq. And both feel that Sinjar and its inhabitants became a pawn for the stronger (Muslim) powers in the region, and that the Western world has forgotten about them. Christians from Sinjar, like many Yazidi, lament the closure of Europe for refugees: "If the way to Europe would be open, nobody would stay in Sinjar. I have four young boys, I would be happy if at least two could go to Europe. I know that everybody who would go to Europe would stay there and would never come back."[59] The same man argues that before IS came, he would have never had the idea of leaving Sinjar: "We had everything, property and land. It was wonderful. We had jobs and everything."[60]

Most of the Iraqi Christians see the end of Christianity in Iraq as a loss, especially because the Aramaic-speaking Christians are now scattered around the world. A Christian woman from Sinjar argues that Christians have no future in Iraq, and she would prefer a collective migration of the community and not an individual one: "Why don't they put us all together in the same place? To Canada or the US. This way we are scattered around the world. One uncle is in Canada, another one in Sweden, and so on."[61]

The fear of losing religious and cultural traditions in an individualized diaspora can also be observed with other religious and cultural minorities from Iraq. Mandaean intellectuals also try to regather the Mandaean diaspora somewhere in exile; for the same reason, most Yazidi try to migrate to Germany, where a large Yazidi diaspora already lives.

Return to Sinjar?

Although some IDPs who lived in the north of Mount Sinjar did return to their towns and villages, most former residents of the city of Sinjar and the southern areas remain on the mountain or in the IDP camps in Kurdistan. While Sinun and Khanasor seem like normal towns again, with a healthy civic life, the city of Sinjar and many villages to the south are still in ruins.

The International Organization for Migration announced that 3,220 families had returned to Sinjar by May 2016.[62] While at least a part of the Yazidi from the north side of Mount Sinjar did return, the Christians had not returned. However, some Babawat had also returned, especially since the Iraqi government took over Sinjar from the Kurds in October 2017. Some also started to repair their houses with the help of Yazidi who had returned earlier.

The events following the Kurdistan independence referendum have increased the insecurity in the region. The Iraqi army took over most of the PDK-controlled areas of Sinjar and left the future status of the region as unclear as it had been previously. Some Yazidi who supported Barzani's PDK fled again from Sinun, now controlled by the YBŞ and its allies. The activities of the Barzani Charity Foundation and the healthcare station of the PDK had to be suspended. The Iraqi government had slowly replaced these activities with its own services for the IDPs in Serdast. Since 2018, insecurity also increased as a result of Turkish attacks against the YBŞ. On August 15, one of the high-ranking YBŞ commanders, Zekî Şengalî, was killed by Turkish forces on his way back from a memorial ceremony in Koço. This was followed by other attacks. The most recent Turkish attack killed YBŞ spokesperson Zardaşt Şengalî on January 15, 2020.

Conclusion

This chapter is a work in progress. Research about the future development of the situation of the IDPs and refugees from the region should and will be continued. The lack of security and the rivalry of different militias and armed groups prevented Yazidi, Christians, and other groups from returning to the Sinjar region. Only a few displaced persons returned to the northern face of Mount Sinjar, while most still live as IDPs inside the Dohuk Governorate. Many would like to migrate to Europe or other countries; however, they remain aware of the difficulties for refugees created by some European states. Many say that they feel abandoned by the international community.

Those willing to return to Sinjar ask for autonomy and international protection. Many survivors say preconditions for returning and rebuilding their villages and towns would include local protection forces and a governorate separate from the Nineveh Governorate. Many adherents of the religious minority groups who lived in Sinjar have lost their trust in a future inside Iraq. They do not connect their problems solely with IS but rather see IS as a continuation of Muslim (Sunni) repression against religious minorities. They generally regard this as a genocide committed by Muslims against the Yazidi and the Christians. Of course, many survivors admit that not "all Muslims" participated in the genocide. However, most victims believed IS's self-presentation and propaganda as the only form of "true Islam." They suffered repression because they were not Muslims, so many of them perceived the perpetrators as Muslims. They see the Sunni Muslims opposing IS as the rare exceptions that stayed humane despite their religion, while true Muslim believers support IS. The self-stylization of IS and its "Islamic" justification for crimes has left a significant and poisonous legacy of distrust in the region.

In a confessional and ethnically mixed region like the Nineveh Governorate, this confessionalized interpretation of conflict creates a heavy burden for the future, especially when victims of such a discourse encounter another confessionalized discourse of self-victimization (i.e. the discourse of Sunni Muslim

Arabs who feel under pressure by the Iraqi army and the PMF, often considered as Shiʿite militias and who often use a confessional iconography).

Religious minorities who survived the violence of the self-proclaimed Islamic State often view violence as a result of religious confessions. The trauma of survivors of such violence often continues long after they leave Iraq. In Austria and Germany, some Yazidi, Christian, or Shiʿite victims of IS suffer re-traumatization when they must coexist with Sunni Muslim refugees in refugee camps.

These minorities also connect their fate with the experiences of other religious minorities who have already vanished from Iraq. A Christian man from Sinjar mentioned the expulsion of the Jews from Sinjar: "My father always told me: Today its Saturday and tomorrow it will be Sunday, which means what happened to the Jews will later on happen to us. And now it happens."[63]

NOTES

1. HUMAN MOBILITY IN THE MIDDLE EAST

1. Stephen Castles, "Twenty-First Century Migration as a Challenge to Sociology," *Journal of Ethnic and Migration Studies* 33, no. 3 (2007): 351–3.
2. See, for example, Douglas S. Massey et al., "Theories of International Migration: A Review and Appraisal," *Population and Development Review* 19, no. 3 (1993): 432; Stephen Castles, Hein De Haas, and Mark J. Miller, *The Age of Migration: International Population Movements in the Modern World* (Basingstoke: Palgrave Macmillan, 2013), 25–53.
3. Gursharan Singh Kainth, "Push and Pull Factors of Migration: A Case Study of Brick Kiln Migrant Workers in Punjab," Munich Personal RePEc Archive (2010): 2, https://mpra.ub.uni-muenchen.de/30036/1/PPM.pdf; Iqbal Ahmed Chowdhury et al., "Internal Migration and Socio-economic Status of Migrants: A Study in Sylhet City, Bangladesh," *American Journal of Human Ecology* 1, no. 4 (2012): 123–33.
4. Susan F. Martin, Sanjula Weerasinghe, and Abbie Taylor, eds, *Humanitarian Crises and Migration: Causes, Consequences and Responses* (London: Routledge, 2014), 5 and 11.
5. Bent Greve, "Labour Migration and Labour Market Integration: Causes and Challenges," in *Migration and Welfare in the New Europe: Social Protection and the Challenges of Integration*, ed. Emma Carmel, Alfio Cerami, and Theodoros Papadopoulos (Bristol: Policy Press, 2012), 88.
6. Alexander Betts, "State Fragility, Refugee Status and Survival Migration," *Forced Migration Review* 43 (2013): 4–6; Sari Hanafi, "Forced Migration in the Middle East and North Africa," in *The Oxford Handbook of Refugee and Forced Migration Studies*, ed. Elena Fiddian-Qasmiyeh et al. (Oxford: Oxford University Press, 2014), 585–6.
7. Douglas S. Massey, "International Migration at the Dawn of the Twenty-First Century: The Role of the State," *Population and Development Review* 25, no. 2 (1999): 307.
8. Douglas S. Massey, "Patterns and Processes of International Migration in the 21st

Century," Conference Paper, Conference on African Migration in Comparative Perspective, Johannesburg, South Africa (2003), 27–8.

9. Catherine Lloyd, "Anti-racism, Racism and Asylum-Seekers in France," *Patterns of Prejudice* 37, no. 3 (2003): 323–40.

10. Castles, De Haas, and Miller, *The Age of Migration*, 4–12.

11. Castles, De Haas, and Miller, *Age of Migration*, 7.

12. Dawn Chatty, *Displacement and Dispossession in the Modern Middle East* (Cambridge: Cambridge University Press, 2010), 1–37; Seteney Shami, "The Social Implications of Population Displacement and Resettlement: An Overview with a Focus on the Arab Middle East," *International Migration Review* 27, no. 1 (Spring 1993): 4–33.

13. Sigrid Faath and Hanspeter Mattes, "Political Conflicts and Migration in the MENA States," in *Migration from the Middle East and North Africa to Europe: Past Developments, Current Status, and Future Potentials*, ed. Michael Bommes, Heinz Fassmann, and Wiebke Sievers (Amsterdam: Amsterdam University Press, 2014), 159–90.

14. European Commission and Eurosat, "Push and Pull Factors of International Migration: A Comparative Report," 2000, x; Kainth, "Push and Pull Factors of Migration," 2; Chowdhury et al., "Internal Migration and Socio-economic Status of Migrants," 123–33.

15. United Nations High Commissioner for Refugees (UNHCR), "Global Trends: Forced Displacement in 2017," 2018, 68, www.unhcr.org/5b27be547.pdf; Internal Displacement Monitoring Centre and Norwegian Refugee Council, "Global Report on Internal Displacement," 2018, 16, www.internal-displacement.org/global-report/grid2018/downloads/2018-GRID.pdf

16. Ibid.

17. Mohamed Kamel Doraï, "State, Migration, and Borders' Fabric in the Middle East," *Frontera Norte* 26, no. 3 (2014): 124.

18. Chatty, *Displacement and Dispossession in the Modern Middle East*, 5.

19. Doraï, "State, Migration, and Borders' Fabric in the Middle East," 121; Update on UNHCR's operations in the Middle East and North Africa (MENA), Executive Committee of the High Commissioner's Programme (2018), 1, www.unhcr.org/5a9fd8b50.pdf

20. UNHCR, "Global Trends: Forced Displacement in 2017," 2018, 6, 71–4, www.unhcr.org/5b27be547.pdf. (By the end of 2017, the number of forcibly displaced Syrians amounted to 12.6 million, which consisted of 6.3 million refugees, 146,700 asylum-seekers, and 6.2 million internally displaced persons [IDPs]. In Iraq, the number of the forcibly displaced was recorded at 3.3 million [360,596 refugees, 272,643 asylum-seekers, and 2.6 million IDPs], while the numbers in Yemen and Libya were 2.1 million [23,553 refugees, 24,642 asylum-seekers, and 2,014,062 IDPs] and 199,013 [11,216 refugees, 6,860 asylum-seekers, and 180,937 IDPs] respectively.) Internal Displacement Monitoring Centre and

Norwegian Refugee Council, "Global Report on Internal Displacement," 2018, 22 and 49, www.internal-displacement.org/global-report/grid2018/down-loads/2018-GRID.pdf. (As of 2017, Syria had the highest number of internally displaced people in the world at 6,784,000 while Iraq had the fourth highest at 2,648,000. Yemen follows as the sixth highest, with 2,014,000 internally displaced people, while Libya has 197,000.)

21. Hanafi, "Forced Migration in the Middle East and North Africa," 585.
22. UNHCR, "Fact Sheet: Timeline and Figures," 2013, www.unhcr.org/5245a72e6. pdf; Senay Özden, "Syrian Refugees in Turkey," Migration Policy Center, 2013, 1, http://cadmus.eui.eu/bitstream/handle/1814/29455/MPC-RR-2013%2005. pdf?sequence=1&isAllowed=y; Kemal Kirişci, *Syrian Refugees and Turkey's Challenges: Going beyond Hospitality* (Washington, DC: Brookings, 2014).
23. William C. Ryan, "The Historical Case for the Right of Sanctuary," *Journal of Church and State* 29, no. 2 (1987): 211; Internal Displacement Monitoring Centre and Norwegian Refugee Council, "Global Report on Internal Displacement," 2018, 22 and 49.
24. Doraï, "State, Migration, and Borders' Fabric in the Middle East," 121, 124, and 128.
25. Karen O'Reilly, *International Migration and Social Theory* (Basingstoke: Palgrave Macmillan, 2012), 62–5; Castles, De Haas, and Miller, *Age of Migration*, 47–9.
26. International Organization for Migration (IOM), "Who Is a Migrant? IOM Definition of 'Migrant,'" UN Migration Agency, www.iom.int/who-is-a-migrant
27. UNHCR, "Migrant Definition," UN Refugee Agency, https://emergency.unhcr. org/entry/176962/migrant-definition
28. Ibid.
29. David Turton, "Refugees, Forced Resettlers and 'Other Forced Migrants': Towards a Unitary Study of Forced Migration," New Issues in Refugee Research, Working Paper 94 (UNHCR, 2003): 1–2, and 8; Julie Peteet, "Unsettling the Categories of Displacement," *Middle East Report* 244 (2007): 2–9.
30. Roger Zetter, "More Labels, Fewer Refugees: Remaking the Refugee Label in an Era of Globalization," *Oxford Journal of Refugee Studies* 20, no. 2 (2007): 179–80, 183–8.
31. Emma Stewart, "Exploring the Asylum–Migration Nexus in the Context of Health Professional Migration," *Geoforum* 39, no. 1 (2008): 223–5.
32. Alexander Betts, *Survival Migration: Failed Governance and the Crisis of Displacement* (Ithaca: Cornell University Press, 2013), 4.

2. BORDERS AND MOBILITIES IN THE MIDDLE EAST: EMERGING CHALLENGES FOR SYRIAN REFUGEES IN "BILAD AL-SHAM"

1. For the purposes of this chapter, the "Middle East" refers to the space belonging to historical Syria, Bilad al-Sham, which geographically comprises the space between

the mountains of Taurus in Turkey and the desert of Arabia, between the Mediterranean and the Euphrates River. From the Hellenist period, the Greeks used the term Coele Syria (hollow Syria) to refer to the area of the Mediterranean and the Euphrates River (in contrast to Syria in Mesopotamia). The Romans used the term for the regions of the Near East between Asia Minor and Egypt belonging to the Roman Empire. The Arabs kept the Roman references. Today's territorial concept (Palestine, Israel, etc.) was first used at the end of the late Ottoman period.

2. This interpretative quest draws on previous research conducted in the Mediterranean region as well as the Mexico–US border region. The best-known comparison is militarized border enforcement, plus humanitarianism, posed against asylum-seeking and irregular migration. However, mobility occurs in more complex ways at these borders, including privileged and other differentiated and sorted mobilities.

3. The "politics of compassion" can be understood from a humanitarian perspective when applied, for example, to migrant children, as there is normally a contradiction between a way of protecting them and a way of discriminating against them (e.g. according to different origins).

4. "Transnationalization or transnational relations implies cross-border ties of individual and collective agents, such as migrants, migrant associations, multinational companies, religious communities, which constitute a social category ... Transnationality denotes a continuum of trans-state ties and practices, ranging from less to more intense and regular. Agents' transnational ties constitute a marker of heterogeneity, akin to other heterogeneities, such as age, gender, citizenship, sexual orientation, cultural preferences or language use," Thomas Faist, "Toward a Transnational Methodology: Methods to Address Methodological Nationalism, Essentialism, and Positionality," *Revue européenne des migrations internationales* 28, no. 1 (2012): 51–2.

5. This refers to the increase of women flows in international migration as well as the incorporation of a new understanding of migrant projects according to the visibilization of gender approaches and that of the role of female economic migration.

6. The "border shift" refers to the multiplication and complexation of borders in a global landscape of neoliberal transformation. See more in Natalia Ribas-Mateos, *Border Shifts: New Mobilities from Europe and Beyond* (Basingstoke: Palgrave Macmillan, 2015).

7. Michel Agier, ed., *Un monde de camps* [A world of camps] (Paris: La Découverte, 2014); David Lagarde, "Mapping the Encampment of the World and Its Consequences on Refugees' Itineraries," chapter presented at the Refugee on the Move Conference, CER-Migracions, Barcelona, 21–22 April 2016.

8. Ibid.

9. The "mobility turn" is applied to a transformation of the social sciences, not only placing new issues on the table but also transcending disciplinary boundaries and putting into question the fundamental "territorial" and "sedentary" precepts, and

it opens the debate on the acceleration of all forms of mobilities, macro or micro mobilities, which are transforming the world.

10. See, for example, "The Vulnerability Assessment of Syrian Refugees in Lebanon," UNHCR/UNICEF/WFP, 2016, www.unicef.org/lebanon/media/676/file/Lebanon-report-4-2016-1.pdf.

11. Fernand Braudel, "Una prueba esencial: La frontera" [An essential test: The border], in *La identidad de Francia: El espacio y la historia* [The identity of France: History and environment] (Barcelona: Editorial Edisa, 1993), 302–3.

12. See, for example, Dawn Chatty, "Introduction: Dispossession and Forced Migration in the Middle East: Community Cohesion in Impermanent Landscapes," in Chatty, *Displacement and Dispossession in the Modern Middle East*, ed. Dawn Chatty (Cambridge: Cambridge University Press, 2010), 1–6.

13. Peter Sahlins, *Boundaries: The Making of France and Spain in the Pyrenees* (Berkeley: University of California Press, 1989).

14. See Timothy J. Dunn, "Immigration Enforcement at the U.S.–Mexico Border: Where Human Rights and National Sovereignty Collide," in *Binational Human Rights: The U.S.–Mexico Experience*, ed. William Paul Simmons and Carol Mueller (Philadelphia: University of Pennsylvania Press, 2014).

15. Judith Butler, "Foreword," in *The Making of a Protest Movement in Turkey: #occupygezi*, ed. Umut Özkirimli (New York: Palgrave Pivot Macmillan, 2014), viii.

16. Mohamed Kamel Doraï, "Palestinian Refugee Camps in Lebanon: Migration, Mobility and the Urbanization Process," in *Palestinian Refugees: Identity, Space and Place in the Levant*, ed. Are Knudsen and Sari Hanafi (London: Routledge, 2010), 125.

17. These figures are constantly updated on UNHCR web pages.

18. Peter Gatrell, "Refugees and Refugee Crises: Some Historical Reflections," World Financial Review, 1 December 2015, www.worldfinancialreview.com/?p=4737. Gatrell underlines the importance of a historical perspective, which would help us reflect on the significance of today's displacement of Syrians and help to highlight their agency instead of viewing them as helpless victims.

19. Mohamed Kamel Doraï, "Ethnography from the Margins: Studying Syrian Refugees' Settlement in Northern Jordan," chapter presented at the Refugee on the Move Conference, Barcelona, 21–22 April 2016.

20. Ibid.

21. See Chiara Denaro, "The Reconfiguration of Mediterranean Migration Routes after the War in Syria: Narratives of the 'Egyptian Route' to Italy (and Beyond)," in *Migration, Mobilities and the Arab Spring: Spaces of Refugee Flight in the Eastern Mediterranean*, ed. Natalia Ribas-Mateos (Cheltenham: Edward Elgar Publishers, 2016).

22. According to Chiara Denaro, "Limits and Borders of the Right to Asylum in the Mediterranean Space. Ethnography of Certain Escape Routes from Syria" (PhD

diss., Universitá Sapienza di Roma, 2017), the routes have been modified since the war in Syria. They can be structured in three migration corridors: Eastern (Turkish–Greek and Turkish–Bulgarian routes), Central (Libyan and Egyptian route), and Western (Spanish–Moroccan sea and land routes).

23. This sorting has become the axis of Heyman's [0]ethnographic studies in recent years.

24. Josiah Heyman, "Cuatro temas en el estudio de la frontera contemporánea, in [Four themes in the study of the contemporary frontier], *El Río Bravo Mediterráneo: Las regiones fronterizas en la época de la globalización* [The Mediterranean Rio Grande: Border regions at the time of globalization], ed. Natalia Ribas-Mateos (Barcelona: Edicions Bellaterra, 2011), 81–98.

25. Jennifer Hyndman, *Managing Displacement: Refugees and the Politics of Humanitarianism* (Minneapolis: University of Minnesota Press, 2000).

26. Giorgio Agamben, *Homo sacer: Il potere sovrano e la nuda vita* (Turin: Einaudi, 1995).

27. Volunteer work was conducted from 24 June to 12 September 2017 in Beirut.

28. Nicholas Blanford, "Case Study: The Lebanon–Syria Border," paper presented at the conference Rethinking International Relations after the Arab Revolutions, Beirut, Universite Saint Joseph, 2016.

29. Nicholas Blanford, "Case Study: The Lebanon–Syria Border," 24.

30. See data by UNHCR, constantly updated page in Lebanon.

31. A century after the Sykes–Picot Agreement to draft borders in the Middle East was signed in 1916 between France and Britain, the region, and the country in particular here, remains a central location of successive conflicts.

32. Interview, Bekaa Valley, July 2017.

33. "The Vulnerability Assessment of Syrian Refugees in Lebanon."

34. Ibid.

35. Ibid.

36. Norwegian Refugee Council (NRC), "Women Refugees in Lebanon and the Consequences of Limited Legal Status on their Housing, Land and Property Rights," Information, Counselling and Legal Assistance Programme, 2016, www.nrc.no/globalassets/pdf/reports/women-refugees-in-lebanon.pdf

37. Interview with NGO worker, Bekaa.

38. Ethnographic notes.

39. Interview, Bekaa Valley, July 2017.

40. Interview with psychologist from a local NGO, summer 2017.

41. Livelihood programs and interventions have been designed and implemented by UNHCR, often in collaboration with humanitarian NGOs. Donors are normally responsible for the design and goal, while governments exert control over legal and policy frameworks. They relate to the supply side and the demands side of refugees' work opportunites.

42. Conference, "Borders of the World: Women's Workshop Project Manager (NGO-Beirut)," Asaffron, Girona, 25 September 2017.
43. Interview with psychologist from a local NGO, summer 2017.
44. When considering Benjamin's Arcades Project, see more in Tim Cresswell, "Towards a Politics of Mobility," *Environment and Planning D: Society and Space* 28, no. 1 (2010): 17–31.
45. Didier Fassin, *Humanitarian Reason: A Moral History of the Present* (Berkeley: University of California Press, 2012); Fassin, "Humanitarianism as a Politics of Life," *Public Culture* 19, no. 3 (2007): 499–520; Fassin, "The Humanitarian Politics of Testimony: Subjectification through Trauma in the Israeli–Palestinian Conflict," *Cultural Anthropology* 23, no. 3 (2008): 531–58.

3. THE BORDERWORK OF HUMANITARIANISM DURING DISPLACEMENT FROM WAR-TORN SYRIA: LIVELIHOODS AS IDENTITY POLITICS IN NORTHERN LEBANON AND SOUTHEAST TURKEY

1. I would like to thank the Center for International and Regional Studies (CIRS) at Georgetown University in Qatar for funding my fieldwork in Lebanon and Turkey. Without the center's financial and intellectual support, this study would not have been possible. I am also indebted to Dr Zeynep Şahin-Mencütek for her invaluable assistance during the Gaziantep fieldwork, and to Muhsin for his hospitality in difficult times. I am also very grateful to Ba'diya from the Halba public library, the staff at the Akkar Network for Development, and Fatima from the International Rescue Committee. I hope one day I will be able to repay the generosity of all the Lebanese, Syrian, and Turkish people who gave some of their precious time to assist me in this research.
2. Polly Pallister-Wilkins, "Humanitarian Borderwork," in *Border Politics: Defining Spaces of Governance and Forms of Transgressions*, ed. Cengiz Günay and Nina Witjes (Berlin: Springer, 2016), 89; Ilana Feldman, "The Challenge of Categories: UNRWA and the Definition of a 'Palestine Refugee,'" *Journal of Refugee Studies* 25, no. 3 (2012): 387–406.
3. This is Baruch de Spinoza's notion, which Ghassan al-Hage draws on in "'Comes a Time We Are All Enthusiasm': Understanding Palestinian Suicide Bombers in Times of Exighophobia," *Public Culture* 15, no. 1 (2003): 65–89.
4. Kemal Kirişci, "Syrian Refugees and Turkey's Challenges: Going beyond Hospitality," Brookings Report, 2014.
5. Fatih Kahraman and Özlem Kahya Nizam, "Multecilik Hallerini Mekan uzerinden Okumak: Gaziantep ornegınde Turkiyelilerin Gozunden Suriyeli kent Multecileri" [The state of immigration upon the environment: example of Gaziantep's Syrian urban refugees in the eyes of the Turkish], *Uluslararası Sosyal*

Araştırmalar Dergisi: The Journal of International Social Research 9, no. 44 (2016): 813.

6. For instance, see "Serious Flaws along Syrian Border Increase Security Risks," *Today's Zaman*, 8 September 2013, www.todayszaman.com/news-325791-serious-flaws-along-syrian-border-increase-security-risks.htm

7. William Walters, "Foucault and Frontiers: Notes on the Birth of the Humanitarian Border," in *Governmentality: Current Issues and Future Challenges*, ed. Ulrich Bröckling, Susanne Krasmann, and Thomas Lemke (London: Routledge, 2011), 138–64.

8. Néstor Rodríguez, "The Battle for the Border: Notes on Autonomous Migration, Transnational Communities, and the State," *Social Justice* 23, no. 3 (1996): 21–37.

9. François Debrix, "Deterritorialised Territories, Borderless Borders: The New Geography of International Medical Assistance," *Third World Quarterly* 19, no. 5 (1998): 827–46.

10. Sara Pantuliano and Eva Svoboda, "International and Local/Diaspora Actors in the Syria Response: A Diverging Set of Systems," working chapter, Humanitarian Policy Group (HPG) at the Overseas Development Institute (ODI), London, 2015.

11. Walters, "Foucault and Frontiers," 138–64.

12. Omar Lizardo, "Is a 'Special Psychology' of Practice Possible? From Values and Attitudes to Embodied Dispositions," *Theory & Psychology* 19, no. 8 (2009): 715.

13. In Gaziantep, as a highly insecure border region at a geopolitical level, and during a post-presidential referendum time span, where domestic political frictions were tangible even though they did not result in material clashes, the political environment proved to be particularly sensitive. This forced the author to often conduct fieldwork in the presence of local policemen, who, in some cases, inhibited the communication with locals or refugees.

14. United Nations Office for the Coordination of Humanitarian Affairs, "Humanitarian Bulletin: Lebanon Issue 24," October 2016, https://reliefweb.int/sites/reliefweb.int/files/resources/OCHA-HumanitarianBulletin-Issue24-October2016_EN.pdf

15. Roula Abi-Habib Khoury, "Rapid Assessment on Child Labour in North Lebanon (Tripoli and Akkar) and Bekaa Governorates" (Beirut: USJ and ILO, 2012), 25.

16. The Arabic transliteration in this chapter follows the (uncodified) commonly accepted rules of the Lebanese dialect. I therefore transcribe terms and sentences in the way local speakers pronounce them, rather than adopting the Standard Arabic transcription scheme, which would be less evocative of lived experience.

17. David Satterthwaite, "The Scale and Nature of Urban Change Worldwide: 1950–2000 and Its Underpinnings," Human Settlement Discussion Chapter Series, International Institute for Environment and Development (IIED), London, 2005, 22.

18. Leah Campbell, "Stepping Back: Understanding Cities and their Systems," working chapter, Active Learning Network for Accountability and Performance in Humanitarian Action (ALNAP), London, 2014, 14.

19. Michel Seurat, *Syrie, l'état de barbarie* [Syria, the state of barbarity] (Paris: Presses Universitaires de France, coll. Proché-Orient, 2012).

20. Interview with the dean of faculty of the American University of Technology, Halba, 2 March 2017.

21. Interview with residents of Halba, 28 February 2017.

22. Interview with Halba resident, 29 February 2017.

23. Ismael Sheikh Hassan and Sari Hanafi, "Insecurity and Reconstruction in Post-conflict Nahr al-Bared Refugee Camp," *Journal of Palestinian Studies* 11, no. 1 (2010): 27–48.

24. Ibid., 40.

25. Conversation with local residents, Halba, February 20, 2017.

26. Faraj T. Zakhour, *Halba fy nisf qarn 1900–1950* (Halba: Dar Zakhour li'l tab'a, an-nashr, wa at-tawzi', 2005), 24.

27. Ibid., 25.

28. A Syrian Workers' Union was actually created in the 1970s; John Chalcraft, "Syrian Migrant Workers in Lebanon: The Limits of Transnational Integration, Communitarian Solidarity, and Popular Agency," European University Institute (EUI) working chapters, Robert Schuman Centre for Advanced Studies (RSCAS), no. 2006/26, Italy, 2006, 4.

29. Ibid., 74.

30. These data have been collected from the local municipality (23 February 2017, Halba).

31. For more details, see: United Nations, "Lebanon Crisis Response Plan 2015–16," www.un.org.lb/library/assets/20151223-LCRP_ENG_Brochure%20(opti-mized)%20(3)-035140.pdf

32. John Chalcraft, *The Invisible Cage: Syrian Migrant Workers in Lebanon* (Stanford, CA: Stanford University Press, 2009).

33. Filippo Dionigi, "Rethinking Borders: The Case of the Syrian Refugee Crisis in Lebanon," *Refugees and Migration Movements in the Middle East* 25 (2017): 22–9.

34. Like in the Gulf Cooperation Council (GCC), the *kafala* system is used to monitor migrant laborers in Lebanon. The laborers are required to have an in-country sponsor, usually their employer, who becomes responsible for their visa and legal status.

35. Maja Janmyr, "UNHCR and the Syrian Refugee Response: Negotiating Status and Registration in Lebanon," *International Journal of Human Rights* 22, no. 3 (2018): 68.

36. Ibid.

37. Francesca Battistin, "IRC Cash and Livelihoods Support Programme in Lebanon,"

Emergency Nutrition Network (ENN) Online, November 2014, www.ennon-line.net/fex/48/irclebanon

38. Chalcraft, "Syrian Migrant Workers in Lebanon."

39. Disaster and Emergency Management Authority of the Republic of Turkey (AFAD), "Barınma Merkezlerinde Son Durum" [Latest situation at shelter centers], 2016, www.afad.gov.tr/tr/ IcerikDetay1.aspx?IcerikID=848&ID=16

40. According to the EU Directive 2001/55/EC on Temporary Protection, enacted in line with Article 91 of the new Law on Foreigners and International Protection (no. 6458), it is an exceptional procedure during an emergency situation that involves a mass influx of displaced persons. According to the EU directive, the duration of temporary protection shall be one year. It may be extended automatically by six-month periods for a maximum of one additional year. Turkey's Temporary Protection Regulation prohibits Syrians under temporary protection from applying for international protection.

41. Kahraman and Nizam, "Multecilik Hallerini Mekan uzerinden Okumak," 808–26.

42. Ibid., 814–16.

43. Ibid., 822.

44. Interview with an insurance company owner, Gaziantep, 14 August 2017.

45. Zeynep Kivilcim, "Legal Violence against Syrian Female Refugees in Turkey," *Feminist Legal Studies* 24 (2016): 205–6; Ali Çarkoglu and Mine Eder, "Urban Informality and Economic Vulnerability: The Case of Turkey," unpublished article, 2006.

46. Ayselin Yıldız and Elif Uzgören, "Limits to Temporary Protection: Non-camp Syrian Refugees in İzmir, Turkey," *Southern European and Black Sea Studies* 16, no. 2 (2016): 207.

47. Arife Karadağ, "Refugees of a City: The Socio-spatial Impacts of those Syrian Refugees Who Arrived in Izmir, Turkey," in *Turkish Migration Conference: Selected Proceedings*, ed. Guven Seker et al. (London: Transnational Press London, 2015).

48. Veronique Barbelet and Caitlin Wake, *The Lives and Livelihoods of Syrian Refugees in Turkey and Jordan* (London: Humanitarian Policy Group, Overseas Development Institute [ODI], 2017), 3.

49. Ibid., 5.

50. Emin Çakılcı, "Do Syrian Refugees a Real Impact on Local Unemployment in Turkey?" *Journal of Human Sciences*, 14, no. 2 (2017): 1213.

51. Mine Eder, "Retreating State? Political Economy of Welfare Regime Change in Turkey," *Middle East Law and Governance* 2, no. 2 (2009): 159.

52. Ibid., 152–84.

53. Ibid., 161.

54. Selim Koru and Omar Kadkoy, "The New Turks: How the Influx of Syrians Is Changing Turkey," *Turkish Policy Quarterly* 16, no. 1 (August 2017): 119–20.

55. Interview with a Turkish citizen working in the export sector, Gaziantep, 14 August 2017.
56. Koru and Kadkoy, "New Turks."
57. Mustafa Kovucu, "The Representation of Syrian Refugees in the Gaziantep's Local Media" (unpublished Master's thesis, Gaziantep University, 2006), 22.
58. Koru and Kadkoy, "New Turks," 121.
59. Taken from ORTADOĞU STRATEJİK ARAŞTIRMALAR MERKEZİ (ORSAM) [Center for Middle Eastern Strategic Studies], "The Impact of Syrian Refugees in Turkey" [in Turkish, translation by author], report no. 195, January 2015, http://tesev.org.tr/wp-content/uploads/2015/11/Suriyeli_Siginmacilarin_Turkiyeye_Etkileri.pdf
60. Jessica Schafer, "Supporting Livelihoods in Situations of Chronic Conflict and Political Instability: Overview of Conceptual Issues," Overseas Development Institute (ODI), working chapter no. 183, London, 2002, 13.
61. Madan Sarup, *An Introductory Guide to Post-structuralism and Postmodernism* (New York: Harvester Wheatsheaf, 1988), 34; Henk van Houtum and Ton van Naerssen, "Bordering, Ordering and Othering," *Tijdschrift voor Economische en Sociale Geografie* 93, no. 2 (2002): 125–36.
62. Livelihoods, defined by the Food and Agriculture Organization (FAO), is: "the physical, social and economic access to sufficient, safe and nutritious food that meets particular dietary needs and food preferences for an active and healthy life." See www.fao.org/economic/ess/ess-fs/en/ for more details.
63. Informal conversation with local traders, Halba, 27 February 2017; interview conducted with two INGO workers, Gaziantep, 13 August 2017.
64. Interview with two INGO workers, Gaziantep, 15 August 2017.
65. Market skill gaps are identified by analyzing the job demand in local markets.
66. In several cases, refugees simply strengthened the skills they had in Syria, but this does not necessarily reflect market gaps. Interview with a local aid worker, Gaziantep, 28 August 2017.
67. Interview with local aid worker, Halba, 1 March 2017.
68. Halba, 22 February 2017.
69. Estella Carpi, "Learning and Earning in Constrained Labour Markets: The Politics of Livelihoods in Lebanon's Halba," Save the Children UK, 2017.
70. Mark Duffield, "The Liberal Way of Development and the Development–Security Impasse: Exploring the Global Life-Chance Divide," *Security Dialogue* 41, no. 1 (2010): 53–76.
71. Carpi, "Learning and Earning in Constrained Labour Markets."
72. Mehmet Duruel, "Suriyeli Sığınmacıların Türk Emek Piyasasına Etkileri Fırsatlar ve Tehditler" [The impact of Syrian refugees on the Turkish labour market: opportunities and threats], *Uluslararası Ekonomik Araştırmalar Dergisi* 3 (2017): 207–22.

73. Carpi, "Learning and Earning in Constrained Labour Markets."

74. Aicha Moushref, "Forgotten Akkar: Socio-economic Reality of the Akkar Region," Mada Association, UNDP, Handicap International and EU Humanitarian Aid, 2008.

75. For the major infrastructural needs across Lebanon after the Syrian refugee crisis, see: UNHCR and REACH, "Multisector Community Level Assessment of Informal Settlements: Akkar Governorate, Lebanon," Assessment Report, November 2014. For more on the infrastructural projects humanitarian agencies have undertaken, see www.flandersinvestmentandtrade.com/export/sites/trade/files/market_studies/Libanon-infrastructureProjects2015.pdf; urban infrastructure has been largely addressed by humanitarian agencies in southern Turkey. See the following UNESCO report, issued by the Gaziantep municipality: http://cmimarseille.org/sites/default/files/newsite/library/files/en/Mr.%20G%C3%B6khan%20Yaman%2C%20Gaziantep%20Metropolitan%20Municipality%20-%20English.pdf

76. Recep Ulusoy and Nebahat Turan, "Gaziantep Ekonomisinin Ortadoğu Açısından Önemi" [The importance of Gaziantep city economy for the Middle East], *Akademik Bakış* 9, no. 18 (2016): 141–65.

77. Interview with local residents, Halba, 24 February 2017.

78. On Turkish border policies: the 1994 regulation defined the need to respond to mass influxes of refugees before the refugees could cross the border into Turkey unless the government was to take a decision to the contrary. In the event that refugees did actually enter Turkey, the regulation called on authorities to keep them in camps as close to the border as possible. See: "Regulation on the Procedures and Principles Related to Possible Population Movements and Aliens Arriving in Turkey Either as Individuals or in Groups Wishing to Seek Asylum Either from Turkey or Requesting Residence Permission in Order to Seek Asylum from Another Country," no. 1994/6169, 30 November 1994, available from www.refworld.org/docid/49746cc62.html. Also, according to a survey conducted by AFAD in 2013, roughly 42 percent and 48 percent of refugees in and outside camps respectively entered Turkey through "unofficial border crossings"; Syrian Refugees in Turkey, 2013 Field Survey Results, 23, www.afad.gov.tr/Dokuman/TR/61-2013123015505-syrian-refugees-in-turkey-2013_print_12.11.2013_eng.pdf. The closure of the Lebanese border, in addition to tougher measures to renew residency permits for refugees, is instead sanctioned by the Presidency of the Council of Ministers, Session of 23 October 2014.

79. For more about refugee e-cards in Lebanon, see "New E-Cards Make Life Easier to Syrian Refugees in Lebanon," World Food Programme, October 13, 2013.

80. Interview with a local aid worker, 28 August 2017.

81. Mona Harb, Ali Kassem, and Watfa Najdi, "Entrepreneurial Refugees and the City: Brief Encounters in Beirut," *Journal of Refugee Studies* 32, no. 1 (2018): 23–41.

82. Carpi, "Learning and Earning in Constrained Labour Markets."
83. Ibid.
84. Interview with the leader of the Akkar Trades Association, Halba, 28 February 2017.
85. The author herself has witnessed such an urban change, as she visited the city first in December 2011.
86. Carpi, "Learning and Earning in Constrained Labour Markets."
87. An IPSOS report states that, out of 1,200 Syrian nationals interviewed, only 13 percent receive direct or indirect aid from any institution or organization (IPSOS, 2017: 4); 85 percent earn their own livelihoods but only 6 percent have a regular income (IPSOS, 2017: 2). IPSOS, "Suriyeli Mülteci Hayatlar Monitörü," Summary Evaluation Report, 2017, http://ingev.org/wp-content/uploads/2017/07/Multeci-Hayatlar-Monitor%C3%BC.pdf
88. Syrian nationals in Turkey can only open large stores or factories by partnering with a Turkish counterpart. This is often believed to be a practical measure to allow authorities to control and monitor sales and financial and legal activities through a Turkish partner (while large companies can easily outsource these services). Interview with a local aid worker, Gaziantep, 29 August 2017.
89. Report of Gaziantep Chamber of Commerce, August 2015, www.gto.org.tr/upload/download/Faaliyet-Raporu-2015–609399.pdf. The attractive cities for Syrian investors have thus far been İstanbul, Gaziantep, Mersin, and Hatay.
90. Interview conducted with INGO officers, Gaziantep, 14 August 2017.
91. UNDP, "Syria Crisis Response Report," March 2017, www.tr.undp.org
92. Hatice Şule Oğuz, "Kulturlerarasi Karsilasmalarin Uzak Ihtimali: Siginmacilik Deneyiminde Gaziantep Ornegi" [The remote possibility of an encounter between cultures: the example of the asylum-seekers in Gaziantep], *Tesam Akademi Dergisi: Turkish Journal of TESAM Academy* 2, no. 2 (2015): 127–65.
93. Out of four shop-runners interviewed, only one was an owner, having migrated to Turkey twenty years earlier. Although local media often report news regarding Syrian refugees' economic empowerment, from a Syrian perspective it is increasingly difficult to open private businesses in Turkey. For example, see: www.hurriyet.com.tr/suriyeli-6-kadin-kursta-meslek-ogrenip-kuafor-40480562
94. Gaziantep, İran pazarı, 15 August 2017.
95. Gaziantep, interview with Turkish nationals, 13 August 2017.
96. Gaziantep, interview with Turkish nationals, 13 August 2017. Indeed, a Syrian shop assistant expressed surprise at seeing my Turkish research assistant entering his shop with me.
97. Gaziantep, 12 August 2017.
98. It is in fact usual to find grammatical errors on Turkish signs related to Syrian shops: *açıktık* rather than *açık* (open), *satlık* rather than *satılık* (on sale), etc. The ban was already enacted in other border locations such as Hatay. See more in

"Municipality Removes Arabic Signs to 'Remove Visual Pollution' in Turkey's South," *Daily News*, 22 May 2017, www.hurriyetdailynews.com/municipality-removes-arabic-signs-to-remove-visual-pollution-in-turkeys-south.aspx?PageID=238&NID=113385&NewsCatID=341

99. Most of the time they rely on the same providers as before the war, according to most of the interviewees. For example, "Sumal Food Corporation," Global Manufacturers, www.gmdu.net/corp-60873.html

100. Gaziantep, İran pazarı, 13 August 2017.

101. Interview with a local aid worker and a factory employee, Gaziantep, 13 and 28 August 2017.

102. All real personal names have been protected. Only the names of NGOs that provided their consent will appear in this chapter. With the lack of official estimates, Syrian Turkmens who fled Syria to relocate to Turkey are counted at between 300,000 and 500,000 in the international media.

103. Interview with Syrian Turkmen refugee, ex-aid provider, and worker, Gaziantep, 13 August 2017.

104. Interviews in Gaziantep, 14 August 2017.

105. Interviews in Halba, 24 February 2017.

106. In Syria and Lebanon, citizenship can legally be transmitted only from the father's side.

107. Interview with a central state official in Halba, 28 February 2017.

108. Informal conversation between the author and a local resident, Halba, 9 March 2017.

109. Interview with Waleed, a local resident, Halba, 20 February 2017.

110. Estella Carpi, "The Everyday Experience of Humanitarianism in Akkar's Villages," Civil Society Knowledge Centre and Lebanon Support, Beirut, 2014.

111. Carpi, "Learning and Earning in Constrained Labour Markets."

112. Henrik Lebuhn, "Local Border Practices and Urban Citizenship in Europe: Exploring Urban Borderlands," *City* 17, no. 1 (2013): 37–51.

113. Chalcraft, *Invisible Cage*.

114. For further details, see Ali Ünal, "Turkey Stands United with Turkmens, Says Foreign Ministry Undersecretary Yalçın," *Daily Sabah*, 15 December 2016, www.dailysabah.com/politics/2016/12/15/turkey-stands-united-with-turkmens-says-foreign-ministry-undersecretary-yalcin

115. Interview with the owner of an insurance company, Gaziantep, 14 August 2017.

116. Gaziantep, 13 August 2017.

117. Walters, "Foucault and Frontiers," 138.

118. For example, see, for Lebanon, "8 Hurt in New Suicide Blasts in al-Qaa after Pre-Dawn Bombings Kill 5, Wound 15," Nahar Net, 27 June 2016, www.naharnet.com/stories/en/212232; and, for Turkey, "Two Killed as Explosion Hits Refugees Near Turkey–Syria Border," Al-Monitor, 6 July 2016, www.al-monitor.com/

pulse/afp/2016/07/turkey-conflict-syria.html; and also in Gaziantep, Joey Millar, "TURKEY BLAST: Massive Explosion Rocks City of Gaziantep Near Border with Syria," *Daily Express*, 25 November 2016, www.express.co.uk/news/world/736686/turkey-blast-explosion-gaziantep-syrian-border

119. Peter Redfield, "Doctors, Borders, and Life in Crisis," *Cultural Anthropology* 20, no. 3 (2005): 329; Didier Fassin, *The Humanitarian Reason: A Moral History of the Present* (Berkeley, CA: University of California Press, 2011).

120. Alessandro Monsutti, "Afghan Migratory Strategies and the Three Solutions to the Refugee Problem," *Refugee Survey Quarterly* 27, no. 1 (2008): 58–73.

121. Katy Long, *The Point of No Return: Refugees, Rights, and Repatriation* (Oxford: Oxford University Press, 2013).

122. Katy Long and Jeff Crisp, "Migration, Mobility and Solutions: An Evolving Perspective," *Forced Migration Review* 35 (2010): 56–7.

123. Maja Janmyr and Lama Mourad, "Modes of Ordering: Labelling, Classification and Categorization in Lebanon's Refugee Response," *Journal of Refugee Studies* 31, no. 4 (2018).

4. HOSTING AND BEING HOSTED IN TIMES OF CRISIS: EXPLORING THE MULTILAYERED PATTERNS OF SYRIAN REFUGE IN THE DAYR AL-AHMAR REGION, NORTHERN BEKAA, LEBANON

1. Census information was provided by the Union of the Municipalities of Dayr al-Ahmar in December 2017. The numbers for Syrians are only indicative: they fluctuate in time as new people arrive and others leave. For instance, during our different fieldworks, the numbers of Syrians we observed in Beshuat varied between 110 people (in the spring) to a mere fifty in the winter, when families go to the region of Tripoli, on the coast, to harvest olives and other winter crops. In April 2017, the president of the municipality estimated their numbers at 150 (interview, 12 April 2017). The figures concerning Lebanese populations represent the number of people registered in the villages and do not reflect the actual number of residents. In Lebanon, people remain registered in their family's place of origin, although they may no longer live there. In the *caza* of Dayr al-Ahmar, estimates are that about 20 percent of the people live there on a permanent basis and 50 percent come solely for the summer.

2. Many Syrians are not registered by the UNHCR. In addition, from 2015 onward, the UNHCR stopped registering Syrians by demand of the Lebanese authorities, which pushed many people into an illegal status.

3. Liisa H. Malkki, *Purity and Exile: Violence, Memory, and National Cosmology among Hutu Refugees in Tanzania* (Chicago: University of Chicago Press, 1995).

4. Cathrine Brun, "Active Waiting and Changing Hopes: Toward a Time Perspective on Protracted Displacement," *Social Analysis* 59, no. 1 (2015): 24. "An agency-in-waiting denotes the capacity to act in the present, in everyday time, based on the

experience of displacement from the subject's history and a critical reflection of the future possibilities framed as waiting and hope."

5. Cathrine Brun defines the state of "permanent impermanence" as the "'everyday time' [that] continues to flow through routinized practices and survival strategies" although "individuals feel stuck in a present that they do not want to inhabit, awaiting a future they cannot reach—a future that is often unpredictable and uncertain." Brun, "Active Waiting and Changing Hopes," 19–37.

6. Fieldwork was conducted in April 2017, in December 2017, and in March 2018.

7. John Chalcraft, *The Invisible Cage: Syrian Migrant Workers in Lebanon* (Stanford, CA: Stanford University Press, 2009).

8. In a speech delivered in 1976, the former Syrian president Hafez al-Asad famously stated that "historically, Syria and Lebanon have formed one single country [*balad wâhid*] and one single people [*sha'b wâhid*]." Quoted in Elizabeth Picard, *Liban– Syrie, intimes étrangers: un siècle d'interactions sociopolitiques* [Lebanon-Syria, intimate strangers: A century of sociopolitical interactions] (Arles: Actes Sud, 2016), 68.

9. Karine Bennafla, "La région de la Bekaa: les mutations d'un espace-frontière entre Syrie et Liban," [The Bekaa region: The mutations of a border region between Syria and Lebanon], *Revue de l'economie méridionale* 1–2, nos. 209–10 (2005): 211–18.

10. Picard, *Liban–Syrie, intimes étrangers*.

11. Karine Bennafla, "Le développement au péril de la géopolitique: l'exemple de la plaine de la Bekaa (Liban)," [Development at risk of geopolitics: the example of the Bekaa plain (Lebanon)], *Géocarrefour* 81, no. 4 (2007): 277–86.

12. Emma Aubin-Boltanski, "La Vierge, les chrétiens, les musulmans et la nation: Liban 2004–2007," [The Virgin, the Christians, the Muslims, and the nation: Lebanon 2004–2007], *Terrain* 51 (2008): 19–29.

13. The Shi'a population who took shelter is remembered by the local population as *duyûf* (guests).

14. Tamirace Fakhoury, "Governance Strategies and Refugee Response: Lebanon in the Face of Syrian Displacement," *International Journal of Middle East Studies* 49, no 4 (2017): 681–700.

15. Ibid., 692.

16. Ibid., 686.

17. Ibid., 688.

18. "Lebanon's Hezbollah to Work with Syrian State on Refugee Returns," Reuters, 29 June 2018, www.reuters.com/article/us-mideast-crisis-lebanon-syria-refugees/ lebanons-hezbollah-to-work-with-syrian-state-on-refugee-returns-idUSKBN-1JP29Q

19. Interview with Imad, Dayr al-Ahmar city, 12 December 2017.

20. Fakhoury, "Governance Strategies and Refugee Response," 689.

21. Ibid.

22. Pseudonyms are used to protect people's identities.

23. Interview with Mikhayl, 11 April 2017.

24. Inter-Agency Coordination Lebanon, "August Statistical Dashboard," August 2017, https://data2.unhcr.org/en/documents/download/60350

25. Census established by the Union of the Municipalities in April 2017.

26. The trade in devotional objects generates about $8,000 per year (interview with Y.K., 7 April 2017).

27. Sahar Al-Attar, "Un développement motivé par des enjeux sociopolitiques," [A development motivated by sociopolitical stakes], *Le commerce du Levant* (30 June 2016), www.lecommercedulevant.com/article/26361-un-dveloppement-motiv-par-des-enjeux-sociopolitiques. Interviews with farmers in the *caza* of Dayr al-Ahmar in 2017 and 2018.

28. Interview with Beshuat farmer, 11 April 2017, and S.F., 6 March 2018.

29. Kamal Hamdan, director of the Consultation and Research Institute, interview, Beirut, 7 April 2017.

30. UNDP-UNHCR, "Impact of Humanitarian Aid on the Lebanese Economy," 10 June 2015, www.lb.undp.org/content/lebanon/en/home/library/poverty/impact-of-humanitarian-aid-undp-unhcr.html

31. The poverty line for Lebanon proposed by the World Bank in 2013 is established at US$ 3.84 per person per day (registered Syrians only). Source: UNHCR, UNICEF and WFP, "Vulnerability Assessment of Syrian Refugees in Lebanon," 2017, https://reliefweb.int/report/lebanon/vasyr-2017-vulnerability-assessment-syrian-refugees-lebanon

32. In some regions, faith-based NGOs are key elements of the humanitarian response. That Dayr al-Ahmar is a Christian area hosting Sunni refugees may explain this situation. See, for instance, Estella Carpi, "The Everyday Experience of Humanitarianism in the Akkar Villages," Civil Society Knowledge Centre, 24 March 2014; Dalya Mitri, "Challenges of Aid Coordination in a Complex Crisis: An Overview of Funding Policies and Conditions Regarding Aid Provision to Syrian Refugees in Lebanon," Civil Society Knowledge Centre, Lebanon Support, 23 May 2014.

33. Dounia el Khoury, WADA founder and president, interview, 7 April 2017; observation in WADA, 18 December 2017.

34. Vocational classes are held at one of the camps on the plain, but the few classes offered to children in Beshuat in 2017 were held under a tent and were stopped after a few months. From an interview with Claire Slaybeh, program officer, Dirâsât, 12 April 2017; and observations in Beshuat and Dayr al-Ahmar.

35. Interview with Katie Seaborne of Oxfam, Zahle, 2 December 2017.

36. For example, Syrian volunteers are present at school during the shift for Syrian children in an initiative supported by the International Rescue Committee; the Norwegian Refugee Council supports information campaigns and support for the registration of children born in Lebanon.

37. With pre-paid cards of $27 per person, per month, delivered to "registered" and "recorded" Syrians (the categorization is explained below).

38. Fakhoury, "Governance Strategies and Refugee Response," 690.

39. The Umam (the Arabic abbreviation for the UN, meaning "nations") is a wide semantic umbrella under which are collated all actors and activities relating to the humanitarian response, from registration of personal status to aid of all kinds.

40. Families buy thicker tarpaulin (called *chawader*) to add on to the UNHCR-provided white tarpaulins as soon as they can afford one (costing between $300 and $400) as it gives more protection from rain, cold, and heat. Favorite *chawader* among the Syrians are former outdoor advertising canvases that bring a colorful look to the camps.

41. Amin Gemayel was the Lebanese president from 1982 to 1988. During the civil war, his stance toward the Syrian authorities fluctuated and was characterized by pragmatism. However, after the Taef agreements of 1990, he went into exile for twelve years mainly due to his disagreement with Syrian policy.

42. Karam, interview with the author, Dayr al-Ahmar city, 12 March 2018.

43. *Haram*, literally "forbidden," is a colloquial expression, here meaning "poor thing."

44. Rana, interview with the author, Dayr al-Ahmar city, 12 March 2018.

45. According to many of the inhabitants of Izz al-Din we talked with in Dayr al-Ahmar in 2017 and 2018.

46. The harvest is hand-gathered leaf by leaf, and involves the subsequent preparation of the leaves.

47. Umm Muhammad, interview with the author, 11 April 2017. Abu Husayn (a land-lord of Btede'i), interview with the author, 6 March 2018.

48. On linkages between labor migrations and refuge, see Nicholas van Hear, "Theories of Migration and Social Change," *Journal of Ethnic and Migration Studies* 36, no. 10 (2010): 1531–6; Van Hear, "Reconsidering Migration and Class," *International Migration Review* 48, no. S1 (2014): S100–21. See also Anthony H. Richmond, *Global Apartheid: Refugees, Racism, and the New World Order* (New York: Oxford University Press, 1994), 343.

49. For Cathrine Brun and Anita Fabos, "making home (in protracted displacement) represents the process through which people try to gain control over their lives and involves negotiating specific understandings of home, particular regimes of control and assistance, and specific locations and material structures." Cathrine Brun and Anita Fabos, "Making Home in Limbo? A Conceptual Framework," *Refuge* 31, no. 1 (2015): 5.

50. Houda Kassatly, "'Enterrer son mort c'est l'honorer': Les réfugiés syriens au Liban à l'épreuve de la mort de leurs proches," ["To bury the dead is to honor him": Families of Syrian refugees in Lebanon put to the death test], *Hommes et migrations, "Réfugiés et migrants au Liban"* 1319 (2017): 105–13.

51. This information was derived from many of our interlocutors in Dayr al-Ahmar.

52. The *mukhtar* is an elected neighborhood- or village-level state representative. He is responsible for issuing residence documents and personal status chapters (granting birth and marriage certificates, preparing ID cards and passports, and authenticating photos).

53. Jean-Claude David and Houda Kassatly, "Les habitants syriens des camps du Liban, ou comment consolider le provisoire," [Syrian inhabitants of camps in Lebanon, or how to consolidate the provisional], *Hommes et migrations, "Réfugiés et migrants au Liban"* 1319 (2017): 77–84.

54. Zeïna, Beshuat, interview with the author, 7 March 2018.

55. The LCRP (2017–2020) aims at a better coordination of the humanitarian relief actions.

56. Shirine Arab, "Laws, Policies and Politics of Forced Displacement in Lebanon: National and Municipal Approaches: Complementarity or Autonomy?" *Conflits et migrations*, ANR, 2017, https://lajeh.hypotheses.org/914

57. That is, in the Dayr al-Ahmar area, the party of the Lebanese Forces.

58. There are seven major families: the Habshi, S'adeh, Quzeh, Fakhi, Kayruz, Khuri, and 'Akkuri.

59. This is not only the Dayr al-Ahmar *caza*, as many other villages and towns in Lebanon have likewise implemented curfews.

60. Latif Quzeh (president of the municipality of Dayr al-Ahmar), interview with the author, 13 December 2017.

61. *Ittihâd al-baladiyyât*: these local unions are established on a voluntary basis among municipalities, usually in order to foster concrete projects that require cooperation, such as irrigation or infrastructure projects.

62. Hamid Kayrouz, interview with the author, 12 April 2017.

63. Posted online on the Janoubia website on 26 July 2016, http://janoubia. com/2016/07/27/العادة-علي-السوري-بن-باسم-الأمن-والو

64. Mashuhr (who conducted a census of the families in the city), interview with the author, 13 December 2017.

65. Emad, Camp Caritas, 14 December 2017.

66. Ahmed, interview with the author, 13 April 2017.

67. Syrians and landlords in Dayr al-Ahmar, interviews with the author, 2017–18.

68. Samir Fakhi (deputy-president of the municipality of Btede'i), interviews on 17 December 2017 and 6 March 2018; see also Josep Zapater, "The Role of Municipalities in Ensuring Stability," *Forced Migration Review* 57 (2018): 12–15.

69. Hamid Kayrouz (president of the municipality of Beshuat), interview with the author, 12 April 2017; Jean Fakhi (president of the Union of the Municipalities of Dayr al-Ahmar), interview with the author, 15 December 2017; Samir Fakhi (deputy president of the municipality of Btede'i), interview with the author, 17 December 2017 and 6 March 2018.

70. Lebanese authorities use the same kind of rhetoric at annual conferences of donors, e.g., help us to help the Syrians or we will not be able to cope.

71. Zahle (UNHCR program officer), interview with the author, 9 March 2018.
72. See Maja Janmyr and Lama Mourad, "Categorising Syrians in Lebanon as 'Vulnerable,'" *Forced Migration Review* 57 (2018): 19–21.
73. "Nâzihûn am lâji'ûn?" [Displaced or refugees?], *Al-Safîr*, 5 February 2013.
74. Ibid.
75. Ibid.
76. Chalcraft, *Invisible Cage.*
77. In February 2013, a resolution by the minister of labor made some professions (previously officially confined to Lebanese) available to Syrian workers, such as electricity and sales ("Syrian Workers in Lebanon: An Assessment of their Rights and Reality," Lebanese Center for Human Rights, 18 December 2013, www.rightsobserver.org/files/Report_Syrian_Workers__ENG_final_(2).pdf). However, on 9 February 2017, a decree (41/1) published in the official journal, no. 7, again limited the activities of the Syrian workers to the agricultural, construction, and waste sectors only. Other sectors are strictly forbidden. See Thierry Boissière and Annie Tohmé Tabet, "Économie de l'éxil, économie de la survie: pratiques et stratégies des réfugiés syriens à Nabaa, un quartier populaire de la banlieue est de Beyrouth," *Critique internationale* (2018).
78. "Intifâda 'ummâliyya fî Dayr al-Ahmar" [Workers riot in Dayr al-Ahmar], *Al-Mudun*, 29 July 2016; "Tahtîm timthâl mâr Charbel fî Dayr al-Ahmar … al-ahâlî yuhaddidûn bi-qata' al-turuq" [Destruction of a St Charbel statue in Dayr al-Ahmar, the locals have threatened to block the roads], *Annahar*, 2 February 2017.
79. Malkki (*Purity and Exile*) has shown how mobile people "out of place" are constructed as dangerous.
80. Hamid (a farmer in Beshuat) and his sister Rima, interview with the author, 8 April 2017.
81. "Tahtîm timthâl mâr Charbel fî Dayr al-Ahmar," *Annahar.*
82. Ibid.
83. Dima and Bassel (a young Syrian couple), interview with the author, 14 December 2017.
84. Mona, interview with the author, 8 March 2018.
85. Karam, Mashuhr and Imad, interview with the author, 13 December 2017.
86. Aubin-Boltanski, "La Vierge, les chrétiens, les musulmans."
87. On the *shawish* and their controversial role in the Syrian camps, see the report of the UNDP: "The Burden of Scarce Opportunities: The Social Stability Context in Central and West Bekaa Conflict," Analysis Report, March 2017; and Malek Abu Kheir, "The Syrian Camps Shawish: A Man of Power and the One Controlling the Conditions of Refugees," *Peace Building in Lebanon* 12 (2016): 9.
88. Inhabitants of Ahmed's camp, interviews with the author, 6 March 2018.
89. Inhabitants of Caritas Camp, interviews with the author, 14 December 2017.

90. Jamila Khoury (director of Dayr al-Ahmar primary and secondary school), interview with the author, 13 December 2017.
91. Five teachers from Dayr al-Ahmar primary and secondary school, interviews with the author, 13 December 2017.

5. DIASPORIC CIRCULARITIES: OMANI-ZANZIBARIS NARRATE EXPERIENCES IN AND OUT OF THE ARCHIPELAGO, 1964

1. Richard Francis Burton, *Zanzibar: City, Island, and Coast* (London: Tinsley Brothers, 1872), 2:1–2.
2. Personal communication, Muscat, Sultanate of Oman, 3 July 2007.
3. *Waliroudi*, episode 21. *Waliroudi* is a Swahili television program that aired on Omani National Television during the lunar month of Ramadan, between June and July 2017, and focused its thirty episodes on the returnees in Muscat. *Waliroudi* is a Swahili word that translates to "returnees."
4. These conversations were held as part of Zones of Peace, Zones of Conflict, a Georgetown University-Qatar program on conflict management and resolution that provides students with real-life applications across the globe. Following a class on the Zanzibar Revolution, I was accompanied by sixteen students to Oman and Zanzibar in 2016. This trip was a rare opportunity that exposed students to the different perspectives on the revolution and the logic behind the labels "revolution" and "genocide" as seen from the point of view of the stakeholders in these locations.
5. Francis Barrow Pearce, *Zanzibar: The Island Metropolis of Eastern Africa* (New York: E. P. Dutton, 1920).
6. Mark Horton and John Middleton, *The Swahili: The Social Landscape of a Mercantile Society* (Malden, MA: Blackwell, 2000). Wamanga is a term Zanzibaris originally used to describe Omani Arab sailors. It has since come to identify all low-status Arab immigrants two almost fully integrated into the economy, setting up as small-scale shopkeepers and copra producers. The Wamanga community allied closely to Arab elites and aristocracy.
7. Sandy Prita Meier, *Swahili Port Cities: The Architecture of Elsewhere* (Bloomington, IN: Indiana University Press, 2016), 139.
8. Ibid., 139–78.
9. Ibid., 139.
10. Nafla S. Kharusi, "The Ethnic Label Zinjibari: Politics and Language Choice Implications among Swahili Speakers in Oman," *Ethnicities* 12, no. 3 (2012): 335–53.
11. Ali Muhsin Al-Barwani, *Conflicts and Harmony in Zanzibar: Memoirs* (Dubai: n.p., 1997).
12. See Saleh Al-Bahry, Facebook post, 20 February 2018, www.facebook.com/groups/Zanzibar

13. Anonymous, Muscat, 2017.

14. William Harold Ingrams, *Zanzibar: Its History and Its People* (London: Frank Cass, 1967), 19–20.

15. Ibid., 28.

16. Omanis critiqued this category as a Western invention by British historians. *Hadimu* means *khadim* or slave in Arabic, and with the Bantu prefix *Wa-*, Zanzibaris such as Juma Aley felt that the term was rooted in the British imperialist policy of divide and rule.

17. Abdulaziz Y. Lodhi, "The Arabs in Zanzibar: From Sultanate to Peoples' Republic," *Institute of Muslim Minority Affairs Journal* 7, no. 2 (1986): 404–18.

18. Ibid., 405.

19. Alastair Hazell, *The Last Slave Market: Dr John Kirk and the Struggle to End the East African Slave Trade* (London: Constable, 2011).

20. Abdul Sheriff, *Dhow Culture of the Indian Ocean: Cosmopolitanism, Commerce and Islam* (New York: Columbia University Press, 2010), 2.

21. Ingrams, *Zanzibar*, 220. Zanzibar and Pemba were British protectorates as per the 1890 Heligoland–Zanzibar Treaty between Germany and the British Empire. From 1913 until Zanzibar's "independence" in 1963, the British Empire appointed its own residents, primarily governors and commissioners in Zanzibar. For more information, see James Stuart Olson and Robert Shadle, eds, *Historical Dictionary of European Imperialism* (New York, NY: Greenwood Press, 1991), 279–80.

22. Lyndon Harries, "The Arabs and Swahili Culture," *Africa: Journal of the International Africa Institute* 34, No. 3 (July 1964), 224–29.

23. *Waliroudi*, episode 3.

24. John Duke Anthony, John Peterson, and Donald Sean Abelson, *Historical and Cultural Dictionary of the Sultanate of Oman and the Emirates of Eastern Arabia*, Historical and Cultural Dictionaries of Asia, no. 9 (Metuchen, NJ: Scarecrow Press, 1976), 126.

25. Ibid.

26. Ibadism is a school of Islam that predates Sunnism and Shiism, dominant in Oman.

27. Personal communication, Muscat, 3 July 2017. The historical fact of Sultan Barghash's mixed race was also discussed in Meier, *Swahili Port Cities*, 104.

28. *Waliroudi*, episode 7.

29. Personal communication, Muscat, 2017.

30. Harries, "Arabs and Swahili Culture," 224–9.

31. Personal communication, Muscat, 3 July 2017. The Afro-Shirazi Party (ASP) was formed in 1957 as a merger between the Afro Party and the Shiraz in Zanzibar. ASP played a significant role in the Zanzibar Revolution in 1964. In 1977, ASP merged with the Tanganyika African National Union (TANU) to form Chama Cha Mapinduzi, the dominant ruling party in Tanzania and the second longest-ruling party in Africa after the National Party of South Africa.

32. Ali Muhsin Al-Barwani was a Zanzibari politician and diplomat under the Sultanate of Zanzibar, and was the only Arab foreign minister of an independent Zanzibar before the establishment of the People's Republic of Zanzibar in 1964.

33. Al-Barwani, *Conflicts and Harmony in Zanzibar*, 129.

34. Ibid., 29.

35. Ibid., 179.

36. John Okello, *Revolution in Zanzibar* (Nairobi: East African Publishing House, 1967).

37. Michael F. Lofchie, *Zanzibar: Background to Revolution* (Princeton, NJ: Princeton University Press, 2015), 48.

38. Bill Ashcroft, Gareth Griffiths, and Helen Tiffin, *Key Concepts in Post-colonial Studies* (London: Routledge, 1998), 118.

39. James Clifford, "Diasporas," *Cultural Anthropology* 9, no. 3 (1994): 302–38.

40. Madawi Al-Rasheed and J. Piscatori, "Transnational Connections and National Identity: Zanzibari Omanis in Muscat," in *Connections and Identities: Understandings of the Arab Gulf*, ed. P. Dresch (London: I. B. Tauris, 2005), 96–113.

41. Garth A. Myers, "Narrative Representations of Revolutionary Zanzibar," *Journal of Historical Geography* 26, no. 3 (2000): 429–48.

42. Ibid., 443.

43. Okello, *Revolution in Zanzibar*, 103.

44. Ibid., 28.

45. Ibid., 33.

46. Patrick Barkham, "Why the Sultan of Zanzibar Took Me under His Wing," *Guardian*, 2 March 2012, www.theguardian.com/lifeandstyle/2012/mar/03/leila-sharp-sultan-of-zanzibar

47. Okello, *Revolution in Zanzibar*, 171.

48. See Norman R. Bennett, *A History of the Arab State of Zanzibar* (London: Methuen, 1978).

49. Al-Barwani in conversation with the Zones of Peace, Zones of Conflict student group, Muscat, 2016.

50. Nasser bin Abdulla Al-Riyami, *Zanzibar Personalities and Events (1828–1972)* (Oman: Beirut Bookshop, 2012), 197.

51. Ibid.

52. Ibid., 146.

53. Abeid Amani Karume was the first president of Zanzibar after the 1964 revolution. After the United Republic of Tanzania was founded, Karume became the first vice president of the United Republic with Julius Nyerere of Tanganyika as president of the new country.

54. Al-Barwani in conversation with the Zones of Peace, Zones of Conflict student group, Muscat, 2016.

55. Al-Barwani in conversation with the Zones of Peace, Zones of Conflict student group, Muscat, 2016.

56. Lofchie, *Zanzibar*, 39.
57. Ibid., 437.
58. Ibid., 157–82.
59. From the Foreign Office to Muscat, no. 26, 17 February 1964, telegram addressed to Aden Acting High Commissioner.
60. Sent by D. J. McCarthy to K. Hickman of Commonwealth Relations, 18 February 1964. Ref. Arab deportation from Zanzibar.
61. Raphael Lemkin, "Genocide as a Crime under International Law," *American Journal of International Law* 41, no. 1 (1947): 145–51.
62. Personal communication, Zanzibar, 2017.
63. Zinjibaris is the ethnic label used in Oman to describe Omanis of Arab descent with historical connections to Zanzibar. This term is discussed in further detail later in the chapter.
64. Al-Riyami, *Zanzibar Personalities*.
65. *Waliroudi*, episode 5.
66. Personal communication, Zanzibar, August 2017.
67. The English, Arabic, and Swahili newspapers that covered the political affairs in the post-1964 period include *Afrika Kwetu, Dawn in Zanzibar, Al-Falaq, Free Zanzibar Voice, Mwanqaza, Al-Nahda, Zanews, Zanzibar Gazzette, El-Najrah*, and the *Tanganiyka Standard*. See Bennett, *History of the Arab State of Zanzibar*.
68. Al-Riyami, *Zanzibar*, 198.
69. Personal communication, Muscat, 2017.
70. Personal communication, Muscat, 3 July 2017.
71. Al-Barwani, *Conflicts and Harmony in Zanzibar*, 134.
72. Al-Riyami, *Zanzibar*, 197–204.
73. Ibid., 199.
74. Ibid.
75. Personal interview, Zanzibar, 2017.
76. Mr M., personal communication, Muscat, 3 July 2017.
77. Annie Bunting, Benjamin N. Lawrence, and Richard L. Roberts, *Marriage by Force? Contestation over Consent and Coercion in Africa* (Athens, OH: Ohio University Press, 2016).
78. Ibid., 37.
79. Personal communication, Zanzibar, August 2017.
80. In Arabic, *Wahadimu* refers to slaves.
81. Al-Riyami, *Zanzibar*, 148.
82. Archival documents, 2 February 1964, no. 19. See A. Burdett, ed., *Records of Oman, 1961–1965*, Archive Editions (Cambridge: Cambridge University Press, 1997).
83. Personal communication, Muscat, 7 July 2017.
84. Pierre Bourdieu, *Outline of a Theory of Practice* (Cambridge: Cambridge University Press, 1977), 16:159–70.

85. Personal communication.
86. See John Duke Anthony's dictionary entry on Ibri: "The most important town of Al Dhahirah province in Oman, Ibri lies approximately halfway between al Buraymi and Nizwa. As a former center for trade in slaves and other commodities, Ibri rivaled and was perhaps more important than al Buraymi. The town's inhabitants are largely from the Ya'aqib and Duru' tribes. It was under the loose control of Imam Hammad bin 'Abd Allah Al-Khalili until ca.1953 when the Imam's *wali* (governor) was driven out. Its recapture by forces of Imam Ghalib bin 'Ali al Hina'i in 1954 was directly responsible for its subsequent occupation by forces of the Sultanate of Oman, who acted in concert with the tribes of the area. Ibri has been part of the Sultanate since that time. I also encountered several references to Ibra and not Ibri. The geographical description of both Ibri and Ibra is the same however."
87. Mr M., personal communication, Muscat, 5 July 2017.
88. J. E. Peterson, "Oman's Diverse Society: Northern Oman," *Middle East Journal* 58, no. 1 (2004): 46.
89. *Waliroudi*, episode 7.
90. Ibid., episode 21.
91. Ibid., episode 1.
92. Ibid.
93. Ibid.
94. Ibid.
95. Saud Bin Ahmed Al-Busaidi, *Memoirs of an Omani Gentleman from Zanzibar* (Oman: Al Roya Press, 2012).
96. *Waliroudi*, episode 1.
97. Ibid., episode 21.
98. Ibid., episode 1.
99. Ibid., episode 5.
100. Personal communication, Zanzibar, August 2017.
101. Kharusi, "Ethnic Label Zinjibari," 338.
102. Ibid., 335–9.
103. Ibid., 335–53.
104. Rogaia Mustafa Abusharaf and Dale Eickelman, eds, *Africa and the Gulf Region: Blurred Boundaries and Shifting Ties* (Berlin: Gerlach Press, 2015), 1.
105. G. Thomas Burgess, Ali Sultan Issa, and Seif Sharif Hamad, *Race, Revolution, and the Struggle for Human Rights in Zanzibar: The Memoirs of Ali Sultan Issa and Seif Sharif Hamad*, no. 119 (Athens, OH: Ohio University Press, 2009), 2.

6. AFGHAN MIGRANTS IN TEHRAN: TOWARD FORMAL INTEGRATION

1. The following individuals provided extensive assistance for the study's fieldwork: Masoumeh Bahrami, Narges Mehrabian, Ameneh Mirzaei, and Tala Rostami.

2. Statistical Center of Iran, "Gozideh-ye natayej-e sarshomari-ye nofus va maskan" [Selected results of census of population and housing], 2011, www.amar.org.ir/Portals/0/sarshomari90/n_sarshomari90_2.pdf

3. "UNHCR Regional Plan: Building Resilience and Solutions for Afghan Refugees in Southwest Asia," United Nations High Commissioner for Refugees (UNHCR), 2016, http://unhcr.org.ir/uploads/news/Afghan%20Resilience%20and%20Solutions%20_FINAL_eng_1.PDF

4. Many citizens of Afghanistan prefer to be called Afghanistani, rather than Afghan; Afghan more correctly refers to the Pashtun population of the country. However, in keeping with the international nomenclature, the term Afghan is used in this chapter.

5. *UNHCR Statistical Yearbook 2014*, UNHCR, 2014, 58, www.unhcr.org/56655f4d8.html; Center for Statistics and Strategic Information, Ministry of Cooperatives, Labor, and Social Welfare (MCLSW), "Vaz'iyat-e mohajerat-e niru-ye kar dar keshvarha-ye jahan" [State of migration among the countries of the world], 2016; see also Bruce Koepke, "The Situation of Afghans in the Islamic Republic of Iran Nine Years after the Overthrow of the Taliban Regime in Afghanistan," Middle East Institute, 2011, www.refugeecooperation.org/publications/Afghanistan/03_koepke.php. Whereas some of Iran's Afghans suddenly found an easier route to migrate to the West and especially Germany in the most recent period, current developments concerning refugee regulations in Europe as well as continued turmoil in Afghanistan mean that their numbers will likely be sustained in Iran.

6. "UNHCR Regional Plan: Building Resilience and Solutions for Afghan Refugees in Southwest Asia," UNHCR.

7. *Amayesh* refers to the surveys for registration of Afghans, conducted by the Iranian government in several rounds. The Iranian government is carrying out a program to register all undocumented Afghanistanis in the country (see "UNHCR Regional Plan").

8. Arne Strand, Astri Suhrke, and Kristian Berg Harpviken, "Afghan Refugees in Iran: From Refugee Emergency to Migration Management," *CMI Policy Brief*, Bergen: CMI/PRIO, 16 June 2004, www.prio.org/Publications/Publication/?x=501; Diane Tober, "'My Body Is Broken Like My Country': Identity, Nation, and Repatriation among Afghan Refugees in Iran," *Iranian Studies* 40, no. 2 (April 2007): 263–85; Maliha Safra, "The Transformation of the Afghan Refugee: 1979–2009," *Middle East Journal* 65, no. 4 (2011): 587–601.

9. Alessandro Monsutti, "Afghan Migratory Strategies and the Three Solutions to the Refugee Problem," *Refugee Survey Quarterly* 27, no. 1 (2008): 58–73; Monsutti, "Migration as a Rite of Passage: Young Afghans Building Masculinity and Adulthood in Iran," *Iranian Studies* 40, no. 2 (2007): 167–85.

10. See UNHCR, "UNHCR Regional Plan"; and Koepke, "Situation of Afghans in

the Islamic Republic of Iran." Domestic advocacy for universal education as well as active participation of some Afghan fighters in the front against ISIS in Syria and Iraq is speculated to have influenced this initiative.

11. "28000 taba'eh-ye khareji dar Iran bimeh-ye ta'min-e ejtemai shodeh-and" [28,000 foreign citizens have been insured], ISNA, 24 February 2016, www.isna.ir/news/95120402772

12. Graeme Hugo et al., "Refugee Movement and Development: Afghan Refugees in Iran," *Migration and Development* 1, no. 2 (2012): 261–79.

13. M. J. Abbasi-Shavazi, and R. Sadeghi, "Socio-cultural Adaptation of Second-Generation Afghans in Iran," *International Migration* 53, no. 6 (2015): 89–110; M. J. Abbasi-Shavazi, Hossein Mahmoudian, and Rasoul Sadeghi, "Family Dynamics in the Context of Forced Migration," in *Demography of Refugee and Forced Migration*, ed. Graeme Hugo et al. (New York, NY: Springer International, 2018), 155–74.

14. Nahid Songhori et al., "Facilitators and Barriers of Afghan Refugee Adolescents' Integration in Iran: A Grounded Theory Study," *Global Social Welfare* 4, no. 4 (2017): 1–10.

15. "Vaz'iyat-e mohajerat-e niru-ye kar dar keshvarha-ye jahan," Center for Statistics and Strategic Information, MCLSW, 14; "Bakhshnameh-ye dowlat: eshteghal-e atba'-e biganeh mamnu' ast" [Government directive: employing foreign citizens is forbidden], Khabaronline, 2 June 2014, www.khabaronline.ir/detail/366263/Economy/5098

16. Tober, "'My Body Is Broken Like My Country.'"

17. Hamid Sepehrdoust, "The Impact of Migrant Labor Force on Housing Construction of Iran," *Journal of Housing and the Built Environment* 28, no. 1 (2013): 67–78.

18. *UNHCR Statistical Yearbook 2014*, UNHCR, 58.

19. "Mosavvabeh-ye vozara-ye ozv-e shoura-ye hamahangi-ye atba'-e biganeh raje' be elhaq-e manateq-e jaded" [Regulation on addition of new regions approved by member ministers of the coordination council of foreign citizens], Majles Research Center, 2002, http://rc.majlis.ir/fa/law/show/121961

20. "Shahrha-ye mamnu' baraye eqameat va tehsil-e afghanha" [No-go cities for Afghan residence and education], Baharnews, 3 June 2012, http://baharnews.ir/news/2756; Farshid Farzin and Safinaz Jadali, "Freedom of Movement of Afghan Refugees in Iran," *Forced Migration Review* 44 (2013): 85–6.

21. Statistical Center of Iran, "Gozideh-ye natayej-e sarshomari-ye nofus va maskan."

22. "Migrants Constitute 88% of Tehran Population Growth," *Financial Tribune*, 27 May 2017, https://financialtribune.com/articles/economy-business-and-markets/65255/migrants-constitute-88-of-tehran-population-growth

23. J. W. Berry, "Acculturation and Adaptation in a New Society," *International Migration* 30, no. 1 (1992): 69–85; Berry et al., "Acculturation Attitudes in Plural

Societies," *Applied Psychology* 38, no. 2 (1989): 185–206; J. W. Berry and D. L. Sam, "Acculturation and Adaptation," in *Handbook of Cross-cultural Psychology*, Volume 3: *Social Behaviour and Applications*, ed. J. W. Berry, M. H. Segall, and C. Kagitcibasi, 2nd ed. (Boston: Allyn & Bacon, 1997).

24. A. Ager and A. Strang, "Understanding Integration: A Conceptual Framework," *Journal of Refugee Studies* 21, no. 2 (2008): 166–91.

25. "International Migration Stock: The 2015 Revision," Department of Economic and Social Affairs, United Nations, 2016, www.un.org/en/development/desa/population/migration/data/estimates2/estimates15.shtml; "Global Trends: Forced Displacement in 2015," UNHCR, 2015, https://s3.amazonaws.com/unhcrsharedmedia/2016/2016-06-20-global-trends/2016-06-14-Global-Trends-2015.pdf

26. Tober, "'My Body Is Broken Like My Country.'"

27. "New York Declaration for Refugees and Migrants," UNHCR, 2016, https://www.unhcr.org/new-york-declaration-for-refugees-and-migrants.html

28. Patricia Ward, "Refugee Cities: Reflections on the Development and Impact of UNHCR Urban Refugee Policy in the Middle East," *Refugee Survey Quarterly* 33, no. 1 (2014): 77–93.

29. Katarzyna Grabska, "Marginalization in Urban Spaces of the Global South: Urban Refugees in Cairo," *Journal of Refugee Studies* 19, no. 3 (2006): 287–307.

30. "The New Urban Agenda," UN-Habitat, 2016, https://habitat3.org/the-new-urban-agenda

31. "Cities Welcoming Refugees and Migrants: Enhancing Effective Urban Governance in an Age of Migration," United Nations Educational, Scientific, and Cultural Organization (UNESCO), 2016, https://unesdoc.unesco.org/ark:/48223/pf0000246558

32. "Global Migration: Resilient Cities at the Forefront," 100 Resilient Cities, 2016, http://action.100resilientcities.org/page/-/100rc/pdfs/Global%20Migration_Resilient%20Cities%20At%20The%20Forefront_DIGITAL%20%28High%20Res%29.pdf

33. Including: municipal council representatives, neighborhood renovation agencies, neighborhood council assistants, municipal authorities, and personnel of other urban service providers.

34. Statistical Center of Iran, "Gozideh-ye natayej-e sarshomari-ye nofus va maskan."

35. District 2 Municipality, "Tarh-e shenasnameh-ye mahallat-e shahrdari-ye mantaqeh-ye 2-ye Tehran" [Characteristics document of District 2], 2010.

36. Statistical Center of Iran, "Gozideh-ye natayej-e sarshomari-ye nofus va maskan."

37. Farnahad Consulting Engineers, "Sima-ye ejtemai-ye mahalleh-y Farahzad."

38. Saravand Consulting Engineers, "Olgu-ye towse'eh-ye mantaqeh-ye do" [District 2 development model], 2005, 12.

39. Ibid., 17.

40. Statistical Center of Iran, "Gozideh-ye natayej-e sarshomari-ye nofus va maskan."
41. Ibid.
42. Tehran Municipality Research Center, "Shenasai-ye khanevarha-ye mahalleh-ye Harandi be surat-e pelak be pelak" [Door-to-door identification of households in Harandi neighborhood], 2015.
43. Five sub-districts inside Tehran's official municipal boundaries make up 23 square kilometers, and two outside the boundaries comprise 7 square kilometers.
44. Tehran Municipality, "Nimrokh-e mahallehha-ye shahr-e Terhan: mantaqeh-ye bist" [Profiles of neighborhoods of the city of Tehran: District 20], 2008.
45. Statistical Center of Iran, "Gozideh-ye natayej-e sarshomari-ye nofus va maskan."
46. Ibid.
47. Tehran has elected council assistants (showrayari) at the district level in addition to municipal council members at the city level.
48. Pricing ranges between 350 and 500 million rials, or in the order of $10,000–12,000.
49. Pricing on average is 200 million rials up front, to be returned after vacating, plus 30 million rials monthly for an 80 square meter space.
50. At the time of fieldwork for this study, the exchange rate was: 1 US dollar = 30,000 rials.
51. This arrangement—called rahn-e kamel in Persian—is perhaps unique to Iran. The landlord makes money by depositing the tenant's up-front payment in a high-interest-rate banking account, returning the whole amount when the tenant moves out.
52. "Matn-e kamel-e tarh-e jaded-e baharestan baraye e'ta-ye tabe'iyat-e be atba'-e khareji" [Complete text of the parliamentary plan to give citizenship to foreigners], Mehrnews, 25 September 2015, www.mehrnews.com/news/2922820
53. Including a butcher shop, fruit shop, and various shops for motorcycle repair, carpets, secondhand home appliances, and garments; stores for carpentry, shoes and bags, and cosmetics; and a real estate agent, as well as a number of restaurants and eateries.
54. "Tehran Fire: Dozens of Firefighters Feared Dead as Tower Collapses," Guardian, 19 January 2017, www.theguardian.com/world/2017/jan/19/tehran-fire-firefighters-killed-tower-collapses-iran
55. Imam Ali Society, "Vaz'iyat-e kudakan-e kar dar dar sokunatgahha-ye faqirneshin-e-Tehran" [Situation of child labor in Tehran's poor settlements], 2015.
56. Naqsh-e Sarzamin Consultants, "Sanad-e chashmandaz-e towse'eh-ye paydar-e mantaqeh-ye Harandi" [Sustainable development vision document of Harandi neighborhood], 2013.
57. Majles Research Center, "Eslahiyeh-ye mosavvabeh-ye akhz-e avarez az mohajeran-e khareji-ye moqim-e shahr-e Tehran" [Correction of regulation on fees to be obtained from foreign migrants residing the the city of Tehran], 2015.
58. "Shohada-ye khareji tabe'iyat-e irani daryaft mikonand" [Foreign martyrs receive Iranian citizenship], ICANA, 17 July 2016, www.icana.ir/Fa/News/303788

7. LIVING WITH UNCERTAINTY: THE STORY OF SUB-SAHARAN MIGRANTS IN LIBYA AND TUNISIA

1. Robert O. Collins and James M. Burns, *A History of Sub-Saharan Africa*, 2nd ed. (Cambridge: Cambridge University Press, 2014), 234.

2. Mustafa O. Attir, "Illegal Migration as a Major Threat to Libya's Security," in *Migration in the Mediterranean: Human Rights, Security and Development Perspectives*, ed. Omar Grech and Monika Wohlfeld (Msida: University of Malta, 2014).

3. "Libya Population," Worldometers, 2018, www.worldometers.info/world-population/libya-population

4. Attir, "Illegal Migration as a Major Threat to Libya's Security," 98.

5. Aderanti Adepoju, Femke van Noorloos, and Annelies Zoomers, "Europe's Migration Agreements with Migrant-Sending Countries in the Global South: A Critical Review," *International Migration* 38, no. 3 (2010): 42–75.

6. Mustafa O. Attir, "Euro-Mediterranean Migrations: From Current Stalemate to Shared Development Perspectives," in *Pursuing Stability and a Shared Development in Euro-Mediterranean Migration*, ed. Emanuela O. Del Re and Ricardo René Larémont (Rome: Aracne, 2017), 234; "Italy to Pay Libya $5 Billion," *New York Times*, 31 August 2008, www.nytimes.com/2008/08/31/world/europe/31iht-italy.4.15774385.html; "Gaddafi Wants EU Cash to Stop African Migrants," BBC, 31 August 2010, www.bbc.com/news/world-europe-11139345; Salah Sarar, "Gaddafi and Berlusconi Sign Accord Worth Billions," Reuters, 30 August 2008, https://uk.reuters.com/article/uk-libya-italy/gaddafi-and-berlusconi-sign-accord-worth-billions-idUKLU1618820080830

7. "Stemming the Flow: Abuses against Migrants, Asylum Seekers and Refugees," Human Rights Watch, 2006, www.hrw.org/reports/2006/libya0906; Hassan Boubakri, "Transit Migration between Tunisia, Libya and Sub-Saharan Africa: Study Based on Greater Tunis," report presented at the Regional Conference on Migrants in Transit Countries: Sharing Responsibility for Management and Protection, Istanbul, 30 September–1 October 2004.

8. Most members of the Libyan sample speak Arabic; however, in the case of those who did not understand Arabic, copies of English and French questionnaires were used.

9. Laura van Waas, "A Comparative Analysis of Nationality Laws in the MENA Region," Tilburg University Law School, September 2014, http://citizenshiprightsafrica.org/wp-content/uploads/2016/04/Tilburg_MENA-Study-2014.pdf

10. Judith Scheele, "The Libyan Connection: Settlement, War, and Other Entanglements in Northern Chad," *Journal of African History* 50, no. 1 (2016): 115–34.

11. Francesco Semprini and Jacob Svendsen, "Libyan Path to Europe Turns into Dead End for Desperate Migrants," *Guardian*, 30 October 2017, www.theguardian.

com/world/2017/oct/30/libyan-migrants-detention-centres-europe-unhcr; Sally Hayden, "New Mafia-Led Militia May be Stopping Refugees from Leaving Libya for Italy," *Independent*, 22 August 2017, www.independent.co.uk/news/world/africa/mafia-refugees-libya-italy-stop-leave-militia-mediterranean-crossing-sabratha-migrant-boats-a7906666.html

12. Martin Richards et al., "Extensive Female-Mediated Gene Flow from Sub-Saharan Africa into Near Eastern Arab Populations," *American Journal of Human Genetics* 72, no. 4 (2003): 1058–64; Paul Lovejoy, *Slavery on the Frontiers of Islam* (Princeton, NJ: Markus Wiener Publishers, 2004); Paul Lovejoy, *Transformations in Slavery: A History of Slavery in Africa*, 3rd ed. (Cambridge: Cambridge University Press, 2011); Bernard Lewis, *Race and Slavery in the Middle East: An Historical Inquiry* (Oxford: Oxford University Press, 1992).

13. United Nations Support Mission in Libya and Office of United Nations High Commissioner for Human Rights, "'Detained and Dehumanized': Report on Human Rights Abuses against Migrants in Libya," UNHCR, 13 December 2016, www.ohchr.org/Documents/Countries/LY/DetainedAndDehumanised_en.pdf

14. "Libya Slave Trade," CNN, 15 November 2017, www.cnn.com/specials/africa/libya-slave-auctions

15. "Libyan Human Rights Body Upset over CNN Report of Slave Auctions in Libya," Libya Observer, 18 November 2017, www.libyaobserver.ly/news/libyan-human-rights-body-upset-over-cnn-report-slave-auctions-libya

16. Ian Drury, "Over One Million Migrants Are 'in the Pipeline' in Libya," *Daily Mail*, 30 March 2017, www.dailymail.co.uk/news/article-4365870/Over-ONE-MILLION-migrants-pipeline-Libya.html

17. Gabriela Baczynska, "Pressure on EU's Southern Borders from African Migrants Seen Persisting in 2018," Reuters, 20 February 2018, www.reuters.com/article/us-europe-migrants-eu-frontex/pressure-on-eus-southern-borders-from-african-migrants-seen-persisting-in-2018-idUSKCN1G42AK

8. INTEGRATING AFRICAN MIGRANTS? GAUGING CITIZEN OPPOSITION TO MIGRANT RESETTLEMENT IN MOROCCO'S CASABLANCA REGION

1. Michael Collyer, "Undocumented Sub-Saharan Africans in Morocco," in *Mediterranean Transit Migration*, ed. Ninna Nyberg Sørensen (Copenhagen: Danish Institute for International Studies, 2006), 136–40.

2. Belachew Gebrewold, *Africa and Fortress Europe: Threats and Opportunities* (Burlington, VT: Ashgate, 2007), 127–71.

3. Some examples include: Hein de Haas, "International Migration and Regional Development in Morocco: A Review," *Journal of Ethnic and Migration Studies* 35, no. 10 (2009): 1571–93; Caroline Zickgraf, "Transnational Ageing and the 'Zero

Generation': The Role of Moroccan Migrants' Parents in Care Circulation," *Journal of Ethnic and Migration Studies* 43, no. 2 (2017): 321–37.

4. Hein de Haas, "Irregular Migration from West Africa to the Maghreb and the European Union: An Overview of Recent Trends," *International Organization for Migration* 32 (2008): 4.

5. "Migration Profile: Morocco," Migration Policy Center, European University Institute-Migration Policy Center (2015): 9.

6. Paul Puschmann, *Casablanca: A Demographic Miracle on Moroccan Soil?* (Leuven: Acco Academic Press, 2011), 22–3.

7. Mohammed Benaziz, "The Question of Race in Morocco," Al-Monitor, 17 January 2014, www.al-monitor.com/pulse/culture/2014/01/racism-black-slavery-morocco.html

8. Ibid.

9. Hisham Aidi, "Morocco: Neither Slave, Nor Negro," Al-Jazeera, 10 April 2016, www.aljazeera.com/indepth/opinion/2016/03/morocco-slave-negro-160330082904386.html. The original slogan was: "Ni Oussif, Ni Azzi, Baraka et Yezzi," combining both French and Arabic dialectical terms. Also, see information on Morocco's "Je ne m'appelle pas Azzi/Masmiytich Azzi" [My name is not Negro] anti-racism campaign: www.libe.ma/Je-ne-m-appelle-pas-Azzi_a48122.html

10. Peter Burns and James G. Gimpel, "Economic Insecurity, Prejudicial Stereotypes, and Public Opinion on Immigration Policy," *Political Studies Quarterly* 115, no. 2 (2000): 201–25; Christian Dustmann and Ian P. Preston, "Racial and Economic Factors in Attitudes to Immigration," *The B.E. Journal of Economic Analysis and Policy* 7, no. 1 (2007): 1–39; Jens Hainmueller and Michael J. Hiscox, "Attitudes toward Highly Skilled and Low-Skilled Immigration: Evidence from a Survey Experiment," *American Political Science Review* 104, no. 1 (2010): 61–84.

11. Jens Hainmueller and Michael J. Hiscox, "Educated Preferences: Explaining Attitudes toward Immigration in Europe," *International Organization* 61, no. 2 (2007): 399–442; Hainmueller and Hiscox, "Attitudes," 61–84.

12. E. Savage, "Berbers and Blacks: Ibadi Slave Traffic in Eighth-Century North Africa," *Journal of African History* 33, no. 2 (1992): 358.

13. Ibid., 351–3.

14. Ibid., 354.

15. Allan R. Meyers, "Class, Ethnicity, and Slavery: The Origins of the Moroccan 'Abid," *International Journal of African Historical Studies* 10, no. 3 (1977): 428.

16. Meyers, "Class, Ethnicity, and Slavery," 430.

17. Eric Ross, "Black Morocco: A History of Slavery, Race, and Islam," *Canadian Journal of African Studies* 49, no. 3 (2015): 551.

18. Benaziz, "Question of Race."

19. Thibaut Dary, "Tirailleurs Africains: l'Empire contre-attaque à Verdun," *Le Figaro*, 5 February 2016, www.lefigaro.fr/histoire/2016/02/25/26001-20160225ART-FIG00204-tirailleurs-africains-l-empire-contre-attaque-a-verdun.php

20. Melani Cammett, "Fat Cats and Self-made Men: Globalization and the Paradoxes of Collective Action," *Comparative Politics* 37, no. 4 (2005): 392.
21. Gabrielle Lynch and Gordon Crawford, "Democratization in Africa 1990–2010: An Assessment," *Democratization* 18, no. 2 (2011): 275–310.
22. Papa Sow, Elina Marmer, and Jürgen Scheffran, "Between the Heat and the Hardships: Climate Change and Mixed Migration Flows in Morocco," *Migration and Development* 5, no. 2 (2016): 294–5.
23. Joris Schapendonk, "Turbulent Trajectories: African Migrants on their Way to the European Union," *Societies* 2, no. 2 (2012): 27.
24. Luisa Martín Rojo and Teun A. van Dijk, "'There Was a Problem, and It Was Solved!' Legitimating the Expulsion of 'Illegal' Migrants in Spanish Parliamentary Discourse," *Discourse and Society* 8, no. 4 (1997): 527.
25. Ibid., 532.
26. Ibid.
27. Schapendonk, "Turbulent Trajectories," 27–41.
28. Emily Pickerill, "Informal and Entrepreneurial Strategies among sub-Saharan Migrants in Morocco," *Journal of North African Studies* 16, no. 3 (2011): 397.
29. De Haas, "Irregular Migration," 12.
30. Ibid.
31. Joris Schapendonk, "Stuck between the Desert and the Sea: The Immobility of Sub-Saharan African 'Transit Migrants' in Morocco," in *Rethinking Global Migration: Practices, Policies, and Discourses in the European Neighbourhood*, ed. Ayse Gunes-Ayata (Ankara: Zeplin, 2008), 133.
32. Ibid.
33. Ferruccio Pastore, Paola Monzini, and Giuseppe Sciortino, "Schengen's Soft Underbelly? Irregular Migration and Human Smuggling across Land Sea Borders to Italy," *International Migration* 44, no. 4 (2006): 95–119.
34. "Migration Profile: Morocco," 9.
35. Graham Keeley and Philip Willan, "850 Migrants Break Through Spain's African Frontier," *The Times*, 21 February 2017, www.thetimes.co.uk/article/850-migrants-break-through-spains-african-frontier-g06qq9smw
36. "More than 200 Migrants Storm Morocco–Spain Border at Melilla," New Arab, 6 January 2018, www.alaraby.co.uk/english/news/2018/1/6/over-200-migrants-storm-morocco-spain-border-at-melilla
37. "Spain and Morocco: Failure to Protect the Rights of Migrants—One Year On," Amnesty International Report, 2006, 11, https://amnestyeu.azureedge.net/wp-content/uploads/2018/10/CeutaandMelillaReportOct2006.pdf
38. Hein de Haas, "Trans-Saharan Migration to North Africa and the EU: Historical Roots and Current Trends," Migration Policy Institute, 2006.
39. Pedro F. Marcelino and Hermon Farahi, "Transitional African Spaces in Comparative Analysis: Inclusion, Exclusion and Informality in Morocco and Cape Verde," *Third World Quarterly* 32, no. 5 (2011): 883–904.

40. Pickerill, "Informal and Entrepreneurial Strategies," 395–7.

41. Kristin Kastner, "Nigerian Border Crossers: Women Travelling to Europe by Land," in *Long Journeys: African Migrants on the Road*, ed. Alessandro Triulzi and Robert Lawrence McKenzie (Boston, MA: Brill, 2013), 36.

42. Laila Zerrour, "Education: 73% des enfants réfugiés sont scolarisés au Maroc," *Aujourd'hui: Le Maroc*, 14 September 2017; Ayşen Üstübici, "Political Activism between Journey and Settlement: Irregular Migrant Mobilisation in Morocco," *Geopolitics* 21, no. 2 (2016): 303–24.

43. Schapendonk, "Turbulent Trajectories," 33.

44. Ayşen Üstübici, "Political Activism between Journey and Settlement: Irregular Migrant Mobilization in Morocco," *Geopolitics* 21, no. 2 (2016): 303–24.

45. Ines Keygnaert et al., "Sexual Violence and Sub-Saharan Migrants in Morocco: A Community-Based Participatory Assessment Using Respondent Driven Sampling," *Globalization and Health* 10, no. 1 (2014): 3.

46. "Morocco to Legalize Some African Migrants," Economist Intelligence Unit: Country ViewsWire, 13 October 2013.

47. Haim Malka, "Morocco's African Future," CSIS Analysis Paper, 2013, 2.

48. "Morocco's New African Ambition," *New York Times*, 28 January 2016.

49. Ibid.

50. Rick Kosterman and Seymour Feshbach, "Toward a Measure of Patriotic and Nationalistic Attitudes," *Political Psychology* 10, no. 2 (1989): 257–74; Cas Mudde, *Populist Radical Right Parties in Europe* (Cambridge: Cambridge University Press, 2007); Tariq Modood, "Muslims and the Politics of Difference," in *The Politics of Migration: Managing Opportunity, Conflict and Change*, ed. Sarah Spencer (Malden, MA: Blackwell, 2003), 100–15.

51. Hainmueller and Hiscox, "Educated Preferences," 399–442. Audrey Smedley and Brian D. Smedley, "Race as Biology is Fiction, Racism as a Social Problem Is Real: Anthropological and Historical Perspectives on the Social Construction of Race," *American Psychologist* 60, no. 1 (2005): 16–26.

52. Joel S. Fetzer, *Public Attitudes toward Immigration in the United States, France, and Germany* (Cambridge: Cambridge University Press, 2000).

53. Ramiro Martinez Jr, *Latino Homicide: Immigration, Violence and Community* (New York: Routledge, 2002).

54. Min Zhou, *Chinatown: The Socioeconomic Potential of an Urban Enclave* (Philadelphia, PA: Temple University Press, 1992).

55. For a survey of the literature on migrants and crime, see Lesley Williams Reid et al., "The Immigration–Crime Relationship: Evidence across U.S. Metropolitan Areas," *Social Science Research* 34, no. 4 (2005): 757–80.

56. Daniel P. Mears, "The Immigration–Crime Nexus: Toward an Analytic Framework for Assessing and Guiding Theory, Research, and Policy," *Sociological Perspective* 44, no. 1 (2001): 1–19.

57. Anna Maria Mayda, "Who Is Against Immigration? A Cross-Country Investigation of Individual Attitudes toward Immigrants," *Review of Economics and Statistics* 88, no. 3 (2006): 510–30; Giovanni Facchini and Anna Maria Mayda, "Does the Welfare State Affect Individual Attitudes toward Immigrants? Evidence across Countries," *Review of Economics and Statistics* 91, no. 2 (2009): 295–314; Jennifer Fitzgerald, K. Amber Curtis, and Catherine L. Corliss, "Anxious Publics: Worries about Crime and Immigration," *Comparative Political Studies* 45, no. 4 (2012): 477–506.

58. Keygnaert et al., "Sexual Violence," 7.

59. Liza Schuster and John Solomos, "Race, Immigration and Asylum: New Labour's Agenda and Its Consequences," *Ethnicities* 4, no. 2 (2004): 267–300.

60. John Sides and Jack Citrin, "European Opinion about Immigration: The Role of Identities, Interests, and Information," *British Journal of Political Science* 37, no. 3 (2007): 477–504.

61. Liza Schuster, *The Use and Abuse of Political Asylum in Britain and Germany* (London: Frank Cass, 2003).

62. Abdel-Qader Yassine, "Reflections on the Fortress," *Al Ahram Weekly*, 7–13 September 2006.

63. George E. Johnson, "The Labor Market Effects of Immigration," *Industrial and Labor Relations Review* 22, no. 3 (1980): 331–41; David Card, "Immigrant Inflows, Native Outflows, and the Local Labor Market Impacts of Higher Immigration," *Journal of Labor Economics* 19, no. 1 (2001): 22–44.

64. Rachel M. Friedberg and Jennifer Hunt, "The Impact of Immigrants on Host Country Wages, Employment and Growth," *Journal of Economic Perspectives* 9, no. 2 (1995): 23–44.

65. Edward E. Leamer and James Levinsohn, "International Trade Theory: The Evidence," in *Handbook of International Economics*, ed. Gene M. Grossmand and Kenneth Rogoff (Amsterdam: North-Holland, 1995), 3:1339–94.

66. Tito Boeri, Gordon H. Hanson, and Barry McCormick, *Immigration Policy and the Welfare System: A Report for the Fondazione Rodolfo Debendetti* (Oxford: Oxford University Press, 2002); Mayda, "Who Is Against Immigration?"; Kenneth F. Scheve and Matthew J. Slaughter, *Globalization and the Perceptions of American Workers* (Washington, DC: Institute for International Economics, 2001); Kevin H. O'Rourke and Richard Sinnott, "The Determinants of Individual Attitudes towards Immigration," *European Journal of Political Economy* 22, no. 4 (2006): 838–61.

67. Neil Malhotra, Yotam Margalit, and Cecilia Hyunjung Mo, "Economic Explanations for Opposition to Immigration: Distinguishing between Prevalence and Conditional Impact," *American Journal of Political Science* 57, no. 2 (2013): 391–410

68. Moshe Semyonov, Rebeca Raijman, and Anastasia Gorodzeisky, "The Rise of Anti-

foreigner Sentiment in European Societies, 1988–2000," *American Sociological Review* 71, no. 3 (2006): 426–49.

69. Shang E. Ha, "The Consequences of Multiracial Contexts on Public Attitudes toward Immigration," *Political Research Quarterly* 63, no. 1 (2008): 29–42.

70. Sides and Citrin, "European Opinion about Immigration."

71. "Régularisation des sans-papiers: 65 % des demandes satisfaites," *La nouvelle tribune*, 10 February 2016, https://lnt.ma/regularisation-papiers-65-demandes-satisfaites

72. Lindsay J. Benstead, "Effects of Interviewer–Respondent Gender Interaction on Attitudes toward Women and Politics: Findings from Morocco," *International Journal of Public Opinion Research* 26, no. 3 (2013): 369–83; Lindsay J. Benstead, "Does Interviewer Religious Dress Affect Survey Response? Evidence from Morocco," *Politics and Religion* 7, no. 4 (2014): 743–60.

73. The response scale to the question of support for the resettlement of African migrants is: 1 (disagree strongly); 2 (disagree); 3 (neither agree nor disagree); 4 (agree); 5 (agree strongly).

74. Charles R. Chandler and Yung-mei Tsai, "Social Factors Influencing Immigration Attitudes: An Analysis of Data from the General Social Survey," *Social Science Journal* 38, no. 2 (2001): 177–88.

75. Kyung Joon Han, "Income Inequality, International Migration, and National Pride: A Test of Social Identification Theory," *International Journal of Public Opinion Research* 25, no. 4 (2013): 502–21; Mikael Hjerm, "Education, Xenophobia and Nationalism: A Comparative Analysis," *Journal of Ethnic and Migration Studies* 27, no. 1 (2001): 37–60.

76. Robert Andersen and Tina Fetner, "Economic Inequality and Intolerance: Attitudes toward Homosexuality in 35 Democracies," *American Journal of Political Science* 52, no. 4 (2008): 952–8.

77. Hainmueller and Hiscox, "Educated Preferences," 399–442.

78. Semyonov, Raijman, and Gorodzeisky, "European Opinion about Immigration," 477–504.

79. The values of all the other right-hand-side variables are fixed at their mean levels when all the predicted probabilities are calculated. The response scale to the question of the religion of African migrants is: 1 (disagree strongly); 2 (disagree); 3 (neither agree nor disagree); 4 (agree); 5 (agree strongly).

80. Dietlind Stolle, Stuart Soroka, and Richard Johnston, "When Does Diversity Erode Trust? Neighborhood Diversity, Interpersonal Trust and the Mediating Effect of Social Interactions," *Political Studies* 56, no. 1 (2008): 57–75.

81. Ronald Inglehart, *Modernization and Postmodernization: Cultural, Economic, and Political Change in 43 Societies* (Princeton, NJ: Princeton University Press, 1997).

82. Jan Pieter van Oudenhoven, Karin S. Prins, and Bram P. Buunk, "Attitudes of Minority and Majority Members toward Adaptation of Immigrants," *European Journal of Social Psychology* 28, no. 6 (1998): 995–1013.

83. The values of all the other right-hand-side variables are fixed at their mean levels when all the predicted probabilities are calculated. The response scale to the question of job competition with African migrants is: 1 (disagree strongly); 2 (disagree); 3 (neither agree nor disagree); 4 (agree); 5 (agree strongly).

84. Jack Citrin et al., "Public Opinion toward Immigration Reform: The Role of Economic Motivations," *Journal of Politics* 59, no. 3 (1997): 858–81; Peter Burns and James G. Gimpel, "Economic Insecurity, Prejudicial Stereotypes, and Public Opinion on Immigration Policy," *Political Studies Quarterly* 115, no. 2 (2000): 201–25; Hainmueller and Hiscox, "Attitudes," 61–84; Hainmueller and Hiscox, "Educated Preferences," 399–442.

85. Malhotra, Margalit, and Hyunjung, "Economic Explanations," 391–410.

86. Colleen Ward and Anne-Marie Masgoret, "Attitudes toward Immigrants, Immigration, and Multiculturalism in New Zealand: A Social Psychological Analysis," *International Migration Review* 42, no. 1 (2008): 227–48.

87. Schapendonk, "Turbulent Trajectories," 27.

88. Burns and Gimpel, "Economic Insecurity," 201–25; Dustmann and Preston, "Racial and Economic Factors," 1–39; Hainmueller and Hiscox, "Attitudes," 61–84.

89. Hainmueller and Hiscox, "Educated Preferences," 399–442.

9. GENDERING THE TRIANGULAR RELATIONSHIP BETWEEN VULNERABILITY, RESILIENCE, AND RESISTANCE: THE EXPERIENCES OF DISPLACED SYRIAN REFUGEES IN JORDAN

1. United Nations Human Commissioner for Rights (UNHCR), "Syria Regional Refugee Response," Operations Portal: Refugee Situations, http://data.unhcr.org/syrianrefugees/country.php?id=107

2. UNHCR Protection Working Group, "2016 Jordan Refugee Response: Protection Sector Operational Strategy," 2016, https://data2.unhcr.org/en/documents/download/43783

3. "Unpacking Gender: The Humanitarian Response to the Syrian Refugee Crisis in Jordan," Women's Refugee Commission Report, March 2014, https://reliefweb.int/sites/reliefweb.int/files/resources/UnpackingGender-WRC.pdf

4. Ibid.

5. "Gender-Based Violence and Child Protection among Syrian Refugees in Jordan, with a Focus on Early Marriage: Inter-agency Assessment," United Nations Women, July 2013, www2.unwomen.org/-/media/field%20office%20jordan/attachments/publications/2014/gbv-cp%20assessment%20jordan.pdf?la=en&vs=1754

6. Caitlin Ryan, "Everyday Resilience as Resistance: Palestinian Women Practicing Sumud," *International Political Sociology* 9, no. 4 (2015): 299–315; Philippe Bourbeau and Caitlin Ryan, "Resilience, Resistance, Infrapolitics and Enmeshment," *European Journal of International Relations* 24, no. 1 (2018): 221–39.

7. Ryan, "Everyday Resilience," 313.

8. Ibid., 309.

9. Bourbeau and Ryan, "Resilience, Resistance, Infrapolitics."

10. Erinn Gilson, "The Perils and Privileges of Vulnerability: Intersectionality, Relationality, and the Injustices of the U.S. Prison Nation," *philoSOPHIA* 6, no. 1 (2016): 43–59.

11. Christian Karner, "Theorising Power and Resistance among 'Travellers,'" *Social Semiotics* 14, no. 3 (2004): 249–71.

12. Judith Butler, Zeynep Gambetti, and Leticia Sabsay, eds, *Vulnerability in Resistance* (Durham, NC: Duke University Press, 2016).

13. Mark Duffield, "Challenging Environments: Danger, Resilience and the Aid Industry," *Security Dialogue* 43, no. 5 (2012): 475–92; Sarah Bracke, "Bouncing Back: Vulnerability and Resistance in Times of Resilience," in Butler, Gambetti, and Sabsay, *Vulnerability in Resistance*, 52–75.

14. Bourbeau and Ryan, "Resilience, Resistance, Infrapolitics."

15. Lauraine Leblanc, *Pretty in Punk: Girls' Gender Resistance in a Boys' Subculture* (New Brunswick, NJ: Rutgers, 1999), 131.

16. Michel de Certeau, *The Practice of Everyday Life* (Berkeley, CA: University of California Press, 1984); James Scott, *Domination and the Arts of Resistance: Hidden Transcripts* (New Haven, NH: Yale University Press, 1990); Michael Hardt and Antonio Negri, *Multitude: War and Democracy in the Age of Empire* (New York, NY: Penguin, 2004); Jocelyn A. Hollander and Rachel L. Einwohner, "Conceptualizing Resistance," *Sociological Forum* 19, no. 4 (2004): 533–54.

17. Karner, "Theorising Power."

18. Rose Weitz, "Women and their Hair: Seeking Power through Resistance and Accommodation," *Gender and Society* 15, no. 5 (2001): 670.

19. James Scott, "Everyday Forms of Resistance," *Copenhagen Journal of Asian Studies* 4, no. 1 (1989): 34.

20. James Scott, *Weapons of the Weak: Everyday Forms of Peasant Resistance* (New Haven, NH: Yale University Press, 1985), 31.

21. Olaf Corry, "From Defense to Resilience: Environmental Security beyond Neoliberalism," *International Political Sociology* 8, no. 3 (2014): 256–74; Jessica Schmidt, "Intuitively Neoliberal? Towards a Critical Understanding of Resilience Governance," *European Journal of International Relations* 21, no. 2 (2015): 402–26.

22. Stephanie M. H. Camp, *Closer to Freedom: Enslaved Women & Everyday Resistance in the Plantation South* (Chapel Hill, NC: University of North Carolina Press, 2004).

23. Elisabeth Olivius, "Constructing Humanitarian Selves and Refugee Others: Gender Equality and the Global Governance of Refugees," *International Feminist Journal of Politics* 18, no. 2 (2016): 270–90.

24. Bracke, "Bouncing Back."
25. Erin K. Baines, *Vulnerable Bodies: Gender, the UN, and the Global Refugee Crisis* (Aldershot: Ashgate, 2004).
26. "Six Years into Exile: The Challenges and Coping Strategies of Non-camp Syrian Refugees in Jordan and the Host Communities," Care International, Department for International Development (DFID), 2016, https://data2.unhcr.org/en/documents/download/51182
27. "In Search of a Home: Access to Adequate Housing in Jordan," Norwegian Research Council (NRC), June 2015, www.alnap.org/resource/20541
28. UNHCR, "2016 Jordan Refugee Response: Protection Sector Operational Strategy."
29. International Labor Organization (ILO), "Work Permits for Syrian Refugees in Jordan," ILO Report, 2015, www.ilo.org/wcmsp5/groups/public/—arabstates/—ro-beirut/documents/publication/wcms_422478.pdf
30. Ibid.
31. Catherine Bellamy et al., "The Lives and Livelihoods of Syrian Refugees," Overseas Development Institute (ODI), March 2017, odi.org/publications/10736-lives-and-livelihoods-syrian-refugees
32. Lewis Turner, "Explaining the (Non-)encampment of Syrian Refugees: Security, Class and the Labour Market in Lebanon and Jordan," *Mediterranean Politics* 20, no. 3 (2015): 386–404.
33. Bellamy et al., "Lives and Livelihoods of Syrian Refugees."
34. UNHCR, "Comprehensive Food Security Monitoring Exercise: Jordan," Operational Portal Refugee Situations, WFP, 2015, http://data.unhcr.org/syrianrefugees/documents.php?page=1&view=grid&WG%5B%5D=40
35. Care International, "Six Years into Exile."
36. HelpAge International, "Hidden Victims of the Syria Crisis: Disabled, Injured and Older Refugees," 9 April 2014, www.helpage.org/newsroom/press-room/press-releases/hidden-victims-radical-change-needed-for-older-disabled-and-injured-syrian-refugees
37. UNICEF, "Running on Empty: The Situation of Syrian Children in Host Communities in Jordan," 2016, www.unicef.org/jordan/Running_on_Empty2.pdf
38. HelpAge International, "Hidden Victims of the Syria Crisis."
39. ILO, "Work Permits for Syrian Refugees in Jordan"; Lewis Turner, "Are Syrian Men Vulnerable Too? Gendering the Syria Refugee Response," Middle East Institute, 29 November 2016, www.mei.edu/content/map/are-syrian-men-vulnerable-too-gendering-syria-refugee-response
40. ILO, "Work Permits for Syrian Refugees in Jordan."
41. UNHCR, "Inter-agency Participatory Assessments," 2014, http://data.unhcr.org/syrianrefugees/working_group.php?Country=107&Id=35

42. United Nations Women, "Gender-Based Violence and Child Protection among Syrian Refugees in Jordan, with a Focus on Early Marriage: Inter-agency Assessment."
43. Care International, "Six Years into Exile."
44. Bellamy et al., "Lives and Livelihoods of Syrian Refugees."
45. Care International, "Six Years into Exile."
46. ILO, "The Rapid Assessment on Child Labour in the Urban Informal Sector in Three Governorates of Jordan (Amman, Mafraq and Irbid)," 2014, https://data.unhcr.org/syrianrefugees/download.php?id=10590; Terre des Hommes International Federation, "Because We Struggle to Survive: Child Labour Report," 2016, www.tdh.ch/sites/default/files/because_we_struggle_to_survive_neuste_version_formatiert_final.pdf
47. ILO, "Rapid Assessment on Child Labour."
48. UNICEF, "A Study on Early Marriage in Jordan," 2014, www.unicef.org/media/files/UNICEFJordan_EarlyMarriageStudy2014-email.pdf
49. ILO, "Work Permits for Syrian Refugees in Jordan."
50. Care International, "Six Years into Exile."
51. United Nations Women, "Gender-Based Violence and Child Protection among Syrian Refugees in Jordan, with a Focus on Early Marriage."
52. Sarah Bailey and Veronique Barbelet, "Towards a Resilience-Based Response to the Syrian Refugee Crisis: A Critical Review of Vulnerability Criteria and Frameworks," UNDP, May 2014, www.odi.org/sites/odi.org.uk/files/odi-assets/publications-opinion-files/9018.pdf
53. UNHCR, "Sexual and Gender-Based Violence: Syrian Refugees in Jordan," March 2014, data.unhcr.org/syrianrefugees/download.php?id=5165
54. Women's Refugee Commission, "Unpacking Gender: The Humanitarian Response to the Syrian Refugee Crisis in Jordan."
55. UNHCR, "Woman Alone: The Fight for Survival by Syria's Refugee Women," 2014, www.refworld.org/docid/53be84aa4.html
56. UNHCR, "Working with Men and Boy Survivors of Sexual and Gender-Based Violence in Forced Displacement," Need to Know Guidance 4, 2012, www.refugeelawproject.org/files/working_papers/Working_with_Men_and_Boy_Survivors_of_Sexual_and_Gender-Based_Violence_in_Forced_Displacement.pdf
57. Marita Eastmond, "Stories as Lived Experience: Narratives in Forced Migration Research," Journal of Refugee Studies 20, no. 2 (2007): 248–64.
58. Um Abed (a woman in her late thirties from Homs), in an interview conducted in Amman, 30 April 2017.
59. A quote literally said by several men in focus groups and individual interviews with men in Amman, Zarqa, and Mafraq.
60. Nehal, in a women's focus group conducted in Amman, 20 April 2017.

61. This quote was literally repeated in several individual interviews conducted with women in Aman, Zarqa, and Mafraq.
62. Abu Yonis (a man in his mid-forties who fled from Damascus), in a men's focus group conducted in Amman, 20 April 2017.
63. Abu Amer (a man in his mid-thirties who fled from Dar'a), in an individual interview conducted in Mafraq, 25 April 2017.
64. Abu Ali (a man in his late forties from Homs), in a men's focus group conducted in Mafraq, 16 May 2017.
65. Hasan (a man in his mid-twenties), in an individual interview conducted in Zarqa, 7 June 2017.
66. Ismael (a man in his early forties who fled from Dar'a), in an individual interview in Zarqa, 3 May 2017.
67. Abu Yonis, focus group.
68. An individual interview conducted in Zarqa, 3 May 2017.
69. Ismael (a man in his early forties who fled from Dar'a), in an individual interview in Zarqa, 3 May 2017.
70. *Basmet ey'n* is the Arabic synonym of the Eye Bio-metric ID, which is the monthly cash transfer provided to vulnerable Syrian refugee families by UNHCR.
71. De Certeau, *Practice*, 26.
72. Ibid.
73. Camp, *Closer to Freedom*.
74. Scott, "Everyday Forms of Resistance," 35.
75. David Butz and Michael Ripmeester, "Finding Space for Resistant Subcultures," *Invisible Culture* 2 (1999): 1–16.
76. De Certeau, *Practice*.
77. Scott, "Everyday Forms of Resistance"; Leblanc, *Pretty in Punk*.
78. De Certeau, *Practice*, 26.
79. Scott, "Everyday Forms of Resistance."
80. De Certeau, *Practice*, 30.

10. "THE WORLD FORGOT US AND EUROPE DOESN'T WANT US": THE SITUATION OF YAZIDI, CHRISTIAN, AND BABAWAT INTERNALLY DISPLACED PERSONS AND REFUGEES FROM SINJAR AFTER THE GENOCIDE OF 2014

1. The PDK (Kurdish: Partiya Demokrat a Kurdistanê) is the ruling party of the autonomous region of Kurdistan in Iraq, dominated by the Barzani family clan.
2. Rojava is the Kurdish name for "Western Kurdistan." It is used for the Kurdish territories of Syria.
3. Jennifer Hillebrecht, "Psychological and Organizational Aspects of Migration of a Special Group of Refugees: The Example of the Special Quota Project Baden-Wuerttemberg with Yazidi Women and Children in Freiburg," in *Refugees and*

Migrants in Law and Policy. Challenges and Opportunities for Global Civic Education, ed. Helmut Kury and Sławomir Redo (Heidelberg: Springer, 2018), 359.

4. Research in Xanke and Mount Sinjar was conducted by the author specifically for this chapter in June and September 2017.

5. Field trips were conducted in January and April 2015, June 2016, and June 2017.

6. Research was conducted in June 2016 and September 2017.

7. Research at Newroz refugee camp was conducted in September 2016.

8. Research was conducted in November 2015.

9. As my Arabic is much better than my Kurdish, and as most of the men in the camps speak Arabic and some of the women do not, it was easier to approach women (often traumatized by their experiences) via a female translator than by myself (as a European male).

10. Birgül Acıkıyıldız, *The Yezidis: The History of a Community, Culture and Religion* (London: I. B. Tauris, 2010), 123.

11. Ibid.

12. Sebastian Maisel, *Yezidis in Syria: Identity Building among a Double Minority* (London: Lexington Books, 2017), 92.

13. Irene Dulz, *Die Yeziden im Irak: Zwischen "Modelldorf" und Flucht* (Berlin: LIT Verlag, 2001), 55.

14. Dietmar W. Winkler, "The Age of the Sassanians: Until 651," in *The Church of the East: A Concise History*, ed. Wilhelm Baum and Dietmar W. Winkler (London: Routledge, 2012), 37.

15. Robert A. Kitchen, "Babai the Great," in *The Orthodox Christian World*, ed. Augustine Casiday (London: Routledge, 2012), 239.

16. Michael Philip Penn, *When Christians First Met Muslims: A Sourcebook of the Earliest Syriac Writings on Islam* (Oakland, CA: University of California Press, 2015), 113.

17. Nelida Fuccaro, *The Other Kurds: Yazidis in Colonial Iraq* (London: I. B. Tauris, 1999), 48.

18. David Gaunt "Sayfo Genocide: The Culmination of an Anatolian Culture of Violence," in *Let Them Not Return: Sayfo—The Genocide against the Assyrians, Syriac and Chaldean Christians in the Ottoman Empire*, ed. David Gaunt, Naures Atto, and Soner O. Barthoma (New York, NY: Berghahn, 2017), 66; Acıkıyıldız, *Yezidis*, 57.

19. Raymond Kévorkian, *The Armenian Genocide: A Complete History* (London: I. B. Tauris, 2011), 375.

20. Interview with a Syrian Orthodox man from Sinjar, now living in a Christian village in Dohuk Governorate, September 2017.

21. Interviews with an Armenian and two Assyrian men from Sinjar, today living in Sweden and Erbil, September 2017 and June 2018.

22. Interview with a Syrian Orthodox man from Sinjar, now living in a Christian village in Dohuk Governorate, September 2017.

23. Nelida Fuccaro, "Communalism and the State in Iraq: The Yazidi Kurds, c. 869–1940," *Middle Eastern Studies* 35, no. 2 (1999): 15.

24. Faleh Jabar, *Ayatollahs, Sufis and Ideologues: State, Religion and Social Movements in Iraq* (London: Saqi, 2002), 131.

25. Martin van Bruinessen, *Mullas, Sufis and Heretics: The Role of Religion in Kurdish Society* (Istanbul: Isis Press Istanbul, 2000), 302.

26. Interview with a Yazidi from Khanasor, September 2017.

27. Interview with a member of the Babawat ethno-religious community who lives in Dohuk, September 2017.

28. Interview with a member of the Babawat ethno-religious community who lived in Sinjar until August 2014, September 2017.

29. Michiel Leezenberg, "The End of Heterodoxy: The Shabak in Post-Saddam Iraq," in *Religious Minorities in Kurdistan: Beyond the Mainstream*, ed. Khanna Omarkhali (Wiesbaden: Harrassowitz, 2014), 247–69.

30. Michiel Leezenberg, "Between Assimilation and Deportation: The Shabak and the Kakais in Northern Iraq," in *Syncretistic Religious Communities in the Near East*, ed. Krisztina Kehl-Bodrogi, Anke Otter-Beaujean, and Barbara Kellner-Heikele (Leiden: Brill, 1997), 155–74.

31. Fuccaro, *Other Kurds*, 192.

32. Christine Allison, *The Yezidi Oral Tradition in Iraqi Kurdistan* (London: Routledge, 2001), 37

33. Concerning the genocidal character of the atrocities against the Yazidi in Sinjar, see: Serhat Ortaç, "Der Angriff auf die Êzîdî in Şingal im Lichte der Genozidkonvention," in *Şingal 2014: Der Angriff des "Islamischen Staates," der Genozid an den Êzîdî und die Folgen; Wiener Jahrbuch für Kurdische Studien 2016, Band 4*, ed. Katharina Brizić et al. (Vienna: Caesarpress, 2016), 9–32; Fazil Moradi and Kjell Anderson, "The Islamic State's Êzîdî Genocide in Iraq: The Sinjār Operations," *Genocide Studies International* 10, no. 2 (Fall 2016): 121–38.

34. Allison, *Yezidi Oral Tradition in Iraqi Kurdistan*, 41.

35. Information from an employee of an international organization who would prefer to remain anonymous.

36. Thomas Schmidinger, "Şingal nach dem Genozid: Die politische und militärische Entwicklung in der Region seit 2014," in *Şingal 2014*.

37. Irene Dulz, "The Displacement of the Yezidis after the Rise of ISIS in Northern Iraq," *Kurdish Studies* 4, no. 2 (2016): 145.

38. Talabani established the Patriotic Union of Kurdistan (PUK) in 1975 and became Iraq's first president after Saddam Hussein in 2005.

39. Thomas Schmidinger, "Şingal: Vom Genozid zum Bürgerkrieg?" in *Sprache—Migration—Zusammenhalt: Wiener Jahrbuch für Kurdische Studien 2017, Band 5*, ed. Katharina Brizić et al. (Vienna: Praesens Verlag, 2017), 260.

40. Schmidinger, "Şingal nach dem Genozid," 34.
41. Interviews with Kurdish journalists from Turkey whose names should not be published under the present circumstances, spring 2017.
42. UNHCR, "Syrian Arab Republic: Countries of Origin of Refugee Population," ReliefWeb, 30 June 2016, https://reliefweb.int/map/syrian-arab-republic/syrian-arab-republic-countries-origin-refugee-population-30-june; and UNHCR, "Syria in Focus," no. 5, 2015, www.unhcr.org/sy/wp-content/uploads/sites/3/2017/03/In-Focus_issue-05_En.pdf
43. Schmidinger, "Şingal nach dem Genozid."
44. Ibid.
45. Dohuk Governorate, Board of Relief and Humanitarian Affairs (BRHA), "IDPs and Refugees in Dohuk Governorate: Profile and General Information," Dohuk, 2016, 10, www.brha-duhok.org/wp-content/uploads/Report%20of%202016.pdf
46. Ibid., 19.
47. Ibid., 56.
48. Eszter Spät, *The Yezidis* (London: Saqi, 1985), 20.
49. Research conducted in January 2015, April 2015, June 2016, May–June 2017, and September 2017.
50. Most interviews were conducted with whole families, as only a few interviews could be done with individuals.
51. Interview with an IDP in Xanke camp, May 2017.
52. Interview with a man from the city of Sinjar, now living in Serdaşt, September 2017.
53. Interview with a woman from the city of Sinjar, now living in Serdaşt, September 2017.
54. He refers to Sura 3 (Ali 'Imran), Verse 85: "And whoever seeks a way other than this way a submission (Islam), will find that it will not be accepted from him and in the Life to come he will be among the losers."
55. Interview with a Syrian Orthodox man from Sinjar, now living in a Christian village in Dohuk Governorate, September 2017.
56. Interview with a Syrian Orthodox man from Sinjar, now living in a Christian village in Dohuk Governorate, September 2017.
57. Interview with a Syrian Orthodox man from Sinjar, now living in a Christian village in Dohuk Governorate, September 2017.
58. Interview with a Syrian Orthodox woman from Sinjar, now living in a Christian village in Dohuk Governorate, September 2017.
59. Interview with a Syrian Orthodox man from Sinjar, now living in a Christian village in Dohuk Governorate, September 2017.
60. Interview with a Syrian Orthodox man from Sinjar, now living in a Christian village in Dohuk Governorate, September 2017.

61. Interview with a Syrian Orthodox man from Sinjar, now living in a Christian village in Dohuk Governorate, September 2017.

62. International Organization for Migration, Iraq Mission (OM-Iraq), "Displacement Tracking Matrix, Iraq Returnee Assessment," preliminary findings from March and May 2016, http://iraqdtm.iom.int/ReturneeLocationAssessment.aspx

63. Interview with a Syrian Orthodox man from Sinjar, now living in a Christian village in Dohuk Governorate, September 2017.

INDEX

Note: Page numbers followed by "*n*" refer to notes. Page numbers in **bold** refer to maps.

INDEX

INDEX

Ryan, Caitlin, 189

Safra, 63
sahel, 58, 63, 64
Saint Charbel (statue), 75
Sassanid Empire, 220
Sayyid Said (sultan of Oman), 13
Schapendonk, Joris, 171, 172, 184
Schmidinger, Thomas, 16
School of Good Shepherd Sisters, 62
Scott, James, 191
Senegal (river), 169
Şengalî, Zardaşt, 236
Şengalî, Zekî, 236
Serdast plateau (Mount Sinjar), 231–2
Şeşo, Haydar, 224–7
Şeşo, Qasim, 224–7
sexual and gender-based violence
    (SGBV), 194–5, 196
sexual politics (Zanzibar), 93–4
Sha'at (Sunni, Shi'a), 68
Shabak communities (Nineveh Plains),
    222, 223
shared houses or rooms (Tunisia), 156
shawish, 28, 77, 258n87
Shekhan, 216, 229
Sheriff, Abdul, 82
Shi'a, 59, 60, 62, 63, 65, 68, 114, 115,
    116, 117, 123, 254n13
Shi'ite party (Hezbollah), 38
Shi'ites, 216, 221, 222, 223
Simele, 229
Singal Protection Units (HPŞ), 224
Sinjar Resistance Units (YBŞ), 225–7,
    228, 230, 231
Sinun, 221, 225, 226, 227, 235
Spain, 166, 170, 171, 172
Spanish and Moroccan economies, 170
state welfare system, 41
    border economy and exports, 42, 45
    livelihoods programs in, 43–7,
        244n41

state-building process, 4, 23
state-centric perspective, 3
Strang, Alison, 106
sub-Saharan African migrants (Mo-
    rocco), 166
    Casablanca–Settat survey, 178–9,
        185
    criminality, 174–6
    ethnicity, 178
    future research, 185
    in North Africa, 166
    interactions and conflicts on arrival
        of, 173–8
    job market competition, 177, 184
    labor migration, 134
    migration danger and cost, 172
    Moroccans' opposition and support
        on integration of, 181–2
    Morocco, political history of,
        168–73
    racism, 174
    religion, 176
    sampling method and result, 179–80
    victims of persecution, 176
Sultan Barghash, 83
Sunni Muslim, 59, 176, 236
Survival Minimal Basket Expenditure,
    44
Swahili (language), 13, 80, 81, 82, 83,
    84, 86, 90, 91, 97, 99, 100, 101,
    259n3
Sykes–Picot Agreement (1916), 23, 27,
    244n31
Syrian "occupation", Lebanon (1976–
    2005), 50, 53
Syrian refugees, 5–6, 13
    Bar Elias, 29–30
    Central Bekaa (Lebanon), 20, 21,
        27–9
    Dayr al-Ahmar (Lebanon), 12
    Gaziantep, 11, 36, 40–2
    Halba, 11, 37–40